Across the Great Divide

ACROSS THE
GREAT

A unique collaborative account of the causes and effects of the financial crisis by

Hoover Institution

and

Brookings Institution

DIVIDE

New Perspectives on the Financial Crisis

EDITED BY

Martin Neil Baily *and* John B. Taylor

CONTRIBUTING AUTHORS

Martin Neil Baily

Sheila C. Bair

Alan S. Blinder

Michael D. Bordo

John H. Cochrane

Ricardo R. Delfin

Darrell Duffie

Douglas J. Elliott

Peter R. Fisher

Randall D. Guynn

Michael S. Helfer

Simon Hilpert

Allan H. Meltzer

Paul Saltzman

Kenneth E. Scott

George P. Shultz

David A. Skeel

Steve Strongin

Lawrence H. Summers

John B. Taylor

Kevin M. Warsh

HOOVER INSTITUTION PRESS

Stanford University | *Stanford, California*

HOOVER INSTITUTION
Stanford University
Stanford, California, 94305-6010
www.hoover.org

BROOKINGS

The Brookings Institution is a private nonprofit organization devoted to research, education, and publication on important issues of domestic and foreign policy. Its principal purpose is to bring the highest quality independent research and analysis to bear on current and emerging policy problems. The Institution was founded on December 8, 1927, to merge the activities of the Institute for Government Research, founded in 1916, the Institute of Economics, founded in 1922, and the Robert Brookings Graduate School of Economics and Government, founded in 1924.

THE BROOKINGS INSTITUTION
1775 Massachusetts Avenue, N.W.
Washington, D.C. 20036
www.brookings.edu

Hoover Institution Press Publication No. 652

Hoover Institution at Leland Stanford Junior University,
Stanford, California, 94305-6010

First printing 2014
22 21 20 19 18 17 16 15 14   9 8 7 6 5 4 3 2 1

Manufactured in the United States of America

Cataloging-in-Publication Data is available from the Library of Congress.
ISBN 978-0-8179-1784-5 (cloth : alk. paper)
ISBN 978-0-8179-1786-9 (epub)
ISBN 978-0-8179-1787-6 (mobi)
ISBN 978-0-8179-1788-3 (PDF)

Contents

Introduction

Martin Neil Baily and John B. Taylor

T he financial crisis of 2008 and the resulting recession devastated the American economy and caused US policymakers to rethink their approaches to major financial crises. Six years have passed since the collapse of Lehman Brothers, but questions persist about the best ways to avoid future financial crises and respond to those that occur anyway.

On October 1, 2013, the Brookings Institution and the Hoover Institution jointly hosted a conference addressing these issues. Twenty-four economic and legal scholars discussed the crisis, its effect on the US economy, and the way ahead. The conference took place simultaneously in Washington, D.C., and Stanford, California, with simulcasting between the locations for maximum interaction among panelists and audience members. A diverse group of panelists made for a day of lively discussion and interesting debate. As participants worked to identify the way forward, they highlighted the need for policies that can adequately help us avoid or deal with future crises. While there was a diversity of views presented, there were some important areas of agreement and the experts agreed on the need for further discussions to expand the range of consensus.

This volume is titled *Across the Great Divide: New Perspectives on the Financial Crisis*. The title is symbolic, first of all, of the range of different groups and opinions brought together, including, for example, those who have been harshly critical of the Federal Reserve Board and those who give high marks to the Fed's rescue efforts and unusual policy measures. In addition, while both Brookings and Hoover are proud of the range of scholars within each institution who embrace different politics and economic philosophies, Brookings is often seen as center left while Hoover is center right. So it was an important step to undertake this joint conference as a way of expanding the dialogue around monetary and regulatory policy. The goal is to maximize agreement in these important policy areas, both of which need continuity in order to give certainty to market participants and citizens that the rules of the game will not change with each swing in the White House or Congress.

This volume focuses on the 2008 financial crisis, the US response, and the lessons learned for future regulatory policy. It contains papers written by the conference panelists and serves to broaden the discussion about potential reforms. After this introductory chapter, Part I of the book explains the causes and effects of the financial crisis. Part II focuses on the role played by the Federal Reserve before, during, and after the 2008 panic. Part III addresses the concept of "too big to fail" (TBTF), and Part IV considers bankruptcy, bailout, and resolution. The volume closes with remarks on the key issues facing financial reforms and thoughts on the key findings of the conference and the way ahead for economic policy.

Causes and Effects of the Financial Crisis

The volume begins with an assessment by Sheila Bair and Ricardo Delfin of the Pew Charitable Trusts on the ways in which corrective regulatory policy often gives rise to new problems and risks in the financial system. They note that new policies which take lessons learned from previous crises into account often develop into blind spots that fuel future crises. They begin by examining five key drivers of the 2008 crisis: highly accommodative monetary policy, the housing bubble, the rise of securitization, the self-regulating markets myth, and the idea of "too big to fail." Bair and Delfin argue that the accommodative monetary policy seen in recent years has biased the financial system toward risk-taking and against risk-aversion. They remind the reader of the positive feedback loop created in the housing market in the years leading up to the 2008 crisis and suggest that financial asset prices and recent Fed actions raise serious questions about the stability of the market as a whole and the possibility of future bubbles. The authors point to the role securitization played in the housing bubble and note that the securitization model was a response to the 1980s savings and loan crisis. They go on to describe the regulatory policy changes that were borne of the failed self-correcting approach to markets, enforcement, and oversight. But they point out that the new command-and-control strategy is also concerning because it risks becoming overly dependent on micromanagement and regulatory discretion. Implicit government support for large financial institutions and government-sponsored enterprises, Bair and Delfin say, hampered discipline within the market and promoted a dangerous level of risk-taking. The paper concludes with suggested practices that temper lesson-learning with responsibility. The authors encourage regulatory policymakers to trust no one, including themselves; to remember what government and markets do well and what they do poorly; and to focus on strong, simple rules. By all means, they say, solve the underlying problem. But we must remain alert to unexpected consequences of our solutions and prepare ourselves to quickly and appropriately address new risks to the financial system.

Lawrence Summers of Harvard University explores whether the US economy is currently in a state of secular stagnation, unable to achieve satisfactory growth and full employment under stable financial conditions as the zero lower bound on nominal interest rates dampens demand below equilibrium levels. Summers supports this hypothesis by noting that the economy merely grew moderately in the five years leading up to the Great Recession, notwithstanding low interest rates and bubbles in financial markets, and failed to pick up even after the recession was over and the financial system repaired. He points to structural changes in the economy which have increased the propensity to save and reduced the propensity to spend and invest, both leading to lower equilibrium real interest rates, and to evidence for negative real interest rates from capital markets and economic research. Based on this analysis of current economic conditions, Summers cautions against both political passivity and unconventional monetary policies aimed at reducing real interest rates. There is little evidence that a passive political stance or pure focus on long-run policies will lead to satisfactory economic growth when the economy is in a liquidity trap. While unconventional monetary policy measures can increase demand by lowering economically important interest rates, they come with undesirable side effects such as boosting unattractive investments, creating uncertainty, and encouraging excessive risk-taking. Instead, Summers recommends raising demand at every possible level of the interest rate by raising government spending, improving inefficient regulations that currently hold back demand, and strengthening long-run supply-side fundamentals to increase consumer and business confidence. Such measures will quickly put the economy back to work and can even reduce future debt burdens.

John Taylor of the Hoover Institution suggests that assessments of the 2008 crisis that look to a narrow stretch of time—usually September through November of 2008—miss the bigger picture. A wider window, from 2003 through 2013, is more useful and reveals that government policy (namely monetary policy, regulatory policy, and an ad hoc bailout policy) played the largest contributing role in the crisis. He takes issue with the deviation from tried-and-true policies and says that these deviations created a boom-and-bust cycle and fueled both the crisis itself and the poor recovery. Specifically, he points to the Fed's low interest rate policy in 2003–2005, unenforced financial regulations, complex Dodd-Frank regulations, "exploding" federal debt, and discretionary monetary policy. Taylor concludes with a ray of hope: if we accept that policy is the problem, we also know that policy, not some other element of the economic system, needs to be fixed. Although he admits that today's policy strategy can't be identical to that of decades past, he nonetheless implores us to return to practices that successfully kept the economy working.

Kevin Warsh, also of Hoover, presents a perspective that complements the others in this section of the volume. He writes that while the US government's policy response to the 2008 crisis remains controversial, we must also take into account the systemic effects of the changes in policy on economic agents. To do so, we need a robust understanding of the behavioral responses to new policies. He thereby explores the role that modeling plays on policy, writing that "getting the model right appears to be a predominant factor in getting policy right." Warsh then focuses on what he calls the new stability agenda of economic policy which has emerged from the financial crisis. He is concerned that this well-intentioned approach to policy will too readily accept "statism" as a means to resist even the more benign turbulence in the economy or in sectors of the economy. Some turbulence, he argues, is not unhealthy for the economy, and indeed it is key to strong, sustainable economic growth and prosperity.

The Federal Reserve Role

The second panel of the conference focused on the role played by the Federal Reserve before, during, and after the 2008 crisis. Alan Blinder of Princeton University opened the dialogue, noting that while the Fed's actions before and during the collapse of Lehman Brothers on September 15, 2008, were generally unsatisfactory, it deserves excellent grades for its subsequent performance. Although not alone in the blame for the events leading up the 2008 crisis, the Fed nonetheless bears a significant portion of the blame because it had unique systemic responsibilities; was and is the *primus inter pares* among financial regulators; and had special consumer protection and mortgage-related responsibilities. In the early 2000s, the Fed ignored the early warning signs of impending economic struggles and ultimately failed to use its legal authority to mitigate the situation. However, it lacked the power to completely fix the problems that created and fueled the 2008 crisis, and the behavior of the Securities and Exchange Commission (SEC) and other regulatory bodies certainly did not help matters. Blinder goes on to describe the Fed's 2002–2004 monetary policy as too loose but ultimately as a minor mistake that caused relatively little harm to the economy. The Fed's biggest mistake, he writes, was allowing Lehman Brothers to fail spectacularly instead of intervening and loaning the necessary funds. After Lehman Brothers failed, however, the Fed addressed the new market circumstances quickly and deftly. Blinder lauds the Fed's use of controversial unconventional monetary policies, but reminds the reader that such policies will eventually have to be wound down.

Michael Bordo, of Rutgers University and the Hoover Institution, presents an examination of the Fed's role in the crisis that is rich in historical analysis. He notes that despite the popularity of comparisons between the Great Depression and the 2008 recession, the crises aren't exactly analogous and "in some respects, basing policy on the lessons of the Great Depression may have exacerbated the recent economic stress and have caused serious problems that could contribute to the next crisis." In the crisis of the 1930s the money supply and the deposit-to-currency-ratio collapsed; in the recent crisis both rose. The 2008 crisis saw none of the commercial bank runs that marked the Great Depression era, and was ultimately an insolvency issue rather than a liquidity issue. The Fed attempted to solve the 2008 crisis using lessons learned from the Great Depression, and in many ways the results were lackluster. Bordo describes the Fed's recent liquidity policy, credit policy, bailouts, and quantitative easing as seriously flawed and damaging to the Fed's reputation.

Peter Fisher of Blackrock joins the conversation with thoughts on how the lessons learned about the Fed from 2008 to 2013 can help guide future policy. He identifies three major lessons from the crisis. First, either the Fed should utilize supervision and regulation to manage excessive leverage or it should "lean against the wind." He stresses the importance of using supervisory tools to promote financial stability. Second, moral hazard is best addressed before, not during, a major economic crisis. He sees the Financial Stability Oversight Council that designates systemically important financial institutions as an important improvement in regulation. And third, the Fed must avoid crafting policies that are short-sighted and must bear in mind potentially perverse consequences. He argues that there is a long list of potentially adverse consequences of the Fed's extraordinary policies. Fisher ultimately recommends that we take this post-crisis opportunity to review the Fed's mandate: we can use lessons learned from the recession to update the Fed's objectives and constraints.

Allan Meltzer of the Hoover Institution devotes his paper to explaining the low inflation and slow growth that have plagued the recovery from the 2008 crisis. He indicates that the flat response to the recent growth of reserves is due to four key problems. First, the Fed mistakenly saw the 2008 crisis as a principally monetary problem and acted accordingly, even though current economic issues are mostly real. Second, the Fed has not announced or adopted a strategy that increases confidence. Third, increased bank reserves are mostly excess reserves; when banks are paid interest on excess reserves they are discouraged from lending. And fourth, credit allocation is not a useful tool to generate expansion. However, Meltzer notes that mistakes made during the 2008 crisis were not all made by the Fed. The administration also made several critical errors on fiscal policy: (1) Congress was given primary responsibility for the American Recovery and Reinvestment Act (ARRA) of 2009; (2) productivity was neglected; (3) individual and corporate taxes were not permanently reduced; and (4) expectation of future tax increases was not addressed. He says that the Fed can't have a long-term impact on real causes of sluggish growth; and the administration's failure to mitigate the public's uncertainty worsened the poor recovery. He concludes by pointing out that the only other slow recovery in US history (1937–1938) was marked by policies similar to those used in the 2008 crisis.

Is Too Big to Fail Over? Are We Ready for the Next Crisis?

Martin Baily and Douglas Elliott of the Brookings Institution open the conversation on "too big to fail," noting that because we can't anticipate the exact nature of the next economic crisis, the financial system must be insulated and stable enough to absorb shocks. Some progress has already been made on this front, particularly through increases in capital ratios and new liquidity requirements. But there is still work to be done. The authors call for policymakers to raise capital and liquidity levels still further for the most systemically important financial institutions. This, they write, widens safety margins, minimizes potential taxpayer and societal losses, and incentivizes voluntary reduction of systemic importance when economically feasible. They also recommend that the legal frameworks for resolution be reformed so that firms (even systemically important firms) can fail without throwing the financial system into disarray. Finally, they suggest we create mechanisms to provide macroprudential oversight to the financial system in order to better manage systemic risks. They reiterate that the financial system is already more resilient to the next shock and conclude by noting that more work is needed, particularly in the areas of public perception, rule implementation, transparency, and quantitative analysis.

John Cochrane of the University of Chicago says that TBTF isn't over, and we're not prepared for the next crisis. Even if we were in a position to address a repeat of the 2008 crisis, history tells us that the next economic crisis will be different from the last one and will require a completely different response. We can, however, reframe our perspective of the 2008 crisis and think of it as a run. It's not institutions that present risk to the financial system, but run-prone assets. While many people resist banning run-prone assets, saying that borrowing will become more expensive and banks unable to transform liquidity and maturity, Cochrane says that this is an outdated notion. He suggests a tax on debt, especially short-term runnable debt, with the goals of decreasing arguments about risk weights and capital ratios, reducing the need for bank asset regulation, and minimizing the current mess of cronyism and politicization that plagues the current regulatory process. The result will be a well-insulated financial system that absorbs booms and busts rather than reliance on regulators to manufacture a world free from market ups and downs.

Darrell Duffie of Stanford University examines the impacts of a possible failure of firms that provide significant financial market infrastructure (FMI). In the United States, FMI firms clear over-the-counter derivatives or tri-party repurchase agreements (repos). Duffie argues that such a failure would have severe adverse effects on the entire financial system. However, existing failure resolution approaches or proposed reforms— whether through administrative procedures under Title II of the Dodd-Frank Act or through bankruptcy law—are not able to resolve these firms in a way that would prevent these effects. For example, the single-point-of-entry approach to resolution would not apply in such cases. Duffie gives the example of two large, complex banks: J.P. Morgan Chase and Bank of New York Mellon. Together they provide about $1.5 trillion of tri-party repo clearing per day in the United States, and they are both engaged in other lines of business that entail risk-taking. A failure of one of these banks would cut off access to tri-party repo financing, which could result in fire sales of securities.

Steve Strongin of Goldman Sachs and his coauthors present an optimistic argument that focuses on the newly strengthened or newly created lines of defense against failure, rather than on the remaining resolution hurdles. Analysis of these three lines of defense—more and better capital, capital incentives for banks to recapitalize early in a stressed situation, and the debt shield—show that the US financial system is far safer today that it was in the past. Although more work needs to be done on reforming resolution processes, these needed improvements should be placed in economic perspective and not used to demonstrate an overall lack of stability in the financial system. He closes by noting that because resolution is needed only in truly extraordinary circumstances, policymakers must conduct thorough cost-benefit analyses of costly proposed solutions.

Bankruptcy, Bailout, Resolution

Randall Guynn of Davis Polk & Wardwell opens the fourth panel with further discussion of the TBTF problem and suggestions for a solution. He describes the TBTF issue as a Hobson's choice between taxpayer-funded bailouts and a potential collapse of the financial system, and notes that the public usually chooses bailout. Guynn suggests a third option, however: a high-speed recapitalization of a financial group that imposes losses on shareholders and other creditors but avoids unnecessary values destruction and preserves the group's going-concern value. After discussing the implications of the Orderly Liquidation Authority (OLA) and the single-point-of-entry recapitalization method, he ultimately suggests a security liquidity provision in Chapter 14 of the Bankruptcy Code. Chapter 14 could more effectively limit the need for OLA if the Federal Reserve were authorized to provide secured liquidity to a bridge financial company if three conditions were met: (1) the bridge financial company is well-capitalized, (2) the liquidity is fully secured, and (3) the liquidity is provided at penalty rates. In cases without sufficient secured liquidity, the bridge financial company would be forced to sell its illiquid assets at fire sale prices. Such fire sales are likely to spread throughout the financial system and put it in serious jeopardy, requiring either OLA or bailouts. Anticipating economic and political arguments against his proposal, Guynn closes by noting that neither the Fed's discount window nor an expanded discount window are bailouts and that no material risk is posed to the Fed by his suggestion.

Ken Scott of Stanford delves further into the need for better bankruptcy resolution and suggestions for improved policy. In an OLA receivership, he says, the receiver uses a "single point of entry" to take over a failed institution and transfer its business to a new bridge company. However, he takes issue with the extent and use of discretionary powers vested in the receiver as part of the OLA process. In particular, he is concerned by the receiver's discretion over which liabilities go to the bridge company and which stay in the debtor's estate; the valuation of assets transferred to the bridge company; and the allocation of losses at both the parent holding company level and the subsidiary level. Scott also addresses major concerns regarding judicial oversight and procedural fairness in the discretionary environment. He concludes that the *ex ante* procedure, which requires the secretary of the treasury to file a petition in US district court in Washington, D.C., and for a judge to determine whether certain statutory conditions are met, is an "empty formality." The *ex post* procedure is also flawed: although there is an appeal process, stays are prohibited, and even if one ultimately received a ruling in one's favor, it may be too late at that point to remedy the situation. He goes on to note that Chapter 14 protocols are far less discretionary and, given their treatment of creditors, are well-equipped to promote disciplined risk-taking and exist in accordance with constitutional standards. However, any transfer of a floundering business to a bridge company gives rise to some problems, whether the transfer happens in Title II or in Chapter 14. Revisions to the bankruptcy code can address some of these issues, but other problems will have to be remedied outside of the bankruptcy code. Scott calls for policymakers to block runs by short-term creditors, assure the bridge company has adequate capital, and clarify liquidity requirements in a way that instills confidence.

David Skeel of the University of Pennsylvania addresses the single-point-of-entry resolution strategy in which bank regulators place a financial institution's holding company into resolution; transfer its assets, short-term liabilities, and secured obligations to a bridge company; and leave its stock and long-term debt behind. Such a transfer would create a well-capitalized new institution. Heralded by some as a regulatory silver bullet, the single-point-of-entry strategy imposes fewer demands on regulators, minimizes the risk to foreign subsidiaries, provides a clear set of rules, and should reduce the risk of runs. Nonetheless, the single-point-of-entry strategy does have several critical vulnerabilities. First, because it provides an option for narrowly targeted intervention, it may increase regulators' willingness to intervene; however, it may discourage regulators from intervening in more complex situations, such as a messy crisis at a major subsidiary. Attempts to resolve such a problem through single-point-of-entry processes might be unsuccessful, or could leave the troubled institution in government hands for years. Regulators are also unlikely to attempt single-point-of-entry resolution on two or more systemically important institutions simultaneously, making this an imperfect tool for handling a major economic crisis. Finally, the single-point-of-entry system dis-incentivizes derivatives monitoring and incentivizes the use of derivatives and other short-term financing options, adding instability to the financial system. Skeel closes by noting that the single-point-of-entry approach shows significant promise as a resolution tool but it does have limitations that make other corrective policies necessary.

Michael Helfer of Citigroup argues that the United States needs both Title II and Chapter 14, saying that "the country needs to have more tools in the toolbox when a large financial institution fails, not fewer." An effective resolution process must feature assurances that liquidity is available, guidelines for qualified financial contracts like derivatives, a responsible authority with the necessary expertise and resources, provisions for continuity of critical services for consumers, and imposition of losses on stockholders, creditors, and responsible management, not taxpayers. Title II addresses these items, and so does Chapter 14, but they are different tools that may not always be used interchangeably. Some crises may respond best to the Title II procedures; others may see best results from Chapter 14. It would be a mistake, Helfer says, to unnecessarily limit regulators' options.

Remarks on Key Issues Facing Financial Reforms

Paul Saltzman of The Clearing House addresses the major problems facing the financial system, highlighting his organization's role in the banking industry, the industry position on key macroprudential rules, and recommendations and observations on how to improve the pace and quality of Dodd-Frank rulemaking. As a recently designated systemically important financial market utility (SIFMU), The Clearing House Association and its membership of eighteen large and diverse commercial banks are directly affected by the topics discussed in this volume and are in a unique position to speak to the ramifications of proposed reforms on the banking industry.

Saltzman expresses concern about macroprudential policy, noting that mistakes made in the macroprudential realm are likely to be correspondingly larger than those made in the microprudential arena, involving macroeconomic consequences that may place the entire economy at risk. Similarly, there is concern within the banking industry that macroprudential regulation could be transformed into a policy that favors certain markets, businesses, or products. Finally, macroprudential regulation is by nature a one-size-fits-all regulatory methodology, and it is challenging at best to apply hard-and-fast rules to varied and distinctive organizations. "Fitting square pegs into round holes is never an easy task," he says.

Saltzman discusses the position of The Clearing House on the topics of capital, long-term debt, the leverage ratio, liquidity, and single counterparty limits. He echoes Helfer by saying that while his organization supports Title II, it also supports legislative and regulatory improvements to the Title I process. He closes with observations and suggestions to enhance the rulemaking process: (1) Dodd-Frank notwithstanding, the pace of rule implementation has already accelerated in the marketplace; (2) when perfect policy simply takes too long to formulate and implement, good and manageable reform starts to look better than perfect; (3) staged implementation is needed because it allows for short-term (if modest) improvements and recognizes that reform work remains unfinished; and (4) more transparent empirical analysis is needed to ensure that reforms work as intended and are in the best interest of the economy.

Concluding Remarks

In his concluding remarks, George Shultz emphasizes that "there was more agreement here than people may have expected at the beginning of the meeting," suggesting therefore that perhaps the conference helped to narrow the great divide.

He began by noting that many at the conference agreed that the Fed should go back to paying zero interest on reserves, and that there was general agreement that a failure of the regulatory system was a significant factor in the financial crisis. Though disagreement remained on why this happened and what should be done about it, in his view, regulatory capture was a big problem, much as George Stigler warned years ago. Reform therefore should focus on simple—easy to understand and monitor—regulatory rules, such as clearly stated capital and liquidity requirements.

Another area of agreement he emphasized was the importance of long-term, strategic thinking. Without clarity in procedures, it's easy to get off track, he said. And he expressed concern about the "legitimate questions [that] were raised about what the Fed has done in an institutional way," noting that the Fed faced the problem of mission creep and that it no longer appeared to be the limited purpose organization it once was.

He agreed with many at the conference that the damage to the financial system had largely been repaired, but worried that the real economy was still growing slowly, despite the huge stimulus from monetary and fiscal policy. The lesson is to concentrate on the real economy—reduce policy uncertainty, get a sound regulatory system in place, and reform the personal and corporate income tax system: "They're the kinds of things that would get the real economy going."

He noted that people at the conference instinctively realized that bailouts change people's behavior in a very undesirable way. Thus we need to look for ways that encourage people in leadership positions to resist bailout and, more generally, have the courage to implement good policy. As he put it: "What I'm saying here is that in order for all of the fascinating and important issues you have been talking about in this conference to work, there have to be some people at the top with guts who are willing to look at these things and see them through. It isn't easy."

PART I

Causes and Effects of the Financial Crisis

CHAPTER 1

How Efforts to Avoid Past Mistakes Created New Ones

Some Lessons from the Causes and Consequences of the Recent Financial Crisis

Sheila C. Bair and Ricardo R. Delfin

> *History doesn't repeat itself, but it does rhyme.*
>
> —MARK TWAIN

Summary

Much has been written about the causes of the 2008 financial crisis. Not enough attention, however, has been focused on how regulators' attempts to correct for behaviors that led or contributed to previous crises—particularly the savings and loan crisis and the Great Depression—created new problems which culminated in the 2008 financial crisis and continue to present ongoing risks to the financial system. In many instances, policies adopted to address the "lessons learned" from one crisis eventually grew into regulatory blind spots and artificial market asymmetries that helped fuel the next. What then are policymakers to do? On one hand, they need to learn from the past and correct for government lapses and missteps of prior years. On the other hand, they need to do so in a way that doesn't create new problems. Government policymakers need not be caught between the proverbial rock (those who cannot remember the past are condemned to repeat it) and a hard place (first, do no harm). This paper seeks to illustrate the observation and offer some thoughts on how we might find a way through this challenge.

Key drivers of the 2008 financial crisis

We begin with a review of commonly cited key drivers of the financial crisis. Much work has been done on these causes,[1] and we do not endeavor

---

The thoughts expressed here are the authors' own and do not necessarily reflect the views of their organizations.

1. See, e.g., Financial Crisis Inquiry Commission, *Final Report*.

to redo that work here. We do, however, seek to highlight how many of these key drivers relate to crises past—and potentially crises future. The particular drivers are:

- Highly accommodative monetary policy
- Housing bubble
- The rise of securitization
- The self-regulating markets myth
- Too big to fail

Highly accommodative monetary policy

The post-Volcker era has been characterized by monetary accommodation in response to periods of market or economic distress, with each round of monetary accommodation making the economy more reliant on the availability of easy credit. The resulting "Greenspan put" contributed to moral hazard by reducing losses (and downside risks) and effectively rewarding "upside" risk-takers at the expense of "downside" risk-avoiders.[2] Given the very long run-up in asset prices—and the cushioning provided by the Federal Reserve to downside shocks—it is not surprising that a bias toward risk-taking and an overconfidence would develop in our financial markets and institutions over time.

Housing bubble

Lower interest rates helped subsidize borrowing and leverage, particularly in housing. Over time, the search for yield among investors (and fees among originators) contributed to a dramatic loosening of mortgage underwriting standards. Increased demand and purchasing power by traditional home-buyers was buttressed by new (and, in some cases, previously unqualified) borrowers and even amateur and professional "flippers."

A positive feedback loop developed: increased housing prices fed increased demand for housing, and increased fee generation, securitization, and various risk-reduction efforts (and faulty risk assumptions) perpetuated increased capacity (and desire) for mortgage-related lending. Home prices rose dramatically.

---

2. See e.g., Miller, Weller, and Zhang, "Moral Hazard"; and G.I. (blog), "Don't you miss the Greenspan Put?"

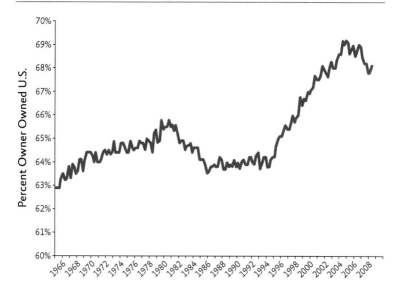

FIGURE 1.1 U.S. Homeownership Rate

Source: Calculatedriskblog.com (http://bp3.blogger.com/_pMscxxELHEg/SIybDq3rcFI
/AAAAAAAACT8/3N9zJHw309E/s1600-h/HomeownershipRateQ22008.jpg)

This feedback loop spread to other parts of the economy as well.
Increases in housing values and desire for mortgage-related lending
brought with them a dramatic increase in consumer spending (and debt
fueled by home equity).[3]

This increase occurred during the same period real incomes were
declining for most households.

Eventually, however, home prices stalled and over-leveraged financial
institutions exposed to trillions of dollars in mortgage-related securities
and derivatives positions began to face losses. They pulled back on issuing
new credit and liquidated positions. A negative feedback loop developed.

Losses on mortgage-backed securities, synthetics, and hedging instruments cascaded through the markets, dramatically reducing aggregate
wealth and contributing to a massive reduction in lending. Consumers—
now facing larger (and potentially resetting adjustable-rate) mortgage
debt, flat or falling housing prices, and a dramatically different economy—stopped spending. GDP and employment fell dramatically.

---

3. See, e.g., Changes in Mortgage-Equity Withdrawal, Quarterly (http://www
.calculatedriskblog.com/2009/03/equity-extraction-data.html).

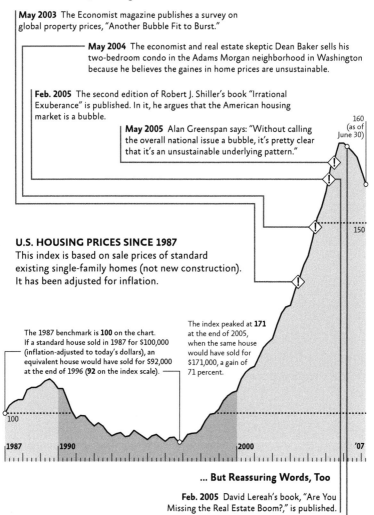

As Prices Soared, Warnings of a Bust ...

May 2003 The Economist magazine publishes a survey on global property prices, "Another Bubble Fit to Burst."

May 2004 The economist and real estate skeptic Dean Baker sells his two-bedroom condo in the Adams Morgan neighborhood in Washington because he believes the gaines in home prices are unsustainable.

Feb. 2005 The second edition of Robert J. Shiller's book "Irrational Exuberance" is published. In it, he argues that the American housing market is a bubble.

May 2005 Alan Greenspan says: "Without calling the overall national issue a bubble, it's pretty clear that it's an unsustainable underlying pattern."

160
(as of June 30)

150

U.S. HOUSING PRICES SINCE 1987
This index is based on sale prices of standard existing single-family homes (not new construction). It has been adjusted for inflation.

The 1987 benchmark is **100** on the chart. If a standard house sold in 1987 for $100,000 (inflation-adjusted to today's dollars), an equivalent house would have sold for $92,000 at the end of 1996 (**92** on the index scale).

The index peaked at **171** at the end of 2005, when the same house would have sold for $171,000, a gain of 71 percent.

100

1987   1990   2000   '07

... But Reassuring Words, Too

Feb. 2005 David Lereah's book, "Are You Missing the Real Estate Boom?," is published.

Feb. 2006 Ben S. Bernanke, the Federal Reserve chairman, says policy makers "expect the housing market to cool but not to change very sharply."

FIGURE 1.2 U.S. Housing Prices Since 1987

Source: New York Times, Sept. 23, 2007 (http://www.nytimes.com/imagepages/2007/09/23 /weekinreview/20070923_BAJAJ_GRAPHIC.html)

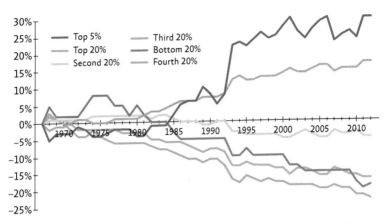

FIGURE 1.3 Change in Share of Total Income, 1967–2012, Relative to 1967, by Percentile

Source: Mother Jones analysis of Census Bureau data (http://www.calculatedriskblog .com/2009/03/equity-extraction-data.html)

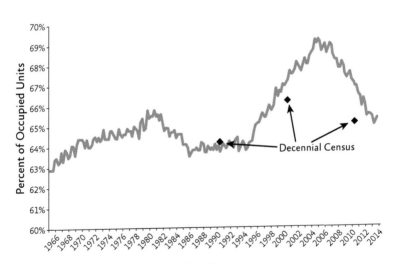

FIGURE 1.4 U.S. Homeownership Rate

Source: Calculatedriskblog.com (http://1.bp.blogspot.com/-y6bOscnRnVc/UnlSaHRE4MI /AAAAAAAAcvQ/-KQAwoA-Ga8/s1600/HomeownershipRateQ32013.jpg)

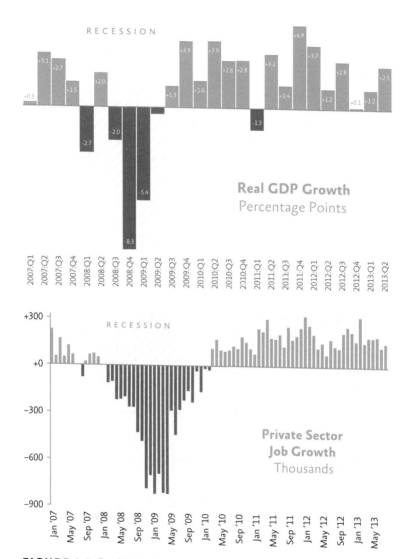

FIGURE 1.5 Real GDP Growth and Private Sector Job Growth

Source: Treasury, "The Financial Crisis Five Years Later: Response, Reform, and Progress" (http://www.treasury.gov/connect/blog/Documents/FinancialCrisis5Yr_vFINAL.pdf)

Crisis response and lessons from crises past

Though the Federal Reserve did increase interest rates in the years leading up to the crisis, it was not in time to stanch inflated housing values. As rates began to normalize in 2006, the housing market turned dramatically. The Fed was forced to reverse course, ratcheting the federal funds rate to near zero and pursuing unprecedented monetary easing (and massive market support) during and after the crisis. Not only did interest rates fall dramatically, the Federal Reserve Board has engaged in a series of positive monetary actions and quantitative easing efforts. Even with this significant support, the economy has been slow to recover.[4]

The ghost of the Great Depression

Fears of the Great Depression were on policymakers' minds during, and after, the crisis.[5] Given that tight money policies exacerbated, perhaps even caused, the Great Depression, it was certainly reasonable and appropriate for the Federal Reserve Board to take action to avoid a repeat. The recent effort, however, has been large and unprecedented, with the Federal Reserve not only using its traditional interest rate tools, but a host of new tools as well, with the aggressive bond buying called quantitative easing (QE) the most discussed. The Board's unprecedented intervention has been taking place for over five years now, and there are reasonable questions about the potential unintended consequences (and future problems) that might result from the Federal Reserve's experiment.

---

4. See, e.g., Percent Job Losses In Post WWII Recessions. http://1.bp.blogspot .com/-ijU6PH-8dt0/UV7FocJzo7I/AAAAAAAAZtM/WUPGUOPBf9g/s1600 /EmployRecMar2013.jpg

5. See e.g., Paulson, *On the Brink,* 255: ("Is this the worst crisis since the Great Depression?" the President asked. "Yes," Ben [Bernanke] replied. "In terms of the financial system, we have not seen anything like it since the 1930s, and it could get worse.") See also AFP, "Bernanke says crisis 'no comparison'": (Still, the Fed chief said lessons learned from the Depression may still apply today, including the "excessively tight monetary policy" that led to higher interest rates and deflation of about 10 percent a year over the first three years of the 1930s. "We have learned from that experience that monetary policy has got to be proactive and supportive of the economy in a situation of difficult financial conditions," he said. "The other part was—the other error, the big mistake that policymakers made in the early '30s was they essentially allowed the financial system to collapse and they didn't do anything about it. The Federal Reserve did no action as the banks failed by the hundreds and the thousands.")

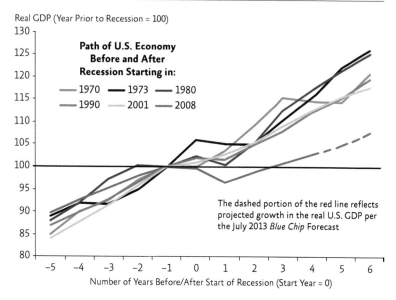

FIGURE 1.6 Path of U.S. Economy Before and After Recessions

Source: FDIC calculations based on data from the Bureau of Economic Analysis

Are new bubbles forming?

While consumers have been de-levering (and large banks have also, to some extent), many are reasonably asking how much of the recent rise in financial asset prices is attributable to market expectations about continued Federal Reserve intervention, and how much is attributable to underlying improvements in economic fundamentals.[6] While many academics and others have sought to analyze and quantify the impact,[7] the markets' reaction to the Federal Reserve's statements has been striking.

While the most obvious example was the dramatic sell-off in Treasuries following the Federal Reserve's April–June 2013 statements about

---

6. We grant that "monetary policy" and "fundamentals" are interrelated: determining "growth" from one is not readily severable from the other analytically. Monetary policy is a part of the system, and increasingly so in the recent past. This growing interrelationship, though, is a part of the concern and unease. Other ways one might ask the question are: "What is the current state of the economy relative to previous economies (on an apples-to-apples/monetary policy) basis?" or "What will happen to these asset prices and the economy when policy accommodation ends?"

7. See, e.g., the excellent work of fellow panelists in this volume.

potentially ending its policy accommodation ("tapering"), the market's response to the Fed's apparent reversal in the summer[8] and the significant reaction to its September 18 surprise "no-taper" news are also illustrative.[9]

While short-term market movements do not a bubble make, the relationship between the Fed's actions and financial asset prices raises legitimate questions about whether and how existing monetary policies designed to avoid the problems of the Great Depression might be creating new risks for the future.[10]

Looking at ten-year treasury yields (TNX), there was substantial volatility around the Federal Reserve's signals of a possible taper in April and May, a spike in yields following (May to September), and significant rebound in bond prices (reduction in yields) after its September "no-taper" surprise.

Equity markets also appear to have responded to Federal Reserve intervention over time.[11]

---

8. See, e.g., Gross, "On the Wings of an Eagle": (This year's April taper talk by the Federal Reserve is perhaps a good example of this forward path of asset returns. Admittedly the reaction in the bond market was rather sudden and it precipitated not only the disillusioning of bond holders, but also an increase in redemptions in retail mutual fund space. But then the Fed recognized the negative aspects of "financial conditions," postponed the taper, and interest rates came back down. Sort of a reverse "Sisyphus" moment—two steps upward, one step back as it applies to yields. . . . Investors now await nervously for news on the real economy as well as the medicine that Janet Yellen will apply to it.)

9. See, e.g., Farrell, "Dow, S&P Hit Record": (The Federal Reserve is not going to slow down the pace of its bond purchases yet. And that was just what investors wanted to hear. The S&P 500 immediately jumped to a new record high, and the Dow quickly followed. The Nasdaq also moved up after the Fed's surprise announcement. All three indexes closed up more than 1 percent. Fed chair Ben Bernanke added fuel to Wednesday's stock rally during his press conference. Bernanke laid out plans to maintain the central bank's "highly accommodative monetary policy" for the foreseeable future, even if the Fed eventually chooses to taper. Bond yields, which have been rising lately, slid back as well as investors bought more bonds. The ten-year Treasury yield fell to 2.71 percent from 2.87 percent earlier in the day. The Fed's moves also pushed down the dollar and drove up commodities. Gold prices spiked more than 4 percent following the announcement. Oil prices rose more than 2 percent.

10. See also Duarte and Rosa, "A Way With Words."

11. Lawler, "Viewpoints": (Indeed, the performance of US equities has been driven by the increased profits of US corporations. QE may have had some effect on earnings, but it did not have a significant impact on equity valuations as measured by price-to-earnings multiples. While it's true that P/E ratios did rise after

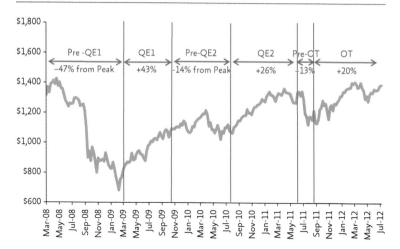

FIGURE 1.7 S&P 500 and Quantitative Easing (QE)

Source: Bloomberg, as of 31 Aug. 2012

Housing prices have also stabilized and rebounded during this period. What happens when the accommodation ends?

The rise of securitization

Funding thirty-year fixed-rate mortgages with short-term, re-pricing deposits proved disastrous in the 1980s savings and loan crisis.[12] In response to that lesson, regulators and market participants sought to replace that traditional funding model with the originate-to-distribute ("securitization") model. Regulators provided strong incentives to banks to securitize mortgages instead of holding them in portfolio. By moving long-term assets off banks' balance sheets, the securitization model would, in theory, create much more resilient banks (and protect the federal safety net) by moving longer-term risk onto large investors who could

---

the announcements of QE2, Twist and Twist 2, the moves were not sustained, and we believe were likely attributable to volatility around market sentiment.)

12. See, e.g., National Commission, *Origin and Causes of the S&L Debacle.* Also see FDIC, *An Examination of the Banking Crises:* (Like mutual savings banks, S&Ls were losing money because of upwardly spiraling interest rates and asset/liability mismatch. Net S&L income, which totaled $781 million in 1980, fell to *negative* $4.6 billion and $4.1 billion in 1981 and 1982.)

appropriately price it and hold it to maturity.[13] While over time, more and more speculation and risk-taking developed in the market, downside fears and concerns were masked, in part, by several factors:

- Mortgages had been traditionally considered one of the safest and least exciting financial products.
- While investors understood traditional mortgage risks (e.g., geographic, interest rate, and refinance risk), the conventional wisdom did not account for the potential for widespread decreases in home prices or for mortgage defaults. Moreover, widespread adoption of nontraditional mortgage features, including steep payment resets, negative amortization, high loan-to-values, and little if any income documentation, created new risks which investors simply did not understand or ignored.
- While leverage increased, so did a host of perceived risk-reducing strategies. In addition to diversifying pools by geographies, mortgage pools and cash flows were tranched and resecuritized into other pools and synthetics—sometimes backed by a financial guarantee/wrap and a first-loss buffer, which was also hedged. Further credit protection could also be purchased on the open market.

---

13. See, e.g., Bies, *Testimony*: 30–31: (When asked about institutions arbitraging assets, Bies noted "Generally they are arbitraging it to the extent I think it is good because they are saying if we can syndicate a loan, securitize an exposure, enter into a derivative transaction, and have someone outside the banking system take on risk, then the bank is stronger and banking system is stronger. The important thing is to understand how it is done. . . . Let me put it in a different perspective. What has evolved really in the last two decades is risk management processes where institutions can keep the risk, and these are sophisticated institutions, can keep the risk they understand best and can manage, and place the remaining risks with other sophisticated investors. These are sophisticated investors because they do have to understand what it is that they are acquiring, whether it is a mutual fund that is looking at the investor direction of that fund, whether it is going into a pension fund, and those fiduciary responsibilities. The buyers of the risk in one way have better information than investors in banks. If you look at data today, we get real-time public data on credit card securitizations that tell you what is happening to current delinquencies and charge-offs. We do not get it if that same credit portfolio is sitting in the bank.")

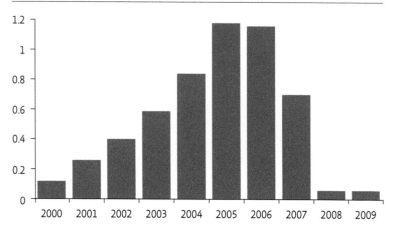

FIGURE 1.8 Issuance of Non-Agency MBS (in trillions)

Source: Wall Street Journal; Data from Inside MBS & ABS (http://securitization.weebly.com /private-label-mbs.html)

Confidence continued even as the nature of the loans—and the funding channels—changed dramatically. Fannie Mae and Freddie Mac (whose underwriting standards helped provide some loan quality control) were losing market share to new "private label" securitizations.[14] This channel not only created a market for traditionally "lower-quality/higher-risk" subprime loans, it also increased the pool of home-buyers (increasing home prices) and the embedded leverage on many consumers' balance sheets. This channel swelled before the crisis and froze after.

Securitization also severed the ownership of the mortgage from the decision to originate and fund it.

- The mortgage production process itself became a profitable, volume (fee)-driven business. The traditional "pull dynamic" of the hopeful home-buyer trying to convince a risk-adverse bank lender was replaced by a new "push dynamic" of a commission/ sales-driven mortgage broker/lender seeking fees and commissions for generating new loans to home-buyers and refinancers.
- Mortgage servicing and workout incentives were also skewed by structures and incentives that made loss mitigation very difficult.

---

14. Mortgage debt held by private label ABS issuers increased from 9 percent of the US total in 2003 to 19 percent in 2006. Source: FDIC.

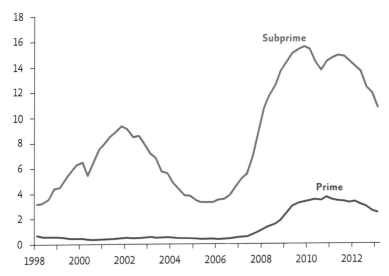

FIGURE 1.9 Conventional Loans in Foreclosure (%)

Source: FDIC Based on Mortgage Bankers Association Data

Because of securitization, mortgages were locked (and sliced) in complicated investment vehicles with complicated rules. Investors with competing interests and those responsible for loan workouts had little or negative economic incentives to mitigate loan losses.

Ironically, in the end many banks (and even the government-sponsored enterprises) ended up bringing many of these risks back onto their books by purchasing mortgage-backed securities and by holding second liens and residual interests. Regulators helped by establishing regulatory capital requirements that first pushed securitization as a way to get loans off of banks' balance sheets and then made it advantageous to bring risky synthetic and securitized loans right back on.

The dramatic rise and fall of short-term wholesale funding

Moreover, while securitization may have sought to reduce some of the longer mortgage risk from traditional bank balance sheets, regulators still permitted significant duration mismatches (this time through increased reliance on short-term wholesale funding). Net repo and fed fund liabilities for private depository institutions and broker-dealers soared in the

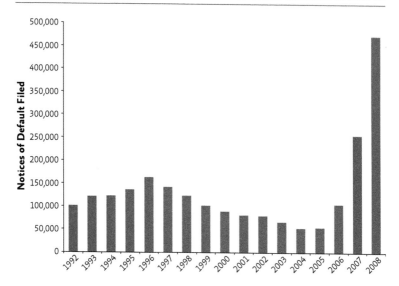

FIGURE 1.10 California Default Notices

Source: Calculatedriskblog (http://www.calculatedriskblog.com/2008/07/dataquick-record
-california-foreclosure.html)

years leading up to the crisis (from under \$1 trillion at the end of 2001 to
\$2.2 trillion in the second quarter of 2006). It is down to \$637 billion in
a post-crisis low.[15]

The self-correcting markets myth

Another key driver was the myth that the market, left to its own devices,
would self-correct and market actors could (and would) best police themselves. This paradigm revealed itself in a variety of policies—and in a general approach to markets, enforcement and market oversight—that allowed
massive risk-taking (and abuse) to grow into a norm and eventually a crisis.

- *Congress: Gramm-Leach Bliley and the Commodity Futures Mod-*
  ernization Act. In spite of the S&L crisis, by the late 1990s to
  mid-2000s significant deregulation came to the financial services—particularly for the largest, most complex firms. After
  years of regulatory softening, in 1999 Congress enacted the

---

15. See Q3, *2013 Federal Reserve Flow of Funds Report.* Available at http://www
.federalreserve.gov/releases/z1/20130925/z1.pdf

Gramm-Leach-Bliley Act, permitting more competition—and more consolidation—among traditionally separated financial services providers (banks, insurance, and broker-dealers). The following year, Congress enacted the Commodity Futures Modernization Act, effectively eliminating oversight over the burgeoning over-the-counter derivatives market.

- *Financial regulators also followed suit.* Perhaps the best example is the Basel II capital framework whereby regulators effectively replaced traditional, standardized regulator-set capital charges with a deferential advanced internal models-based approach that allowed companies to build their own models and effectively set their own capital requirements (subject to regulatory oversight of the model) amid expectations of effective self-policing and counterparty/market-policing. During this period of massive changes in the mortgage market, the Office of the Comptroller of the Currency (OCC) thwarted state efforts to impose mortgage lending standards by granting the banks it regulated—including the nation's largest—preemption of state-imposed consumer protections. At the same time, the Federal Reserve Board refused to use its authority under the Home Ownership and Equity Protection Act to adopt mortgage lending standards, even though it was the only federal agency with power to set national standards for bank and nonbank mortgage originators.

These approaches were central to the pre-crisis period and failed dramatically,[16] spawning a new approach.

From hands-off to command-and-control?

Given past regulatory shortcomings—and clear examples of systematic abuse, gaming, and manipulation—we have seen a significant change in direction. Congress, in the Dodd-Frank Act (DFA), not only laid the groundwork for a new regulatory regime, it required minimum standards for mortgages (section 1411), floors for capital at the largest firms (section 171), and enhanced standards for the largest firms (section 115).

---

16. See e.g., Greenspan, *Testimony*: (. . . those of us who have looked to the self-interest of lending institutions to protect shareholders' equity [myself especially] are in a state of shocked disbelief. Such counterparty surveillance is a central pillar of our financial markets' state of balance. If it fails, as occurred this year, market stability is undermined.).

International regulators have strengthened the capital regimes to establish a leverage ratio (a complete turnaround from the Basel II era), and US regulators have promulgated a supplemental leverage ratio for the largest firms and an FBO (foreign banking organizations) rule that would require the establishment of an intermediate holding company to help ensure that sufficient capital exists to buffer—and potentially resolve—a foreign institution's US operations. These efforts are radical departures from the former paradigm—and positive developments. But five years after the crisis, they have yet to be fully implemented.

That being said, there is some cause for concern too. To compensate for past regulatory shortcomings, the new approach risks becoming too reliant on regulatory discretion and judgment and on micro-management of business activities. Though increased regulatory vigilance and skepticism are welcome, there has been too little focus on writing strong, simple rules that are difficult to game and easy to understand, implement, and enforce, and too much reliance on "stress testing" which, while helpful, is a discretionary process heavily reliant on supervisory judgment. Bank capital rules are a good example, where the regulators continue to rely on highly complex, model-driven formulas which have little, if any, credibility in the market place, especially when there are simpler, readily available alternatives such as strengthened leverage ratios and standardized risk weights. Similarly, the Volcker Rule promises to be highly complex and highly reliant on supervisory judgment.

In general, regulators have not tackled the perverse economic incentives that lie at the heart of many of the problems. For instance, their re-proposal would eviscerate Dodd-Frank's mandate to require mortgage securitizers to maintain "skin in the game," allowing them to pass along 100 percent of the default risk on securitized mortgages to investors. And they have given insufficient attention to compensation systems that are heavily influenced by short-term ROE (return on equity) and trading profits, which give rise to incentives to take on leverage and proprietary trading profits. Instead, there is significant reliance on examiners to detect and correct for imprudent behaviors (a questionable strategy given the inherent difficulties of megabank management and boards to fully understand and control risk-taking within their organizations). And scant reliance has been placed on increasing market discipline to address excessive risk-taking by, for instance, requiring stronger, more meaningful disclosure of risks in large banks' financial statements and regulatory filings such as the Title 1 mandated "living wills."

Too big to fail

Consistent with the incentives created by these policies, large institutions became significantly larger and more complex. When markets turned—and instability spread throughout the system—the problem of too-big-to-fail was clearly revealed. During the pre-crisis period, implied government support for the government-sponsored enterprises and large financial institutions diluted market discipline and created strong incentives to take outsized risks with excessive levels of leverage.

Real progress on reform

Significant progress has been made on this problem—but it is not yet resolved. The DFA established a mechanism under Title I to apply consolidated oversight, living will requirements, and enhanced prudential standards on large, complex financial institutions. It also enables the FDIC to resolve potentially systemic entities that cannot be resolved safely in bankruptcy. Though more work is needed (e.g., to establish legal structure simplification and minimum long-term debt requirements to provide additional loss absorbency in a failure) the tools are in place to end too-big-to-fail if the regulators are willing to use them.[17]

Some had suggested that the requirements for systemically important financial institutions (SIFIs) would be a "badge of honor," but the evidence thus far does not support that view as large institution funding costs have widened relative to "small enough to fail" regional banks.

Are clearinghouses the new GSEs?

One area for newfound concern, though, is clearinghouses. While the DFA prohibited one-off bailouts and established the "scarlet letter" Title I SIFI regime, clearinghouses are treated differently. The act's derivatives provisions substantially increase the amount of transactions that must go through clearinghouses, dramatically raising the size and interconnectedness of these institutions. While this level of size and interconnection should make these firms ripe for oversight under Title I, they

---

17. See, e.g., the Dodd-Frank Act, Section 165(d)(5), which permits the Federal Reserve Board and the FDIC to jointly impose a host of requirements, including divestiture of certain assets or operations, on institutions that fail to submit resolution plans that credibly facilitate orderly liquidation in bankruptcy.

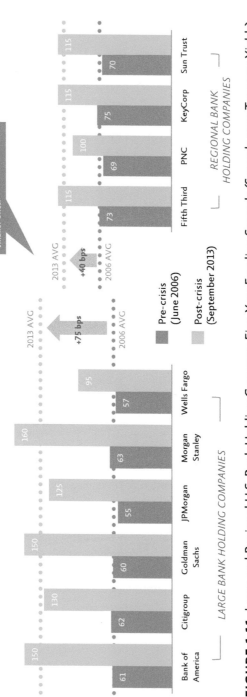

FIGURE 1.11 Large and Regional U.S. Bank Holding Company Five-Year Funding Spreads (Spreads over Treasury Yields)

Source: Treasury, "The Financial Crisis Five Years Later: Response, Reform, and Progress"

are in fact specifically carved out of Title I[18] and placed under a much weaker Title VIII backstop provision for designated financial market utilities (DFMUs). In addition, while SIFIs receive no benefits from their designation, DFMUs do, thus obtaining access to Federal Reserve Board services and potential emergency lending.[19] When we add to this mix the fact that clearinghouses remain regulated by the chronically underfunded Commodity Futures Trading Commission and Securities and Exchange Commission, we are left with a recipe that is surprisingly similar to the pre-crisis GSEs (government-sponsored enterprises) and Office of Federal Housing Enterprise Oversight (OFHEO): enormous, for-profit, financial institutions that are massively interconnected to a potentially captive market, being regulated by outmanned and underfunded regulators.

In an effort to address instability in the over-the-counter derivatives market by moving most derivatives into central clearing, these policies may be creating new sources of instability from "too-big-to-fail" for-profit clearinghouses that are explicitly designed for government support if they get into trouble. A better solution would be to eliminate their special status as DFMUs and regulate them under Title I.

Conclusion

Governments never learn. Only people learn.
—MILTON FRIEDMAN

Let us hope the dedicated people in charge of our regulatory system this time will learn not just from the immediate past but from the broader past as well. Let us hope in trying to avoid the most recent financial crisis that we also avoid the kinds of mistakes that can lead to new ones. A few principles that might help us move forward, responsibly:

Trust no one, including yourself. This mindset would help us avoid repeating the overly deferential approach of the pre-crisis years without falling into an overly discretionary, command-and-control type of regulatory framework that can dramatically undermine effective management and sound markets.

---

18. Dodd-Frank Act, Sec. 102(a)(4).
19. Ibid., Sec. 806.

Remember what government and markets do well (and badly). Government is good at establishing and enforcing basic rules of the road that can protect innocent third parties, helping to solve collective action problems, and working to ensure an equal playing field for participants engaging in the same activity. When governments do this, and do it consistently, markets can grow and work.

Governments, however, have a weakness for making exceptions and carve-outs that contribute to complexity and often lead to asymmetries and abuse. They are also terrible at admitting mistakes, setting or determining asset prices, fostering market discipline, and recognizing the inherent difficulties in the consolidated supervision of large, complex financial institutions.

Markets do well at discounting information and setting asset prices. They are also far better at innovating—when they are held accountable for their mistakes and are operating on an equal playing field. When market participants are not accountable for their mistakes (e.g., because of lack of oversight and enforcement or because counterparties and investors are uninformed or mistaken about the dynamics) or when they have artificial advantages (e.g., through capital frameworks, legal carve-outs, or implicit government support), they will take full advantage, and often with leverage.

Focus on strong, simple rules. If policymakers operate with a healthy skepticism of others and themselves, and accept that no person (and no model) can be trusted to predict the future, they are left with two choices: (1) break up financial institutions into sufficiently small discrete parts so that they can compete and fail with minimal externalities; or (2) establish strong, simple rules that (while not perfect) provide a reasonable buffer to account for our uncertainty and are radically easier to understand, implement, and enforce. This approach must be combined with meaningful disclosure of risks being undertaken by large, complex financial institutions so that market discipline can complement regulatory efforts.

Either of these options is superior over time to the "mega-institutions and little oversight" approaches that contributed to the Great Depression and the 2008 Crisis or the "mega-institutions and mega-bureaucracy" command-and-control model that we are risking. The "strong, simple rules and market discipline" approach, however, is far more achievable in the near term. It may be bad for the lawyers, consultants, and compliance professionals who profit from complexity, but it would be far better for the rest of us.

Solve the underlying problem (and, even then, remain alert). One significant cause of markets and regulatory complexity is policymakers' willingness[20] to make ad hoc exceptions and minor "fixes" that over time morph into hyper-complex rules and systems.[21]

Moreover, once a policy is implemented, few things have proven more dangerous than overconfidence. Throughout the crisis we saw markets—and regulators—take steps that they thought were responsible and risk-reducing that turned out to be massively risk-enhancing. Some of these problems (like too-big-to-fail) are particularly difficult to eliminate over time.

References

Agence France-Presse. "Bernanke says crisis 'no comparison' to Great Depression," December 1, 2008, http://www.google.com/hostednews/afp/article /ALeqM5gzwiRk81qjTxmJYcbbCuXLWX0urA?hl=en.

Bies, Susan. *Testimony Before the Joint Hearing of the Subcommittee on Financial Institutions and Consumer Credit and the Subcommittee on Domestic and International Monetary Policy, Trade, and Technology, House Financial Services Committee, "Basel II: Capital Changes in the U.S. Banking System and the Results of the Impact Study,"* May 11, 2005, http://www.gpo.gov/fdsys/pkg /CHRG-109hhrg25388/pdf/CHRG-109hhrg25388.pdf.

Dodd-Frank Wall Street Reform and Consumer Protection Act (Dodd-Frank Act), Public Law 111–203, July 21, 2010.

---

20. We recognize that other factors, particular the policymaking "process," also contribute to this complexity. Prudent policymaking is often hamstrung by a process built for gridlock, small fixes or complexity-creating compromise. Strong, simple solutions are often the most difficult to enact.

21. One need look no further than the evolution of money market fund reform for an example of this phenomenon. Rather than accepting and addressing its "original sin" of permitting a stable net asset value (NAV), we have seen the SEC implement new reform after reform. Over the years it has tightened the scope of eligible securities, reduced maturities, increased disclosure, and strengthened liquidity requirements, among other things. See SEC, "Proposed Rule." Now the agency is considering either (1) "gates and fees" or (2) stable NAV carve-outs for certain investors ("retail") and asset categories ("agencies").

Duarte, Fernando, and Carlo Rosa. "A Way With Words: The Economics of the Fed's Press Conference." Federal Reserve Bank of New York, November 2013, http://libertystreeteconomics.newyorkfed.org/2013/11/a-way-with-words-the -economics-of-the-feds-press-conference.html.

Farrell, Maureen. "Dow, S&P Hit Record After Fed Holds Off on Taper." *CNN Money,* September 18, 2013, http://money.cnn.com/2013/09/18/investing /stocks-markets/.

Federal Deposit Insurance Corporation. "The Savings and Loan Crisis and Its Relationship to Banking," in *An Examination of the Banking Crises of the 1980s and early 1990s,* vol. 1, 2000, http://www.fdic.gov/bank/historical /history/167_188.pdf.

Financial Crisis Inquiry Commission. *The Financial Crisis Inquiry Report: Final Report of the National Commission on the Causes of the Financial and Economic Crisis in the United States,* January 2011, http://www.gpo.gov/fdsys /pkg/GPO-FCIC/pdf/GPO-FCIC.pdf.

G.I., "Don't you miss the Greenspan Put?" *Free Exchange* (blog). *The Economist,* August 11, 2011, http://www.economist.com/blogs/freeexchange/2011/08 /markets-and-fed.

Greenspan, Alan. *Testimony Before House Committee on Oversight and Government Reform,* October 23, 2008, http://clipsandcomment.com/wp-content /uploads/2008/10/greenspan-testimony-20081023.pdf.

Gross, William H. "On the Wings of an Eagle." Pimco *Investment Outlook,* December 2013, http://www.pimco.com/EN/Insights/Pages/On-the-Wings -of-an-Eagle.aspx.

Lawler, Patrick M. "QE and the Equity Market: Is the Fed Driving or Along for the Ride?" Pimco *Viewpoints,* October 2012, http://www.pimco.com/EN /Insights/Pages/Is-the-Fed-Driving-or-Along-For-the-Ride.aspx.

Miller, Marcus, Paul Weller, and Lei Zhang. "Moral Hazard and the U.S. Stock Market: Analyzing the 'Greenspan Put,'" Peterson Institute for International Economics, 2002, http://www.iie.com/publications/wp/02-1.pdf.

National Commission on Financial Institution Reform, Recovery, and Enforcement. *Origins and Causes of the S&L Debacle: A Blueprint for Reform: A Report to the President and Congress of the United States,* 1993.

Paulson, Henry M., Jr. *On the Brink: Inside the Race to Stop the Collapse of the Global Financial System.* New York: Business Plus, 2010.

Securities and Exchange Commission. "Proposed Rule on Money Market Fund Reform," 2013, http://www.sec.gov/rules/proposed/2013/33-9408.pdf.

CHAPTER 2

Low Equilibrium Real Rates, Financial Crisis, and Secular Stagnation

Lawrence H. Summers

The past decade has been a tumultuous one for the US economy, characterized by the buildup of huge excesses in financial markets during the 2001–2007 period; the Great Recession and its containment; and, finally, a recovery that has been very slow by historical standards and insufficient to bring the economy back even close to the levels of output that were anticipated before the recession. The containment of the Recession was no easy feat, since economic conditions initially looked worse than in the early months of the Great Depression. However, the economy is still struggling five years later, and the correct diagnosis of its ailment is requisite for applying the appropriate treatment going forward.

Hence, in this paper I will therefore discuss what I label the new secular stagnation hypothesis. This hypothesis asserts that the economy as currently structured is not capable of achieving satisfactory growth and stable financial conditions simultaneously. The zero lower bound on base nominal interest rates, in conjunction with low inflation, makes the achievement of sufficient demand to bring about full employment problematic. If and when ways can be found to generate sufficient demand, they will likely be associated with unsustainable financial conditions. Secular stagnation was first suggested by Alvin Hansen in the late 1930s,[1] but did not prove relevant given the rise in demand due to World War II and the massive pent-up demand for consumer and investment goods after the war. The difficulty that the US economy has had for many years in simultaneously achieving full employment, strong growth, and

I am indebted to Simon Hilpert for extensive and excellent assistance in turning my conference presentation into the current paper.

1. Alvin H. Hansen, "Economic Progress and Declining Population Growth," *American Economic Review* 29, no. 1 (1939): 1–15.

financial stability suggests that secular stagnation should be considered anew. Moreover, the problems of achieving sufficient demand appear to be even more serious in Europe and Japan than in the United States. I will argue that secular stagnation is a scenario supported by both theory and evidence, and therefore is an important contingency to be ensured against. I will also discuss the policy approaches that could raise demand and thus help avoid stagnation woes.

Economic facts and a hypothesis

Any explanation of US economic developments in the years leading up to the Great Recession of 2007–2008, and the five years since, has to grapple with two important facts. First, prior to the crisis, the economy grew only at a moderate rate and did not overheat. The unemployment rate stayed above 4 percent and did not plummet to historic depths (figure 2.1). Similarly, capital utilization did not rise to historically unusual levels (figure 2.2) and there were no reports of significant shortages in labor markets. This is remarkable, since multiple factors combined to substantially boost aggregate demand: monetary policy kept interest rates low, the absence of effective action by financial regulatory authorities and a breakdown of risk controls brought about excessive leverage in the financial sector, and the housing markets were characterized by the presence of large and manifestly unsustainable asset bubbles.

Second, even after the financial system was repaired, the real economy did not pick up, and growth remained sluggish. The LIBOR OIS spread (London Interbank Offered Rate, Overnight Indexed Swap), a proxy for financial distress, was reduced to regular pre-crisis levels by 2009 (figure 2.3); credit default swaps on major financial institutions, which measure the costs of insuring against a default, quickly normalized (figure 2.4); and taxpayer funds outstanding to major financial institutions were largely repaid by the end of 2010 (figure 2.5). All three factors reflect the swift and successful containment of the crisis and a substantial normalization of conditions in the financial sector. Nonetheless, the broader economy has not returned to normal—the recovery has only kept up with population growth and normal productivity growth, but it has not produced the catch-up growth required to reach the economy's potential. Figure 2.6 shows the path of actual GDP (gross domestic product) and potential GDP as predicted in 2007. With GDP growth limited since the aftermath of the crisis, there has been almost no gain in output relative

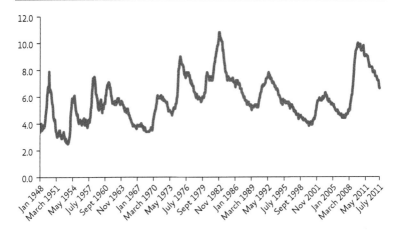

FIGURE 2.1 Civilian unemployment rate

Source: US Department of Labor, Bureau of Labor Statistics

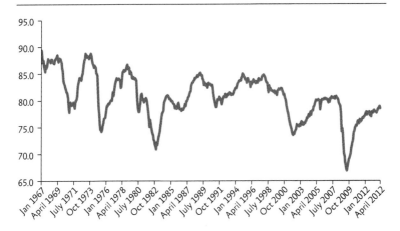

FIGURE 2.2 Total capital utilization

Source: Board of Governors of the Federal Reserve System

to the previously predicted potential. In the labor market, very limited progress in restoring the employment ratio (share of the adult population that is working) to pre-crisis levels has been made (figure 2.7), even adjusting for demographic changes (figure 2.8).

The sluggishness of the recovery is counterintuitive on the theory that the root cause of the output downturn was the financial breakdown in the fall of 2008. As an analogy, consider episodes characterized by a telephone

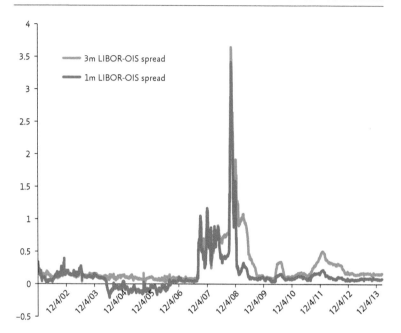

FIGURE 2.3 LIBOR-OIS spread

Source: Bloomberg

connection problem, a power failure, or a breakdown of the transportation system. While GDP would plummet during such episodes, after telephone connectivity was restored, power turned back on, or transportation restarted, we would expect the path of GDP to return to normal. For a time, GDP would be above normal as inventories were replenished and people caught up with the spending they were unable to do during the period of failure. However, this has not proved the case for the "financial power failure" of 2007–2008: now that the central connections have been repaired, there has been no sign of catch-up, abnormally rapid growth, or a closing of slack.

The point here may be put starkly. It has been over fifteen years since the US economy achieved satisfactory and sustainable growth. The Great Recession of 2007–2008 and subsequent slow recovery followed the 2003–2007 period, which was characterized by bubbles in the financial markets. Before that was the 2001 recession, which was preceded by the Internet bubble.

In Japan, it has been a generation since growth approached the 3 percent level that was thought of as a conservative estimate of its potential

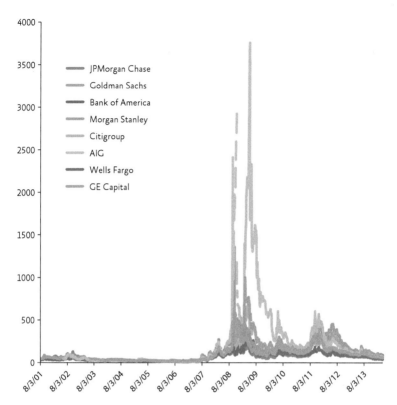

FIGURE 2.4 CDS spreads (bp) on major financial institutions

Source: Bloomberg. Eight largest holding companies as of December 31, 2013
https://www.ffiec.gov/nicpubweb/nicweb/top50form.aspx.

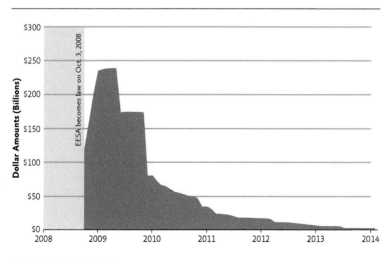

FIGURE 2.5 TARP repayment

Source: US Department of the Treasury, TARP Tracker

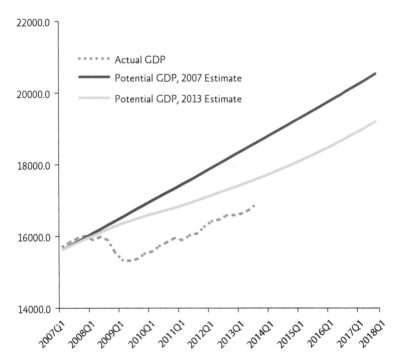

FIGURE 2.6 Output gap (billions, 2013 USD)

Source: Congressional Budget Office

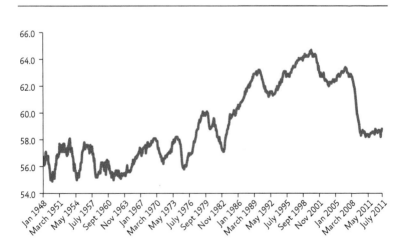

FIGURE 2.7 Civilian employment ratio

Source: US Department of Labor, Bureau of Labor Statistics

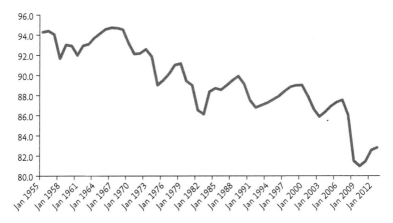

FIGURE 2.8 Employment ratio for men ages 25–54

Source: Organisation for Economic Co-Operation and Development

throughout the 1980s. And the European economy, like the American economy, had unsustainable finance in the pre-2008 period and has had manifestly unsatisfactory growth in output and employment since that time (figure 2.9).

Modern macroeconomics in either its New Keynesian or New Classical version cannot provide a satisfactory account of this situation. First, it is a premise of standard formulations of both schools of thought that fluctuations are cyclical around a path of what is labeled as normal or trend or potential GDP, so that shortfalls of output in one period are on average matched by excesses of output in another. In New Classical models, the fluctuations are frequently seen as optimal responses to changing economic conditions. In New Keynesian models, fluctuations are treated as undesirable, but policy can only aspire to reduce the variance of output over time, not to raise its average level. Clearly, what is required to account for the experience of recent years in the industrialized world is a theory of why output is continually depressed relative to potential for a protracted period. Models that see stabilization policy as an exercise in minimizing the amplitude of fluctuations around a given mean have little to contribute to explaining a prolonged period of stagnation a fortiori, as do models which presume the optimality of outcomes.

Second, models in the dominant macroeconomic traditions attribute adverse outcomes to some form of wage or price rigidity. In recent years, the industrial world has been below target inflation despite depressed

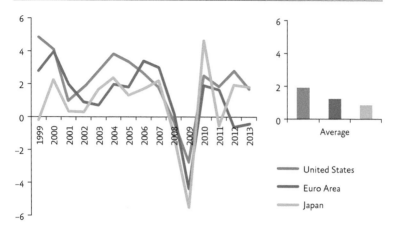

FIGURE 2.9 Economic growth in the US, Euro Area, and Japan

Note: The Euro Area contains the fifteen OECD countries that are members of the euro area (Austria, Belgium, Estonia, Finland, France, Germany, Greece, Ireland, Italy, Luxembourg, Netherlands, Portugal, Spain, Slovak Republic, Slovenia).
Source: OECD Economic Outlook 2013 (projections for 2013).

levels of output and employment. Greater flexibility of wages and prices would have exacerbated the situation both by further reducing inflation and by raising real interest rates—thereby depressing output. So, if anything, in the current context wage and price rigidity are sources of stability rather than fluctuation.

The secular stagnation hypothesis

The tentative hypothesis of secular stagnation provides an explanation for the growth patterns just described. Suppose that structural changes in the US and global economy led to a substantial increase in the propensity to save and a substantial reduction in the propensity to spend and invest. Then, the real interest rate as the price on saving is supposed to fall until supply and demand equilibrate. However, short-term safe interest rates cannot fall below zero because people would substitute holding currency for holding debt instruments that pay a negative yield. Since instruments that carry risk have a spread beyond safe instruments and since longer-duration debt has higher yields than shorter-duration debt, a zero bound on safe government short-term rates implies a lower bound, albeit above zero, on a broad range of other interest rates that are relevant for firms' and households' decisions.

With a lower bound on nominal interest rates, savings and investment cannot be equated by the price channel and hence must be equated by a reduction in output. This view explains both facts: if equilibrium real interest rates were low or negative, then the economy would fail to overheat or contain significant slack prior to the downturn even with artificially inflated demand. Also, if equilibrium real interest rates were not attainable following the crisis, then full employment would not materialize even after the financial system was repaired.

Elsewhere I have presented[2] a variety of reasons for believing that the equilibrium real interest rates have fallen. These include (1) decreasing population growth and possibly declining technological change; (2) an increase in the tendency to save associated with changes in the income distribution, with more income being retained by corporations, going to owners of capital, and going to those with higher incomes and presumably low propensity to consume; (3) a reduction in the demand for investment associated with technological changes that reduce the level of capital investment necessary to carry out a given quantum of economic activity; and (4) the accumulation of substantial holdings of liquid government debt by emerging market central banks.

Responding to secular stagnation doubts

Concerns about the possibility of secular stagnation have profound policy implications. Before analyzing candidate policy responses, two substantial doubts about the accuracy of the secular stagnation diagnosis need to be addressed.

First, is growth about to accelerate in the United States and much of the industrialized world? After all, fears of secular stagnation when raised in the 1930s were proven wrong. If acceleration is imminent, there is little need for great alarm about secular stagnation. Some recent economic indicators—like the strength of the stock markets and the end of the sharp fiscal contraction—provide grounds for optimism. However, consensus forecasts have predicted that escape velocity would be around the corner for several years, but have been belied by lingering stagnation. Addi-

---

2. Lawrence H. Summers, "U.S. Economic Prospects: Secular Stagnation, Hysteresis, and the Zero Lower Bound," keynote address at the National Association for Business Economics conference, February 24, 2014; forthcoming in *Business Economics* (2014).

tionally, Japan failed to achieve its predicted escape velocity in the 1990s, despite implementing a zero interest rates following its financial crisis in the late 1980s; now, Japan has a level of output only a little more than half of what was forecast twenty years ago. Moreover, even if the economy accelerates, this provides no assurance that prolonged growth at regular real interest rates is possible. Across the industrial world, inflation is below target levels and shows no sign of picking up—a strong suggestion of a chronic and substantial shortfall in demand.

Second, and related, why should we believe that the economy will not return to normal levels of output and capacity without additional unconventional policy? Have real interest rates really declined so substantially that the zero bound is much more relevant than in the past? As just noted, there are a range of factors that would suggest substantial declines in equilibrium real interest rates.

Beyond these theoretical factors, empirical evidence also indicates a reduction in the real rate of interest. The interest rate on Treasury Inflation-Protected Securities (TIPS), which is a measure of the real interest rate, has been declining since mid-2007, with the exception of a single spike in early 2009. Figure 2.10 shows the interest rates on five-, ten-, twenty-, and thirty-year TIPS. The five- and ten-year real interest rates have been negative for substantial periods between 2011 and 2013, with the five-year rate dropping to as low as –1.67 percent in September 2012. Even the twenty-year TIPS rate dropped into negative territory for a prolonged period in the latter half of 2012.

A related analysis has been performed by Thomas Laubach and John C. Williams,[3] who seek to determine the equilibrium real interest rate for the US economy by using sophisticated statistical techniques to estimate the real interest rate necessary for demand and potential supply to be equated. Their calculations (depicted in figure 2.11) suggest that equilibrium real rates are now negative and have been trending downward for a long time.

Both the abundance of theoretical reasons for a decrease in demand and the available empirical evidence thus indicate that the US economy is plausibly incapable of generating demand sufficient to exhaust potential output, corroborating secular stagnation concerns.

---

3. Thomas Laubach and John C. Williams, "Measuring the Natural Rate of Interest," *Review of Economics and Statistics* 85, no. 4 (November 2003): 1063–1070.

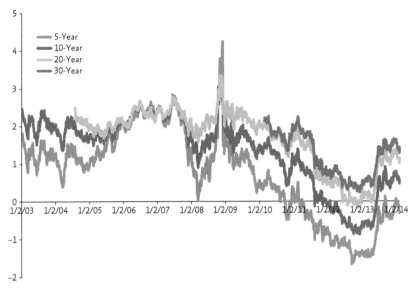

FIGURE 2.10 Real interest rates as measured by returns on Treasury Inflation-Protected Securities (TIPS).

Source: Board of Governors of the Federal Reserve System

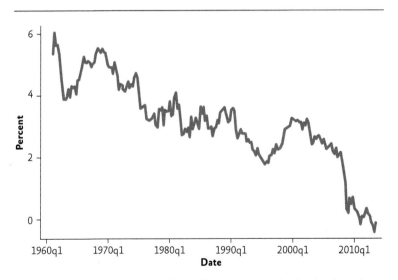

FIGURE 2.11 Estimate for the real interest rate by Laubach and Williams (2003)

Source: Updated estimates from John Williams's home page, http://www.frbsf.org /economic-research/economists/john-williams/.

Policy prescriptions

Given the concern that demand is constrained by the lower bound on the nominal interest rate, there are three potential policy approaches. The first and least satisfactory is passivity. Perhaps the situation will right itself or policies that promise an increased emphasis on long-run macroeconomic rectitude will improve matters. But there is little evidence anywhere in the industrialized world that such policies in the face of liquidity trap conditions are availing. Early work suggesting the efficacy of fiscal consolidations in stimulating economic activity has been convincingly discredited by research at the International Monetary Fund (IMF) and in other places.[4]

The second alternative is to use monetary policy to engineer lower real interest rates consistent with the zero lower bound on the nominal interest rate. This involves keeping the federal funds rate near zero and taking unconventional monetary policy actions that aim aggressively at reducing risk and term premiums, so that the economically important risky or longer-term interest rates can be reduced. This strategy is more attractive than doing nothing, but has multiple problematic aspects. First, it is questionable whether investments that are not attractive at already negative real interest rates, but only get implemented when real interest rates fall even further, will be productive. Second, these new and unconventional policies create uncertainty, as markets puzzle about the strategy of winding down quantitative easing and about the effect of forward guidance on investors' beliefs. Third, as Jeremy Stein[5] and others have pointed out, reducing interest rates through unconventional monetary policy

---

4. See, for instance, IMF, "Will It Hurt? Macroeconomic Effects of Fiscal Consolidation," chapter 3 of the IMF's October 2010 "World Economic Outlook"; Jaime Guajardo, Daniel Leigh, and Andrea Pescatori, "Expansionary Austerity: New International Evidence," IMF Working Paper WP/11/158 (2011); Christina D. Romer and David H. Romer, "The Macroeconomic Effects of Tax Changes: Estimates Based on a New Measure of Fiscal Shocks," *American Economic Review* 100 (2010): 763–801; and Alan J. Auerbach and Yuriy Gorodnichenko, "Measuring the Output Responses to Fiscal Policy," *American Economic Journal: Economic Policy* 4, no. 2 (2012): 1–27.

5. Jeremy C. Stein, "Overheating in Credit Markets: Origins, Measurement, and Policy Responses," speech at the "Restoring Household Financial Stability after the Great Recession: Why Household Balance Sheets Matter" research symposium sponsored by the Federal Reserve Bank of St. Louis, St. Louis, Missouri, February 7, 2013.

leads investors to increase risk-taking and leverage, thus raising the likelihood of bubbles. The argument that macroprudential policies can be used to contain such financial excesses is a chimera—unconventional monetary policy stimulates the economy precisely by increasing asset values and the ability to borrow, which prudential regulation aims to address. In addition, macroprudential policies rely on the ability of regulatory agencies to spot and curb bubbles—the same regulators who were unable to discern that Lehman Brothers, Wachovia, Washington Mutual, and Bear Stearns were undercapitalized even a week before they failed. Regulatory approaches that do not require regulators to be able to outguess markets are preferable. These include sharp increases in capital and liquidity requirements and the provision of swift and forceful resolution authority. Finally, there are distributional concerns: policy measures that drive down interest rates to inflate asset values benefit those who hold the assets, which are disproportionately the wealthy.

The third and most promising policy option is to spur spending at every possible level of the real interest rate. The most direct way to do this is through fiscal policy action. Consider infrastructure investments, which not only increase productivity and thereby raise GDP, but also stimulate demand in an economy that is demand-constrained. As such, fixing John F. Kennedy International Airport in an environment with a construction unemployment rate in the double digits by issuing long-term debt at very low interest rates should be highly attractive.

When the growth rate exceeds the interest rate, which will likely be the case for a long time for short-term debt, the debt-to-GDP ratio will decline if the government issues debt and rolls over the debt to cover interest payments. Elsewhere, I have demonstrated[6] that in the model of the US economy used for the forecasting and analysis of monetary policy at the Federal Reserve Board, a five-year fiscal impulse in the context of a nominal short-term interest rate at the zero lower bound leads to a lower debt-to-GDP ratio in twenty-five years. The model (1) assumes that government expenses do not contribute to utility or productivity—they are simply goods that are produced and contribute to GDP, but then are thrown into the ocean; and (2) does not take into account public debt at the local and state levels. Both are model simplifications that understate the real-world effect of expansionary fiscal policy on GDP growth, so that

---

6. Lawrence Summers and David Reifschneider, ongoing analysis for speech at National Association for Business Economics, 2014.

the future debt-to-GDP ratio would likely be even lower than the model predicts.

But public investment is just one way to boost demand. There are ample opportunities to improve the efficiency of regulation in ways that would stimulate demand, particularly in the energy sector. One example in the United States would be to allow exports of fossil fuels. In general, a concerted effort to promote competitiveness to increase net exports would raise demand in a single nation without the need to lower interest rates. However, such a strategy would not work for the world as a whole. Finally, long-run supply-side fundamentals such as policy measures that ensure the sustainability of entitlement programs, provide for tax reform, and facilitate investments in labor force skills and innovation can contribute to confidence and thereby boost demand in the short term.

Conclusion

Economic developments over the past decade raise concerns about secular stagnation. In a sufficiently low inflation environment, it may be impossible to attain real interest rates consistent with full employment. Even if it is possible, monetary policy actions that keep short-term nominal interest rates near zero by reducing term and risk premiums raise the likelihood of financial excesses and future crises. However, secular stagnation is not inevitable. We can ensure both adequate economic growth and financial stability with the right policy choice: a commitment to structural increases in demand. Embracing this objective will require a sea change in contemporary economic thinking.

CHAPTER 3

Causes of the Financial Crisis and the Slow Recovery

A Ten-Year Perspective

John B. Taylor

When I told my colleague, Alvin Rabushka, about the topic of this panel, he sent me a list of 210 reasons for the fall of the Roman Empire, and facetiously added "ditto" for the financial crisis. The view that there are a host of reasons for the financial crisis—or a perfect storm where many things went wrong simultaneously—is not uncommon. It allows policymakers, financial market participants, and economists to point to someone else's actions or theories to deflect blame and say "it's not my fault." And such a long list avoids the tough political decisions about how to move forward and undertake needed but difficult reforms.

Fortunately, the evidence points to a much narrower set of causes and perhaps even to an underlying common cause for the financial crisis and the poor performance of the economy since the crisis. At least that is what I have found in my research during the five years since the crisis, as summarized in Taylor (2009, 2012, 2013).

When looking for possible causes of big historical events—especially at the time of anniversaries of the event—it is tempting to concentrate on a small window of time around the event. For the financial crisis that would be the months of September, October, and November 2008. It was then that the stock market crashed, interest rate spreads spiked, and extreme financial stress spread around the world. Figure 3.1 below focuses on the drop in the Standard & Poor's 500. You can see the huge crash in the first part of October. From October 1 to October 10 the Dow Jones Industrial Average index fell 2,399 points.

This paper was presented at the Joint Conference of the Brookings Institution and the Hoover Institution on "The US Financial System—Five Years after the Crisis" at the panel "Causes and Effects of the Financial Crisis," October 1, 2013.

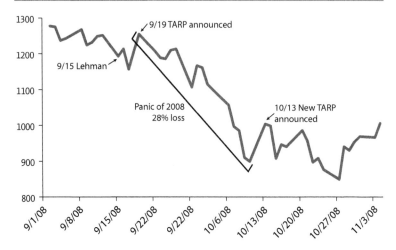

FIGURE 3.1 The Standard & Poor's 500 during the Panic of 2008.
Source: FRED (Federal Reserve Economic Data), Federal Reserve Bank of St. Louis

But focusing only on this slice of time can be very misleading. If one is considering monetary policy, for example, there are big differences between the policy during the panic and the policy before and after the panic. In a presentation at the annual Jackson Hole, Wyoming, conference in August 2013, International Monetary Fund Managing Director Christine Lagarde (2013) argued that "unconventional monetary policies . . . helped the world pull back from the precipice of another Great Depression." That conclusion might well apply to the monetary policy *during* the panic. But if one also considers monetary policy before and after the panic, the possibility arises that this policy helped bring us to the precipice and then helped create forces which delayed the recovery. When you widen the window—to include not only the five years since the panic ended but also the five years before the panic began—you get a more complete assessment and the lessons are clearer.

Such a ten-year view shows that the underlying cause was not some exogenous forces or inherent defects with market systems that inevitably placed the economy on that precipice. Rather, the cause was largely government policy; in particular, monetary policy, regulatory policy, and an ad hoc bailout policy. Simply put, we deviated from economic policies that had worked well for nearly two decades. Ironically, a major effect of the crisis has been to perpetuate many of these policies, making recovery from the crisis much harder.

Monetary policy

First, consider monetary policy. My empirical research, which was conducted before the panic, showed that the Federal Reserve held interest rates excessively low starting about ten years ago. It was a big deviation from the kind of policy that had worked well for more than twenty years in the 1980s and 1990s. Figure 3.2, below, illustrates this deviation. It shows the inflation rate going back to the 1950s along with two flat lines: one indicating an inflation rate of 4 percent and one indicating inflation at 2 percent. The little boxes indicate the stance of monetary policy during several periods in terms of the setting of the federal funds rate. The late 1960s and 1970s were a period in which monetary policy wasn't working very well. Inflation started picking up in the late 1960s and continued into the 1970s. You can see the reason: the federal funds rate was only 4.8 percent when the inflation rate was about 4 percent—a very low real interest rate, and certainly not enough at that point to tame the upward pressure on inflation. So inflation picked up.

Starting in the early 1980s the Fed moved to a better monetary policy. In 1989, for example, figure 2 shows that the federal funds rate was much higher for the same inflation rate as in the late 1960s. And that policy continued through the 1990s. In 1997 the federal funds rate was 5.5 percent when the inflation rate was 2 percent.

But then policy went off track, and that is the main point illustrated in this historical chart. In the period before the crisis—especially around 2003–2005—monetary policy was inappropriate for the circumstances. The federal funds rate was only 1 percent in the third quarter of 2003 while the inflation rate was about 2 percent and rising. The economy was operating pretty close to normal. The Fed's federal funds rate was below the inflation rate, completely unlike the policy in the 1980s and 1990s and similar to the 1970s.

So it was a shift to a much different policy. Not coincidentally, at this time there was an inflection point in housing price inflation. The monetary action helped accelerate the housing boom. Even if long-term fixed-rate mortgages were not affected much, the policy made low teaser rates on adjustable-rate mortgages possible.

During the five years since the panic ended, many researchers have carefully studied this period before the crisis and have confirmed these effects of monetary policy on housing. Jarocinski and Smets (2008) and Kahn (2010), using entirely different empirical methods, found such

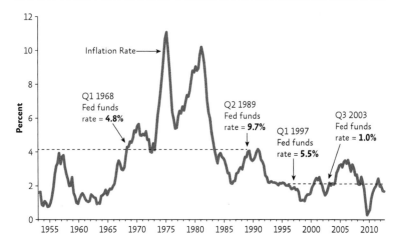

FIGURE 3.2 Changes in monetary policy leading up to the crisis.

Source: FRED, Federal Reserve Bank of St. Louis

effects on housing in the United States during this period. Bordo and Lane (2013) have shown effects of such policies on housing in a longer study of US history.

Other researchers have found evidence that the policy of very low rates caused a search for yield and encouraged risk-taking. Empirical research by Bekaert, Hoerova, and Lo Duca (2013), for example, found that "lax monetary policy increases risk appetite (decreases risk aversion)."

There is also evidence from Ahrend (2010) at the Organisation for Economic Co-operation and Development (OECD) that the same thing happened in Europe. The European Central Bank (ECB) held the interest rate too low for Greece, Ireland, and Spain. These countries are where the booms and excesses in the housing markets were most pronounced. So there is international corroboration of the initial findings.

Regulatory policy

Second, there was a deviation from sound regulatory policy. The main problem was not insufficient regulations, but rather that regulators permitted violations from existing safety and soundness rules. Hundreds of regulators and supervisors were on the premises of large financial institutions, but they allowed too many institutions to take too many risks.

Wallison (2011) makes the case that federal government housing policy effectively forced risky private sector lending—through affordable-housing requirements for Fannie Mae and Freddie Mac and lax regulation of these institutions—without any change in risk aversion. The irresponsible regulation of Fannie and Freddie allowed these institutions to go well beyond prudent capital levels. Regulatory capture was clearly evident, as Morgenson and Rosner (2011) document in the case of Fannie and Freddie. They showed that government officials took actions that benefited well-connected individuals and that these individuals in turn helped the government officials. This was a mutual-support system which drove out good economic policies and encouraged bad ones. It thereby helped bring about the financial crisis and sent the economy into a deep recession.

Though there is debate about the impact of the Securities and Exchange Commission (SEC) decision in April 2004 to relax the capital ratio rules for the very large broker-investment banks, including Bear Sterns and Lehman Brothers, at the least it raised risk by allowing those institutions to do their own risk weighting. There's a great deal of research still needed here, but that decision certainly is a symptom of the problems of regulatory policy during this time.

Ad hoc bailout policy

The third policy problem was an ad hoc bailout policy that upset many Americans and was, on balance, destabilizing.

The inevitable bust and defaults that followed the boom and risk-taking induced by monetary policy and regulatory policy started as early as 2006. At first, the Fed misdiagnosed the problem, arguing that widening interest rate spreads in the money market were not signs of the resulting damage to bank balance sheets but rather a pure liquidity problem. The Fed thus treated the problem by pouring liquidity into the interbank market via the 2007 Term Auction Facility.

When risk spreads did not respond and financial institutions began to falter, the Fed followed up with an on-again, off-again bailout policy which created more instability. When the Fed bailed out Bear Stearns' creditors in March 2008, investors assumed Lehman's creditors would be bailed out. Whether or not it was appropriate to bail out Bear Stearns' creditors (in this case I tend to give the benefit of the doubt to the policymakers in the room), it was inappropriate not to lay out a framework

TABLE 3.1 Stock markets around the world before and after Lehman failure and TARP rollout

Date	S&P	FTSE	DAX	CAC	IBOVESPA	NIKKEI
September 12	1252	5417	6235	4333	52393	12215
September 15	1192	5204	6064	4169	48419	11609
September 19	1255	5311	6134	4325	53055	11921
October 10	899	3932	4544	3176	35610	8276

S&P   United States, Standard and Poor's 500. Source: FRED
FTSE   United Kingdom, FTSE 100 Index. Source: Yahoo Finance
DAX   Germany, Deutscher Aktien Index. Source: Yahoo Finance
CAC   France, CAC 50, Cotation Assistée en Continu. Source: Yahoo Finance
IBOVESPA   Brazil, Bolsa de Valores do Estado de São Paulo Index. Source: Yahoo Finance
NIKKEI   Japan, Nikkei 225 Stock Average. Source: FRED
FRED refers to Federal Reserve Economic Data, Federal Reserve Bank of St. Louis

for future interventions. (A number of us recommended that at a conference in the summer of 2008.) With no framework other than implicit support for a rescue of creditors, many people were surprised when they were not rescued. With policy uncertainty rising, the panic in the fall of 2008 began.

The policy uncertainty continued as the Troubled Asset Relief Program (TARP) was rolled out and then radically altered in midstream. From the time that the TARP was announced on September 19, 2008, until a new TARP was put in place, equity prices experienced a major decline. The same thing occurred in other countries. The timing is almost exactly the same as shown in table 3.1. As it shows, the S&P 500 was higher on September 19—following a week of trading after the Lehman Brothers bankruptcy—than it was on September 12, the Friday before the bankruptcy. This indicates that some policy steps taken after September 19 worsened the problem.

Again, consider figure 3.1, which shows in more detail what was happening during this period. Note that the stock market crash started at the time TARP was being rolled out. Though it is hard to prove, I believe the brief and incomplete three-page request from the US Treasury for the TARP legislation, the initial rejection, and the flawed nature of the plan to buy toxic assets were all factors in the panic. When former Treasury Secretary Hank Paulson appeared on CNBC on the fifth anniversary of the Lehman Brothers failure, he said that the markets tanked, and he came to the rescue; effectively, the TARP saved us. Appearing on the same show minutes later, former Wells Fargo chairman and CEO Dick Kovacevich—

observing the same facts in the same time—said that the TARP caused the crash and made things worse.

Five years since the crisis

So now let's look at what has happened since the crisis. Ironically, the legacy of the crisis has been to continue and even double down on the deviations from good policy that led to the crisis. And that, in my view, is the explanation for why we have added another five years of economic disappointments. In many ways the policies resemble the policies that got us into this mess with the uncertainty, the unpredictability, the unprecedented nature, and the failure to follow rules and a basic strategy. The crisis itself has given more rationale to "throw out the rule book," to do special, unusual things.

To illustrate this in the case of monetary policy, consider figure 3.3 below. It deserves careful study in analyzing the causes and effects of policy. Figure 3.3 shows reserve balances held by banks at the Fed. It is a measure of liquidity provided by the Fed.

The first part of the figure illustrates what represents good monetary policy before the crisis. You can see a small blip around September 9, 2001. With the physical damage in lower Manhattan, the Fed provided what was then an amazing $60 billion of liquidity to the financial markets. You can hardly see it in the figure, but it was beautiful monetary policy: the funds were put in quickly and removed quickly. There is another expansion of liquidity during the panic of fall 2008; again, this largely represents good lender-of-last-resort policy, including the swaps with foreign central banks and loans to US financial institutions. When the panic subsided in late 2008 this lender-of-last-resort policy began to wind down, as it should have.

But as shown in figure 3.3, the liquidity increases didn't end. Instead we saw a massive expansion of liquidity with quantitative easing: QE1, QE2, and QE3. It has been completely unprecedented. There's really no way for such a massive policy to be predictable or rules-based. I know that the intentions were good, but there is little evidence that this policy has helped economic growth or job growth. Those of us who were concerned about the QE way back in 2009 said, "Well, what about the exit?" And these are exactly the concerns that we have seen realized in the market this year. In the year since QE3 started, long-term Treasuries and mortgage-backed securities have risen rather than fallen as the Fed predicted with this policy.

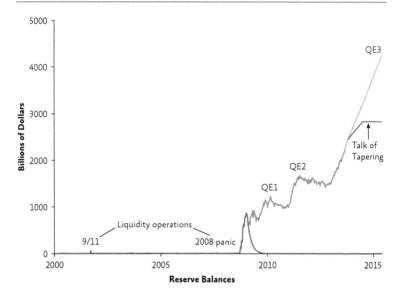

FIGURE 3.3 Shifting from liquidity operations to unconventional monetary policy.

Source: FRED, Federal Reserve Bank of St. Louis

The suggestion in May and June 2013 by the Fed that there would a tapering of QE3 is also illustrated in figure 3.3. That tapering was post-poned and the Fed went back to QE3 as originally implemented with a great deal of uncertainty remaining. Later in the year the Fed announced a clever strategy for reducing its purchases. But the "taper tantrum" of May–June 2013 shows that anticipations of a difficult exit are part of the reason why this unconventional monetary policy has not been effective.

Figure 3.3 also serves as a reminder that the magnitudes of quantitative easing are very large and that this is a very unusual policy. Indeed, the magnitudes on that graph are completely unprecedented. So we are facing a very interventionist, unconventional, unpredictable policy. After good lender-of-last-resort policies during the panic of 2008, the Fed has doubled down since 2009 on the interventionist policies of 2003–2007, and this has raised questions about its independence and credibility. In this sense the impact of the crisis has not been good for the future of monetary policy.

Figure 3.3 also shows why, when referring to unconventional monetary policy, it is important to distinguish between these massive asset purchase programs from 2009 onwards and the liquidity operations during the panic of 2008.

I believe this interventionist policy orientation has spread to other kinds of policy, including the Keynesian temporary fiscal stimulus packages. These have not led to sustained recovery. Indeed, they have necessitated their own reversals, resulting in volatility. There is nothing that needs to be partisan about this view. Both political parties have been responsible for the changes in policy.

The stimulus package of 2008, for example, was enacted in the George W. Bush administration. It increased personal disposable income because of the rebate in that package. But consumption did not increase as policymakers hoped. Consumption went nowhere but down, even though the stimulus package was supposed to jump-start the economy. This temporary action did to consumption exactly what Milton Friedman would have predicted: very little.

There are many other examples showing that these kinds of temporary discretionary policies—sometimes aimed at particular sectors—have not worked. Another example is the "cash for clunkers" program (the Car Allowance Rebate System), which occurred in 2009. It was supposed to jump-start the economy. Some people argued very strongly that this would help increase and sustain economic growth. There was a little bit of an effect, as far as we can tell, but then it diminished quickly and was offset by declines a few months later. And this was a very short span of this expansion, just within the year 2009. It's hard to see how this could be anything positive in terms of jump-starting the economy and getting the expansion moving again.

On the regulatory front, the changes are mixed but, on balance, negative for the economy. Dodd-Frank did some good things, including eliminating the Office of Thrift Supervision. But it also left us with hundreds of new rules, many of which have not been written, creating a great deal of uncertainty, especially for smaller banks. Even with the Orderly Liquidation Authority in Title II of Dodd-Frank, I am concerned that the bailout mentality and "too-big-to-fail" attitude remain problems. Creditors are likely to benefit more than they would in bankruptcy under Title II, and that is why we have proposed a reform of the bankruptcy code (Chapter 14) as part of the Resolution Project at the Hoover Institution. Still, without higher levels of capital or subordinated debt, I fail to see how the immensely large and complex institutions will be resolved. That leaves the incentive for even the toughest treasury secretary to do a bailout again on a large scale.

The danger is not only the so-called moral hazard but the uncertainty that this policy causes. "Is there going to be a bailout?" investors ask. "What's going to happen? What's the policy? Is it going to be a Lehman? Is it going to be a Bear Stearns?" We just don't know, and that is a concern I have about the policy itself.

Alternative views

In sum, there is considerable evidence that our economic troubles in recent years—not only the financial crisis but also the weak recovery—are due to ineffective and counterproductive government policy interventions. There are, of course, alternative views, including what I call the Reinhart and Rogoff view and the Summers view.

The Reinhart and Rogoff view

One widely discussed view of the recovery is that it has been weak because the recession and the financial crisis were severe. This alternative view is based largely on the book *This Time Is Different* by Carmen Reinhart and Kenneth Rogoff (2009). In this book they argue that history shows that severe financial crises are normally followed by weak recoveries. This view is frequently cited by government officials as the reason why policy has not been the problem.

But there are a number of problems with this view. Michael Bordo and Joseph Haubrich (2012) found that the "weak recovery is normal" result does not actually characterize American history. Bordo summarized these findings in a September 27, 2012, *Wall Street Journal* article, "Financial Recessions Don't Lead to Weak Recoveries." In discussing the view that weak recoveries follow deep recessions, Bordo wrote, "The mistaken view comes largely from the 2009 book *This Time Is Different,* by economists Carmen Reinhart and Kenneth Rogoff . . . " and he then showed that US data disprove their findings. Recent research by David Papell and Ruxandra Prodan (2012) also concludes "that the current recovery for the US has been slower than the typical recovery from severe recessions associated with financial crises."

Figure 3.4 summarizes the main message from the American experience with recoveries from deep recessions associated with financial crises. The bars show the growth rates in the period immediately following deep recessions. These have been stronger than recoveries following shallower recessions, averaging about 6 percent per year. The growth rate over a

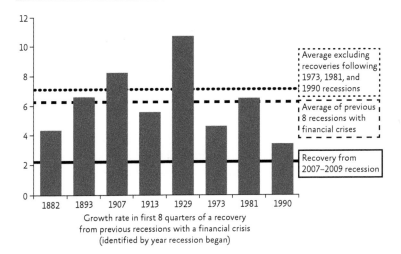

FIGURE 3.4 Economic growth following recoveries from deep recessions with financial crises.

Source: National Bureau of Economic Research (NBER) web page "Tables from *The American Business Cycle,*" http://www.nber.org/data/abc/, and FRED, Federal Reserve Bank of St. Louis.

comparable period in this recovery is about 2 percent per year. So the recovery from the recent deep recession of 2007–2009 is a clear exception from US experience.

One of the reasons for the disagreement with the findings of Reinhart and Rogoff relates to differences in how one defines recovery. When you define recovery as starting from the trough, the current US recovery is clearly relatively weak compared to recoveries from past deep recessions with financial crises. This is the standard way to define recovery as explained, for example, in an introductory economics text by Taylor and Weerapana (2012): the recovery is "the early part of an economic expansion, immediately after the trough of a recession." But if you include the downturn itself in the definition, which is what Reinhart and Rogoff do, you can get a different answer because the downturn and the recovery are mixed together.

The Summers view

An entirely different explanation for our poor economic performance during the past decade was outlined by Larry Summers at the Brookings-Hoover conference and later at a November 8, 2013, IMF conference. It is summarized in chapter 2 in this volume. Following are the key elements of the Summers view.

First, in the years before the crisis and recession, "arguably inappropriate monetary policies and surely inappropriate regulatory policies" should have caused the economy to overheat. This should have shown up in demand pressures, rising inflation, and boom-like conditions. But the economy failed to overheat, and there was significant slack. As Summers put it at the Brookings-Hoover conference, "There is almost no case to be made that the real US economy overheated prior to the crisis."

Second, in the years since the crisis and recession, the recovery should have been quite strong once the panic was halted. But the recovery has been very weak. Employment as a percentage of the working-age population has not increased, and the gap between real GDP and potential GDP has not closed.

Third, a decade-long secular decline in the equilibrium real interest rate explains both the lack of demand pressures before the crisis and the slow growth since the crisis. This decline in the equilibrium real interest rate offset any positive demand effects of the low interest rate policy before the crisis. And with the zero interest rate bound, the low equilibrium interest rate leaves the economy weak even with the current monetary policy.

Summers's first point is inconsistent with some important facts. Inflation was not steady or falling during the easy money period from 2003 to 2005. It was rising. During the years from 2003 to 2005, when the Fed's interest rate was too low, the inflation rate for the GDP price index doubled from 1.7 percent to 3.4 percent per year. On top of that there was an extraordinary inflation and boom in the housing market as demand for homes skyrocketed, and home price inflation took off, exacerbated by the low interest rate and regulatory policy. Finally, the unemployment rate got as low as 4.4 percent, well below the natural rate and not a sign of slack.

As I have described above, the second point that the recovery has been weak is clearly true. I have been writing about this weakness since the recovery began. The book *Government Policies and the Delayed Economic Recovery* by Lee Ohanian, Ian Wright, and me (2012) shows the distressing picture of the employment-to-population ratio on the cover. Indeed, these are the facts that we are trying to explain in this conference.

Regarding the third point, there is little direct evidence for a savings glut. In my 2009 book on the crisis *(Getting Off Track: How Government*

Actions and Interventions Caused, Prolonged, and Worsened the Financial Crisis), I examined the claim that there was a savings glut and found evidence to the contrary. Globally, savings rates had fallen going into the crisis, and the United States was running a current account deficit, which means national saving below investment. But the factual problem with Summers's first point sheds doubt on the whole "low equilibrium real interest rate" explanation.

Concluding remarks

To conclude, the explanation for the financial crisis and weak recovery laid out here fits the facts of the past ten years very well. Deviations from good economic policy have been responsible for the very poor performance. Such policy deviations created a boom-bust cycle and were a significant factor in the crisis and slow recovery.

Such deviations include the Fed's low interest rate policy in 2003–2005 and the lax enforcement of financial regulations—both deviations from rules-based policies that had worked in the past. These were largely responsible for the boom and the high level of risk-taking, which ended in the bust in 2007 and 2008. Other more recent deviations are the hundreds of new complex regulations under Dodd-Frank, the vast government interventions related to the new health care law, the temporary stimulus packages such as cash for clunkers which failed to sustain growth, the exploding federal debt that raises questions about how it will be stopped, and a highly discretionary monetary policy that has generated distortions and uncertainty.

Moreover, as summarized here, this view that "policy is the problem" stands up quite well compared to either the Summers "secular stagnation" view or the Reinhart-Rogoff "it's due to the financial crisis" view.

Finally, I note that there is a very optimistic implication of what I have been arguing here. If you take the view that policy is the problem, then you know what to do to fix the problem: change the policy. This means mainly getting back to policy principles that worked in the past—that worked before all these tragic events happened. It would mean a more predictable monetary policy, a more rules-based regulatory policy, and an aversion to bailouts rather than a too-big-to-fail mentality. Of course, the world is changing and applying these principles will not mean exactly the same policy strategy as in the two decades before the last one. But the economy worked pretty well in those days, and it's not working well now.

References

Ahrend, Rudiger. 2010. "Monetary Ease: A Factor Behind Financial Crises? Some Evidence from OECD Countries." *Economics: The Open Access, Open Assessment E-Journal* 4.

Bekaert, Geert, Marie Hoerova, and Marco Lo Duca. 2013. "Risk, Uncertainty, and Monetary Policy." European Central Bank working paper 1565.

Bordo, Michael D., and Joseph G. Haubrich. 2012. "Deep Recessions, Fast Recoveries, and Financial Crises: Evidence from the American Record." Working paper 12–14, Federal Reserve Bank of Cleveland.

Bordo, Michael, and John Landon-Lane. 2013. "Does Expansionary Monetary Policy Cause Asset Price Booms: Some Historical and Empirical Evidence." NBER Working Paper 19585.

Jarocinski, Marek, and Frank R. Smets. 2008. "House Prices and the Stance of Monetary Policy." Federal Reserve Bank of St. Louis *Review,* July/August: 339–65.

Kahn, George A. 2010. "Taylor Rule Deviations and Financial Imbalances." Federal Reserve Bank of Kansas City *Economic Review* Q-II: 63–99.

LaGarde, Christine. 2013. "The Global Calculus of Unconventional Monetary Policies." Federal Reserve Bank of Kansas City, Jackson Hole Economic Policy Symposium: Global Dimensions of Unconventional Monetary Policy, August 23.

Morgenson, Gretchen, and Joshua Rosner. 2011. *Reckless Endangerment: How Outsized Ambition, Greed, and Corruption Led to Economic Armageddon.* New York: Times Books.

Ohanian, Lee E., John B. Taylor, and Ian J. Wright, eds. 2012. *Government Policies and the Delayed Economic Recovery.* Stanford, CA: Hoover Institution Press.

Papell, David, and Ruxandra Prodan. 2012. "The Statistical Behavior of GDP after Financial Crises and Severe Recessions." Working paper, University of Houston.

Reinhart, Carmen, and Kenneth Rogoff. 2009. *This Time Is Different: Eight Centuries of Financial Folly.* Princeton, NJ: Princeton University Press.

Taylor, John B. 2009. *Getting Off Track: How Government Actions and Interventions Caused, Prolonged, and Worsened the Financial Crisis.* Stanford, CA: Hoover Institution Press.

Taylor, John B. 2012. *First Principles: Five Keys to Restoring America's Prosperity.* New York: W.W. Norton.

Taylor, John B. 2013. "The Effectiveness of Central Bank Independence versus Policy Rules." *Business Economics,* July.

Taylor, John B., and Akila Weerapana. 2012. *Principles of Economics, 7th Edition.* Mason, OH: South-Western Cengage Learning.

Wallison, Peter J. 2011. "Three Narratives about the Financial Crisis." *Cato Journal* 31 (3).

CHAPTER 4

Rethinking Macro
Reassessing Micro-foundations

Kevin M. Warsh

> *"[I]t appears that policymakers, if they wish to forecast the response of citizens, must take the latter into their confidence. This conclusion, if ill-suited to current econometric practice, seems to accord well with a preference for democratic decision-making."*
>
> —ROBERT LUCAS, 1976

It has been about five years since the economy buckled under the force of the global financial crisis. It happened much as Hemingway (1926) described how a person goes bankrupt. "Two ways," Hemingway wrote, "Gradually, then suddenly."

Well, the pattern of recovery has not followed the pattern of the crash. The recovery of the United States' economy can only be characterized as gradual. We hear repeated talk of escape velocity and confident, model-based predictions of sustained economic liftoff. There remain, however, insufficient real data—as of yet—to support the proposition. Instead, more than four years into recovery, we are growing accustomed to rationalizations that excuse economic malaise and comparisons to comfort us along the lines of at-least-we-are-doing-better-than-they-are.

Economists debate what transpired. Many hold the view that the period of steady growth and stable prices that preceded the crisis—the so-called Great Moderation—was largely the result of well-implemented macroeconomic policies. But the long period of benign economic results bred a complacency that sowed the seeds of crisis.

I am grateful to John Cogan, Stan Druckenmiller, Darrell Duffie, Chad Jones, Nellie Liang, Vincent Reinhart, George Shultz, Jeremy Stein, John Taylor, Jake Carney, Karen Reichgott, and John Abraham for helpful comments and discussion.

So, they ask, what should be done to return to the prosperity of the Great Moderation without inviting a repeat of the crisis? The emerging consensus has it that a grant of new powers to central bankers and regulatory authorities will go a long way to righting the ship. The standard tool-kit of periodic doses of fiscal and monetary stimulus (or restraint) should do its part to ensure economic growth and price stability. The zero-lower-bound constraint on interest rates can be managed effectively through asset purchases and forward guidance, the new vanguard of monetary policy. The tool-kit should be supplemented further, authorities tell us, with newfangled macroprudential policies that can be mastered to ensure macroeconomic stability.[1]

We are at a critical policy conjuncture, both in assessing macroeconomic policy and in evaluating the prospects for our economy. Many economic policymakers are convening in forums—publicly and privately—to "rethink macro." In my remarks, I will offer my own modest contributions to this undertaking.[2]

Economists disagree on the macroeconomic policy choices made in recent years, including the Federal Reserve's expansive asset purchase program and the new macroprudential regulatory regime. But there should be broad agreement that these policies are fundamentally different than practiced previously.

In some sense, these new policies have a common, understandable motivation: to bring greater stability to the financial markets and the economy. In practice, however, we should be particularly wary of top-down policies that risk undermining the economy's micro-foundations. If new macro-policies fundamentally alter the reaction functions of individuals and businesses, then that would go a long way to explaining why many leading policymakers and econometric models continue to err systematically in forecasting the performance of the economy.

I posit that changes in the conduct of macroeconomic policy may well be altering the underlying micro-foundations of the economy. Reviewing these micro-foundations of macro—the behavior of individuals, households, and firms—is essential to evaluate optimal policy and understand the future contours of the economy.

---

1. See, for example, Yellen (2012).

2. This paper is focused on the conduct of US policy, but the themes are applicable more broadly.

Lucas critique revisited

In the 1970s, Bob Lucas, Tom Sargent, Ned Phelps, and others challenged some of the leading macroeconomic forecasting models of their day. They worried that excessive enthusiasm for certain stylized macro models led policymakers—and the real economy—astray.

They took issue with the existing macroeconomic frameworks that were built largely on the relationship among aggregated data, such as consumption, spending, and investment. Their scholarship recognized that economic actors do not tend to react passively to policy changes. Individuals, households, and firms are not easily fooled. Instead, they tend to see through short-term policy fixes and assess the medium-term implications of changes in government policy on their everyday economic decisions.

Under the going theory that it "takes-a-model-to-beat-a-model," Lucas *et alia* applied new techniques and methods to improve the discipline of economics. In some sense, they recognized starkly the dynamic interaction between macro-policymakers and micro-economic actors.

Building on this literature, most of today's dynamic stochastic general equilibrium (DSGE) models seek to simultaneously incorporate rigidities—such as prices and wages—and rational expectations. The impact of any change in monetary policy is then calibrated, including a potential behavioral response. Note that these tend *not* to be real business cycle models which incorporate explicitly the decisions of individual agents.

So, are these models likely to be reliable predictors of the actual contours of the economy?

Even the latest generation of DSGE models does not incorporate a financial sector. In effect, the models assume that liquidity and risk can be intermediated with sufficiently low friction so as to not materially affect economic outcomes. Some strides have been made to correct this omission (Bernanke and Gertler 1995). But considerably more attention is required. As the financial crisis and its aftermath made clear, financial frictions are of first-order importance to the macroeconomy. If not, the failure of financial intermediaries during the crisis should not have caused such losses to the overall economy. If the financial sector were not of great import to the real economy, the imperative to reform our regulatory structure would also be sorely misplaced.

Of even greater consequence, today's leading macroeconomic models are structured to be mean-regressing. The economy is thought to respond similarly to prior economic periods. But these models lose much of their predictive capacity when policy regimes change. When confronted with persistently large tracking errors, forecasters (including at the Fed) now often resort to importing subjective "add-factors" to massage the model outputs, seeking to reconcile the differences between the predicted outcomes and the stark reality of slow growth.

As Lucas reminded us more than forty years ago, "any change in policy will systematically alter the structure of economic models . . . for the question of short-term forecasting, or tracking ability of econometric models . . . this conclusion is of only occasional significance . . . [but] for issues involving policy evaluation, in contrast, it is fundamental" (Lucas 1976).

In some sense, the Lucas critique—as it came to be known—was not just an academic debate taking place inside ivy-covered walls. It was about a fundamental rethink to help reconcile economic theory with economic policy, and economic policy with economic reality. While the economics profession learned much since the so-called rational expectations school emerged, the critique reminds us that the adoption of new policy regimes alters the structure of models, which consist of the decision rules of economic agents.

So, how can the notion underlying the Lucas critique inform our current economic predicament?

Today—perhaps even more so than in the late 1970s—getting the model right appears to be a predominant factor in getting policy right. Central bankers talk regularly about policy that is data-dependent and forecast-dependent. They go out of their way to describe their models' assumptions and outputs. They laud transparency and consider it a foremost virtue in the conduct of policy. Their forecasts for GDP, employment, and inflation tend to drive the policy debate, both inside the corridors of the Federal Open Market Committee (FOMC) and among financial market participants. The resulting policy judgments have large and consequential effects on the economy.[3]

If, for example, the Federal Reserve's FRB/US model—among the foremost DSGE models—estimates that the unemployment rate will remain

---

3. Given the shortcomings of leading models and the large tracking errors of forecasts, it is not obvious why model-centric policy should predominate. A compelling alternative would include a broader review of financial market conditions and real-time economic data to be considered alongside a broad range of model-based outputs.

above the natural rate of unemployment for a couple more years, that tends to weigh heavily on the staff's judgmental forecast. In my experience, the staff forecast then plays a central role—maybe even an anchoring role—from which many members of the FOMC make their individual forecasts. The latest iterations of the Fed's model, if they are believed, provide ample rationale for continuation of highly accommodative policy.

But what happens if the reaction function of economic agents changed along with policy regimes after the crisis of 2008?

This change in micro-behavior could be, in part, a function of the crisis itself. Economic agents never experienced an environment akin to the panic of 2008 and its resulting shock to wealth, confidence, and incomes. Nor should we downplay the impact on our citizenry of the failure or near-failure of many financial firms with various degrees of attachment to the US government, including Fannie Mae, Freddie Mac, and the largest banks.

Changes in the micro-foundations could also be a function of the macroeconomic policy response which differed markedly from historical precedent. In both cases, we should not be surprised if there were a different post-crisis economic response by our fellow citizens.

What is so new about policy? Consider the following:

- A renewed belief by policymakers that large, temporary government stimulus (e.g., Economic Stimulus Act of 2008 and American Recovery and Reinvestment Act of 2009) could be timed, sized, and deployed effectively to offset private shortfalls in demand.
- An unprecedented monetary policy response, which became more aggressive even as time elapsed from the depths of the financial crisis.
- A more expansive role, if not responsibility, for central banks as default providers of aggregate demand.
- A complex, novel macroprudential regulatory framework to oversee banks and systemically important financial firms.

I don't wish to devote these remarks to any detailed critique of particular policy choices. But these new policies share a common, if unexplored, narrative: they represent regime change. A broad, new financial stability agenda has become our government's primary policy objective. Stability is the new dominant guidepost for policy, its North Star.

The new stability agenda

Economists and policymakers have long struggled to draw lines between stability and efficiency (Sargent 2011). The line-drawing in the post-crisis era appears to be moving to favor macro-policies that elevate stability over efficiency. This is understandable and, by some lights, necessary. But, of no less consequence, I worry that the new stability agenda now in vogue seeks to do far more under the high-sounding auspices of stability than simply mitigating tail risks.

What is this stability about?

If it's about making our financial system more resilient to shocks, then it strikes me as consistent with past motivations, if not practice. Ensuring that the plumbing of the financial system works to promote prosperity is a noble and worthy pursuit. The Fed's creation a century ago, arising from the Panic of 1907, was aptly focused on mitigating future crises. Growth and employment are well-served if policymakers are able to reduce the likelihood of cataclysmic disruptions in financial intermediation, which would otherwise imperil the allocation of savings to profitable investment opportunities.

But, in practice, upon surveying the broad suite of new policies, the new stability agenda may be something quite different, something untested, with implications unclear. The new stability agenda appears at least as focused on smoothing macroeconomic aggregates as on mitigating tail risks. It seems keen, in effect if not intent, to remove significant risk from financial markets—even in benign times—as if volatility itself were anathema to prosperity. The new stability regime seems committed to taming the normal business cycle, as though economic growth that deviates somewhat from trend intrinsically and systematically harms long-term prospects.[4]

I worry that the new stability agenda, however well-intentioned, is more inclined to accept statism than risk the consequences of dynamism. It thereby risks undermining the micro-foundations of macro. To achieve

---

4. Central bankers have long sought to minimize large deviations in output, employment, and inflation from target in the conduct of monetary policy. So, macroeconomic aggregates have long mattered. But I contend that the new stability agenda, including the Fed's large, direct, and prolonged participation in long-term funding markets, represents a quantitative and qualitative break with past practice, especially with respect to changing the resulting incentives of economic agents.

long-run stability, we must be accepting of considerable turbulence along the way. Turbulence or, more aptly, economic vitality is scarcely an unhealthy condition. It may be essential at the micro-economic level to achieve sustainable macroeconomic prosperity. Yet, if economic vitality is frowned upon in the new policy regime, then we might be lessening the economy's long-run potential.

Seeking to banish recessions is a fundamentally different endeavor than taking steps to avoid another financial panic. A look back at the Great Moderation offers some key—perhaps unexpected—insights on the interaction between micro-economic foundations and macroeconomic outcomes.

The Great Moderation unmasked

The moderation of the business cycle marked the generation that preceded the financial crisis. It is easy to review the period with some longing. It's understandable that the desire to return to a period of reduced volatility of aggregate economic data—GDP, employment, industrial production, inflation—is motivating policymakers.

But, if we are seeking to return to those halcyon days without the pernicious after-effects, we should be clear what the period was really all about.

The Great Moderation is a great misnomer. The seeming stability of the aggregate data during the Great Moderation belied significant disruption at the household and firm level. The period was marked by extraordinary changes at the level of individuals, households, and businesses. And this vitality served to propel growth, standards of living, and, yes, aggregate stability for more than a generation.

Taylor (1998) was among the first to note the reduction in aggregate macro-volatility and improved economic outcomes during the "long boom." He rightfully assigned a significant portion of the credit to the improved conduct of monetary policy. Indeed, during the 1980s and 1990s, central bankers established—and followed—a clearer policy framework which contributed to the superior outcomes that marked the era.[5]

---

5. I am persuaded that improved conduct of macroeconomic policy, including monetary policy, was an important contributor to better economic outcomes during much of the Great Moderation. Especially since the financial crisis, however, the conduct of broad macroeconomic policies changed. This paper seeks to better understand the resulting behavioral responses of key economic agents.

McConnell and Perez-Quiros (2000) and Stock and Watson (2002) demonstrate the extent of the moderation across the US economy beginning in the early 1980s. They offer a range of explanations for the benign macroeconomic outcomes, including acceleration to a services-oriented economy and less severe exogenous shocks to supply and demand.

Dynan, Elmendorf, and Sichel (2006) add to the growing literature on the year-over-year volatility of earnings and income at the household level. Their review of disaggregated data from households shows greater economic uncertainty during the Great Moderation than in prior periods. Although aggregate economic activity became less volatile than previously, individual households appear to have faced more volatile economic circumstances.

The careful data work of Davis and Kahn (2008) is consistent with these findings. When they consider household-level consumption changes, they "find no evidence of a decline in volatility after 1980. The evidence on individual earnings uncertainty points to a longer-term rise, not a decline."

What helps to explain this apparent divergence? Greater access to financial products—and the concomitant ability of individuals to offset shortfalls in income—helps to soften the blow from income shocks. In addition, the greater heterogeneity of households means that changes in income are less correlated with their peers. Other leading explanations include innovation in inventory management, allowing firms to be more nimble in their use of labor and capital.

The growth models of Aghion and Howitt (1992) describe a simple model of growth through creative destruction. Growth results from technological progress being undertaken by competing firms seeking to innovate. These innovations positively affect an entire economy, notwithstanding near-term turbulence. New research and development beget economic profits, which raise wages for highly skilled workers until the next innovation makes the prior enhancements obsolete.

That stronger growth and muted volatility arise from vitality inside of the economy should be of little surprise to those familiar with Silicon Valley. Schumpeter's creative destruction finds its exemplar in the area around Stanford University. Disruptive technologies threaten incumbent firms and workers with impunity, but this difficult transition should not be confused with weaker growth or macro-instability.

In my view, then, both economic theory and empirical data from the Great Moderation suggest that the period of macro-stability was consistent with micro-instability. It may well be that disruptions in the micro-foundations of the economy were a necessary condition for the benign macro-conditions of the period.

If the new primary objective of our nation's public policy, however, is to stabilize macro-fluctuations, then harm may be done to the Schumpeterian dynamics that are crucial to economic growth. Leaving growth considerations aside, it is not even apparent that a new stability agenda will achieve the macroeconomic stability to which it aspires.

Let's turn to the possible effects of these new macroeconomic policies. The task is to judge—as much as practicable—the impact of changes in macroeconomic policy on the micro-foundations of the real economy. I will review possible changes in reaction functions of banks and business in the new regime. The changing decision calculus likely has significant consequences for individuals and households as well. Considerably more attention is owed to the actual behavioral responses of economic agents to changes in macroeconomic policy.

The new financial regulatory regime: de-risking the banking business?

In regulatory policy, the new stability brigade is in full force. Inspired by the Dodd-Frank Act (DFA), a new financial architecture is being implemented. The new financial oversight regime represents not just a change in rules and an escalation in boots-on-the-ground to police financial firms. It fundamentally changes the roles, responsibilities, and institutional design of our government's oversight of financial institutions.

Purportedly to resolve conflicts and confusion among more than a dozen regulatory authorities, the law did something to which Washington leaders are long accustomed: it created a committee. And it appointed the secretary of the treasury as the chair of the new committee, the Financial Stability Oversight Council (FSOC), a break with two decades of practice that sought to insulate regulators from political influence.

Today, the FSOC's constituent members, including the Fed and nine other voting members, are in the midst of reorganizing themselves to fulfill their new responsibilities. With characteristic understatement, Ben Bernanke, chairman of the Fed at the time, acknowledged the difficult task at hand (Bernanke 2012):

> "The crisis, the recession it sparked, and the subsequent slow recovery . . . demonstrated that we have much to learn about the workings

and vulnerabilities of our modern, globalized financial system and its interactions with the broader economy. In responding to these stressful financial and economic developments, the Federal Reserve and other central banks have had to deploy a variety of new tools and approaches to carry out their responsibilities in the area of macroprudential supervision, with the objective of promoting financial stability and reducing the likelihood and costs of a future financial crisis. Although much progress has been made, we are still at an early stage in understanding how best to meet these new macroprudential responsibilities."

My intention, however, is not principally to critique the new law or its implementation, or to suggest what might constitute more significant regulatory reform of our largest financial firms (Warsh 2012a). Rather, it is to highlight the possible consequences of the new regime on the decision-making of key economic agents and to suggest that the effects on the overall economy should not be dismissed. In fact, the effects of these changes go well beyond our ability to forecast.

A new, comprehensive set of rules for banking—virtually any new set of rules—can, over time, be constructive or destructive to the microfoundations of the economy. But when these rule changes are still largely unknown more than three years after the reforms were enacted into law, there is good reason to be concerned about their detrimental effects. Since DFA was enacted, 848 pages of statutory text expanded to 13,789 pages of new regulation, more than 15 million words. And, according to Davis, Polk & Wardwell, this represents only 39 percent of required rule-makings, with much of the remainder well past legislative deadline (Davis Polk 2013).

In addition, the banking "reforms" are not likely to be known even once the DFA-designated rule-makings are ostensibly complete. Jeremy Stein, a member of the board of governors of the Federal Reserve, describes the difficulty in calibrating this broad set of authorities (Stein 2013a). A longer period of adjustment to the rules is likely to prevail.

"One way to resolve this tension is to refrain from putting ourselves in the position of having to make a once-and-for-all decision in a setting of substantial uncertainty. Rather, it might be preferable to try to learn from the incoming data and adjust over time, particularly since the recent changes to capital regulation already on the books may represent an informative experiment . . . For example, the capital-surcharge schedule proposed by the Basel Committee for globally important systemic banks may be a reasonable starting point. However, if after some time it has not delivered much of a change in the size and complexity of the largest of banks, one might conclude that the implicit tax was too small and should be ratcheted up. . . . Of course, I recognize that its gradualist nature presents practical challenges . . . "

The behavior of financial intermediaries during a period of prolonged limbo is particularly vexing. Might the firms reduce the extension of credit to the real economy until the final capital rules are ultimately adjudicated? Shrinking their asset base may prove far more attractive than raising new capital and thereby diluting their firms' existing equity holders.

The legislation also promises a new remit in overseeing a complex, interconnected financial system: macroprudential oversight. In the decade before the financial crisis, many authoritative reports—replete with compilations of aggregate data—suggested that the global financial system was fundamentally sound. With the benefit of hindsight, a deeper review would have found significant infirmities. So, the search for a new approach to overseeing the banking system is necessary and understandable.

Macroprudential oversight scarcely sounds like an Orwellian plot. But what is it exactly? I don't know. There remains precious little economic literature or policy practice to provide informed guidance.

Adrian, Covitz, and Liang (2013) are among the first, and most knowledgeable, to conceptualize this new regime. Given the high costs to the economy of fragile financial institutions, the new regime is intended to implement policies "preemptively" to ensure greater financial stability. They lay out a laudable principal objective: "Macroprudential policies are designed to reduce vulnerabilities to mitigate the amplification of negative shocks, and also to pre-position institutions so that they can absorb shocks."

The Fed has assuredly made progress in its monitoring regime. But the task of identifying bubbles or vulnerabilities is daunting. Suffice it to say that the new macroprudential policy tools, including tools to assess and to pop asset bubbles, are still a subject of considerable debate among policymakers.

The Adrian-Covitz-Liang framework is especially useful in helping to frame the policy trade-offs when pursuing the new macroprudential remit. Evidently, there is no free lunch policy to be pursued. Instead, they highlight how policies that seek to reduce the likelihood of systemic crises may do so only by raising the costs of financial intermediation in non-crisis periods.

The framework implicitly asks how much "sand in the gears" of financial intermediation a country is prepared to accept. Several unresolved questions follow:

- What will be the effects on the cost and availability of credit to businesses and households?
- Will the added costs of financial intermediation correspond to a material reduction in the odds of a negative systemic event?
- If the initiatives pursued in the name of macroprudential oversight turn out to be detrimental to growth, are we confident that longer-term stability benefits are attainable?

Moreover, the new remit may well conflict with the Fed's conduct of monetary policy. Are lower employment and lower macroeconomic risk preferable to higher employment and higher macroeconomic risk? When such a conflict occurs, how should it be resolved? By whom? How much confidence must the authorities have in their own judgment to decide? Will the Fed make that judgment in its independent conduct of monetary policy? Or will it be resolved by the treasury secretary as the head of the FSOC?

It is also critical to understand the new decision-making calculus of the largest banks in this new regime. How are the executives and boards of directors likely to respond to an avalanche of new and changing rules, an overlapping set of regulators, and a new overseer endowed with a new remit when the downside risks are apparent and the upside gains are impossible to observe? Might the largest banks fight the new regime fiercely? Or are they more likely to decide that fighting their overseers is a battle that cannot be won?

We have long worried that our largest financial institutions were "too big to fail." Under DFA, these firms are redefined as systemically important financial institutions (SIFIs). If recent behavior is any indication, I fear they will most likely become public utilities.

In my judgment, the temptation for SIFIs to become public utilities is a troubling development. Significant political science literature suggests that the tensions and uncertainties among regulators and those regulated are often ultimately resolved by truce, by negotiated settlement, or by implicit arrangement. Fannie Mae and Freddie Mac are only the latest examples of entities that became quasi-public utilities over time while retaining some quasi-private attributes. And as their demise makes apparent, the "constructive ambiguity" associated with these firms turned out to be neither constructive nor ambiguous.

Some large "systemically important" firms may well be willing to accept new, permanent government masters and supplementary public purposes in order to protect their privileged status. In so doing, they may be persuaded to apportion some of the economic rents—gained in part by virtue of being perceived as backed by the government—to the official sector as a sort of peace offering.

For many of the banks themselves, this might not be an irrational response. John Mack, the former chairman and CEO of Morgan Stanley, captured the sentiment recently (Lucchetti and Steinberg 2013) when he reportedly advised his successor, James Gorman: "Your number one client is the government."

This new regime may be useful for large bank executives, boards of directors, bondholders, or even shareholders. But the consequences for our financial and economic system may be far less comforting. A small number of large public utilities atop the banking sector would invariably change the business of banking. The uneven playing field may well be creating perverse incentives for the erstwhile competitors of the biggest firms—small and medium-sized banks and other financial intermediaries. More work should be done to evaluate better the resulting impact on credit flow to businesses, households, and individuals in the real economy.

The public utility model is at odds with the best of US economic history. The new regime may be more consistent with statism than dynamism, more consistent with short-run stability than growth-enhancing vitality. And, over the medium term, we should query whether this new policy regime is useful to achieve either a higher growth trajectory for our economy or a mitigation of tail risks. And even if the public utility model makes the business of banking less volatile in most periods, it may be riskier still in times of significant financial stress.

The new monetary policy regime: boosting business capital expenditures?

In the depths of the financial crisis, a newly aggressive, volatility-reducing monetary policy was instituted by the Federal Reserve. It represents an important component of the broader stability agenda.

The United States was suffering from old-fashioned panic, in which volatility measures jumped and asset prices fell dramatically. Quantitative easing, as it came to be known, was established. QE1's objectives included stopping the run on wholesale funding, infusing liquidity into the banking system, and improving market functioning. The panic, ultimately, was averted and the recession turned to a recovery, albeit a muted one.

The expansion and extension of the Fed's asset purchase program (so-called QE2 and QE3) was instituted to accelerate the pace of the economic recovery, according to its proponents. The refined goal was to transmit the Fed's aggressive policies through financial markets to strengthen aggregate demand. As a massive buyer of Treasury and mortgage securities, the Fed removed significant duration and associated volatility from financial markets. It thereby enticed new investors—unnatural buyers—into the market, especially for riskier assets like housing and equities.[6]

Risk assets, like stocks, rallied at least as much as the Fed expected. The Standard & Poor's 500 and the Russell 1000 are up more than 150 percent since the recovery began in March 2009. Lower measured market volatility is also consistent with higher asset prices. The VIX (Volatility Index) averaged less than fifteen during the last twelve months. That is 60 percent lower measured equity volatility than the crisis average and nearly 30 percent lower than the long-term average.

What about the predicted strengthening of the real economy? Increases in asset values and net worth were predicted to have significant follow-on wealth and confidence effects that would thereby bolster the real economy.

Let's isolate one critical cog in the transmission mechanism of QE: did higher share prices induced in part by monetary policy translate into significantly higher business investment?

---

6. Still, legitimate questions can be raised about QE's long-term consequences. But what is the optimum quantum of volatility removal from markets? Can the Fed's QE permanently lower volatility in markets? Or is it akin to the law of conservation of matter, in which actual volatility is neither created nor destroyed, but simply moved from one place to another and from one time period to another? See, for example, similar concerns expressed by Jeremy Stein in remarks delivered at a symposium sponsored by the Center for Financial Studies (Stein 2013b): "If the Fed's control of long-term rates depends in substantial part on the induced buying and selling behavior of other investors, our grip on the steering wheel is not as tight as it otherwise might be."

Pre-tax corporate profits represent a record of more than 12 percent of GDP. These profits have no doubt been aided by lower interest rates, cost savings, and significant productivity improvements. This explains in part the significant share price appreciation during the last four years. QE proponents believe, quite reasonably, that the aggressive asset purchase regime supported additional share price appreciation.

Historically, high share prices are associated with increased business confidence and higher capital expenditures. But when comparing business investment patterns during this cycle to history, the results are clearly disappointing. Despite a contraction far more severe than the six previous cycles, recovery of real non-residential fixed investment delivered only a moderate improvement from trough levels. As figure 4.1 below makes clear, investment is only slowly returning toward its pre-recession highs.

In fact, real non-residential fixed investment remains roughly 1.5 percent below its pre-recession peak, substantially lower than the last six post-recession recoveries in which previous peaks were surpassed by nearly 20 percent after a similar period of time.

Business investment is also lagging most forecasters' projections. The Philadelphia Federal Reserve Bank survey of professional forecasters, for example, consistently overestimated investment growth (by approximately 1 percentage point per annum) throughout this period. Model-based forecasts, such as those employed by Macroeconomic Advisers, also point to errors of similar magnitude in overestimating investment growth post-crisis.

There is a common litany of explanations for the lack of capital investment by the private sector, including lack of aggregate demand, regulatory uncertainty, and Washington dysfunction.

Might there be another reason why the historical regression broke down?

I posit that QE-induced share price appreciation is not fully internalized by corporate chieftains. They are unsure if monetary policy at the zero lower bound can usher in a stronger real economy. While pleased with their stock performance, corporate leaders question whether their share prices will remain elevated in a post-QE world. So, company executives are not taking their elevated share prices at face value and investing accordingly. Instead, they appear to be looking through some of the share price appreciation, concluding that it was bolstered by a surge in QE that

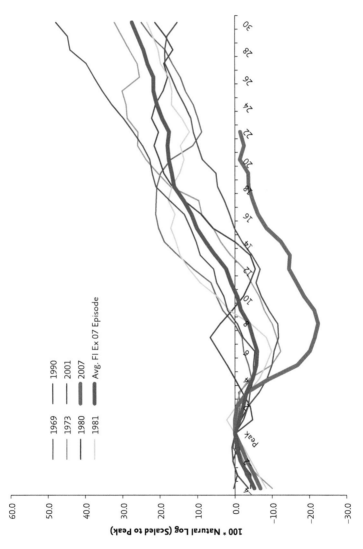

FIGURE 4.1 Real non-residential fixed investment—quarters after business cycle peaks.

Source: Morgan Stanley Research

may not persist. So, they remain underinvested relative to past economic cycles and recent share performance.

If true, we might have to wait until an exit from QE before an actual acceleration in capital expenditures on long-lived assets is observed. Company executives may then be in a position to evaluate their unaffected share price—that is, uninfluenced by QE—before committing to a more robust investing regime. Well-intended macro-policy—solving for higher share prices and lower market volatility by use of non-conventional tools—may have changed micro-behavior. Leading econometric models may be unable to account for such behavioral responses.

Ultimately, a sustainable equilibrium will be established between asset prices and the real economy. But given the novelty of the government's policy response, it is difficult to know whether the current mix of low market volatility, higher prices for risk assets, and modest economic recovery puts the United States on a path toward sustained improvement in the next year or two. In the alternative, the aggressive macroeconomic response may have lowered potential GDP and created a pretense of stability that is susceptible to an unexpected deterioration in conditions. Business leaders may well be confronted by the same riddle. It's no surprise, then, that capital expenditures continue to fall short of forecasts.

Closing comments

The efficacy of the US government's post-crisis macroeconomic policy response is the subject of considerable debate. The reaction function of key economic agents, however, is worthy of considerably more discussion and empirical assessment. We should seek to better understand the particular behavioral responses of economic agents to policymakers' novel designs.

The broad suite of new policies may be changing the micro-foundations of macro, threatening the supply and demand sides of the real economy. The new regulatory architecture might be altering the decision-making of credit providers and users alike. The resulting public utility banking model could well be causing banks and their customers to act differently than forecasted. Lagging business capital expenditures are another illustration of how the promised benefits of new macroeconomic policy may be faltering due to the behavioral responses of key economic decision-makers.

As a result, more of the burden of economic growth is being placed on the pocketbook of consumers. Yet, consumption spending has generally disappointed model-based predictions and policymakers' expectations. Consumers may have initially pulled back on their spending due to the shock caused by the panic of 2008. But, in spite of massive monetary intervention, consumers may continue to hesitate taking the bait, reckoning that the novel policy regime will not deliver a recovery nearly as robust as they had grown accustomed to observing in prior periods.[7]

Just five years after the financial crisis, the instinctive preference for stability over turbulence is understandable. But we should be humble in any undertaking that seeks to remove substantial turbulence, upend the business cycle, or reorder stability and growth in an economy that is dependent on millions of decisions made every day far afield from Washington.

References

Adrian, Tobias, Daniel Covitz, and Nellic Liang. 2013. "Financial Stability Monitoring." Federal Reserve Board Finance and Economics Discussion Series 2013–21: 2.

Aghion, Philippe, and Peter Howitt. 1992. "A Model of Growth Through Creative Destruction." *Econometrica* 60 (2): 323–351.

Bernanke, Ben S. 2012. "Opening Remarks." Remarks delivered at the Federal Reserve conference on central banking, Washington, D.C., March 23.

Bernanke, Ben S., and Mark Gertler. 1995. "Inside the Black Box: The Credit Channel of Monetary Policy Transmission." *Journal of Economic Perspectives* 9 (4): 27–48.

Cochrane, John. 2013. "Three Views of Consumption and the Slow Economy." *The Grumpy Economist* (blog), February 3.

Davis Polk. 2013. *Dodd-Frank Progress Report*. New York: Davis Polk & Wardwell. October: 4.

Davis, Steven J., and James A. Kahn. 2008. "Interpreting the Great Moderation: Changes in the Volatility of Economic Activity at the Macro and Micro Levels." *Journal of Economic Perspectives* 22 (4): 155–180.

Dynan, Karen E., Douglas W. Elmendorf, and Daniel E. Sichel. 2006. "Can Financial Innovation Help to Explain the Reduced Volatility of Economic Activity?" *Journal of Monetary Economics* 53 (1): 124–150.

---

7. See, for example, Cochrane 2013.

Dynan, Karen E., Douglas W. Elmendorf, and Daniel E. Sichel. 2008. "The Evolution of Household Income Volatility." The Brookings Institution, February.

European Central Bank. 2013. *Financial Stability Review*. May. Frankfurt am Main, Germany: ECB.

Hemingway, Ernest. 1926. *The Sun Also Rises*. New York: Charles Scribner's Sons.

Lucas, Robert. 1976. "Econometric Policy Evaluation: A Critique." *Carnegie Rochester Conference Series on Public Policy* 1 (1): 19–46.

Lucchetti, Aaron, and Julie Steinberg. 2013. "Life on Wall Street Grows Less Risky." *Wall Street Journal*, September 9.

McConnell, Margaret M., and Gabriel Perez-Quiros. 2000. "Output Fluctuations in the United States: What Has Changed Since the Early 1980s?" *American Economic Review* 90 (5): 1464–1476.

Sargent, Thomas J. 2006. "Ambiguity in American Monetary and Fiscal Policy." *Japan and the World Economy* 18 (3): 324–330.

Sargent, Thomas J. 2011. "Where to Draw Lines: Stability Versus Efficiency." *Economica* 78 (310): 197–214.

Sargent, Thomas, and Neil Wallace, 1976. "Rational Expectations and the Theory of Economic Policy." *Journal of Monetary Economics* 2 (2): 169–183.

Stein, Jeremy. 2013a. "Regulating Large Financial Institutions." Remarks delivered at the Rethinking Macro Policy II conference sponsored by the International Monetary Fund, Washington, D.C., April 17: 7.

Stein, Jeremy. 2013b. "Yield-Oriented Investors and the Monetary Transmission Mechanism." Remarks delivered at Banking, Liquidity, and Monetary Policy symposium sponsored by the Center for Financial Studies in Honor of Raghuram Rajan, Frankfurt, Germany, September 26: 7.

Stock, James H., and Mark W. Watson. 2002. "Has the Business Cycle Changed and Why?" NBER Working Paper 9127.

Taylor, John B. 1998. "Monetary Policy and the Long Boom." Remarks delivered at the Homer Jones Lecture, Southern Illinois University, April 16.

Warsh, Kevin. 2010. "Regulation and its Discontents." Remarks delivered at the New York Association for Business Economics, New York, February 3.

Warsh, Kevin. 2011. "The Financial Repression Trap." *Wall Street Journal*, December 6.

Warsh, Kevin. 2012. "Regulatory Reform: A Practitioner's Perspective." Remarks delivered at the Seventh Annual Morrison & Foerster Lectureship, Stanford Law School, April 25.

Warsh, Kevin. 2012. "Who Deserves Credit for the Improving Economy?" *Wall Street Journal*, April 8.

Wieland, Volker, Tobias Cwik, Gernot J. Müller, Sebastian Schmidt, and Maik Wolters. 2012. "A New Comparative Approach to Macroeconomic Modeling and Policy Analysis." *Journal of Economic Behavior & Organization* 83 (3): 523–541.

Yellen, Janet L. 2012. "Pursuing Financial Stability at the Federal Reserve." Remarks delivered at the Fourteenth Annual International Banking Conference, Federal Reserve Bank of Chicago, November 11.

PART II
The Federal Reserve's Role

CHAPTER 5

Federal Reserve Policy Before, During, and After the Fall

Alan S. Blinder

The exact dating of the financial crisis that gripped the world and precipitated a severe worldwide recession late in the last decade is somewhat up in the air—even a bit arbitrary. I favor August 9, 2007—Paribas Day—as the start date, but other choices are equally plausible; and the run-up to the crisis surely extends back years before that. The signal event of the entire sorry episode, however, is clear. It happened on September 15, 2008, when Lehman Brothers filed for bankruptcy. Pretty much everything that hadn't fallen apart previously came crashing down after Lehman Day. The crisis also truly went global at that time.

Correspondingly, my evaluations of the Federal Reserve's policy actions are dramatically different pre- and post-Lehman Day. In brief, the Fed deserves mixed but rather poor grades for the years and days leading up to (and including) the fateful Lehman decision, but quite excellent grades thereafter. Most of this short paper is devoted to explaining that last sentence.[1]

Before the Fall

There is almost universal agreement that regulatory neglect, especially in the mid-2000s, helped set the stage for the financial crisis—and that while some of the regulators' somnolence was obvious only after the fact, much of it was obvious beforehand.[2] There is so much blame to go around the regulatory community that it is nice (for the Fed) that blame can be shared among six different agencies (in the United States) plus the US Congress (e.g., for passing the odious Commodity Futures Modernization Act [CFMA] in 2000). Yet the Federal Reserve gets, and probably

---

1. For much greater detail on the issues discussed here, and many other issues as well, see Blinder (2013).

2. See Financial Crisis Inquiry Commission (2011).

merits, a healthy share of the blame because (a) it was the only regulator with systemic responsibilities (tacit then, explicit now), (b) it was (and remains) the *primus inter pares* among financial regulators, and (c) it had been assigned by Congress special responsibilities for both mortgages and consumer protection.

Starting with some perspicacious warnings from then-Governor Ned Gramlich as early as 2000, continuing through an early 2002 article by economist Dean Baker, and including numerous press reports in 2003 and 2004, the Fed had ample warnings that something—indeed much—was amiss in the residential mortgage market, especially in the subprime sector.[3] It ignored them all. Notably, the Fed and other bank regulators did not need to go to Congress for any additional authority in order to crack down on the patently unsafe and unsound lending practices, or on the abusive and even predatory loan terms, that were visible all around them. Their pre-existing legal authority was ample; they just didn't use it. And under malign neglect, bad went to worse.[4] For this abysmal performance, all of America's bank regulators, including the Fed, deserve a failing grade.

But that was not all. Financial regulators allowed far too much leverage to build up in the system. Prominently, the Securities and Exchange Commission (SEC) permitted what can only be called reckless levels of leverage at the nation's five giant investment banks. The Federal Reserve and the Office of the Comptroller of the Currency (OCC) seemed either unaware of or unfazed by the hyper-leveraged structured investment vehicles (SIVs) that sprouted alongside the balance sheets of many of the biggest commercial banks. The Office of Thrift Supervision was an embarrassment—and was subsequently abolished. No one seemed to pay any attention to the titanic amounts of leverage embedded in certain derivatives, which were exploding in volume, perhaps because Congress had instructed regulators not to look. Leverage embedded in derivatives poses particularly difficult challenges for regulators since, while most derivative contracts start at a zero net position (hence are neither an asset nor a liability), they can move sharply in either a negative or a positive direction. It is the exposure, not the literal amount of leverage (assets divided by capital), that matters.

---

3. See Baker (2002), Temkin, Johnson, and Levy (2002), and Andrews (2004).

4. In (undeserved) fairness, the most outrageous mortgage lending probably happened outside the regulated banking industry. But what went on inside banks was bad enough.

One good question to ask is: could the Fed have stopped the leverage binge with the weapons at its disposal at the time? Certainly not fully, and certainly not by itself. For example, the SEC was needed to deal with the most serious leverage addicts: the big investment banks. That said, the Fed and the OCC could and should have arched more eyebrows sternly at bankers, informed themselves better about SIVs, and worried more about exposures from derivatives than they did. Much more. And that would have helped.

So far, I've dealt only with regulatory *behavior*, which was not a pretty picture. But there were also huge problems with the regulatory *structure*, which was plagued by both silos and gaps. Prior to the crisis, as now, we had too many bank regulators. Partly for that reason, the Fed would often run into jurisdictional roadblocks when it sought to cross over the border between the bank holding company (the Fed's jurisdiction) and the bank (the OCC's jurisdiction). Worse yet, the central bank had essentially no regulatory window into the pure investment banks. In addition, most of the shadow banking system—including, prominently, mortgage brokers and mortgage banks—were effectively unregulated. The situation in the over-the-counter derivatives business was even worse, since CFMA actually *banned* their regulation. None of this was the Fed's fault.

But what about monetary policy? Some critics have blamed the Fed's low-interest-rate policy in 2002–2004 (the Fed started tightening in June 2004) for encouraging leverage, providing the raw material for risky "carry trades," and, in general, aiding and abetting speculation such as the housing bubble.[5] With the benefit of hindsight, the Fed probably did keep money and credit too loose for too long. But unlike its regulatory laxity, that "error" was far from obvious contemporaneously. After all, the US economy was struggling to escape from the slow "jobless recovery" that followed the 2001 recession. The compound average annual growth rate of real GDP from the third quarter of 2001 through the first quarter of 2003 was a paltry 1.9 percent. It looked like the economy needed help.

Perhaps more fundamentally, one can ask whether short-term interest rates that were, say, even 1–2 percentage points higher, and mortgage rates that were perhaps 0.6–1.2 percentage points higher, would have stopped the housing bubble in its tracks.[6] The case of the United Kingdom, where

---

5. One prominent example is Taylor (2009).

6. Interest rates 3–4 percentage points higher would have almost certainly caused another recession.

the Bank of England kept short rates well above Federal Reserve levels throughout, suggests not. So does common sense when prospective home-buyers were expecting (no doubt, irrationally) 10–20 percent capital gains *per year*. Notice also that the housing bubble did not burst even after the Fed started raising the federal funds rate in June 2004. (The funds rate eventually went up by a cumulative 425 basis points.) House prices kept rising for at least another two years.[7]

So I agree that the Fed kept monetary policy too loose for too long in 2002–2004. But that "mistake" was small, forgivable under the circumstances, and may not have done much harm.

The Panic of 2007–2009

On monetary policy, the Federal Open Market Committee (FOMC) was a little slow on the draw, seeing the continuing financial crisis as more of a technical issue regarding illiquidity than a macroeconomic issue calling for monetary easing. For example, it was still calling high inflation its "predominant policy concern" as late as its August 7, 2007, meeting—just two days before Paribas Day! The committee was soon having second thoughts about that judgment. But it did not cut interest rates until September 18, and then it waited another agonizing six weeks before cutting rates again. The Fed only really seemed to "get it" in December 2007. But once the FOMC started moving in earnest, it moved fast, lending huge amounts and lowering interest rates. The federal funds rate, which had been at 5.25 percent on September 17, 2007, was down to virtually zero by December 16, 2008. Its interest-rate reactions dwarfed, e.g., those of the European Central Bank.

The Fed's massive emergency lending, much of it under the pliable section 13(3), followed the lines Bagehot had prescribed in 1873—sort of. The central bank lent freely against collateral that, if not always "good," was at least decent, and charged a (very small) penalty rate. And just as Bagehot prescribed, the Fed's lending rose from about zero on Lehman Day to a titanic $1.5 trillion and then receded "naturally" back to about zero as the panic eased and banks no longer needed central bank credit. It was, as it should have been, a temporary operation.

---

7. The words "at least" connote that housing prices peaked at different times, depending on which prices index you use.

Finally, however, I should mention what I believe was the Fed's biggest error of all: letting Lehman Brothers fail so messily, in a jumble of bankruptcy proceedings.

First, it must be admitted that:

- The Fed would have been crawling out on a long limb had it rescued Lehman without approval from the Treasury; so the US Treasury shares the blame.[8]
- There was legitimate concern about how much good collateral Lehman could have posted to secure Federal Reserve loans under section 13(3); but on the other hand, the Fed was the legal judge of that.
- The Fed and the Treasury tried hard, right up to the last minute, to broker a "private sector solution" whereby some other large financial institution (Bank of America? Barclays?) would buy Lehman. Once push came to shove, they did not view Lehman as a good opportunity to teach a moral hazard lesson, even though Treasury Secretary Henry Paulson had suggested as much earlier.

All that said, if the Fed and the Treasury had realized how terrible things would get if Lehman were allowed to fail, it seems to me that the central bank could have labeled enough of Lehman's collateral as "good enough" to justify the necessary loans—much as it had done for Bear Stearns (using J.P. Morgan as a vehicle) just six months earlier.[9] Indeed, I think a significant part of the stunning market reactions to the Lehman failure stemmed from the starkly different treatments accorded to Lehman (let it fail) versus Bear (save it).

After the Bear Stearns operation, markets presumed that many large financial institutions (FIs) were too big or too connected to fail. After Lehman Brothers failed, the rulebook went out the window, no FI looked safe

---

8. Within days of the Lehman disaster, the Treasury, which had claimed it had no money it could use legally to save Lehman, found $50 billion in the Exchange Stabilization Fund to support the endangered money market mutual fund industry.

9. The Fed lost nothing on $29 billion worth of Bear Stearns assets that J.P. Morgan viewed (in March 2008) as too risky to take on its own balance sheet. Might that have happened with the Lehman assets, too, once the crisis passed?

anymore, and the rout was on. It was a monumental error with catastrophic consequences. If the Treasury and the Fed were going to take a moral hazard stand somewhere, it should have been over Bear, not Lehman.

Once Lehman crashed and burned, and the far-reaching and frightening consequences started to become clear, the Fed's performance improved markedly and admirably. But the Fed did not win a lot of public accolades or support. As Barney Frank astutely observed, "No one has ever gotten reelected where the bumper sticker said, 'It would have been worse without me.' You probably can get tenure with that. But you can't win office."[10]

True, but the Fed's strong actions probably kept a terrible situation from mushrooming into an all-out catastrophe.[11] Like the Troubled Asset Relief Program (TARP), to which Ben Bernanke lent his personal and the Fed's institutional power and prestige, many of the Fed's emergency actions were bold, intelligent, and imaginative. When things started crashing all around him, there was no playbook sitting on Fed Chairman Ben Bernanke's bookshelf. The Fed (and the Treasury) had to improvise on the fly. I shudder to think about what might have happened had the Federal Reserve behaved in 2008–2009 as it did in 1930–1931. Fortunately, so did Bernanke.

After Lehman, the Fed intervened in unprecedented ways, first to save and then to resuscitate dying (or dead) markets for commercial paper (CP) and mortgage-backed securities (MBS). The CP rescue program resulted in a temporary bulge in the central bank's balance sheet, the acceptance of some (though not much) credit risk, and a tacit foray into credit allocation. It was a portent of things to come. The MBS purchase program, which is still in progress, led to a huge and long-lasting expansion of the Fed's balance sheet, the acceptance of even more credit risk, and a quite explicit effort to allocate more credit to mortgage finance. In each respect, the Fed stuck its neck out, and critics brayed that it was going astray. In each respect, in my view, the Fed deserves kudos for being right.

Bernanke also made an intellectual break with previous episodes of quantitative easing (QE), as practiced mainly in Japan. (He tried to change

---

10. Quoted in *Washington Post,* July 21, 2009. I found this quotation in Wilson (2012, 251). By the way, you *can* get tenure with that!

11. Blinder and Zandi (2010) estimated that without the many "financial policies," which included TARP, the unemployment rate would have risen nearly 3 percentage points more than it did.

the name, too—to "credit easing." But "QE" stuck.) In Japan, the focus of QE was on the *liabilities* side of the Bank of Japan's balance sheet. The central idea was to throw massive amounts of excess reserves into the banks on the hope that they would put some of them to work. As practiced by the Fed, however, the focus of QE was on the *assets* side of the central bank's balance sheet—what the Fed bought. Bernanke emphasized imperfect substitutability and "portfolio balance" effects that would lower interest rates (even on assets the Fed was not buying), raise stock prices, and probably—though the Fed never emphasized this—lower the dollar exchange rate. Hence the Fed's official term for QE: large-scale asset purchases (LSAPs).

Of course, these two approaches are more like two sides of the same coin than alternatives because balance sheets must always balance. Whenever the Bank of Japan does QE operations to boost bank reserves, it must also decide which assets to buy. Whenever the Fed does LSAPs, it simultaneously raises bank reserves *pari passu,* which is why I call it an *intellectual* break. But appraisals of Japanese-style QE naturally focus more on credit and money creation, whereas appraisals of American-style LSAPs naturally focus more on movements in interest rates and stock prices.

After the Fall

The outright panic ended in the spring of 2009. One of the main reasons was the highly successful "stress tests" on nineteen systemically important financial institutions (SIFIs)—not all of which were banks—that Secretary of the Treasury Tim Geithner had announced in February. The tests themselves were carried out by all the bank regulatory agencies working together, but the Fed was clearly in first chair.

We see these 2009 stress tests now as a smashing success—and instrumental to ending the crisis. But it is easy to forget that they were a riverboat gamble at the time.[12] Two opposite risks loomed large. If the stress tests were seen as too easy, markets might have viewed them as a whitewash, concluded that the problems with the big banks were far deeper than suspected—and panicked. If the stress tests had turned up a much greater need for bank capital than they did, markets might have deemed the announced capital needs impossible to meet—and panicked. The regulators managed to thread the needle with credible—and

---

12. Remember, e.g., that Europe's first bank stress tests were a miserable failure.

amazingly transparent[13]—stress tests that estimated capital needs that, while not trivial, were manageable. After that, confidence in the banking system came back rapidly.

Once the stress test results were in, financial markets bounced back quickly and vigorously, but the economy did not. Several data revisions later, we see that annual GDP growth over the next two years (from the second quarter of 2009 to the second quarter of 2011) averaged just 2.25 percent. At the time of the Brookings-Hoover conference (October 2013), the unemployment rate, which peaked at 10 percent, was still 7.3 percent—and most knowledgeable observers thought the downward movement of the official unemployment rate *overstated* the improvement in the labor market. For example, the employment-to-population ratio barely budged.

The reasons for the sluggish recovery are many and varied—and a subject for another day. But they had induced the FOMC, by the time of the conference, to stick with its near-zero interest-rate policy for nearly five years; and the near-zero federal funds rate will probably last another two or more.[14] In addition, the Fed has rolled out one QE policy after another, the latest (QE3) being an almost-equal blend of buying long Treasuries and buying agency MBS.

These unconventional monetary policies (UMPs) have been controversial since their inception—and still are. I give the FOMC mostly high marks for its UMPs. Others do not. Apart from the fact that "hawks" virtually always want tighter monetary policy than "doves" do, I find this controversy rather puzzling. After all, most UMPs are just continuations of conventional monetary policies into a world in which the federal funds rate can no longer be pushed down.

Think about QE in Treasuries, for example. Under normal conditions, when the Fed wants to give the economy a boost, it goes out into the marketplace and purchases Treasury securities, mostly T-bills. That's called "open-market operations," and we teach the basic idea in Economics 101. (I know because I teach Economics 101.) But QE is just another form of open-market operations. The two differences are that

---

13. Prior to the stress tests, the Fed and other bank regulators virtually never released information about the conditions of specific banks. That was considered highly confidential.

14. The Fed's Survey of Economic Projections as of September 18, 2013, showed that only four of seventeen Federal Reserve governors and Reserve Bank presidents thought the funds rate would rise before the end of 2014; another twelve thought that would happen by the end of 2015.

(a) when open-market operations are conducted at the zero lower bound, the federal funds rate cannot fall any further, and that (b), partly for that reason, the Fed acquires longer-dated Treasury notes and bonds, rather than bills, to try to push down intermediate and long rates. Another quantitative-but-not-qualitative difference is that QE in Treasuries seems to have rather low bang for the buck. For that reason, the magnitudes of Federal Reserve purchases must be large.

QE in MBS raises some other issues, including the unveiled attempt to channel more credit into the housing sector. But is that really so different, in its effects, from conventional monetary policy? Under normal conditions, when the Fed buys T-bills and lowers interest rates to raise aggregate demand, the strongest expansionary effects are always felt in the housing market—and conversely when the Fed tightens. QE in MBS is designed to have precisely such a "biased" effect. But when buying MBS, the credit allocation is explicit and highly visible, whereas it is tacit and (to some extent) hidden under conventional monetary policy.

Has QE worked? Should it be continued, tapered down, or even eliminated? Opinions vary. The overwhelming weight of the empirical evidence seems to say that the various episodes of QE have pushed down interest rates, although the post-QE1 effects are far smaller than those from QE1—which, after all, rescued the moribund MBS market.[15] Krishnamurthy and Vissing-Jorgenson (2013) even suggest, somewhat surprisingly, that the impacts on rates may not spread very far along the yield curve or the risk curve. Critics of QE don't dispute these findings (much). Mainly, they argue that any such benefits must be weighed against the market-distorting and/or potentially inflationary (eventually!) effects.

Curiously, the undisputed fact that the economy is still weak is used by both proponents and opponents of continuing QE to bolster their arguments. The pro-QE camp argues that the economy still needs more support from monetary policy. The anti-QE side argues that the Fed has little to show for trillions of dollars of QE.

Are there other options? For more than three years, I have been urging the Fed to lower—probably into negative territory—the interest rate it pays on excess reserves (IOER). The idea is to blast some of the current mountain of excess reserves out of the banks and get these dollars

---

15. See, for example, Gagnon, Raskin, Remache, and Sack (2011); D'Amico and King (2013); Hamilton and Wu (2012); and Krishnamurthy and Vissing-Jorgenson (2011, 2012, 2013).

functioning, as they do in normal times, as "high-powered" money. Notice that, to the extent this effort works, cutting the IOER might actually enable the Fed to trim its balance sheet somewhat without, on net, withdrawing monetary stimulus.

Looking ahead

What are some questions and concerns about the future?

Most obviously, the Fed must eventually exit from most or all of its remaining UMPs—mainly, the near-zero interest-rate policy and the vast expansion of its balance sheet. Designing and implementing a strategy for doing so (an exit strategy) entails many tricky questions, such as when to exit (when to start and when to finish), how to exit (e.g., should the Fed let assets run off or sell them actively?), and the proper sequencing. Each of these issues has been discussed extensively, both by the Fed itself and by outside observers. Needless to say, the books will not be closed on UMPs until the Fed has exited—gracefully, I hope. Let me raise just two questions about the Fed's exit strategy to date.

First, the FOMC's announced sequencing seems destined to steepen the yield curve. Why? Because it begins with tapering back on QE3 purchases, then perhaps allowing some assets to run off, both of which will probably happen well before the FOMC begins to raise the federal funds rate. Thus, intermediate and long rates seem almost certain to rise while the short end of the yield curve is anchored near zero, thereby steepening the yield curve. It is far from obvious to me why the Fed wants to steepen the curve as opposed to, say, letting it drift upward in a more-or-less parallel manner. After all, the FOMC has been relying for five years now on *flattening* the yield curve as the best way to inject more stimulus into the economy. If the FOMC has reasons to steepen the curve as it exits, it should articulate them. I haven't heard any.

Second, FOMC spokespersons from Bernanke on down have been trying to talk the market into the implausible proposition that the timing of tapering has no bearing on the timing of the eventual increases in the funds rate. Thus, for example, when the Fed surprised markets by seeming to advance the expected start date for tapering to September 2013,[16] the central bank apparently expected that the "announcement" would *not* advance the market's perceived start date for interest rate hikes. Unre-

---

16. Which, just prior to the conference, it decided not to do.

alistic thinking like that, I believe, was one major reason why the Fed was surprised at the market's strong reactions to its tapering "hints" in May–June 2013.

Why do I call this unrealistic? Because the decision to taper and the decision to raise interest rates depend on the same factors: the economy's growth prospects, especially for improvements in labor market conditions, and the continued quiescence of inflation. When one moves up or back in time, so does the other. Thus, unlike (apparently) many on the Fed, I think it was perfectly rational for the markets to shift the forward curve upward when Bernanke started talking about tapering. In my view, the Fed should banish from its thinking the implausible proposition that it can separate expectations of tapering from expectations of rate increases. It is much more likely that, as one moves up, so will the other.

A second set of issues pertains to what comes after the exit. In particular, should the Federal Reserve return to the *status quo ante,* or should it retain some aspects of its recent/current unconventional monetary policies?[17] As one concrete and important example, consider the Fed's multipronged efforts (via QE and forward guidance) to flatten the yield curve.

Back in the old days of conventional monetary policy, many central banks had only one instrument of monetary control that they actually used: the overnight interbank lending rate (in the United States, the federal funds rate). That self-imposed limit created a kind of shell-game aspect to monetary policy because no important economic transactions take place at the federal funds rate. Rather, moving the funds rate was a way to *influence,* but not to *control,* the financial variables that really affect economic activity: the entire constellation of interest rates, stock prices, exchange rates, and the like. The slippage between, say, the funds rate and the ten-year Treasury rate was a major source of uncertainty for monetary policymakers. Indeed, I used to play a little guessing game when I was vice chairman of the Fed: when we moved the funds rate by X basis points, how much would the ten-year rate move? I was decent, but certainly not terrific, at this game.

I bring up this point because various sorts of UMPs, especially direct purchases of Treasury notes and bonds, can be viewed as ways to reduce the slippage between the funds rate and, say, the ten-year rate by purchasing ten-year bonds directly or by giving pointed and specific forward guidance. Is it so clear that the Fed and other central banks

---

17. I have written on this at greater length in Blinder et al. (2013).

should relinquish this ability as part of the return to normalcy? Or have we learned something useful that can make monetary policy more effective?

A third set of issues surrounds "too big to fail." Title II of Dodd-Frank (Orderly Liquidation Authority) abolishes TBTF de jure, and the FDIC has recently published its single point of entry (SPOE) plan for doing so in practice.[18] Many critics, however, remain skeptical, refusing to believe SPOE will work de facto. It will have to be used before we know for sure, and if many SIFIs are teetering on the brink at once in a systemic crisis (as in September-October 2008), it may be difficult to put it into effect.

A related point involves section 13(3) of the Federal Reserve Act— the emergency lending authority. To prevent the Fed from invoking 13(3) on behalf of a single troubled institution (e.g., saving AIG), Congress amended it to require that any special lending facility have "broad-based eligibility" rather than be tailored to suit a single firm ("no more bail-outs"). Some observers worry that this restriction will seriously weaken the Fed's ability to contain future systemic crises. That's possible, but I am less worried. It seems to me that, in a crisis, the Fed should have no trouble defining a *class* of eligible borrowers who need emergency loans. So the new section 13(3) should not be an operational constraint on the Fed's ability to fight a systemic crisis.

Finally, I must at least mention the almost-unexplored continent: macroprudential policy. That ugly word connotes the uncharted territory *between* monetary policy and *micro*prudential policy—where traditional safety-and-soundness considerations meet macroeconomic concerns. Macroprudential policy is still in its infancy—even in those countries that are already (or are on the verge of) practicing it. In the United States, we are still clearly in the thinking stage, at the Fed and elsewhere.[19] And it needs a lot of thinking.

The contrast with conventional *macroeconomic* monetary policy could hardly be more stark. When deploying conventional monetary policy, there is just one instrument—the overnight interest rate—and a lot of evidence (not all of it in agreement!) on how it works. When we venture into the realm of macroprudential policy, we encounter a long list of potential instruments (e.g., loan-to-value ratios, cyclically variable capital and/or liquidity requirements, etc.), but not much of a knowledge base

---

18. See FDIC and Bank of England (2012).

19. Principally, at the Treasury's new Office of Financial Research.

on which to appraise their relative efficacies. So there is a lot of spadework for the Federal Reserve, the Treasury, and others to do.

Here's one example: what should a central bank do in the face of a (suspected) asset price bubble? An emerging point of view holds that the bank shouldn't raise the overnight interest rate to burst the bubble because that's a poorly targeted instrument and because it might also burst the economy. Instead, the argument goes, the central bank should use conventional supervisory and macroprudential instruments to lean against—and, in the limit, burst—the bubble. But which one or ones? I don't raise this as a rhetorical question. I don't think anyone knows the answer.

Which seems an appropriate place to end this essay.

References

Andrews, Edmund L. 2004. "The Ever More Graspable, and Risky, American Dream." *New York Times,* June 24. http://www.nytimes.com/2004/06/24 /business/the-ever-more-graspable-and-risky-american-dream.html ?pagewanted=all&src=pm.

Baker, Dean. 2002. "The Run-up in Home Prices: Is It Real or Is It Another Bubble?" CEPR Briefing Paper, Center for Economic and Policy Research, Washington, DC, August, http://www.cepr.net/documents/publications /housing_2002_08.pdf.

Blinder, Alan S. 2013. *After the Music Stopped: The Financial Crisis, the Response, and the Work Ahead.* New York: Penguin Press.

Blinder, Alan S., Thomas J. Jordan, Donald Kohn, and Frederic S. Mishkin. 2013. *Exit Strategy: Geneva Reports on the World Economy 15.* Geneva, Switzerland: International Center for Monetary and Banking Studies, September. London: Centre for Economic Policy Research.

Blinder, Alan S., and Mark Zandi. 2010. "How the Great Recession Was Brought to an End." *Moody's Analytics,* July 27, http://www.economy.com/mark-zandi /documents/End-of-Great-Recession.pdf.

D'Amico, Stefania, and Thomas B. King. 2013. "Flow and Stock Effects of Large-Scale Treasury Purchases: Evidence on the Importance of Local Supply." *Journal of Financial Economics* 108 (2) (May): 425–48.

Federal Deposit Insurance Corporation and Bank of England. 2012. "Resolving Globally Active, Systemically Important, Financial Institutions." Joint White Paper, December 10.

Financial Crisis Inquiry Commission. 2011. *The Financial Crisis Inquiry Report: Final Report of the National Commission on the Causes of the Financial and*

Economic Crisis in the United States. Washington, DC: US Government
Printing Office.

Gagnon, Joseph, Matthew Raskin, Julie Remache, and Brian Sack. 2011. "The
Financial Market Effects of the Federal Reserve's Large-Scale Asset Purchases." *International Journal of Central Banking* 7 (1) (March): 3–44.

Hamilton, James D., and Jing Cynthia Wu. 2012. "The Effectiveness of Alternative Monetary Policy Tools in a Zero Lower Bound Environment." *Journal of
Money, Credit, and Banking* 44, no. S1 (February): 3–46.

Krishnamurthy, Arvind, and Annette Vissing-Jorgensen. 2011. "The Effects of
Quantitative Easing on Interest Rates: Channels and Implications for Policy."
Brookings Papers on Economic Activity 42 (2) (Fall): 215–87.

Krishnamurthy, Arvind, and Annette Vissing-Jorgensen. 2012. "The Aggregate
Demand for Treasury Debt." *Journal of Political Economy* 120 (2) (April):
233–67.

Krishnamurthy, Arvind, and Annette Vissing-Jorgensen. 2013. "The Ins and
Outs of Large-scale Asset Purchases." Paper presented at Federal Reserve
Bank of Kansas City, Jackson Hole Economic Policy Symposium: Global
Dimensions of Unconventional Monetary Policy, August 22–24.

Taylor, John B. 2009. *Getting Off Track: How Government Actions and Interventions Caused, Prolonged, and Worsened the Financial Crisis.* Stanford, CA:
Hoover Institution Press.

Temkin, Kenneth, Jennifer E. H. Johnson, and Diane Levy. 2002. *Subprime Markets, the Role of GSEs, and Risk-Based Pricing.* US Department of Housing
and Urban Development. Washington, DC: US Government Printing Office.

Washington Post. 2009. "Transcript. The House Holds a Hearing on the
Semi-Annual Report of the Fed on Monetary Policy." *WP Politics,* July 21.
http://www.washingtonpost.com/wp-dyn/content/article/2009/07/21
/AR2009072101505.html.

Wilson, Daniel J. 2012. "Fiscal Spending Jobs Multipliers: Evidence from the
2009 American Recovery and Reinvestment Act." *American Economic Journal: Economic Policy* 4 (3) (August): 251–82.

CHAPTER 6

The Federal Reserve's Role

Actions Before, During, and After the 2008 Panic in the Historical Context of the Great Contraction

Michael D. Bordo

Introduction

The financial crisis of 2007–2008 has been viewed as the worst since the Great Contraction of the 1930s. It is also widely believed that the policy lessons learned from the experience of the 1930s helped the US monetary authorities prevent another Great Depression. Indeed, Ben Bernanke, the chairman of the Federal Reserve during the crisis, stated in his 2012 book that, having been a scholar of the Great Depression, his understanding of the events of the early 1930s led him to take many of the actions that he did.

This chapter briefly reviews the salient features of the Great Contraction of 1929–1933 and the policy lessons learned. I then focus on the recent experience and examine the key policy actions taken by the Fed to allay the crisis and to attenuate the recession. I then evaluate Fed policy actions in light of the history of the 1930s. My main finding is that the historical experience does not quite conform to the recent crisis and, in some respects, basing policy on the lessons of the earlier crisis may have exacerbated the recent economic stress and have caused serious problems that could contribute to the next crisis.

The Great Contraction story

The leading explanation of the Great Contraction from 1929 to 1933 is by Milton Friedman and Anna Schwartz in *A Monetary History of the United States: 1867 to 1960* (1963a). They attributed the Great Contraction from 1929 to 1933 to a one-third collapse of the money supply brought about by a failure of Federal Reserve policy to prevent a series of banking panics

For helpful comments, I thank Allan Meltzer, Ashoka Mody, and David Wheelock. For valuable research assistance, I thank Antonio Cusato.

from 1930 to 1933. The Friedman and Schwartz story was augmented by Bernanke (1983). Like Friedman and Schwartz, he attributed the Great Contraction to monetary forces and especially the collapse of the banking system. However, unlike them, he placed less emphasis on the effects via the quantity theory of money on spending and more on the consequences of the collapse of the banking system in raising the cost of financial intermediation and creating a credit crunch.

The Great Contraction was preceded by the Wall Street boom and rapidly growing economy of the Roaring Twenties. The Friedman and Schwartz story began with the Fed tightening policy in early 1928 to stem the stock market boom. Fed officials believing in the real bills doctrine were concerned that the asset boom would lead to inflation. Recent evidence suggests that the stock market boom, as well as an earlier housing boom in the mid-1920s, was in part fueled by the Federal Reserve's pursuit of an expansionary monetary policy beginning in 1926 (White 2009; Bordo and Landon-Lane 2013b).[1]

The subsequent downturn beginning in August 1929 was soon followed by the stock market crash in October. The New York Fed reacted swiftly to the stock market crash by lowering its discount rate, lending heavily to the money center banks, and purchasing government securities in the open market. This action prevented the stock market crash from leading to a banking panic as had often occurred before the establishment of the Federal Reserve System. Thereafter requests by the New York Fed to the Board for additional easing were rejected and the Fed failed to prevent four banking panics that followed between October 1930 and March 1933.

According to Friedman and Schwartz, the banking panics worked through the money multiplier to reduce the money stock (via a decrease in the public's deposit currency ratio). The panic in turn reflected what Friedman and Schwartz called a "contagion of fear" as members of the public—fearful of being last in line to convert their deposits into currency—staged runs on the banking system, leading to massive bank failures. In today's terms this would be a liquidity shock.

The collapse in money supply in turn led to a decline in spending and, in the face of nominal rigidities, especially of sticky money wages, and

---

1. In 1931 Adolph Miller, member of the Federal Reserve Board, blamed the stock market crash and the depression on Benjamin Strong, former governor of the New York Fed, for keeping interest rates unusually low in 1926 to help Britain stay on the gold standard. This policy, he argued, fueled the Wall Street boom.

also a decline in employment and output (Bordo, Erceg, and Evans 2000). The process was aggravated by banks dumping their earning assets in a fire sale and by debt deflation (deflation which increased the real value of nominal debt), which weakened the net worth of firms and households and weakened bank balance sheets.

According to Friedman and Schwartz, had the Fed acted as a proper lender of last resort (as it was established to be in the Federal Reserve Act of 1913), it would have offset the effects of the banking panics on the money stock and prevented the Great Contraction.

The principal exception to the Fed's inaction was a brief interlude from April to August 1932 when, under pressure from the Congress, the Fed engaged in a massive $1 billion open market purchase ($16 billion in today's prices or 2 percent of 1932 GDP). This expansionary monetary policy reversed the decline in money supply, greatly reduced interest rates, and led to a quick revival in industrial production and real output. In many respects the 1932 interlude was a prelude to the policies of quantitative easing in Japan in the 2000s and in the United States today.

The Fed reversed course and ended the purchases in the summer of 1932 because of its fear of the expansionary policy rekindling stock market speculation and inflation and threatening gold convertibility. The depression continued, culminating in the banking panic in early 1933. Friedman and Schwartz posit that had the expansionary policy continued, the contraction would have ended much earlier than it did.

An extensive literature has posited several explanations for the Fed's failure as a lender of last resort (Bordo and Wheelock 2013). These include: 1) flaws in the System's structure which impeded coordination between the Federal Reserve Board and the Reserve banks, especially after the death of Benjamin Strong in 1928 (Chandler 1956; Friedman and Schwartz 1963a); 2) devotion to the gold standard which kept the Fed from following expansionary policies to offset banking panics (Temin 1989; Eichengreen 1992); 3) adherence to a flawed policy framework that relied on nominal interest rates and the level of discount window borrowing as policy guides (Meltzer 2003; Wheelock 1991); and 4) the failure of the Federal Reserve Act to provide a discount mechanism and money market environment of the sort that enabled the Bank of England and other European central banks to function effectively as lenders of last resort.

This was manifest in three flaws: 1) the reluctance of member banks to turn to the discount window in times of stress (the "stigma problem"); 2) the Fed's limited membership and the fact that, except in extreme circumstances, only member banks had access to the discount window; and 3) the restrictive eligibility requirements on collateral posted for borrowing at the Fed's discount window.

The Great Contraction ended in March 1933 when newly elected President Franklin Delano Roosevelt declared a one-week nationwide banking holiday during which bank examiners weeded out the insolvent banks. The institution of the Federal Deposit Insurance Corporation (FDIC) in 1934 solved the problem of panics. FDR also ended the link to the gold standard in April 1933 and later devalued the dollar by close to 60 percent. A rapid recovery and reflation from 1933 to 1936 was fueled by expansionary Treasury gold and silver purchases and a rise in commodity prices. This was helped by the devaluation and by gold inflows induced by capital flight from Europe, which increased the money supply (Romer 1992). The Federal Reserve, which continued to maintain its policy of inaction, had little to do with the recovery (Meltzer 2003).

The Roosevelt administration blamed the banks, other financial institutions, and the Federal Reserve for the contraction. The Banking Acts of 1933 and 1935 made significant changes in the structure and authority of the Federal Reserve System. The acts concentrated policymaking authority within the Board of Governors, expanded the Fed's ability to lend on the basis of any sound collateral, and authorized the Fed to lend to nonfinancial firms in a crisis (section 13(3)).

In addition, the banking system was subject to major reform, including the introduction of federal deposit insurance; the forced separation of commercial and investment banking (Glass-Steagall Act); the regulation of deposit interest rates (regulation Q of Glass-Steagall); and strict limits on market entry. These reforms were intended to enhance the Fed's ability to respond to crises while making the banking system less vulnerable to instability (Bordo and Wheelock 2013, 34).

The Federal Reserve, after many years of denial and hostility to Friedman and Schwartz, accepted their lessons from the Great Contraction. On the occasion of Milton Friedman's ninetieth birthday, Ben Bernanke apologized for the Fed: "I would like to say to Milton and Anna: regarding the Great Depression. You're right. We did it. We're very sorry. But thanks to you, we won't do it again" (Bernanke 2002).

In his 2012 lectures Bernanke emphasized two great shortcomings of the Fed in the Great Contraction: its failure to serve as a lender of last resort and its failure to use its tools of monetary policy to prevent deflation and the collapse of real economic activity. These lessons were not forgotten in the Fed's response to the crisis of 2007–2008 and the Great Recession.

The Crisis of 2007–2008 and the Great Recession

Like the 1929–1933 episode, the crisis of 2007–2008 in the United States was preceded by an asset price boom—in house prices. The end of the boom set in motion forces that triggered the crisis of 2007–2008. Government intervention in housing markets going back to the 1930s served as the backdrop to the crisis. The Federal Housing Administration and Fannie Mae were set up to encourage the development of the mortgage market and to provide housing finance.

In subsequent decades and especially in the 1990s, as argued by Rajan (2010), successive administrations and Congress pushed for affordable housing using the government-sponsored enterprises (GSEs) and allowed them to reduce their capital requirements. Lending was encouraged and rising prices raised the GSEs' profits, leading them to take on more risk. The FHA in the 1990s also took on riskier mortgages, reduced the minimum down payment to 3 percent, and increased the size of mortgages that would be guaranteed. The housing boom came to its climax in the George W. Bush administration, which urged the GSEs to increase their holding of mortgages to low-income households (Rajan 2010, 37). Between 1999 and 2007 national house prices doubled, according to the Standard and Poor's Case-Shiller repeat sales index.

The private sector also contributed heavily to the boom in an environment of loose regulation and oversight by the Federal Reserve and other agencies as they recognized that the GSEs would backstop their lending. During this period lending standards were reduced and practices like NINJA (no income, no job, no assets) and NO-DOC (no documentation) loans were condoned. These developments led to the growth of the subprime and Alt A mortgages which were securitized and bundled into mortgage-backed securities and then given triple-A ratings. Mortgage-backed securities (MBS) were further repackaged into collateralized debt obligations (CDOs). Credit default swaps (CDSs) provided insurance on many of these products. Financial firms ramped up leverage and avoided regulatory oversight and statutory capital requirements with special purpose vehicles (SPVs) and special investment vehicles (SIVs). These factors encouraged a lending boom (Bordo and Meissner 2012).

The boom was fueled by expansionary monetary policy by the Federal Reserve after the tech bust of 2001. Low policy rates were kept in place until 2005 to prevent the economy from slipping into a Japan-style deflation. John Taylor (2007) has led the indictment of the Fed for fueling the housing boom in the early 2000s. Based on the Taylor Rule (Taylor 1993) he showed that the federal funds rate was as low as 3 percentage points below what a simple Taylor Rule would generate for the period 2002–2005. Taylor then simulated the path of housing starts had the Fed followed his rule over the period 2002–2005. His calculations suggest that most of the run-up in housing starts from 2002–2005 would not have occurred.[2]

The default on a significant fraction of subprime mortgages after the collapse of house prices produced spillover effects around the world—via the securitized mortgage derivatives into which these mortgages were bundled—to the balance sheets of investment banks, hedge funds, and conduits (which are bank-owned but off their balance sheets) which intermediate between mortgage and other asset-backed commercial paper and long-term securities. The uncertainty about the value of the securities collateralized by these mortgages spread uncertainty through the financial system. All of this led to the freezing up of the interbank lending market in August 2007.

In an attempt to allay what it perceived as a liquidity crisis, the Fed then both extended and expanded its discount window facilities and cut the federal funds rate by 300 basis points. A principal innovation was the Term Auction Facility (TAF) which allowed banks to bid anonymously for funds from the Fed. It was designed to encourage banks to go to the discount window by avoiding the "stigma problem" which had been so important in the 1930s.

The crisis worsened in March 2008 with the rescue of investment bank Bear Stearns by JP Morgan, backstopped by funds from the Federal Reserve. The rescue was justified on the grounds that Bear Stearns' exposure to counterparties was so extensive that a worse crisis would follow if it were not bailed out. The March crisis also led to the creation of a number of new discount window facilities whereby investment banks could access the window and which broadened the collateral available for discounting.

---

2. For supporting evidence for many countries and over long periods, see Bordo and Landon-Lane (2013a and 2013b) and Ahrend, Cournede, and Price (2008).

The next major event was a Treasury bailout and partial nationalization of the insolvent GSEs, Fannie Mae and Freddie Mac, in July 2008 on the grounds that they were crucial to the functioning of the mortgage market.

Events took a turn for the worse in September 2008 when the Treasury and Fed—in an attempt to prevent moral hazard—allowed investment bank Lehman Brothers to fail in order to discourage the belief that all insolvent institutions would be saved. It was argued that Lehman was both in worse shape and less exposed to counterparty risk than Bear Stearns. After the crisis, Bernanke (2012a) argued that Lehman was allowed to fail because it was deemed insolvent and because the Fed lacked the legal authority to rescue it.

The next day the authorities bailed out and nationalized the insurance giant AIG, fearing the systemic consequences for collateralized default swaps if it were allowed to fail. The fallout from the Lehman bankruptcy then turned the liquidity crisis into a full-fledged global credit crunch and stock market crash as interbank lending effectively seized up on the fear that no banks were safe.

To stem the post-Lehman financial market panic, the Fed invoked section 13(3) of the Federal Reserve Act to extend the discount window to nonbank financial institutions and financial markets. The Fed created special liquidity facilities to provide funding to the money market mutual funds (MMMFs) which were clobbered by the collapse of Lehman and then to the commercial paper market that was funded by the MMMFs. Facilities for broker-dealers, asset-backed securities, and many other institutions and markets were created. Bernanke (2012a) justified the extension of access to the discount window as perfectly consistent with Walter Bagehot's (1873) strictures because they were backed by collateral (although not made at penalty rates). These policies, he argued, prevented the collapse of the global financial system.

In the ensuing panic, along with Fed liquidity assistance to the commercial paper market and the extension of the safety net to the money market mutual funds, the US Treasury (in the week after Lehman and AIG) sponsored its Troubled Asset Relief Plan (TARP) whereby $700 billion could be devoted to the purchase of heavily discounted mortgage-backed securities and other securities to remove them from the banks' balance sheets and restore bank lending. The initial TARP package, which was only a two-and-a-half-page document, was rejected by the Congress, precipitating a major stock market crash and a spike in the OIS-Libor spread (the difference between the overnight indexed swap rate and the London interbank offered rate). TARP was later passed and, rather than in the original intent, most of the funds were used to recapitalize the major banks after a series of stress tests.

According to Taylor (2009), the uncertainty associated with the passage of TARP and the two about-faces between Bear Stearns and Lehman and then AIG were the key causes of the panic in September 2008, rather than the collapse of Lehman.

The crisis immediately spread to Europe and to the emerging market countries as the global interbank market ceased functioning. The Fed set up extensive inter-central-bank swap lines to keep open international liquidity. The United Kingdom authorities responded by pumping equity into British banks, guaranteeing all interbank deposits, and providing massive liquidity. The European Union countries responded in kind. These actions ended the impending sense of financial doom.

After the financial crisis eased, the US economy continued to implode. Expansionary Federal Reserve policy at the end of 2008 lowered the federal funds rate to zero. Once the policy rate hit the zero nominal bound, the Fed initiated its policy of large-scale asset purchases (LSAPs), commonly known as quantitative easing (QE)—open market purchases of long-term Treasuries and mortgage-backed securities. The original justification for this unorthodox policy was the portfolio adjustment mechanism of Friedman and Schwartz (1963b), Brunner and Meltzer (1973), and Tobin (1969). However, the QE program was supposed to affect the economy by a signaling channel as well.[3] In addition to these channels, Woodford (2012) has emphasized the importance of forward guidance: communication by the Fed on the pace and timing of its QE purchases. He argues that forward guidance is much more important than the actual purchases. The Fed since 2012 has adopted this approach with, so far, limited success.

LSAP 1, which began in November 2008, was intended to purchase $1.75 trillion of long-term securities, most of which were in agency MBS (mortgage-backed securities held by GSEs). It was followed in March 2010

---

3. Krishnamurthy and Vissing-Jorgensen (2011, 2013) have argued that the portfolio balance channel works through two narrow channels: a capital constraint channel and a security channel. They find that the purchase of MBS via their two channels has a stronger and more widespread impact than the purchase of long-term securities whose impact is much more localized.

by LSAP 2, in which the Fed would purchase $600 billion of long-term Treasury bonds, and the Maturity Extension Program (MEP), which was a swap of short-term for long-term securities to extend the maturity of the Fed's portfolio. It was then followed by LSAP 3, in which the Fed purchased both MBS and long-term Treasuries.

Debate swirls over how effective the LSAP policies have been. LSAP 1 lowered long-term yields from 30 to 90 basis points depending on the study (Bernanke 2012b suggested they were higher).[4] LSAP 2 was much less effective, lowering long-term Treasury bonds by, at most, 20 basis points.

These purchases more than tripled the Fed's balance sheet and have been held as excess reserves by the banks. Bernanke (2012b) posits that the LSAP programs increased real output by 3 percent and employment by two million jobs and effectively attenuated the recession in July 2009. This, he argued, made the unusually slow recovery from the Great Recession considerably faster than would otherwise have been the case.

The Financial Crisis of 2007–2008 and the Great Contraction compared: the Fed has misinterpreted history

Bernanke (2012a) and others have invoked the Great Contraction and especially the banking panics of 1930–1933 as a good comparison to the financial crisis and Great Recession of 2007–2009. In several figures below I compare the behavior of some key variables between the two events. I demarcate the crisis windows in the Great Contraction using Friedman's and Schwartz's dates. For the recent period I use Gorton's (2010) characterization of the crisis as starting in the shadow bank repo market and then changing to a panic in the shadow banking system and the universal banks after Lehman failed in September 2008 (light gray shading).

The signature of the Great Contraction was a collapse in the money supply brought about by a collapse of the public's deposit currency ratio, a decline in the banks' deposit reserve ratio, and a drop in the money multiplier (see figures 6.1 to 6.4). In the recent crisis, the M2 money supply did not collapse; indeed, it rose, reflecting expansionary monetary policy (figure 6.1). Similarly, the deposit currency ratio did not collapse in the recent crisis—it rose (figure 6.2). There were no runs on the commercial banks because depositors knew that their deposits were protected by federal

---

4. Taylor and Stroebel (2012) find that purchases of MBS had virtually no impact.

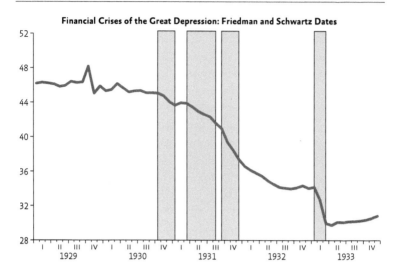

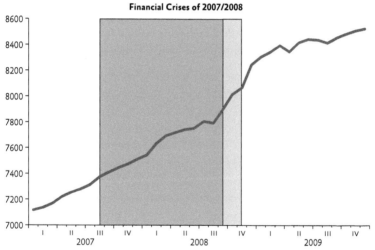

FIGURE 6.1 Money Stock (M2)

Source: Bordo and Landon-Lane (2010)

deposit insurance, which was introduced in 1934 in reaction to the bank runs of the 1930s. The deposit reserve ratio declined (figure 6.3), reflecting an increase in banks' excess reserves induced by open market purchases and a positive spread between the interest rate on excess reserves and the federal funds rate, rather than by a scramble for liquidity as in the 1930s. The money multiplier declined in the recent crisis, reflecting the same

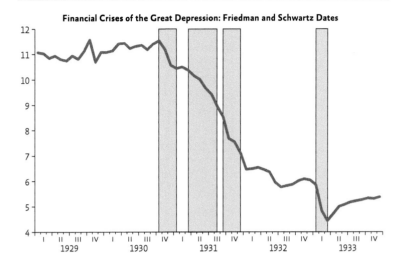

Financial Crises of the Great Depression: Friedman and Schwartz Dates

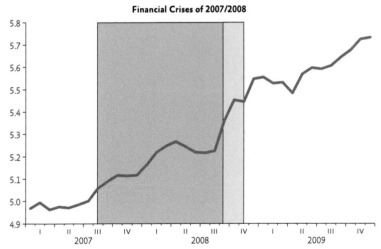

Financial Crises of 2007/2008

FIGURE 6.2 Ratio of Deposits to Currency in Circulation

Source: Bordo and Landon-Lane (2010)

forces (figure 6.4). Moreover, although a few banks failed in the recent crisis the numbers were miniscule relative to the 1930s, as were deposits in failed banks relative to total deposits.

Thus the recent financial crisis and recession was not a pure Friedman-and-Schwartz money story. It was not driven by an old-fashioned contagious banking panic. But as in 1930–1933, there was a financial crisis.

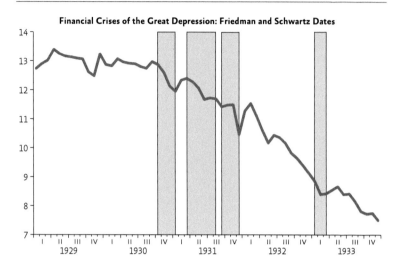

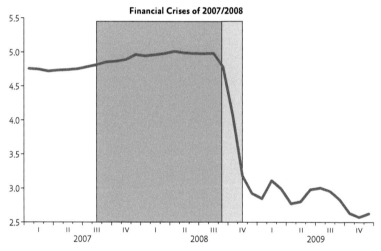

FIGURE 6.3 Ratio of Deposits to Reserves

Source: Bordo and Landon-Lane (2010)

It reflected a run beginning in August 2007 on the institutions that make up the shadow banking system, which was not regulated by the central bank nor covered by the financial safety net. These institutions held much lower capital ratios than the traditional commercial banks and hence were considerably more prone to risk. When the crisis hit they were forced to engage in major deleveraging involving a fire sale of assets into a falling

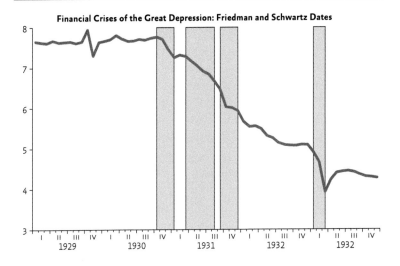

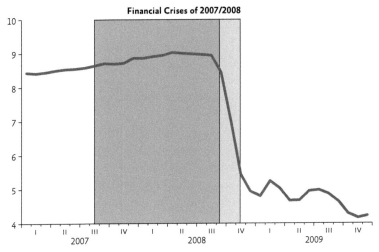

FIGURE 6.4 Ratio of M2 to Monetary Base

Source: Bordo and Landon-Lane (2010)

market, which in turn lowered the value of their assets and those of other financial institutions. A similar negative feedback loop occurred during the Great Contraction, according to Friedman and Schwartz (Bordo and Landon-Lane 2013c).

According to Gorton (2010), the crisis centered in the repo market (sale and repurchase agreements) which had been collateralized by opaque (subprime) mortgage-backed securities by which investment banks and some universal banks had been funded. The repo crisis continued through 2008 and then morphed into an investment bank crisis after the failure of Lehman Brothers in September 2008. It peaked with the collapse of the money market mutual funds after the Reserve Primary Fund "broke the buck" and liquidity for the commercial paper market dried up (Blinder 2013, chapter 6) (see figure 6.5). The crisis led to a credit crunch which led to a serious (but, compared to the Great Contraction, not that serious) recession. See figure 6.6 which compares the Baa-ten year composite Treasury spread between the two historical episodes. This spread is often used as a measure of credit market turmoil (Bordo and Haubrich 2010). As can be seen, the spike in the spread in 2008 is not very different from that observed in the early 1930s.

Unlike the liquidity panics of the Great Contraction, the deepest problem facing the financial system was insolvency. This was only recognized by the Fed after the September 2008 crisis. The problem stemmed from the difficulty of pricing securities backed by a pool of assets, whether mortgage loans, commercial paper issues, or credit card receivables. Pricing securities based on a pool of assets is difficult because the quality of individual components of the pool varies. Unless each component is individually examined and evaluated, no accurate price of the security can be determined. As a result, the credit market was confronted by financial firms whose portfolios were filled with securities of uncertain value: derivatives that were so complex the art of pricing them had not been mastered. The credit market thus was plagued by the inability to determine which firms were solvent and which were not. Lenders were unwilling to extend loans when they couldn't be sure that a borrower was creditworthy (Schwartz 2008).

Taylor (2009) buttresses the critique of the Fed's liquidity policy. He shows that the sharp reduction in the federal funds rate from 5.25 percent to 2 percent between August 2007 and April 2008 was significantly below what the Taylor Rule predicted. This overly expansionary monetary policy led to a sharp depreciation in the dollar and a run-up in commodity prices in 2008. In addition, Taylor and Williams (2009) provide evidence that the TAF had little impact in reducing the OIS three-month Libor spread—a measure of risk and liquidity effects. This suggests that the spread largely reflected counterparty risk.

Thus an important shortcoming of the Fed's reading of the history of the Great Contraction was initially to treat the recent crisis as primarily a

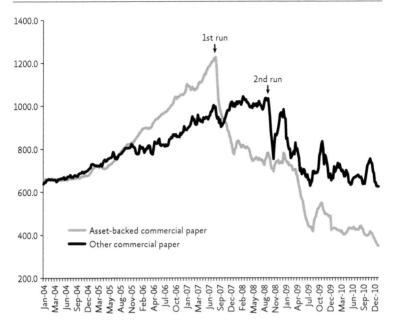

FIGURE 6.5 Commercial Paper (Billions of Dollars)

Source: Federal Reserve Bank of St. Louis

liquidity crisis. The key problem of the crisis of 2007–2008 was not liquidity but insolvency—especially the fear of insolvency of counterparties.

Another hallmark of the recent crisis which was not present in the Great Contraction was that the Fed and other US monetary authorities engaged in a series of bailouts of incipient and insolvent firms deemed too systematically connected to fail. These included Bear Stearns in March 2008, the GSEs in July, and AIG in September. Lehman Brothers had been allowed to fail in September 2008 on the grounds that it was insolvent, that it was not as systematically important as the others, and—as was stated well after the event—that the Fed did not have the legal authority to bail it out.

Finally, a comparison could be made between the 1930s experience and the recent crisis in the use of the LSAPs to attenuate the recession. In the spring of 1932, under pressure from the Congress, the Fed began conducting large-scale open market operations. Unlike the recent experience, the economy had not yet reached the zero lower bound and short-term rates were about 2 percent. In its open market purchases, the Fed did

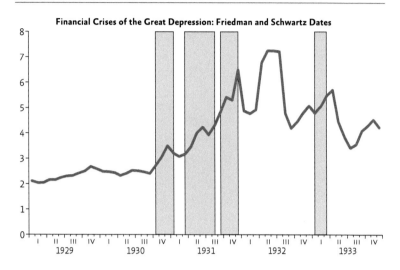

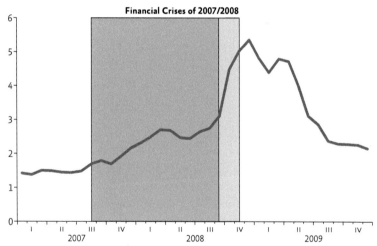

FIGURE 6.6 Quality Spread (Baa-10 year T-Bill)

Source: Bordo and Landon-Lane (2010)

not restrict its purchases to short-term securities but bought government securities at all maturities up to ten years. According to Friedman and Schwartz[5] (1963a) and Meltzer (2003), the policy, although unfortunately

---

5. Landon-Lane (2013) examined the counterfactual effect of a policy like the LSAPs in the period after 1934 when short-term interest rates had reached the

short-lived, did succeed in turning around the economy. M2 stopped declining and flattened out; and the monetary base and Federal Reserve credit picked up, as did bank credit (see figure 6.7). Also, industrial production and real GDP began expanding after a lag. Interest rates reversed their rise and dropped like a stone. Unlike the recent LSAPs, the bond purchases were not locked up in the banks' excess reserves. The Fed did not pay interest on reserves.

By comparison, the recent LSAPs did not significantly increase the M2 money supply or bank credit and most were locked up in bank reserves by the spread of a bit less than 25 basis points between the interest on excess reserves and the federal funds rate. As a consequence, neither M2 nor bank lending increased much and long-term Treasury yields fell less than their counterparts in the 1930s, although the sizes of the purchases were much greater (see figure 6.8).

There are many differences between the two cases, but the comparison still seems relevant. The Fed through its LSAP policy—by locking up reserves in the banking system—tied at least one hand behind its back and prevented a monetary expansion which could have stimulated a faster recovery than did occur.

Conclusion: some policy lessons from history

(1) Overly expansive liquidity policy

From the banking panics of the 1930s, the Federal Reserve learned the Friedman and Schwartz lesson of the importance of conducting an expansionary open-market policy to meet all the demands for liquidity (Bernanke 2012a). In the recent crisis, the Fed conducted highly expansionary monetary policy in the fall of 2007 and from late 2008 to the present. Taylor (2009) has argued that Fed liquidity policy was too expansionary in the fall of 2007 and early 2008. This reduced the exchange value of the dollar and helped stimulate a commodity price boom.

However, according to Hetzel (2012), Fed monetary policy was actually too tight through much of 2008 as seen in a flattening of money growth and

---

zero lower bound. He showed that had the Fed not followed its inactive policy but instead conducted bond purchases of comparable magnitude to those done between 2008 and 2012 it would have lowered long–term bond yields by similar magnitudes—about 20 basis points—as the recent Fed policy. This policy would have likely accelerated the Treasury-driven recovery.

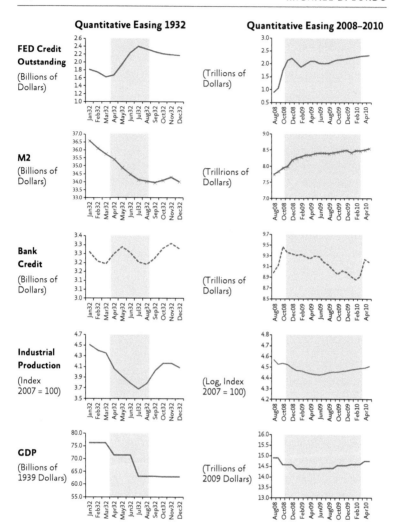

FIGURE 6.7 FED Credit Outstanding, M2, Bank Credit, IP and GDP; 1932 and 2008–2010

Source: Federal Reserve Bank of St. Louis

the monetary base and high real interest rates. Although the Fed's balance sheet surged, the effects on high-powered money were sterilized. These actions may have reflected concern that rising commodity prices at the time would spark inflationary expectations. By the end of the third quarter of 2008 the sterilization ceased, evident in a doubling of the monetary base.

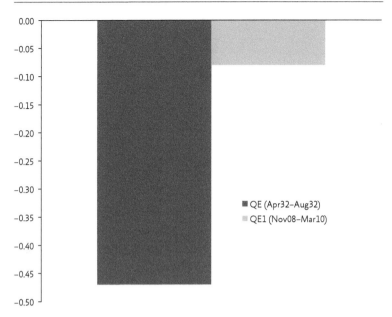

FIGURE 6.8 Changes in the Ten-Year Treasury Bond Yield

Note: In percentage points, difference between the interest rate during the last month of the program and the month previous to the program beginning.
Source: Federal Reserve Bank of St. Louis

(2) Credit policy

The Fed, based on Bernanke's (1983) analysis that the 1930s banking collapse led to a failure of the credit allocation mechanism, adopted credit policy—providing credit directly to markets and firms the Fed deemed most in need of liquidity—in contrast to delivering liquidity directly to the market by open market purchases of Treasury securities and leaving the distribution of liquidity to individual firms to the market. The choice of targeted lending instead of an imperial liquidity provision by the market exposed the Fed to the temptation to politicize its selection of recipients of its credit (Schwartz 2009). In addition, the Fed's balance sheet ballooned in 2008 and 2009 with the collateral of risky assets including those of nonbanks. These assets were in part backed by the Treasury. The Fed also worked closely with the Treasury in the fall of 2008 to stabilize the major banks with capital purchases and stress testing. Moreover, the purchase of mortgage-backed securities combined monetary with fiscal policy. Many of these actions referred to by Goodfriend (2011) as credit policy have impinged upon the Fed's independence and have weakened its credibility.

(3) Bailouts

Undoubtedly the most serious policy error that occurred in the crisis of 2007–2008 was the bailouts that the Fed and other US monetary authorities engaged in of incipient insolvent firms deemed too systematically connected to fail. These included Bear Stearns in March 2008, the GSEs in July, and AIG in September. The investment bank Lehman Brothers had been allowed to fail in September on the grounds that it was basically insolvent and not as systemically important as the others. One wonders: if Bear Stearns had been allowed to fail, could the severe crisis in September/October 2008 have been avoided? Had Bear Stearns been closed and liquidated, it is unlikely that more demand for Fed credit would have come forward than what actually occurred. The fact that general creditors and derivative counterparties of Bear Stearns were fully protected by the merger of the firm with JPMorgan Chase had greater spillover effects on the financial services industry than would have been the case had a receiver been appointed who would have frozen old accounts and payments as of the date of the appointment. Fewer public funds would have been subjected to risk. When Drexel Burnham Lambert was shut down in 1990 there were no spillover effects.

Furthermore, assume, as the Fed argued at the time, that there would have been a crisis in March like the one that followed Lehman's failure in September. Would it have been as bad as the latter event? Assume that the moral hazard implications of bailing out Bear Stearns led the remaining investment banks and other market players to follow riskier strategies than otherwise on the assumption that they also would be bailed out. This surely made the financial system more fragile than otherwise, so that when the monetary authorities decided to let Lehman fail the shock that ensued and the damage to confidence were much worse (Bordo 2008).

In addition, in response to Bernanke's (2012a) claim that legally the Fed could do nothing to save Lehman, the history of financial crises provides examples when monetary authorities bent the rules and rescued "insolvent banks" whose failure would have otherwise led to a panic. The chairman's statement that the Fed was legally prevented from rescuing Lehman reads like an *ex post hoc ergo propter hoc* justification to cover the Fed's tracks from what turned out to be a disastrous decision.

(4) Quantitative Easing

Finally, the quantitative easing policy that was followed since late 2008 was deliberately hampered by the Fed's decision not to reduce the spread between the interest on excess reserves and the federal funds rate to zero. It was based on a fallacious argument that reducing the spread would destroy the money market mutual fund industry. This policy discouraged the banks from lending (Blinder 2013; Hall 2013; Woodford 2012). The successive LSAP policies involved discretion and were not based on rule-like behavior (Taylor 2009).

The forward guidance policy which accompanied quantitative easing has also not been rule-like. Rather than stick to its announced conditions for tapering its bond purchases and its eventual exit from the LSAP policy, the Fed has based its policy on very short-run considerations.

In addition, keeping interest rates low for many years has created growing distortions in the economy. These include: financial repression, as in the 1940s, imposing a burden on savers; the discouraging of savings; potential capital losses to banks when the Fed finally exits; losses on the Fed's balance sheet as rates rise; reduced transfers to the Treasury; and policy uncertainty which threatens bank lending and investment.

In conclusion, the crisis of 2007–2008 had similarities to the 1930s Great Contraction in that there was a panic in the shadow banking system. But it was not a contagious banking panic that required massive infusions of liquidity as in the 1930s. It was largely a solvency crisis based especially on fear of the insolvencies of counterparties. The Fed was slow to recognize this and injected too much liquidity into the economy in 2007. When it did recognize the problem in 2008 it instituted credit policies which have threatened its independence. It also engaged in massive bailouts of large, interconnected financial institutions which were deemed too essential to fail. This engendered moral hazard for future bailouts. Despite these issues, the Fed avoided the fate of the Great Depression.

Finally, when short-term interest rates hit the zero lower bound the Fed began following quantitative easing policies. Once the recession ended these policies were continued to speed up an unusually slow recovery. The attempt at stimulus once the economy returned to positive growth did not add much traction. It also has had perverse and potentially negative long-lasting effects on the real economy and on future growth. QE as well as the credit policies followed during the crisis have been based on discretion and not the rule-like approach to monetary policy followed during the Great Moderation. These actions have damaged the Fed's hard-earned credibility. It will take a long time to regain it.

References

Ahrend, Rudiger, Boris Cournede, and Robert Price. 2008. "Monetary Policy, Market Excesses, and Financial Turmoil." Organisation for Economic Co-operation and Development, Economics Department working paper 597.

Bagehot, Walter. 1873. *Lombard Street: A Description of the Money Market*. London: Henry S. King & Co.

Bernanke, Ben S. 1983. "Non-Monetary Effects of the Financial Crisis in the Propagation of the Great Depression." *American Economic Review* 73 (3): 257–76.

Bernanke, Ben S. 2002. "Remarks by Governor Ben S. Bernanke at the Conference to Honor Milton Friedman, University of Chicago." November 8.

Bernanke, Ben S. 2012a. *The Federal Reserve and the Financial Crisis*. Princeton, NJ: Princeton University Press.

Bernanke, Ben S. 2012b. "Opening Remarks: Monetary Policy since the Onset of the Crisis." Federal Reserve Bank of Kansas City, Jackson Hole Economic Policy Symposium: The Changing Policy Landscape. August 31.

Blinder, Alan. 2013. *After The Music Stopped: The Financial Crisis, The Response, and the Work Ahead*. New York: Penguin Press.

Bordo, Michael. 2008. "An Historical Perspective on the Crisis of 2007–2008." NBER Working Paper 14569.

Bordo, Michael, Christopher Erceg, and Charles Evans. 2000. "Money, Sticky Wages, and the Great Depression." *American Economic Review* 90 (5): 1447–1463.

Bordo, Michael, and Joseph Haubrich. 2010. "Credit Crises, Money, and Contractions: An Historical View." *Journal of Monetary Economics* 57 (1): 1–18.

Bordo, Michael, and John Landon-Lane. 2010. "The Lessons from the Banking Panics in the United States in the 1930s for the Financial Crisis of 2007–2008." NBER Working Paper 16365.

Bordo, Michael, and John Landon-Lane. 2013a. "Does Expansionary Monetary Policy Cause Asset Price Booms: Some Historical and Empirical Evidence." NBER Working Paper 19585.

Bordo, Michael, and John Landon-Lane. 2013b. "What Explains House Price Booms? History and Empirical Evidence." NBER Working Paper 19584.

Bordo, Michael, and John Landon-Lane. 2013c. "The Banking Panics in the United States in the1930s: Some Lessons for Today." In *The Great Depression of the 1930s: Lessons for Today*, edited by Nicholas Crafts and Peter Fearon, chapter 7. New York: Oxford University Press.

Bordo, Michael, and Christopher Meissner. 2012. "Does Inequality Lead to a Financial Crisis?" NBER Working Paper 17896.

Bordo, Michael, and David Wheelock. 2013. "The Promise and Performance of the Federal Reserve as Lender of Last Resort, 1914–1933." In *The Origins, History, and Future of the Federal Reserve: A Return to Jekyll Island*, edited by Michael Bordo and William Roberds. New York: Cambridge University Press.

Brunner, Karl, and Allan H. Meltzer. 1973. "Mr. Hicks and the 'Monetarists.'" *Economica* 40 (157): 44–59.

Chandler, Lester V. 1956. *Benjamin Strong, Central Banker.* Washington, DC: Brookings Institution.

Eichengreen, Barry. 1992. *Golden Fetters: The Gold Standard and the Great Depression, 1919–1939.* New York: Oxford University Press.

Friedman, Milton, and Anna Jacobson Schwartz. 1963a. *A Monetary History of the United States, 1867–1960.* Princeton, NJ: Princeton University Press.

Friedman, Milton, and Anna J. Schwartz. 1963b. "Money and Business Cycles." Supplement, *Review of Economics and Statistics* 45 (1): 32–64.

Goodfriend, Marvin. 2011. "Central Banking in the Credit Turmoil: An Assessment of Federal Reserve Practice." *Journal of Monetary Economics* 58 (1): 1–12.

Gorton, Gary. 2010. *Slapped By the Invisible Hand: The Panic of 2007.* New York: Oxford University Press.

Hall, Robert. 2013. "The Natural Rate of Interest, Financial Crises, and the Zero Lower Bound." Federal Reserve Bank of Kansas City, Jackson Hole Economic Policy Symposium: Global Dimensions of Unconventional Monetary Policy. August 23.

Hetzel, Robert. 2012. *The Great Recession: Market Failure or Policy Failure?* New York: Cambridge University Press.

Krishnamurthy, Arvind, and Annette Vissing-Jorgensen. 2011. "The Effects of Quantitative Easing on Interest Rates: Channels and Implications for Policy." *Brookings Papers on Economic Activity.* Fall.

Krishnamurthy, Arvind, and Annette Vissing-Jorgensen. 2013. "The Ins and Outs of LSAPs." Federal Reserve Bank of Kansas City, Jackson Hole Economic Policy Symposium: Global Dimensions of Unconventional Monetary Policy. August 23.

Landon-Lane, John. 2013. "Would Large Scale Asset Purchases Have Helped in the 1930s? An Investigation of the Responsiveness of Bond Yields from the 1930s to Changes in Debt Levels." Rutgers University. http://www.cleveland fed.org/research/Conferences/2012/current_policy/final/landon-lane_final .pdf.

Meltzer, Allan H. 2003. *A History of the Federal Reserve, Vol. 1: 1913 to 1951.* Chicago: University of Chicago Press.

Rajan, Raghuram. 2010. *Fault Lines: How Hidden Fractures Still Threaten the World Economy.* Princeton, NJ: Princeton University Press.

Romer, Christina D. 1992. "What Ended the Great Depression?" *Journal of Economic History* 52 (4).

Schwartz, Anna J. 2009. "Origins of the Financial Market Crisis of 2008." *Cato Journal* 29 (1).

Stroebel , Johannes, and John B. Taylor. 2012. "Estimated Impact of the Federal Reserve's Mortgage-Backed Securities Purchase Program." *International Journal of Central Banking* 8 (2): 1–42.

Taylor, John B. 1993. "Discretion versus Policy Rules in Practice." *Carnegie-Rochester Conference Series on Public Policy* 39: 195–214.

Taylor, John B. 2007. "Housing and Monetary Policy." Remarks at Federal Reserve Bank of Kansas City, Jackson Hole Economic Policy Symposium: Housing, Housing Finance, and Monetary Policy. August 31.

Taylor, John B. 2009. "The Financial Crisis and the Policy Responses: An Empirical Analysis of What Went Wrong." NBER Working Paper 14631.

Taylor, John B., and John C. Williams. 2009. "A Black Swan in the Money Market." *American Economic Journal; Macroeconomics* 1 (1): 58–83.

Temin, Peter. 1989. *Lessons from the Great Depression.* Cambridge, MA: MIT Press.

Tobin, James. 1969. "A General Equilibrium Approach to Monetary Theory." *Journal of Money, Credit, and Banking* 1 (1): 15–29.

Wheelock, David. 1991. *The Strategy and Consistency of Federal Reserve Monetary Policy, 1924–1933.* New York: Cambridge University Press.

White, Eugene. 2009. "The Lessons from the Great American Real Estate Boom and Bust of the 1920s." NBER Working Paper 15573.

Woodford, Michael. 2012. "Methods of Policy Accommodation at the Interest-Rate Lower Bound." Federal Reserve Bank of Kansas City, Jackson Hole Economic Policy Symposium: The Changing Policy Landscape. August 31.

CHAPTER 7

Mistakes Made and Lessons (Being) Learned

Implications for the Fed's Mandate

Peter R. Fisher

W hat have we learned about the role of the Federal Reserve over the last five years that might help guide the Fed in the future?

First, before the crisis the Federal Reserve raised interest rates too slowly, given its hands-off approach to supervision. From this we learned that either the Fed needs to "lean against the wind" in managing interest rates or that efforts should be made to constrain excessive credit growth and leverage through supervision and regulation. But to do neither should be unacceptable.

Second, we learned that during a crisis is the wrong time to address moral hazard. The seeds of the 2008 debacles of Bear Stearns and Lehman Brothers were sown in 1999. This is when negotiations leading up to the Gramm-Leach-Bliley Act missed the opportunity to bring major nonbank financial firms inside a stronger supervisory framework. Not addressing the moral hazard of large nonbank financial firms relying on implicit Fed support was the critical mistake. Both supervision and discount window access should have been extended to reflect market realities. However, while we need the Fed to be able to act as an effective lender of last resort in a crisis we also need to be able to limit the exercise of lender-of-last-resort powers so that their use remains exceptional. How to strike this balance is another dilemma for monetary policy.

Third, since the crisis the Fed has vigorously pursued polices aimed at reviving the economy but in doing so is conceiving of its mandate over too short a horizon. The Fed's actions since 2010 have been premised on the reasoning that only present evidence of excessive inflation pressures or of financial instability should limit the use of its monetary policy powers in pursuit of maximum employment. This presumes that there are no other limits on how much aggregate demand monetary policy can or should borrow from the future in order to fill a perceived deficiency in current demand. This ignores too many potentially perverse consequences that may contribute to a weaker economy and greater deflationary pressures in the future. The Fed's current interpretation of its mandate obscures these longer-term, intertemporal trade-offs.

Each of these lessons poses a dilemma for the conduct of monetary policy. Together, they suggest the need for a fundamental review of the Fed's mandate. How can we incorporate financial stability into the Fed's objectives with more than lip service? How can the Fed be an effective lender of last resort without that becoming a metaphor for all of monetary policy? How can we lengthen and broaden the Fed's horizon so that the important intertemporal trade-offs become a more explicit consideration in the Fed's decisions?

We may not be ready to draft legislation. But surely scholars and citizens should take the occasion of both the fifth anniversary of the crisis and the Fed's own centenary to consider what we have learned that could better guide the Fed in the future.

Address leverage—one way or another

From 2003 to 2006 the Fed was too slow to raise interest rates, given its reluctance to use supervisory tools to address the buildup of debt, leverage, and house prices.

There were, of course, important failings of the private sector that contributed to the financial crisis. But agency problems and misaligned incentives, excessive and poorly designed compensation arrangements, imperfect accounting and disclosure practices that produce incomplete and lagged information, excessive leverage, and liquidity illusions, as well as under-paid and poorly equipped supervisors, are not the novel inventions of the early years of the twenty-first century. These are enduring features of our financial system.

What *was* different this time was that, after 2001, the Fed tried hard to stimulate the economy in general and the housing sector in particular. Then, beginning in 2004, the Fed raised interest rates slowly and predictably while maintaining a hands-off approach to the supervision of financial institutions in general and the mortgage market in particular.

Credit bubbles can be observed when lending takes place against momentum in asset prices rather than income. Bankers and lenders are always and everywhere tempted to chase the apparently wider net-interest margins on loans to riskier borrowers without properly accounting for the higher probability of default. This reaches an acute stage when lenders ignore the borrowers' ability to repay debt from income and rely, instead, on the expectation of future increases in the value of collateral. The core responsibility of bank supervisors is to ensure that bank managers control these risks, ground their credit judgments in the income of borrowers, and force loans to be valued consistent with a realistic probability of default.

The asset quality of bank balance sheets—and the asset quality of nonbanks whose liabilities come to be accepted as close substitutes for bank liabilities—is of profound concern to monetary policy because this is where most money comes from. Seen in this light, financial stability should be the lens through which we view monetary and price stability.

In 2004, instead of addressing financial stability concerns with supervisory tools, the Fed appears to have taken financial stability as a reason to raise rates slowly. Concerns about a repetition of the bond market sell-off of 1994, when the Fed had last begun to raise rates from low levels, contributed to the Fed's gradual approach. Unfortunately, the risks were more symmetric. While the Fed thought that raising rates slowly might avoid a disruptive deleveraging of the financial system, its seemingly cautious approach encouraged a much greater buildup of leverage which, ultimately, contributed to the severity of the financial crisis.

If we are to continue to use monetary policy to promote good economic outcomes—in employment and consumer prices—then financial assets will necessarily be the shock absorbers we use to stabilize aggregate demand. As long as this is the case, the Fed should not be squeamish about raising rates. In 1994 the Fed was not squeamish; it raised rates deliberately and forcefully. The bond market, Mexico, Orange County, California, and others did not find a "Greenspan put" that year. And the following year, 1995, was the beginning of a period of sustained gains in economic output and employment for the United States.

What have we learned? In the future, the Fed should either temper its use of interest rate tools to place greater emphasis on financial stability *and thus necessarily place less emphasis on its employment and price stability objectives* or it should employ other supervisory tools to avoid a buildup of leverage and to promote financial stability.

Preferably the Fed would do some of both. It would moderate its use of interest rates in managing employment and price stability so as to promote financial stability and it would also be more willing to employ its existing—as well as new—supervisory tools. These might include higher equity for banks and financial intermediaries as well as two-way margin collateral for all trading exposures. Perhaps they ought even to include minimum and counter-cyclical home equity requirements for home-buyers.

Next time we should not be left on the horns of the dilemma of a Fed that pursues an employment goal and a price stability constraint in the short run and that is unwilling to use either interest rates or supervisory tools to promote financial stability. To be successful, the Fed will need to know when and how to employ supervisory tools or interest rate policies at just the right time. This, in turn, will require getting financial stability inside the Fed's objectives and reaction function.

Address moral hazard before the crisis

The seeds of the 2008 debacles of Bear Stearns and Lehman Brothers, and perhaps others like AIG, were sown in 1999. We recognized then that large, nonbank financial firms lacked effective prudential supervision and regulation and also lacked access to the Fed's routine lending facilities. Leading up to the Gramm-Leach-Bliley Act, the Fed tried to get authority over nonbank firms that were part of bank holding companies. Other countries were eager for the United States to establish stronger prudential supervision over both the major broker-dealers and other nonbank financial firms like AIG and GE Capital. After the rapid growth and increasing prominence of nonbank financial firms in the 1980s and 1990s, this would have been the right time to establish a new supervisory regime and to extend discount window access to these firms in return for Fed supervision—which is where things ended up with the large broker-dealers in 2008 after the crisis. This was a missed opportunity and one that Congress bears some responsibility for.

Think how different the events of 2008 would have been had Bear Stearns and Lehman Brothers already had almost a decade of experience of access to the Fed's discount window, inside a stronger supervisory regime.

The Fed needs to be able to lend to those financial intermediaries whose liabilities are accepted as close substitutes for its own. Ensuring that these firms can remain liquid is a key purpose of central banks and how central bank lending facilities can stabilize the banking system.

Once upon a time, it was only the liabilities of the major clearinghouse commercial banks that were accepted by other financial and commercial firms as "money good" and substitutes for the Fed's own liabilities. But over the course of the 1990s, with the growth of the repo market of collateralized short-term lending and of the nonbank financial firms themselves, the overnight liabilities of broker-dealers, in particular, came to be accepted as close-enough substitutes for money good. They came to be accepted as a zero-volatility, zero-credit-risk store of value and means of exchange within the financial system and by nonfinancial firms. The Fed could have tried to resist this through supervision and regulation. But once it happened, the Fed needed to assure itself that the balance sheets backing those liabilities were sound and that there were assets of sufficient quantity and quality that could be liquefied if needed.

The creation of the Financial Stability Oversight Council in the Dodd-Frank legislation, together with its power to designate firms as "systemically important financial institutions" and thereby subject them to Fed oversight, is an important improvement in our supervisory process but represents only a half-step toward addressing the lender-of-last-resort problem. This is because access to the Fed's discount window is still restricted to a narrower category of intermediaries.

Inside the perimeter of firms whose liabilities are close substitutes for the Fed's own, the Fed needs to be able to assure itself of the quality of these firms' balance sheets and to provide both routine discount window lending and lender-of-last-resort facilities in a crisis. But the history of banking is the history of new forms of money evolving both on the edges of the commercial banks' balance sheets and on the balance sheets of other firms outside the perimeter of banking. Because of this, the Fed needs to be able to lend "beyond the perimeter" as is recognized in section 13(3) of the Federal Reserve Act.

The Dodd-Frank Act restricts the Fed's 13(3) authority both by requiring certain disclosures when it is used and by requiring that lending cannot be to individual firms but only to participants "in any program or facility with broad-based eligibility."[1] This gets moral hazard exactly backwards.

The new restriction does not preclude the Fed from lending to a particular firm but requires that the Fed be prepared to lend to other similar firms as a cost of lending to a particular firm. This is likely to cause the Fed to delay lending to a particular firm until there is at least some basis

---

1. Federal Reserve Act, section 13, http://www.federalreserve.gov/aboutthefed/section13.htm.

for thinking the entire class of firms may be at risk. But waiting until the whole class is at risk is to wait too long.

More importantly, moral hazard is *greater* when the Fed lends to a broad class of nonbank firms as opposed to an individual firm. The shareholders and executives of an individual firm *can* face "failure" in the form of losses, censure, and disgrace after the fact. But the shareholders and executives of a broad-based class of firms *will not* all face after-the-fact failure or censure precisely because they are members of a broad class whose individual responsibility will be obscure. As a consequence of the Fed lending to a broad class it will be harder to hold accountable shareholders and executives of even an individual, troubled firm that may have been the initial cause for concern. Once the crisis has been deemed sufficiently systemic to warrant lending to a broad class, it will also be harder, not easier, to hold anyone accountable.

Lending under section 13(3) "beyond the perimeter" of the Fed's normal authorities will always be a judgment call. There will necessarily be uncertainty about whether just liquidity or solvency is at stake. With hindsight, many of us are comfortable sustaining the seemingly contradictory opinions that we *dislike* the fact that the Fed *did* support Bear Stearns in March 2008 and we *dislike* the fact that the Fed *did not* lend to Lehman Brothers that September. This underscores the judgment-call nature of these decisions.

John Taylor is certainly right that the disparate treatment of troubled firms in September 2008 made matters worse by creating uncertainty over how their capital structures would be treated by the authorities.[2] But the greater mistake, in my view, was made in 1999 when Congress failed to get all of the major broker-dealers, as well as other nonbank financial firms, inside a stronger supervisory regime and the Fed's discount window authority.

We should not risk a repetition of the events of September and October 2008. Moral hazard is a bad thing but the loss of employment and output is much worse.

But now the Fed faces the challenge of trying to address moral hazard after having been willing to provide all manner of lender-of-last-resort facilities in 2008 and 2009. There is now a widespread impression that the Fed will always provide the market as a whole with a put option—made

---

2. See John Taylor's chapter in this volume, Chapter 3, "Causes of the Financial Crisis and the Slow Recovery."

worse by the amendment to section 13(3) which requires broad-based eligibility. How the Fed can both hold the power to be a vigorous lender of last resort in the next crisis and also unwind the expectation that it will insure financial markets against all bad outcomes creates a second dilemma for monetary policy.

Address the long-term, intertemporal trade-offs

Since the end of the financial crisis, the Fed is making the mistake of conceiving of its mandate over too short—and too narrow—a horizon. This permits the Fed to avoid articulating the difficult intertemporal trade-offs that it is making.

Since 2010 the Fed has used its powers to try to stimulate the US economy quickly, pursuing its dual mandate without apology in the short run. The observed benefits of the Fed's extraordinary actions are, at best, mixed. At the same time, the list of potential costs is longer and more worrisome than acknowledged and the Fed has not offered a cost-benefit framework that can assess whether the costs outweigh the benefits. The Fed has given no apparent weight to the risk that its actions might retard the economy's performance or add to deflationary pressures. Yet these are precisely the potential costs that deserve the closest scrutiny.

1. Things changed in 2010. The case for the Fed's extraordinary actions in 2008 and 2009 was a different one. Stabilizing the financial system and avoiding a too-rapid deleveraging of the financial and household sectors required a strong response from the Fed.

But 2010 was supposed to be the year in which the Fed began to normalize monetary policy. While the Fed expected to hold the federal funds rate down for a considerable period, Chairman Bernanke explained in his semi-annual testimony on February 24 that the Fed would be ending its program of balance sheet expansion: "We have been gradually slowing the pace of these purchases in order to promote a smooth transition in markets and anticipate that these transactions will be completed by the end of March."[3] But six months later, at Jackson Hole, the chairman

---

3. Ben S. Bernanke, testimony accompanying the "Semi-annual Monetary Policy Report to the Congress," February 24, 2010, Committee on Financial Services, US House of Representatives, www.federalreserve.gov/newsevent/testimony /bernanke20100224a.htm.

foreshadowed that the Fed would again start expanding its balance sheet, which was subsequently confirmed at its meeting on November 3.[4]

To solve for the zero-nominal interest rate boundary, the Fed has used forward guidance, balance sheet expansion, and extension of the maturity of its asset holdings. These actions are intended to engineer a lower-for-longer path of short-term rates, a portfolio channel rebalancing of the collective private portfolio into riskier assets, and a compression of the term premium, respectively, so as to increase consumption via a wealth effect, increase consumption and investment via greater credit creation, increase employment and output, and avoid deflation.

2. The observed benefits of the Fed's actions are, at best, mixed. Figure 7.1 depicts percent changes in level terms, from the time of Bernanke's 2010 Jackson Hole speech through the end of June 2013, for three different measures of credit conditions, full-time employment, real gross domestic product, house prices, and equity markets.

The increase in equity values, as represented by the Standard & Poor's 500, dominates the results, rising 53.4 percent over the thirty-four-month period. Nonfinancial business credit outstanding rose 4.7 percent and the S&P/Case-Shiller national house price index rose 7.4 percent. Real GDP grew by 5.7 percent, full-time employment by 3.8 percent, and domestic financial credit and household credit outstanding declined by 3.6 percent and 2.5 percent, respectively.

These results suggest the greatest impact on the wealth effect—in equity and house values—and also a noticeable impact on business credit. But any impact on GDP and employment is hard to see and household credit and financial sector credit outstanding continued to decline. In defense of the Fed's actions, it is argued that as we lack the counterfactual we don't know how much worse things would have been. This is always true with macroeconomic policy and, thus, is not an entirely satisfying justification for such an extraordinary monetary policy experiment.

There is also a less flattering counterfactual. In February 2010 the Fed expected to end its balance sheet expansion in March of that year (while

---

4. Ben S. Bernanke, "The Economic Outlook and Monetary Policy," remarks delivered at the Federal Reserve Bank of Kansas City, Jackson Hole Economic Symposium on Macroeconomic Challenges: The Decade Ahead, August 27, 2010, http://www.federalreserve.gov/newsevents/speech/bernanke20100827a.htm; and Statement of the Federal Open Market Committee, press release, November 3, 2010, http://www.federalreserve.gov/newsevents/press/monetary/20101103a.htm.

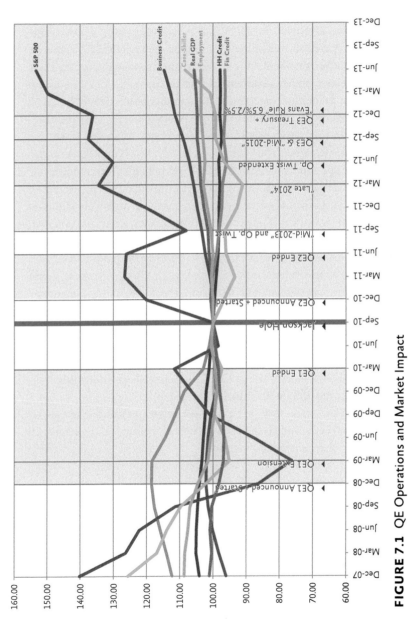

FIGURE 7.1 QE Operations and Market Impact

Source: Federal Reserve, Financial Accounts of the U.S.; Department of Commerce, Bureau of Labor Statistics, Standard & Poors

maintaining low interest rates). The Fed also then projected a central tendency for real growth of GDP of 3.4 to 4.5 percent for 2011 and 3.5 to 4.5 percent for 2012.[5] In the autumn the Fed resumed asset purchases and, with the exception of the one hiatus, continued its purchases through 2011, expanded them in 2012, and continued through 2013. But growth in 2011 and 2012 turned out, in fact, to be appreciably lower than the Fed's 2010 projections, with GDP growth of 1.8 percent in 2011 and 2.8 percent in 2012.[6] So the Fed did much more quantitative easing than it expected to do and the results, in terms of GDP, were much worse than expected.

Of course, this harsh counterfactual does not disprove the benefits of the Fed's policies. There were noticeable "head winds" from the financial crisis in Europe and from the tightening fiscal policy as a consequence of the waning of the original Obama administration stimulus program and the debt ceiling debate and ratings downgrade of Treasury securities in 2011. But the Fed's focus has been on improving the outlook for the labor market. So far there is little evidence that three years of extraordinary actions by the Fed have done anything to improve the labor market—at least not yet to the Fed's own satisfaction.[7]

3. The list of potential costs is longer and more worrisome. In his 2012 Jackson Hole speech, Bernanke acknowledged four potential costs of the Fed's Large Asset Purchase Program. The risks were that:

- The Fed's ongoing purchases and large securities holdings might impair the functioning of securities markets.
- The size of the Fed's balance sheet might reduce confidence in the Fed's ability to exit from these policies and thereby un-anchor inflation expectations.

---

5. Federal Reserve Monetary Policy Report to the Congress, "Part 4, Summary of Economic Projections," February 24, 2010, http://www.federalreserve.gov /monetarypolicy/mpr_20100224_part4.htm.

6. US Department of Commerce, Bureau of Economic Analysis, NIPA Table 1.1.1, http://www.bea.gov/iTable/iTable.cfm?ReqID=9&step=1#reqid=9 &step=3&isuri=1&903=1.

7. Citing "cumulative progress toward maximum employment and the improvement in the outlook for labor market conditions" at its meeting on December 18, 2013, the Federal Open Market Committee decided to "modestly reduce" the pace of its balance sheet expansion, http://www.federalreserve.gov/news events/press/monetary/20131218a.htm.

- Financial stability might suffer from an imprudent reach for yield by investors.
- The Fed might incur losses on its large securities holdings if there were an unexpected rise in interest rates.[8]

Bernanke subsequently also mentioned the negative impact on savers from exceptionally low interest rates.[9]

The impaired functioning of securities markets and the negative impact on savers are costs that one could weigh against benefits. However, the chairman gave short shrift to the negative impact on savers, observing that since savers will benefit once the economy recovers there was no need to dwell on the negative consequences for savers who, after all, play other roles.[10] Moreover, the other costs identified by Bernanke are not costs that one would weigh against benefits to decide whether to pursue these policies.

The portfolio balance channel seeks to encourage portfolio investors to buy riskier assets in place of Treasury and mortgage-backed securities that the Fed has purchased. So the Fed is trying to engineer a chase for yield, with rising equity markets and compressing credit spreads viewed as a sign of success. Thus, an imprudent chase for yield would amount to "too much of a good thing" rather than a reason not to pursue such policies.

Similarly, a rise in interest rates sufficiently enduring to generate losses for the Fed implies that there would be a recovery in the economy sufficient to push nominal interest rates higher. This cost would most likely be a consequence of success, rather than an independent bad outcome.

An un-anchoring of inflation expectations is the only cost Chairman Bernanke associated with reduced confidence in the Fed's ability to exit its policies.[11] This seems quite optimistic. There are other risks worth considering. Reduced confidence in the Fed's ability to exit could undermine improvements in the availability of credit and reverse the wealth effect,

---

8. Ben S. Bernanke, "Monetary Policy since the Onset of the Crisis," remarks at the Federal Reserve Bank of Kansas City, Jackson Hole Economic Policy Symposium: The Changing Policy Landscape, August 31, 2012, http://www.federalreserve.gov/newsevents/speech/bernanke20120831a.htm.

9. Ben S. Bernanke, "Five Questions about the Federal Reserve and Monetary Policy," speech at the Economic Club of Indiana, Indianapolis, October 1, 2012, http://www.federalreserve.gov/newsevents/speech/bernanke20121001a.htm.

10. Ibid.

11. Bernanke, "Monetary Policy since the Onset of the Crisis."

thereby washing out too quickly the expected benefits of balance sheet expansion. Indeed, over the spring and summer of 2013 we observed that the Fed's "taper talk" caused a much greater tightening in financial conditions than the Fed intended or expected.

The list of potential costs is longer and more worrisome. William White has offered a compelling list of unintended consequences of ultra-easy monetary policy which is worthy of attention.[12] The slightly narrower category of perverse consequences that could retard the economy's recovery and increase the risk of deflation should be of particular concern.

First, the Fed's asset purchase program, and particularly its efforts to suppress the term premium, risk accentuating the liquidity trap in which we find ourselves. Some investors with some of their capital may chase yield as the Fed intends. But the risk of a future backup in interest rates also discourages long-term lending as the low returns available do not compensate for the potential future volatility in interest rates. While the Fed sees the compression of the term premium as a way to stimulate credit creation, at extremely low levels, this risks increasing investors' liquidity preferences.

Second, pinning the risk-free rate close to zero may be discouraging business fixed investment. Nonfinancial business leaders and corporate planners view the spread between the risk-free rate (as reflected in short-term interest rates) and their expected hurdle rates of return (less a term premium) as a risk premium for their projects. The wider this spread the riskier their projects appear. While perhaps their hurdle rates are too high, they are reluctant to lower their hurdle rates in part because of perceptions that the Fed is manipulating the term premium.

While the Fed has focused its policies on pushing portfolio investors to rebalance into riskier assets, the extended period of low short-term rates risks dampening business investment. In this way, the Fed may be encouraging corporate share buybacks as the "safer" investment decision, helping propel equity values higher but diminishing business investment and job creation from what it might otherwise have been. Driving up equity values so significantly may also be suppressing the normal forces

---

12. William R. White, "Ultra Easy Monetary Policy and the Law of Unintended Consequences," Federal Reserve Bank of Dallas, Globalization and Monetary Policy Institute, Working Paper 126, revised September 2012, http://www.dallasfed .org/assets/documents/institute/wpapers/2012/0126.pdf.

of creative destruction in the economy, permitting weak management to hide behind elevated share prices.

Third, there is the risk that what investment does take place reflects a substitution of capital for labor. While the Fed's actions alone are unlikely to be able to cause such an outcome, exceptionally low interest rates for an extended period might support such a substitution. Given the prolonged weakness of the labor market, it seems an oversight not to consider this as a potential cost of the Fed's actions.

Fourth, the Fed's pursuit of a wealth effect—through higher equity values and home prices—is clearly contributing to the inequality of wealth and income. The rebuttal that income inequality is principally a consequence of globalization and technological change overlooks the self-evident consequence of driving asset prices higher as principally benefiting those who hold these assets or who earn their income from changes in those assets' prices—primarily those in financial services and real estate. A higher stock market may increase the propensity to consume of those who own stocks, but this group has a low propensity to consume relative to income—rich people can afford to save, poor people cannot. The reality of stagnant median incomes and rising wealth for the few is unlikely to contribute to an increased propensity to consume among the broader population who do not hold financial assets.

Fifth, the extended period of extraordinary monetary policy has had the effect of increasing capital flows into developing economies (just as the threat of "tapering" in mid-2013 partially reversed these flows). By providing a greater impetus for capital to flow into these countries, the Fed's extraordinary policies have likely contributed to higher levels of investment than might otherwise have occurred. This, in turn, could be contributing to the downward pressure on wages in the United States and other developed economies. It could also contribute to future deflation pressures when this additional productive capacity comes back to haunt us in the next downturn.

4. What might Keynes have thought? In *The General Theory* Keynes considered the question of whether monetary policy alone could be effective in stimulating economic activity. He saw several limits:

"If, however, we are tempted to assert that money is the drink which stimulates the system to activity, we must remind ourselves that there may be several slips between the cup and the lip. For whilst an increase in the quantity of money may be expected, *cet. par.,* to reduce the rate of interest, this will not happen if the liquidity-preferences of the public are increasing more than the quantity of money; and whilst a decline in the rate of interest may be expected, *cet. par.,* to increase the volume of investment, this will not happen if the schedule of the marginal efficiency of capital is falling more rapidly than the rate of interest; and whilst an increase in the volume of investment may be expected, *cet. par.,* to increase employment, this may not happen if the propensity to consume is falling off."[13]

Keynes's concern was that increases in liquidity preferences and decreases in the efficiency of capital and the propensity to consume would limit the effectiveness of efforts to hold down the rate of interest as a means of stimulating economic activity. But it also seems appropriate to ask whether the effort to solve the zero-rate boundary with ultra-low interest rates might contribute to the very conditions that Keynes thought would limit the impact of monetary policy.

For example, to the extent that extraordinary efforts to pull down the term premium create the conditions of a liquidity trap, this would tend to increase the public's liquidity preferences from what they otherwise would be, offsetting the beneficial impact of any increase in the quantity of money.

While there is some evidence of a recent decline in the efficiency of capital,[14] whether this is a consequence of the Fed's polices or simply an exogenous phenomenon is hard to discern. But one purpose of easy monetary policy is to stimulate investment that would otherwise have appeared uneconomic. Thus, we should not be surprised if a prolonged period of extraordinarily low interest rates was followed by an increase in the ratio of capital to output (or capital to labor, for that matter). Keynes's observation that lower interest rates will not increase investment if the efficiency of capital is falling more rapidly would then come into play.

Finally, the propensity to consume might be falling off for demographic reasons and this would limit the effectiveness of monetary policy.

---

13. John Maynard Keynes, *The General Theory of Employment, Interest, and Money* (Cambridge, UK: Macmillan Cambridge University Press, 1936), chapter 13, section III.

14. Andrew Smithers, *The Road to Recovery: How and Why Economic Policy Must Change* (Chichester, UK: John Wiley & Sons, 2013), 221–224.

However, if the low interest rates for savers caused by the Fed's actions were discouraging the animal spirits of consumers, and increasing their propensity to save, then the Fed's actions would be accentuating the demographic factors holding down the propensity to consume. In this way, extraordinary policies could be contributing to a "falling off" of the propensity to consume and, thereby, reducing the likelihood that increased investment would lead to an increase in employment.

Thus, Keynes's skepticism that monetary policy alone can stimulate the system to activity also suggests several ways of explaining the apparently diminishing impact of the Fed's extraordinary actions.

5. The intertemporal trade-offs are not obviously beneficial. To stimulate economic activity, monetary policy can really only do two things: it can take aggregate demand from foreigners or it can borrow aggregate demand from the future. To take demand from foreigners a central bank can try to engineer a weaker currency. But many factors influence exchange rates, particularly trade policies and capital flows and the economic performance and policies of the nations on the other side of the exchange rates. To borrow aggregate demand from the future a central bank can engineer lower interest rates to stimulate current consumption and investment at the expense of future consumption and investment.

How much should we attempt to borrow from the future? Putting aside financial stability concerns for the moment, is the risk of *higher* inflation and inflation expectations the only limit? What if the risks are more symmetric? What about the risk that borrowing too much demand from the future might engender deflationary conditions?

With hindsight, wouldn't we accept somewhat less employment and output from 2003 to 2007 in order to avoid so much lost from 2008 to 2013? Might we have borrowed too much demand for housing from the future? Could the excess or mal-investment in housing in those earlier years, apart from the effects of the financial crisis, be part of what is weighing on current conditions? It matters what trend we think we are on.

If we think we are on a trend of rising propensities to consume and to borrow and monetary policy borrows a little consumption and investment from the future and successfully nudges us back to higher growth, without more inflation, then the intertemporal trade-off will appear successful. When we get to the future we will be glad.

If we borrow too much demand from the future, and we push up against other constraints in the economy, the additional demand brought into the present can generate inflationary pressures—or asset bubbles and financial instability. In these cases, the intertemporal trade-offs are less favorable.

But what if we are on a trend of declining propensities to consume and to borrow? If we then borrow demand and savings from the future, we might find that when we get to the future it is diminished. Having brought consumption and investment into the present, we will have less consumption and more debt in the future but also more output—exactly a prescription for deflationary pressures.

While the goal of the Fed's extraordinary actions—or that of any stimulative policy—may be to push the economy off a low growth path and onto a higher one in the future, good intentions do not assure good outcomes.

Lowering the reward for savings and the cost of borrowing *might* stimulate current consumption and output in such a way as to put future output on a higher path, even accounting for higher private debt levels. (Similarly, it is possible that a fiscal policy of a debt-financed increase in government spending—particularly if directed to investment rather than to consumption—*might* raise both current and future output.) But this "just right" outcome is not guaranteed and certainly involves an inter-temporal trade-off in reducing future net saving. The debt burden stimulated by highly accommodative monetary policy might not generate much additional current demand and might also restrain future consumption and investment, providing a lower future growth path and a "deflationary" outcome—similar to the path we appear to have been on over the last decade.

More attention has been focused on the potential for a "demand-induced" inflationary outcome in which highly accommodative monetary policy stimulates too much credit and too much demand—with the Fed noting the lack of inflationary pressures and critics anticipating an eventual rise in inflation, even as many measures of inflation have gradually declined. But there is also the risk of a "diminished capacity" inflationary outcome in which demand does not accelerate but a decline in the economy's productive potential eventually leads to capacity constraints and inflationary pressures on a lower future growth path.

Whatever macroeconomic theories one may wish to apply, a thorough cost-benefit analysis would consider a much wider range of potential costs than the Fed has enumerated and at least assess the risks of all four of these potential outcomes and the intertemporal trade-offs they involve.

The Fed, however, has imagined a world in which it need only focus on the risks of either too little growth and employment or too much demand and inflation. By ignoring the risks of other outcomes the Fed has narrowed both its horizon and its vision of its mandate.

We should have a fundamental review of the Fed's mandate

What seems at first to be a debate about the means of conducting monetary policy turns out to be a debate about the appropriate ends of monetary policy. It turns out to be about what we think monetary policy can or should accomplish.

The Fed's current mandate and modus operandi don't incorporate financial stability concerns, don't provide guidance on how to use and to limit lender-of-last-resort authority, and don't include a framework for addressing all of the important intertemporal trade-offs nor the time horizon over which they should be considered. But these are critical challenges the Fed will face.

Section 2A of the Federal Reserve Act states that the Fed ". . . shall maintain long run growth of the monetary and credit aggregates commensurate with the economy's long run potential to increase production, so as to promote effectively the goals of maximum employment, stable prices, and moderate long-term interest rates."[15]

The current dual mandate interpretation of these words is not the only reasonable interpretation. For a number of years, Fed officials thought the most reasonable interpretation was to strive for stable prices, defined as a rate of inflation sufficiently low so as not to influence household and business decisions, as a precondition for achieving maximum employment. The current dual mandate interpretation reverses this, seeking maximum employment subject to a constraint of stable prices. The Fed has decided that the meaning of stable prices is 2 percent inflation but has interpreted maximum employment to be too difficult to specify and to vary across time.

I would not want to see the Fed's mandate reduced only to price stability because this would likely make it harder to incorporate financial stability concerns, to articulate how to act as a lender of last resort, or to consider the longer-term trade-offs.

---

15. Federal Reserve Act, Section 2A, http://www.federalreserve.gov/about thefed/section2a.htm.

While we have had much criticism of Congress and recent presidents for fiscal policy that borrows too much, the Federal Reserve also needs to ponder how much we can or should borrow from the future.

Putting aside politics and the dysfunction of our national legislature, Section 2A does not appear to be the best statement of a central bank mandate that we can imagine. Now would be a good time to consider how to articulate the Federal Reserve's objectives and constraints in light of what we have learned.

CHAPTER 8

A Slow Recovery with Low Inflation

Allan H. Meltzer

Afer almost five years of recovery, the unemployment rate remains well above postwar norms, and much of the decline in the rate results from discouraged workers leaving the labor force. The largest part of recent new job placements are part-time jobs, many at relatively low wages. The number of people in poverty is at a record high. An administration that came into office promising to narrow the gap between middle class and highest income has seen the gap widen. Their statements and speeches do not reflect the fact that the outcome of administration policy is the opposite of its rhetoric.

These and other results come after massive fiscal stimulus and unprecedented expansion of bank reserves. The popular conclusion among financial analysts is that inflation remains low because the economy grows slowly. Monetary history does not give unambiguous support to that proposition. Economies with high inflation have not uniformly or even generally experienced high growth. As recently as the 1970s, the United States had rising inflation without high real growth or high employment. Paul Volcker frequently offered the anti-Phillips curve proposition: high unemployment and high inflation are positively related. He said that the way to lower the unemployment rate was to reduce expected inflation, and it worked as he said.

In the paper that follows I offer explanations of the current low inflation and the slow growth in this recovery.

The slow recovery and low inflation

Federal Reserve actions always have many critics. One very unusual difference now is that criticisms do not come only from financial markets and academics. Paul Volcker and Alan Greenspan have joined Taylor, Bordo, me, and others.

Thanks to John Taylor for helpful comments.

The Federal Reserve has a strong sense of cohesion and loyalty. I cannot recall a previous example of former chairmen publicly criticizing the policy and actions of their successors. Even the outspoken Marriner Eccles did not criticize Thomas McCabe nor did Martin publicly criticize Burns. But both Volcker in a speech to the New York Economics Club (Volcker 2013) and Greenspan on television urged, in Volcker's words "a more orthodox central banking approach."

My criticism of recent actions is in a historical context. It reflects some problems the Federal Reserve has had often: political pressures, politicized actions, neglect of the real and nominal distinction, excessive response to monthly and quarterly data, and neglect of the role of money and credit markets. One indication of a political influence is the use of Federal Reserve policy to allocate credit. See Goodfriend (2012).

I will discuss two issues. First, why is there so little inflation despite highly expansive Federal Reserve actions? Second, why is the recovery so much slower than after other recessions?

Not only is the economic recovery slow, it has failed to reduce the poverty rate. The unemployment rate has fallen, but new full-time jobs are scarce. Much of the fall in the unemployment rate resulted from discouraged workers leaving the labor force. And many of the new jobs are part-time, low-wage jobs, not the types of jobs that encourage spending. On the whole a miserable record.

Inflation remains low because, up to the time of writing, early August 2013, money growth is not excessive. The central monetarist proposition is in Milton Friedman's well-known words: "Inflation is always and everywhere a monetary phenomenon." Since money growth is low, inflation remains low.

We have never before experienced excessive reserve growth accompanied by moderate money growth. That's what we have now. In the year to late July 2013, the Fed increased bank reserves 34 percent. For the half year, the rate is a 69 percent annual rate. Money growth, M2, rose 6.9 percent for the year to date, and 5 percent annual rate for six months. Similar outcomes are found in earlier years of QE2 and QE3. Through most of its history the Fed ignored money growth, claiming that monetary velocity is unstable, and they repeat that error now. The statement is often true of quarterly velocity, but not true of annual velocity, as shown by data for 1919 to 1995 in Meltzer (2009). The Fed's reason for disregarding money growth is an example of its concentration on monthly and quarterly data and neglect of persistent changes.

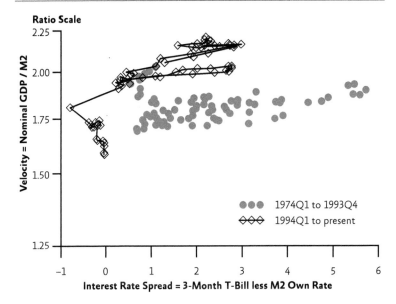

FIGURE 8.1 M2 Velocity and Interest Rate Spread

The St. Louis Fed data plot M2 velocity against the spread of the three-month T-bill less the own rate on M2. Figure 8.1 shows that relation has remained stable in this cycle despite exceptionally low interest rates.

The QE programs piled up excess reserves in the banks to more than $2 trillion in late July 2013. Some say this shows a liquidity trap. Utter nonsense! The traditional meaning of a liquidity trap defined the trap as a condition in which increases in money had no effect on interest rates, prices, and output. See Brunner and Meltzer (1968). Increases in equity market prices, reductions in long-term interest rates, and changes in the exchange rate accompany reserve additions. A hint in June that the Fed may soon "taper" the size of reserve additions dramatically raised long-term interest rates. Advocates of a liquidity trap explanation should read the literature. None of the price changes should occur.

The Fed entered the crisis after a period of low interest rates in 2003 to 2005 that served to finance the boom. It responded to the start of the Great Recession and the credit crisis by flooding the markets with liquidity. This prevented a collapse of the payments system. One can criticize some actions such as failure to charge a penalty rate, but the prompt and massive response deserves commendation. That good start was not followed by a long-term strategy.

The five years of recovery after 2008 are the slowest in the postwar. I propose two main reasons. First, the Fed failed to recognize that the slow recovery reflected real economic problems, not principally monetary problems. Second, Obama administration policies deterred investment and employment, delaying recovery.

Keynesian analysis of the recession and recovery interpreted the decline as a decline in (nominal) aggregate demand. By decisively lowering interest rates and increasing bank reserves, policy expected to restore aggregate demand. The actions known as QE2 and QE3 had, at most, a modest effect on recovery. Two main reasons are that many of the problems were real, not monetary, and more than 95 percent of the increase in reserves had no effect on money or bank credit growth. The entire expansive effect was the first-round effect on interest rates, the exchange rate, and asset prices. Instead of expanding loans and money, banks increased excess reserves. By paying interest on excess reserves, policy encouraged the reserve accumulation. Paying interest on excess reserves increases market efficiency in normal conditions, so it should be ended now and restored later.

The Federal Reserve made a traditional error, an error repeated many times. They equated monetary expansion to the first-round effects on interest rates, exchange rates, and asset prices. They ignored any subsequent effects from growth of money and credit. A better policy would have expanded money and credit growth more and excess reserves less. That would have provided more stimulus and avoided the problem posed by more than $2 trillion of excess reserves.

The Fed pays a quarter percent interest on bank excess reserves. Those earnings would go to the Treasury, thus the taxpayers, if the Fed did not pay interest on excess reserves. Instead domestic and foreign banks currently receive $5 billion a year, and rising.[1]

The Fed's balance sheet has more than $2 trillion of excess reserves currently. At best, it will take years to bring its balance sheet back to the former low level of excess reserves. A proper policy would announce a strategy and implement it. If a new recession comes, the strategy would adjust; it will take a long-term strategy, a rule-like policy, to unwind the massive accumulation of excess reserves. I find no reason for making the decision about a long-term problem depend on the moving monthly unemployment rates.

---

1. I recognize that in a more normal economy, payment of interest on excess reserves increases market efficiency.

The idle excess reserves remain a threat to future inflation, not current inflation. Currently the large bank excess reserves are one source of another problem—the slow growth of bank lending during this recovery.

In a typical postwar recovery, banks lend to new businesses, to small businesses, first-time home-buyers, and other high-risk borrowers. Current low rates make such loans unprofitable. Raising rates enough to cover expected losses would invite criticism or worse from the new consumer credit agency. Lending on risky mortgages would increase foreclosures. Banks can earn a quarter percent risk-free by holding excess reserve. Many have repaired their capital position, paid dividends and bonuses using earnings from excess reserves. The payments by the Fed to domestic and foreign banks would be paid to the Treasury, reducing the budget deficit, if the Fed reduced the interest rate on excess reserve to zero.

Low interest rates encourage borrowing, but they also discourage lending to risky borrowers. Instead of holding more excess reserves, banks would lend to new and other risky borrowers at rates that covered expected losses. With the current hostility toward banks and the new consumer credit regulator, raising interest rates for small borrowers would invite criticism and regulation. The banks avoided the criticism.

Some point to revived housing and auto markets. At the time this is written, there is no evidence of a substantial increase in mortgage loans to the public. Existing houses are purchased mainly by real estate investment companies and speculators, not principally by individuals. That's an unusual and risky housing recovery.

Auto loans are an exception. I conjecture that default risk is mitigated by the banks' ability to repossess autos if owners default. That option is less valuable for mortgage loans that default given experience in the recent past with mortgage foreclosures.

Another problem with recent monetary policy is that it relied excessively on credit allocation, especially mortgage purchases (Goodfriend 2012). And the Fed failed to recognize that the slow recovery was not principally a monetary problem that they could solve. It was mainly the result of real problems, an anti-business, pro-tax-increase, and heavy-regulation policy.

To sum up, the four main reasons for sluggish response to massive reserve growth are:

- The US economic problems are mainly real, not monetary.
- The Federal Reserve has not adopted and announced a strategy, based on a policy rule that increases confidence.

- Most of the additions to bank reserves sit idle as excess reserves. Paying interest on excess reserves and privatize regulation discourages lending.
- Credit allocation is an ineffective way to generate economic expansion.

The expansion in perspective

Only one other recovery in US history was a slow recovery with unemployment rates that remained far above full employment levels or even the level reached at the previous peak. After winning re-election in 1936, President Roosevelt adopted policies, and took actions, that businesses regarded as hostile.

Hostility toward business shows in the slow increase in business investment after 1937 and 2008. Investment is the weakest part of both recoveries. Table 8.1 shows the available data.

Table 8.1 uses data that are close to comparable for the two periods; identical series are not available. I would prefer to use real values of investment, but real investment is not available for a comparable series in 1937–41 in the source data. Fortunately prices are relatively stable in both periods.

In both periods, investment and employment rose slowly. In 2012 both investment and employment are below their previous peaks in 2007. War mobilization and changed economic policy enabled employment to rise above both 1929 and its 1937 peak by 1940. Investment did not pass both peaks until 1941.

After his 1936 re-election, President Roosevelt's policies became more populist. His failed effort to "pack" the Supreme Court is well-known. Other actions included an active anti-trust policy by the Justice Department, a Temporary National Economic Commission very critical of business practices, an excess profits tax, and increased regulation including a minimum wage. The administration did not intervene to stop the auto workers union from occupying General Motors buildings, a violation of property rights. Investment and employment growth reflect the belief that the administration had an anti-business orientation. When the president called businessmen "economic royalists" in a speech, these concerns grew and uncertainty, the enemy of investment, rose.

Populism ended with the start of re-armament and war. The hostile rhetoric ended. President Roosevelt appointed two leading Republicans to his cabinet as secretaries of war and navy. Soon after, he appointed the head

TABLE 8.1 Investment and Employment in Two Slow Recoveries

	1937–41			2008–12	
Year	Gross Private Domestic Investment[a]	Total Wage and Salary Workers[b]	Year	Private Fixed Investment[c]	Total Private Employment[d]
1937	11.8	31,026	2008	2128.7	114,342
1938	6.5	29,209	2009	1703.5	108,321
1939	9.3	30,618	2010	1679.0	107,427
1940	13.1	32,376	2011	1818.3	109,411
1941	17.9	36,554	2012	2000.9	111,826

a/in billions. Economic Report, January 1967, p. 225
b/in thousands. Economic Report, January 1967, p. 242
c/in billions. Economic Report, March 2013, p. 346
d/in thousands. Economic Report, March 2013, p. 378
Source: Economic Report of the President, 1967 and 2013, Chair of the Council of Economic Advisers

of General Motors to supervise production for war. Business responded by investing, expanding, and hiring. Patriotism overcame populism.

In the current slow recovery from the Great Recession, the Bush administration started fiscal expansion by increasing spending in its last year in office. The Obama administration added more than $800 billion of additional spending. It claimed that the economy was in dire need of substantial stimulus. With great fanfare, it announced spending for state and local governments, project-ready construction, food stamps, and much else.

The program was based on a simplistic Keynesian belief that any deficit-financed spending in recession adds to output and employment. This is a mistake. Following a decade of limited benefit in Japan, years of trillion-dollar annual US deficits have generated a small response here. Proponents have been left to claim that much worse results were avoided, a proposition that may be true but is hard to support with evidence. A more useful criticism would compare the administration's policy to the tax reduction and increased defense spending of the early 1980s. Following that policy produced substantially greater growth in GDP, as shown in table 8.2. I will return to reasons for the weak response to the 2009 fiscal program.[2]

---

2. A large number of studies estimate the response to government spending. Some report a multiplier greater than one. Others find it is less than one. There is no consensus eghty years after the *General Theory*.

TABLE 8.2 GDP Growth after Recessions

Year	Annual GDP Growth	Year	Annual GDP Growth
2011	0.6	1983	4.5
2012	3.1	1984	7.2
1972	5.6	1933*	13.5
1973	5.9	1934*	7.6

*Balke Gordon quarterly data from first quarter.
Source: Economic Report of the President, 2011 and 2013, Chair of the Council of Economic Advisers

Table 8.2 shows real GDP growth in the first two years after the trough in several postwar periods and after the Great Depression of 1929–32.

The data reinforce the point made many times. The recovery is sluggish compared to either the recovery following the Great Depression or the recoveries during some earlier postwar recessions.

Alesina (2009) and his co-authors showed that the most effective stimulus programs reduce tax rates. Expenditure increases are much less potent and less reliable. As for President Obama's favored tax increases, they have depressing effects.

Research by President Obama's first chair of the council showed that tax increases slowed growth by 3 percentage points for each 1 percentage point increase in tax rates (Romer and Romer 2010). Many other studies support the conclusion that fiscal stimulus was poorly designed. Other problems with fiscal policy programs are discussed below.

The most important development of macroeconomic research of the past several decades is the integration of expectations into dynamic macro models. Without accepting that rational expectations apply equally to all markets, most economists now accept that expectations of future costs and benefits are a critical part of the response to policy actions. Did it not occur to prominent administration economists that continued large deficits increased expected future tax rates? And didn't they anticipate that taxing highest income earners would reduce saving and investment?

We know that the sustained growth of any economy comes from two sources, growth of the labor force and productivity growth. The first has slowed in most developed countries following the decline in the live birth rate after the postwar baby boom ended. The United States' labor force growth has benefited from immigration, but that too has declined. Productivity growth results from the use of more productive capital and from increased labor efficiency. Productivity growth remained strong during

2009 and 2010. One result was lower demand for labor. Firms could satisfy sluggish demand growth by producing more per existing worker.

For the years 2007–12, lower, non-farm productivity growth is only 1.6 percent, a full percentage point less than 2000–07. For the manufacturing sector, the drop is much greater, a decline from 3.9 percent in 2000–07 to 1.8 percent in 2007–12.

Slower sustained or underlying growth rates affect producer expectations about the path to which the economy returns in a recovery. Lower expected growth and the threat of increased taxation reduce investment. Without doubt, investment growth has been slow in this recovery.

Porter and Rivkin (2012) asked 10,000 Harvard Business School alumni about decisions to locate plants. The respondents cited a complex US tax code, an ineffective political system, a weak public education system, poor macroeconomic policies, convoluted regulation, deteriorating infrastructure, and a lack of skilled labor as reasons for not investing in the United States. Most of the decisions were to move investment out of the United States.

The standard analysis of the speed of recovery is Friedman (1969). The speed at which our economy returns to its growth path increases with the depth of the preceding recession. This proposition implies that rates of recovery from the Great Recession should be faster than average, not slower than average. See also Bordo and Haubrich (2012). An explanation of the role of policy as a cause of the slow recovery is called for.

Fiscal policy mistakes

The more than $800 billion fiscal expansion voted in 2009 is widely believed to have failed to restore economic growth. I believe the administration made several mistakes.

The first mistake was to give the Congress principal responsibility for the details of the spending program. Congress chose a package of changes that redistributed income, always a concern for Congress. For example, money was sent to the states to cover some of their budget deficits. State and local employees avoided layoffs. Payments went to teachers, police, and firemen. The recipients surely knew that their receipts were not a permanent subsidy. The administration forecast that the stimulus would create 640,000 jobs, of which 325,000 were teachers kept from layoffs.

Standard theory implies that the teachers would save as much of a temporary benefit as they could, spend as little as possible, expecting that layoffs would come when the transfer ended. That was what happened.

Another large part of the 2009 stimulus was for construction. The administration sent Vice President Biden to show their effort to get "ready projects" underway. Alas, when the president finally recognized that there were very few "ready projects" two years later, most of the money had not been spent.

The second mistake was neglect of productivity. In his very thorough book, *Money Well Spent?* Michael Grabell (2012), a journalist, reported on the overestimates, mistaken reports, and successes and failures of the stimulus program. Economists could not agree on the size of the economy's response. Few, if any, recognized that the effectiveness of any spending program, private or public, depends on the productivity of the resources used. This point was made by Martin Bailey (1962) in a book widely used almost fifty years ago. The late Nobelist James Tobin, a prominent Keynesian economist, told me that he regarded Bailey's book, though written at Chicago, as the best book on standard Keynesian economics. I agree. Alas, its influence declined. The role of productivity of resource use disappeared.

A third related mistake neglects the evidence from earlier recessions. The response to permanent tax reduction is a persistent change in incomes of households and business. The strong response to the Reagan tax cuts and defense spending increased productivity in the use of resources, so the stimulus was strong.

Critics point out that the Clinton tax increases were followed by a sustained expansion. I believe this mistakes the tax increases with the balanced budget that followed. A federal balanced budget is rare. Since 1930 only two presidents, Eisenhower and Clinton, achieved balanced budgets in two consecutive years or longer. Budget balance signals that future tax increases are unlikely. Because the economy grows, sustained budget balance makes expected future tax reduction more likely. Lower expected rates increase investment.

Fourth, the proponents of deficit spending also err by neglecting the expected future tax increases required to reduce the deficit. There may have been a time when the public believed that government spending would increase income enough to generate revenue to balance the budget. Many have learned from more than eighty years of deficits in many countries not to believe that outcome. Large deficits, especially deficits that finance low productivity spending, encourage the belief that future tax rates will increase. This lowers further the response to fiscal stimulus.

Administration policy increased costs and uncertainty about returns to investment especially. The Porter and Rivkin data, cited earlier, confirm this. Monetary stimulus cannot offset these burdens. They are real.

Start with President Obama's repeated demands for higher tax rates on incomes over $250,000 and more recently his request for limits on the amounts that can be saved in 401 retirement plans. It is not surprising that investment lags badly in this recovery. These taxes would fall most heavily on the country's largest savers. No one should expect President Obama to sign a deficit reduction bill that doesn't include more revenue. Will there be an agreement? How much would taxes increase? Uncertainties of this kind are real also.

Next look at the direct effects of the Affordable Care Act on employment. Estimates of the increase in labor cost vary, but many businesses have reduced hours of work to shelter many of their employees from the costs imposed by the act. In recent data, the number of new full-time jobs is dwarfed by part-time jobs. And employers hire fewer workers. The Environmental Protection Agency raises energy costs. The National Labor Relations Board tries to strengthen unions. Businesses see these efforts as cost increases that slow investment, growth, and employment. And they increase uncertainty.

The large budget deficit and uncertainty about future tax rates leave open the size of after-tax returns to new investment. Actions that increase labor costs shift remaining investment demand toward robotics and other labor substitutes, reducing employment demand.

If Congress agreed to the tax increase on upper incomes, uncertainty would be lower but the expected return to capital would be lower also. Firms respond to the current uncertainty by holding multibillions of cash assets. The high tax rate on repatriating earnings leaves many of the earnings abroad.

There is general agreement that future deficits are unsustainable. Neither presidents nor Congress have adopted a plan to control spending or pay for it. Serious proposals by President Obama's deficit commission, or by Congressman Paul Ryan, are not adopted and not even seriously considered. These failures of government are a major source of uncertainty about our future.

Administration policy is not the only real problem. Export demand is held back by the faltering European economy. Increased regulation adds to costs and uncertainty of future returns. Slower growth in China lowers real demand as well. We have an enormous foreign debt. The only way we can service that debt is by increasing exports and reducing imports. Shale gas is a great help, if the EPA doesn't prevent drilling by increasing costs. More uncertainty.

Better policy programs

To improve results, the Federal Reserve should commit to a rule or quasi-rule such as the Taylor rule that aims at both reduced unemployment (or relatively stable output growth) and expected inflation. The rule incorporates the dual mandate that Congress approved and that the public seems willing to support. When the Federal Reserve followed it closely from 1985 to 2002, it produced the longest period of relatively stable growth with low inflation and short, mild recessions in Federal Reserve history.

The Federal Reserve should use models that include credit, money, and assets. See Brunner and Meltzer (1993), Meltzer (1995), Taylor (1995), and Tobin (1969). The central problem of stability requires that policy acts in a way that induces the public to hold money, bonds, and real capital at equilibrium values consistent with stable output growth and low inflation. As in Issing (2005), it should use annual monetary growth as a second monetary pillar.[3]

Adopting a rule is a first step. The next step is to strengthen incentives to follow the rule. The Federal Reserve has much more authority than accountability. Neither Governor Harrison nor the Federal Reserve Board were fired for causing the Great Depression, but President Hoover, Secretary Mellon, and many members of Congress lost their positions. Arthur Burns and the Board of Governors were not fired, but President Carter and many members of Congress were.

To increase accountability, the Federal Reserve should announce an objective, the combination of inflation and unemployment rate or output growth rate that it expects to achieve over several years, most likely two or three. If it fails to achieve its objective, it must offer an explanation and submit resignations. The president can accept the explanation or the resignations. Several countries, starting with New Zealand, have adopted

---

3. Issing and Wieland (2013, 432) wrote: "The most important reasons for the U.S. Federal Open Market Committee's disappointing performance during this period (the Great Inflation) can be seen in the continuation of a discretionary monetary policy . . . "

this arrangement. It has not produced resignations, to my knowledge, but it has enhanced incentives to concentrate on medium-term objectives.

A peculiarity of the emphasis given to current and near-term events is that monetary policy operates with a lag. Policy actions today cannot do much about output, employment, or inflation in the near term. No less important is that intense pressures to do something about current problems often induce the Fed to adopt current actions that make it more difficult to resolve long-term problems. Some current examples: how can the Federal Reserve reduce the trillions of excess reserves without increasing inflation and/or unemployment? Adding to excess reserves to respond to a current economic slowdown exacerbates the problem. Some propose higher inflation as a way of reducing unemployment and the value of our enormous debt. This again either presumes a persistent trade-off, contrary to 1970s and 1980s experiences, or it postpones the return to stability.

Excessive attention to short-term changes neglects the distinction between permanent and temporary changes that is central to standard economic analysis. Several examples of recent neglect of this distinction are available:

- The claim that growth slowed in the summer of 2010 and deflation and recession would follow misled the Federal Reserve. By early autumn, these forecasts and conjectures proved incorrect. The Federal Reserve eased. Most of the additional reserves added to excess reserves.
- In the exceptionally warm winter of 2012, US economic growth rose. There was no way to know for months whether the improvement was a temporary response to a mild winter or a persistent improvement. By late spring, it was clear that the increased expansion was temporary.
- Federal Reserve officials discuss publicly whether and when they should end QE. Removing more than $2 trillion of excess reserves will take years of applying a consistent strategy. Why does it matter whether the start occurs with an unemployment rate of 7.5 percent or 7.0 percent, or some other non-recession number?

These examples can be extended almost endlessly.

A common response to my concern about future inflation is that future inflation is not a problem because the Federal Reserve can always raise its interest rate enough to slow inflation. In principle, this is certainly true.

But practice, I fear, is different. Business, labor, and members of Congress are not indifferent about the level of interest rates. When the 1921 Board allowed rates to rise above 6 percent, Congress discussed curtailing its authority. I claim in my history that was a major reason why the Board resisted raising the discount rate in 1928–29 before the depression. Secretary Morgenthau in the 1930s was often alarmed and threatening if interest rates rose by even small amounts. After World War II, the Federal Reserve would not end wartime-pegged long rates until it gained the support of some influential members of Congress, especially Senator Paul Douglas. And more than thirty members of the Senate sponsored legislation in summer 1982 to force Paul Volcker's FOMC to reduce interest rates.

The Federal Reserve has reason to be concerned about congressional intervention. Legislative threats are common. Between 1973 and 2010, members of Congress introduced 1,575 bills in the House and 728 bills in the Senate. About 75 percent die without further action [Hess and Shelton 2012]. No one knows whether one will gather support.[4]

In its first one hundred years, the Federal Reserve has never announced a lender-of-last-resort policy. Every banking crisis brings some actions, but there is never an announced rule. Bagehot's famous criticism of the Bank of England's policy did not fault its actions. Bagehot's ([1873] 1926) criticism was that the Bank did not announce its policy in advance. My proposals for financial stability remove the nearly four hundred regulations in the Dodd-Frank law and adopt four rules:

1. A clearly stated rule governing the lender of last resort. Bagehot's rule, lend freely against good collateral at a penalty rate, remains appropriate.
2. Protect the payments system, not the bank, banks, or bankers.
3. By implementing the first two rules, prevent the problem from spreading to other banks and financial institutions.
4. Require regulated large banks to hold at least 15 percent equity capital against all assets.

When these rules were in force, they prevented bank crises.

Bagehot's criticism of the Bank of England applies to the Federal Reserve. By announcing and following a policy rule, the Federal Reserve

---

4. The Federal Reserve should act to restore independence. See especially Calomiris (2013).

would notify banks about what it will and will not do. It gives them an incentive to hold collateral acceptable for discount at the Reserve Banks. It reduces uncertainty, surely a gain during crises. It also reduces the expected gain from failing banks asking Congress to press the Federal Reserve or others for bailouts. And if banks follow the rule by holding collateral and larger equity reserves, fewer fail.

A policy rule for too-big-to-fail should not be the main way to prevent failures. Far more important is a rule that prevents most failures. Congress should enact equity capital standards for banks. I propose that beyond some minimum size, equity capital requirements should increase with asset size up to a maximum of 20 percent of assets. Losses would be borne by stockholders. The Federal Reserve and other regulators would monitor capital requirements. Outside auditors would certify that the requirements are met. Equity capital of 15 to 20 percent would restore capital for large banks to where it was in the 1920s (Meltzer 2012).

Equity reserves should replace much regulation of asset portfolios. We learned that in the period well before the mortgage and financial market collapse that hundreds of federal regulators observed portfolio decisions at all the major banks without opposing any. Banks evaded risk-based capital requirements by putting risk assets in separate entities. Regulators permitted the evasion. There are many additional examples of forbearance and evasion. Equity reserves on all bank assets would be a more effective way of enforcing prudent lending.

One further recommendation applies to money market funds. They exist only because the Federal Reserve and Congress maintained ceiling rates for bank time deposits during years of rising inflation. These are mutual funds that have a special privilege. When prices of their asset portfolio would require them to pay less than one dollar per dollar of nominal deposits, they do not mark deposits to market. They use the dollar price. This rule is inconsistent with the mark-to-market requirement of all other mutual funds. Partially repealing the rule is a step in the right direction. It should be repealed for all deposits, not just business deposits.

Conclusion

The slow recovery from the Great Recession results from the mistaken policies and anti-business rhetoric of the administration. That rhetoric adds to the real source of slow growth by increasing uncertainty and threatening to increase tax rates and regulations on investors.

The Federal Reserve cannot have a lasting effect on real, non-monetary causes of low demand growth. And it reduces its short-term responses by encouraging growth of idle excess reserves.

No less disturbing are the failures of economists serving in policy positions to publicly and seemingly privately fail to explain to administration officials including the president that, whatever beliefs one holds about regulation and the distribution of income, administration rhetoric and policy actions are a major reason for slow growth.

Two observations can only be suggestive, but the only previous slow recovery, from the 1937–38 recession, shows very similar responses of investment and employment. That time the economist Jacob Viner, a Treasury adviser, to his credit, delivered the message to President Roosevelt. We should not expect less professionalism now.

References

Alesina, Alberto, and Ardagna, Silvia. 2009. "Large Changes in Fiscal Policy: Taxes versus Spending." National Bureau of Economic Research Working Paper 15438.

Bagehot, Walter. (1873) 1962. *Lombard Street: A Description of the Money Market.* Homewood, IL: Richard D. Irwin Inc.

Bailey, Martin. 1962. *National Income and the Price Level.* New York: McGraw-Hill.

Bordo, Michael, and Joseph Haubrich. 2012. "Deep Recessions, Fast Recoveries, and Financial Crises: Evidence from the American Record." National Bureau of Economic Research Working Paper 18194.

Brunner, Karl, and Allan H. Meltzer. 1968. "Liquidity Traps for Money, Bank Credit, and Interest Rates." *Journal of Political Economy* 76 (1).

Brunner, Karl, and Allan H. Meltzer. 1993. *Money and the Economy: Issues in Monetary Analysis.* Cambridge, UK: Cambridge University Press.

Calomiris, Charles. 2013. "How to Promote Fed Independence: Perspectives from Political Economy and US History." Working paper copied at Columbia University.

Friedman, Milton. 1969. "The Monetary Studies of the National Bureau." In *The Optimum Quantity of Money and Other Essays,* chapter 12. Chicago: Aldine.

Goodfriend, Marvin. 2012. "The Elusive Promise of Independent Central Banking." Keynote lecture, Institute for Monetary and Economic Studies, Bank of Japan.

Grabell, Michael. 2012. *Money Well Spent? The Truth Behind the Trillion-Dollar Stimulus, the Biggest Economic Recovery Plan in History.* New York: Public Affairs.

Hess, Gregory D., and Cameron A. Shelton. 2012. "Congress and the Federal Reserve." Claremont McKenna College working paper.

Issing, Otmar. 2005. "Why Did the Great Inflation Not Happen in Germany?" Federal Reserve Bank of St. Louis *Review* 87 (2): 329–35.

Issing, Otmar, and Volker Wieland. 2013. "Monetary Theory and Monetary Policy: Reflections on the Development over the Last 150 Years." *Jahrbucher fuer Nationaloekonomie und Statistik* 233 (3): 423–45.

Meltzer, Allan H. 1995. "Monetary, Credit, and (Other) Transmission Processes: A Monetarist Perspective." *Journal of Economic Perspectives* 9 (4): 49–72.

Meltzer, Allan H. 2009. *A History of the Federal Reserve, Vol. 2, Book 2: 1970–1986.* Chicago: University of Chicago Press.

Meltzer, Allan H. 2012. "More Regulation Is Not the Answer." Testimony before the House Financial Services Committee, June 6.

Porter, Michael, and Jan Rivkin. 2012. "Choosing the United States." *Harvard Business Review* 90 (3): 80–91.

Romer, Christina D., and Romer, David H. 2010. "The Macroeconomic Effects of Tax Changes: Estimates Based on a New Measure of Fiscal Shocks." *American Economic Review* 100 (3): 763–801.

Taylor, John B. 1995. "The Monetary Transmission Mechanism: An Empirical Framework." *Journal of Economic Perspectives* 9 (4): 11–26.

Tobin, James. 1969. "A General Equilibrium Approach to Monetary Theory." *Journal of Money, Credit, and Banking* 1 (1): 15–29.

Volcker, Paul A. 2013. "Central Banking at a Crossroad." Copied from the *Economic Club of New York*, May 29.

PART III

Is Too Big to Fail Over?
Are We Ready for the Next Crisis?

CHAPTER 9

How Is the System Safer?
What More Is Needed?

Martin Neil Baily and Douglas J. Elliott

T he recent severe financial crisis underlined the need for our financial system to operate with sufficient safety margins. Fortunately, very considerable progress has been made in improving safety through a combination of law, regulation, and voluntary private sector responses to the lessons of the crisis.

We will focus in this paper on the improvements in some of the key safety margins, particularly the actions to:

1. Substantially raise bank capital requirements to reduce both the probability of failure and the potential cost of such failures. If a troubled bank's capital falls below the new, higher requirements, the Federal Deposit Insurance Corporation (FDIC) can intervene while there is still substantial shareholder money available to cushion creditors and, ultimately, taxpayers.

2. Create new bank liquidity requirements that should have similar benefits to the capital increases. Liquidity shocks are a major source of the risk of bank failures, so improving a bank's ability to handle such shocks reduces the probability of failure. Further, buying time to react should reduce economic losses that would be caused by the need to quickly secure liquidity even on damaging terms.

3. Raise capital and liquidity levels still further for the most important financial institutions. This provides an incentive for a firm to voluntarily reduce its systemic importance, if that can be done economically, and also widens safety margins to reduce potential taxpayer and societal losses.

4. Reform the legal approaches to resolution of troubled financial institutions so that it becomes feasible to allow even important

---

Olivia Rosenthal provided substantial assistance in preparing the section on resolving large institutions.

financial firms to fail without severe disruption to the financial system as a whole, while placing the costs of failure on the shareholders and holders of long-term unsecured debt at the holding company.

5. Create mechanisms to provide macroprudential oversight for the financial system. This describes a set of tools to try to manage overall systemic risks, such as by requiring higher capital levels in boom times, when the risk of a bubble developing is greatest.

The rest of this paper will elaborate on these points.

Substantially raising bank capital requirements

The most critical margin of error for a bank is that supplied by its capital. Capital, in its simplest form, represents the portion of the value of a bank's assets that is not legally required to be repaid to anyone and is therefore available to cover losses. The purest and strongest form of capital is therefore common equity, the funds paid in by the original purchasers of a bank's common shares, plus the accumulated profits and losses of the bank. Common shareholders are the owners of the bank and benefit or lose based on the bank's performance rather than on any guaranteed return. Common equity is the strongest form of capital because it: (a) is perpetual, with no automatic right to a future repayment, (b) has no right to a minimum periodic payment, such as a dividend or interest payment, and (c) has the lowest repayment priority of any security in a bankruptcy or other insolvency proceeding.

Capital directly protects depositors, transactional counterparties, other customers, and investors in the bank's debt. It indirectly protects taxpayers by ensuring that someone other than these protected parties bears the loss, without the government having to step in with a rescue package. This margin for error is very valuable to all the other constituents of a bank, particularly because it is entirely flexible. The source of the loss can come from any cause: one does not have to guess in advance what the problem might be and provide specific protection for that eventuality.

There are other securities that also perform capital's critical function of protecting other investors or depositors in the financial instruments of a bank. For example, a perpetual preferred share never needs to be repaid and ranks behind all claimants on the estate of a bankrupt institution, except for common shareholders. If it is non-cumulative, meaning there is no right to receive in the future any dividends that are skipped because of financial difficulties, then it also does not represent a cash drain on a bank that is in trouble and chooses not to pay its preferred shares. Because they are shares, the holders do not have the legal right to force the company into bankruptcy for nonpayment of dividends. Thus, this security provides almost as much protection to all the other constituents of a bank as common equity does.

There are still other forms of securities that provide a weaker version of capital. For example, cumulative perpetual preferred shares give less protection because they have the right to eventually be paid any dividends that were skipped, but they have all the other protective characteristics. A preferred share with a very long maturity, say thirty years, is much like a perpetual preferred share as long as the maturity date is so far off that it does not affect the behavior of other investors. (If a bond holder will be paid off in five years, he is unlikely to care much whether the preferred has no claim to repayment at all or no claim for thirty years.) Perhaps the weakest form of capital that still can reasonably be considered capital is a subordinated bond. It fails the key tests of capital for a going concern, since there are required payments both at maturity and on interest payment dates, enforceable by the right to push a bank into insolvency.

In terms of avoiding failure, therefore, subordinated debt is much inferior to higher levels of capital, such as equity. However, the existence of such debt can be very important in the event of failure. As we discuss later in this paper, unsecured debt issued by the financial holding company is part of the cushion that protects taxpayers in the event of bankruptcy or when FDIC resolution is invoked.

In retrospect, it is clear that banks and many other financial institutions were generally quite under-capitalized prior to the financial crisis. Capital levels for banks should be set so that there is a very low probability that any losses will spread beyond the common shareholders and other suppliers of capital. Instead, many financial institutions went bankrupt in the financial crisis and many more might have done so had there not been massive government intervention.

Capital levels, and the quality of that capital, are now quite substantially higher than during the boom years. Much of this is the result of market responses. Debt holders, uninsured depositors, customers, and even many investors in common stock are leery of dealing with an under-capitalized financial institution. Capital levels had only sunk so low during the boom because there was a wide perception that economic and financial risks were also very low. The crisis demonstrated the fallacy of this thinking and it became difficult for banks to compete effectively without improving their capital substantially.

Regulators have pushed capital levels still higher by raising the minimum levels that they insist banks meet. Some of this occurred on an ad hoc basis, but the larger effect comes from longer-term changes in the global agreements on appropriate capital levels and their translation into national law and regulation. In particular, the global agreement known as Basel III requires sharply higher capital, and of better quality, than was allowed before the crisis. (Basel III is the term used for the third version of the Basel Accord on Bank Capital, which builds on the original accord agreed upon twenty-five years ago. The Basel rules are reached by consensus at the Basel Committee on Bank Supervision and are voluntarily implemented in national law and regulation. There are implementation differences of importance, but the standards generally apply in all the most significant banking jurisdictions.)

In the United States, rules based on the Basel III standards will start to apply this year, although the higher requirements are phased in over a few years. In practice, most banks are positioning themselves to be in compliance with the ultimate rules by 2014 or soon thereafter, rather than taking advantage of the transition period.

Regulators in the United States effectively use three different capital standards, requiring capital exceeding the maximum of these three levels: a ratio of capital to risk-weighted assets (RWA); a simple "leverage ratio" of capital to total assets; and the level of capital required under a stress test, which applies only to the largest banks.

The first measure attempts to calculate the level of risk in a bank's portfolio of loans and investments and to ensure that capital is adequate to cover that risk. RWA is therefore the risk-weighted total amount of assets held by the bank. That is, the total value of each asset is multiplied by a percentage reflecting its risk level and this adjusted amount is added across all assets to produce a total risk-weighted asset figure. The percentage weighting for each category ranges from 0 percent, for extremely safe investments such as cash and US government securities, to 100 percent for riskier classes of assets. In a few cases, the levels exceed 100 percent for certain very risky assets, such as loans in default or imminent danger of default and the riskiest tranches of securitizations. Commitments to lend that are not carried on the balance sheet are converted to an asset amount using weightings that depend on the type of commitment, with those that are certain to be drawn down receiving 100 percent weightings. These asset-equivalent amounts are then treated as if they were already on the balance sheet, with their effect on total RWA depending on the riskiness of their type of credit.

For example, residential mortgage loans often have a 50 percent risk-weighting, so that a $1 million mortgage would generate a risk-weighted asset of $500,000. If a bank were trying to hold capital equal to 10 percent of its RWA, then it would need $50,000 of capital to cover this mortgage. If, instead of making a loan immediately, the bank made a commitment to lend in the future should the homeowner wish, then the $1 million commitment might be treated as equivalent to, say, a $750,000 loan. After applying the 50 percent risk-weighting, this would produce an RWA of $375,000 and a need for capital of $37,500.

Those banks that have significant trading books use a different set of rules to determine the capital needed to back those trading positions. These calculations attempt to capture both the overall market risk of different types of securities and the specific credit or other risks that apply to particular securities. Market risks are calculated based on a "value at risk" (VAR) formula that looks at the historic distribution of price movements. The idea is to use the level of loss from an unlikely severe market movement, such as one that occurs only 1 percent of the time in the chosen historical period, and then to multiply this by a factor to add further conservatism. The specific techniques and weightings used under the previous version of the Basel Accord (Basel II) are now viewed as unsatisfactory in light of their performance in the recent financial crisis and have been revised to be considerably more conservative.

US bank regulators also require that banks maintain sufficient capital to meet a "leverage ratio" test, which is measured simply as the amount of capital divided by total assets, without regard to risk weighting, averaged over the period. Basel III will add a leverage ratio to global standards as well.

The largest US banks also undergo a stress test in which a particularly adverse economic environment is postulated and banks must use their models, under the guidance of the regulators, to estimate how much capital they would have at the end of the period. These stress tests remain relatively ad hoc, changing considerably from year to year based on changes in the regulators' perceptions of the economic risks and also evolving over time as regulators attempt to refine and improve their risk measurement approaches.

In recent years, the stress tests have become the binding regulatory capital constraint on the banks subject to the tests, producing higher minimum requirements than the other methods. This may be a natural and useful result in a crisis period or immediately thereafter, but it would be disturbing if it became the long-term norm. The stress tests have many flaws as the binding constraint. They have not been derived by the kind of multiyear global consultative process that has allowed the Basel rules to be refined. They have not even gone through a normal US rule-making process whereby there is adequate public discussion of how they are structured and why. For that matter, even the subjects of the test are not fully aware of how the regulators will decide to adjust the results of the banks' internal models, since the authorities have been afraid that transparency would lead to gaming. Further, the tests are ad hoc and change considerably from year to year.

If there is a decision to use the stress tests as the main regulatory constraint on capital, then there should be much more discussion of the rationale for this and there need to be important changes to fix the flaws.

The Basel III rules are substantially more conservative than the earlier US rules or than the Basel II rules that were adopted by most of the world but had not yet been put into place in the United States. Basel III is more conservative than Basel II in a number of key ways, five in particular, which will be explored below:

- Higher quality of capital
- Higher required capital levels
- Higher levels of risk-weighted assets
- Much higher capital for trading positions
- Leverage ratios

1. Higher quality of capital: The Basel rules allow banks to count a number of instruments beyond common equity as capital, with the strongest being considered part of "tier 1," which counted for most purposes as if it were common equity. Weaker instruments fell into "tier 2" or, for limited purposes, an even weaker bucket called "tier 3." In practice, ratios using tier 1 capital tended to be the most binding on the banks, since it was considerably easier and less expensive to sell tier 2 securities than those that fell into tier 1.

The financial crisis demonstrated that the weakest forms of capital provided little real protection in a severe, widespread crisis. In particular, subordinated debt proved to be of almost no public policy value because it was not considered feasible to allow so much of the financial system to be restructured in insolvency proceedings. Outside of such circumstances, subordinated debt has no capital features, since it requires fixed payments that can be enforced by putting a firm into bankruptcy. Similarly, the ability to skip or defer payments on preferred shares proved to be of less value than expected, because of the signaling effects of that deferral. It would certainly have sent a negative signal about the specific bank that skipped a payment, but there was also concern that it would then make it much harder for other banks to roll over their preferred securities or to raise capital through issuing new preferred shares, because of the contagion effects.

As a result, the Basel III rules mean that some securities that counted in tier 1 under the previous rules now fall in tier 2 and a number of tier 2 securities no longer count at all, especially since the former tier 3 category has been completely abolished.

Further, Basel III puts constraints on how much of certain items can be counted as capital. In particular, the treatment of intangible assets is tougher. The value of a firm's assets usually includes some assets that have value, but which are neither financial instruments nor physical in nature. Most intangible assets at banks derive from the difference between the amount the bank paid in the past for another bank and the book value of the acquired bank's assets at the time of the purchase. The presumption is that the sales price represents the fair value of the bank, since it was arrived at in an arm's-length negotiation, so intangible assets must exist that were worth the difference between the price and the book value. The biggest banks have grown through many acquisitions, so this type of intangible asset can represent a large figure for them.

Mortgage servicing rights represent another large category of intangible assets for banks. Servicers normally make a profit, often substantial, on the mortgages they handle. As a result, banks have developed a market to buy or sell the right to be the servicer for the remaining life of a portfolio of mortgages.

Intangible assets usually represent genuine value, but they can be difficult to turn into cash in a crisis and they can lose value if a bank's overall franchise deteriorates. Both disadvantages are particularly true of the goodwill taken on in acquisitions, which can be almost impossible to monetize in a crisis. In recognition of these difficulties, Basel III subtracts from the value of common equity the amount of intangible assets, with a few exceptions. Mortgage servicing rights are allowed in an amount up to 10 percent of tier 1 common equity. If the balance sheet shows more, then the level of assets and the level of common equity are reduced by the overage.

Two other categories of assets are partially excluded. Deferred tax assets whose value is dependent on future profits are also limited to 10 percent of tier 1 common equity, since their value can fall sharply when a bank becomes troubled. Equity investments in nonconsolidated financial institutions face the same limitation for a different reason: there is concern that a problem at, for example, an insurer would end up hitting the capital both of that insurer and of a bank with a significant stake in that firm.

In addition, the aggregation of these three categories is capped at a total of 15 percent of tier 1 common equity. In the case of all three categories, there was a significant minority that wished to exclude these assets completely from tier 1 common equity; the partial exclusion was the result of a compromise.

2. *Higher required capital levels:* The minimum level of the ratio of capital to risk-weighted assets is higher in absolute terms. Under Basel II, tier 1 capital had to be at least 4 percent of RWA and common equity had to "predominate," generally interpreted as being at least half the total. Thus, 2 percent of RWA had to be in the form of common equity. Under Basel III, tier 1 capital must be at least 6 percent of RWA and at least 4.5 percent of RWA must be in the form of common equity. Thus, the safest and most expensive form of capital underwent more than a doubling of the minimum requirements. The minimum total of capital remains at 8 percent of RWA, meaning that tier 2 capital can only fill 2 of the 8 percentage points of RWA going forward, whereas Basel II allowed tier 2 and 3 capital to total up to 4 percentage points.

However, this considerably understates the true required increase. Basel III adds a new "capital conservation buffer" of 2.5 percent of RWA, which must be in the form of tier 1 common equity. If a bank does not maintain this full buffer on top of its base minimum, then various actions will be required to conserve capital, including limitations on dividend payments and on bonuses. The constraints are onerous enough, and the signaling effects severe enough, that it is clear that managements will work hard to avoid dipping into this buffer, although it will be there to deal with emergencies. Thus, the minimum level of tier 1 common equity effectively increases from 2 percent of RWA under Basel II to 7 percent under Basel III, more than tripling.

Basel III also calls for national authorities to have the right to impose a counter-cyclical capital buffer of up to 2.5 percent of RWA if they believe that financial conditions are too loose. This is one of the macroprudential measures that are discussed in more detail later. It is *not* expected that this buffer would be employed under most circumstances, but it would be available for use in boom times.

3. Higher levels of risk-weighted assets: As part of designing Basel III, the committee spent considerable effort reviewing the risk weights that were applied to the different types of assets. There was a consensus that many of the risk weights had been too low under Basel II and therefore there were a number of increases to them going forward.

4. Much higher capital for trading positions: Under the previous Basel rules, the amount of capital required for positions held in the trading book was often quite a bit lower than the same position would have required outside that book. This was principally because trading positions were judged based on the volatility of prices, using the assumption that a security held for trading could be liquidated within ten days and that it was possible to estimate how much of a loss that might entail, based on historical data about prices. In retrospect, the historical data generally reflected the recent, much quieter market environment, especially for new types of securities and other financial instruments for which there was relatively little history. In consequence, a series of revisions were made that took effect in advance of Basel III. These are known, perhaps inevitably, as Basel II.5.

Most basically, there are definitional changes that make it harder to take a banking book position and move it to the trading book in order to gain from potentially lower risk-weightings. The risk-weighting calculations were also toughened considerably, with Standard & Poor's reporting a resultant tripling of the average risk-weighting for such assets at eleven European banks that it surveyed in 2012.[1]

One important change is to use a "stressed value at risk" (SVAR) measurement in addition to a normal VAR calculation. In essence, VARs calculate a potential loss on a position by assuming that historical patterns of

---

1. Standard and Poor's, "Basel 2.5 Increases The Squeeze On Investment Banking Returns," last modified May 14, 2012, http://www.standardandpoors.com /ratings/articles/en/us/?articleType=HTML&assetID=1245334380388.

trading prices hold and that a low-probability bad outcome occurs, such as a loss on a ten-day holding period that is worse than the losses experienced 99 percent of the time historically. Generally, although not always, banks used the most recent year for their probability calculations. Stressed VARs instead must be calculated using a one-year period of historical market conditions that would have produced a substantial loss, which might be a year from the recent financial crisis. Several other important technical changes were made to try to ensure that market risk was truly fully accounted for.

5. *Leverage ratios:* Basel III added a feature to Basel II that was already in place in the United States, albeit with different details. Earlier versions of Basel used only one set of capital requirements, those related to the risk-weighted asset calculations. The new version adds a second minimum requirement, based on a leverage ratio, with the binding constraint being whichever calculation produces the higher minimum for a bank. The leverage ratio is calculated by dividing total tier 1 capital by the total assets of the bank, with some adjustments to the assets, particularly the addition of a number of off-balance-sheet exposures.

The intention of the Basel Committee was clearly to continue to use the risk-weighted measures as the normal method for determining the minimum required capital, but with the addition of the leverage constraint to avoid problems that might arise from risk weightings that prove to be too low.

Most developed banking systems did not use a leverage ratio, unlike the United States, and therefore it was decided to provide an extensive transition period. The leverage ratio is to be reported by banks starting in 2015, with its use as a binding regulatory constraint starting in 2018.

The United States already had a leverage ratio, albeit calculated somewhat differently. Banks are required to maintain a 3 percent leverage ratio if they are considered "strong" by supervisors or a 4 percent ratio otherwise. However, for a bank to be considered "well-capitalized," and therefore benefit from some automatic regulatory flexibility, its ratio must be at least 5 percent.

One of the most important differences between the existing US rules and the Basel III rules as they will be applied in most countries relates to our accounting systems. In the United States, we use generally accepted accounting principles (GAAP) as promulgated by the Financial Accounting Standards Board under the authority of the Securities and Exchange

Commission (SEC). Most nations use International Accounting Standards (IAS) as promulgated by the International Accounting Standards Board (IASB). There are significant differences that are relevant to financial institutions. In particular, derivatives exposures are generally carried on a gross basis under IAS, whereas GAAP carries them on a net basis, where offsetting exposures to a single counterparty are netted if there is a master netting agreement between the firms, as is usually the case. It has been reported that the size of Deutsche Bank's balance sheet is almost twice as big under IAS rules as under GAAP, although it would be rare for the difference to be this pronounced. (Deutsche Bank has very large derivatives exposures that magnify the differential.)

Basel III provides considerable guidance as to how derivatives and similar exposures should be calculated for leverage ratio calculations, although there still remains a residual difference because of the basic national accounting rules and regulatory discretion in the application of the Basel rules. The US federal banking agencies have indicated that, on average, a sampling of banks in this country that are sophisticated enough to be allowed to use the "advanced approaches" option for capital calculations would have a denominator for the Basel III leverage calculations that is 1.43 times the balance sheet size that was previously used in US leverage ratio calculations.

The US regulatory agencies recently proposed for comment the concept of setting a supplementary US leverage ratio for the largest banks at 5 percent of assets for consolidated banking groups and 6 percent for the banking entities within those groups. If the 1.43 multiple holds true, this would imply leverage ratios of 7.15 percent and 8.52 percent under the old US calculations. The new rules would take effect at the beginning of 2018.

An argument that is made for using a leverage ratio calculation is that it is simple and provides a backup safety measure that avoids the possibility of financial institutions gaming the risk-weighted capital ratio. A downside of a simple leverage ratio is that if it becomes the binding constraint on financial institutions, this may encourage them to hold riskier assets that promise higher expected returns. Corporations set target rates of return on equity, arguing they must do this to remain viable in a competitive market environment. If required to hold additional capital, they will look for ways to raise returns in order to meet their return targets, especially if additional risk in the portfolio of assets is not understood by markets.

There is a considerable literature on the question of the costs of bank capital and whether or not the cost of equity (and hence the company's target rate of return) will decline if banks take steps to become safer or rise if banks become riskier. Certainly there are steps banks can take that are visible to shareholders and that reduce risk, and these should lower the cost of equity. But it is apparent that in the run-up to the crisis the shareholders of many financial institutions had insufficient sense of the riskiness of the portfolios of these institutions. Taking excessive risk was a major factor in the crisis; leverage ratio regulation should avoid promoting such behavior in the future.

Total effect of changes incorporated in Basel III

It is now possible to get a fair estimate of the total impact of Basel III on minimum capital requirements because large banks have generally begun disclosing their capital ratios under both the old and the new rules.

Figure 9.1 shows the differences in capital requirements for a set of large US bank groups as calculated on a Basel III basis as compared to the Basel II.5 rules. On average, the stricter Basel III rules reduce the reported tier 1 common equity ratio by 2.4 points.[2] The full difference between the earlier US rules and Basel III would be higher, as there were some effects from moving to Basel II.5 from the earlier US rules.

Improvements in bank capital in recent years

The total increase in key capital ratios since the crisis is very striking, clearly showing a large increase in margins for error in the system. Another chapter in this book[3] illustrates the magnitude of the capital changes at US banks. Using a consistent Basel I basis, tangible common equity rose from 4.6 percent of risk-weighted assets in the fourth quarter of 2007 to 11.6 percent in the third quarter of 2013, as shown in Figure 9.2 .

---

2. These figures are taken from 10-Q statements filed with the SEC for the third quarter of 2013, the latest figures available. The purpose here is to show how changes in the Basel guidelines have affected the capital ratios for the large banks. We recognize that there are alternative ways of calculating capital ratios. For example, Thomas Hoenig posts comparative measures on his web site, www .fdic.gov/about/learn/board/hoenig/capitalizationratios2q13.pdf.

3. See chapter 12 of this volume: Steve Strongin, "Too Big to Fail from an Economic Perspective."

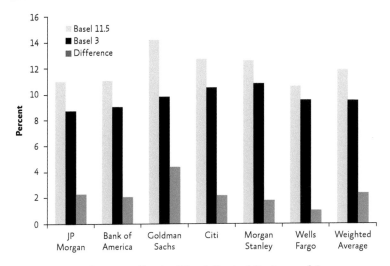

FIGURE 9.1 Common Equity Tier 1 Capital Ratio as of September 30, 2013

Note: Weighted Average based on risk-weighted assets under Basel II.5 standards.
Source: SEC filings

Creation of new bank liquidity requirements

Capital is arguably the most important safety buffer, since it provides the resources to recover from substantial losses of any nature and also gives those dealing with the bank confidence in its safety. However, the proximate cause of a bank's demise is usually a liquidity problem that makes it impossible to survive a classic "bank run" or a modern equivalent, such as an inability to access the debt markets for new funding. It is entirely possible for the economic value of a bank's assets to be more than sufficient to cover all of its claims and yet for that bank to go bust because its assets are illiquid and its liabilities have short-term maturities.

In fact, a primary reason for the existence of central banks is to assist with this problem through a "lender-of-last-resort" function. Central banks are intended to halt bank runs against solvent institutions by lending against sound collateral to provide the liquidity necessary to pay out claims in a crisis. This function is not intended to be a bailout of an insolvent bank, nor would such a bank have sufficient truly sound collateral to be able to borrow the necessary funds from the central bank. However, the difficulty of placing a value on the assets offered as collateral means

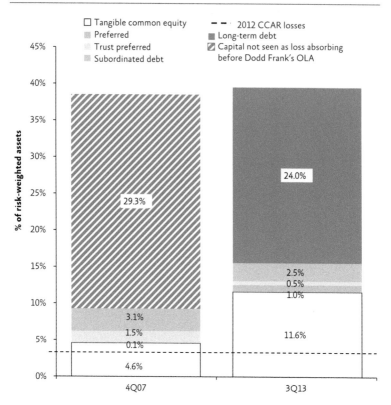

FIGURE 9.2 Loss-absorbency among US G-SIFI banks

Source: Steve Strongin, "Too Big to Fail from an Economic Perspective," chapter 12 in this volume.

that it can be hard to tell for sure whether a bailout may be occurring. It also raises the risk that a truly solvent bank will not receive the appropriate central bank funding due to a misunderstanding of the actual asset values.

The recent financial crisis underlined the importance of the lender-of-last-resort function as well as the practical and political difficulties in its use on a widespread basis. As a result, regulators and the markets now demand that banks be considerably more liquid than was required before the crisis. One of the major miscalculations made by most of the market players and the regulatory community was a belief, often unstated, that the high levels of market liquidity typical of the preceding decade would make it possible to sell assets readily without too large a haircut. This proved to be wrong.

In the Basel III rules, regulators have, for the first time, designed global standards for the minimum liquidity levels to be held by banks. Before this, there were a few countries that had quantitative minimum requirements, but the large majority, including the United States, relied on subjective regulatory judgment as to when liquidity levels were so low that a bank should be forced to remedy them. In practice, very little was done to force banks to shore up liquidity.

The Basel III liquidity rules, which will be phased in starting in 2015, rely on two minimum ratios. The first is a "liquidity coverage ratio" which is a kind of stylized stress test to ensure that a bank would have the necessary sources of cash to survive a thirty-day market crisis. It appears that thirty days was chosen as the relevant period because it was viewed as long enough for central banks and governments to take the necessary emergency measures to calm a widespread market crisis of liquidity.

The second is the "net stable funding ratio," which tries to ensure that a bank's balance sheet would be more than covered by stable long-term funding sources. The idea is to keep banks from engaging in excessive "maturity transformation" whereby they fund long-term obligations with short-term sources of cash.

Liquidity coverage ratio

The liquidity coverage ratio (LCR) is calculated by dividing the bank's level of high-quality liquid assets by the projected cash claims over the next thirty days. Basel III specifies what will be considered high-quality liquid assets. Very safe, very liquid assets, including government bonds and cash held at central banks, are considered to be tier 1 assets. Safe and liquid assets of other types, including specified categories of private securities, are considered to be in tier 2 and are subject to haircuts of up to 50 percent on their value to represent the potential loss in a fire sale during a time of crisis. Tier 2 assets may constitute no more than 40 percent of the total.

Basel III also specifies what percentage of assets with an indefinite maturity, such as demand deposits, will be assumed to run off. In practice, retail deposits tend to be "sticky" and not to move, especially when they fall within the deposit guarantee limits, and therefore little run-off is assumed from them. Corporate deposits are less sticky and are assumed to run off in greater volume. Assumptions are also specified about drawdowns of cash through lines of credit and other instruments where banks have promised to loan money up to certain limits if requested. Crisis times tend to result in many of these lines being drawn down.

Banks will be required to maintain LCRs of 100 percent or more; that is, to have sources of cash more than sufficient to cover their expected outflows over the assumed thirty-day crisis period. However, the Basel Committee has indicated that national regulators should allow the ratio to fall below 100 percent when a bank or the system is in trouble. Absent this guidance, the sources of cash would essentially be tied up and unavailable to handle the very type of crisis they are intended to protect against. That said, banks in normal times will almost certainly target a ratio above 100 percent in order to maintain a safety buffer to protect them from potential regulatory actions. They will also be loath to fall below 100 percent even in a time of crisis, although circumstances may force them to do so. Financial markets will react similarly and may substantially penalize banks that open themselves up to regulatory actions by allowing their ratios to decline to near or below 100 percent.

Net stable funding ratio

The net stable funding ratio (NSFR) is the level of stable sources of funds divided by the level of assets adjusted for their ability to be liquidated. Stable sources of funds consist of tier 1 and tier 2 capital, other preferred shares, liabilities with a maturity of more than one year, and portions of those liabilities with unspecified maturities, such as demand deposits. As with the LCR, the haircuts applied to the latter category depend on the degree of perceived stickiness. The need for stable funding is reduced from the initial level of total assets by the exclusion of portions of the assets that can readily be sold. The haircuts that are applied are based on the relative degree of liquidity and therefore the ease of sale in troubled times and the potential impact of fire sale conditions.

As with the LCR, the NSFR is required to remain above 100 percent, with some flexibility for crisis times. Managements are likely to hold liquidity buffers above these levels and will be pressured by investors to do so, in order to avoid potential regulatory actions.

Liquidity improvements in recent years

A recent study by the Clearing House Association,[4] an industry trade group, provides some revealing figures on the substantial improvements already made in the industry's liquidity position in response to the lessons of the crisis and in anticipation of future regulation. It found that US commercial banks in aggregate reduced their reliance on wholesale funding by well over one-third from the peak in 2008 to the second quarter of 2012. Wholesale funding fell from about 30 percent of total funding to roughly 18 percent. Further, it found that commercial banks went from being significant net users of short-term funding prior to the crisis to net suppliers in recent years. Specifically, the volume of short-term liabilities minus short-term assets fell from 10 percent of total assets to –6 percent.

Raising capital and liquidity levels further for the most important financial institutions

Regulators in the United States and globally drew another conclusion from the financial crisis, which is that some financial institutions have a level of systemic importance that means they should be held to even greater standards of safety. Such institutions are often referred to as systemically important financial institutions (SIFIs). The higher standards are generally viewed as serving a double purpose. The most straightforward is because they are perceived as likely to do more damage in a crisis than other institutions would. In addition, they are often perceived to benefit from an unfair subsidy in their borrowing costs based on the assumption by creditors that the government would have to rescue such important institutions if a crisis flared up. Since higher safety standards generally come with a cost, the differential in safety margins serves as a direct offset to any market subsidy.

SIFIs are required to carry tier 1 common equity to RWA of up to 3.0 points more than the standard requirements, depending on the degree to which they are determined to be systemically important. Initially, the

---

4. The Clearing House, "Assessing the Basel III Net Stable Funding Ratio in the Context of Recent Improvements in Longer-Term Bank Liquidity," TCH Research Report, August 2013, https://www.theclearinghouse.org/~/media/Files /Association%20Documents/20130829%20TCH%20Study%20Assessing%20 the%20Basel%20III%20Net%20Stable%20Funding%20Ratio%20in%20the%20 Context%20of%20Recent%20Imprrovements%20in%20Bank%20Liquidity.pdf.

most critical banks, such as J.P. Morgan, are required to carry 2.5 points more of capital, with the 3.0 level available as a deterrent to the further aggregation of systemic importance. Other SIFIs have lower requirements, down to 1.0 point more of capital for the lowest tier.

Resolving large complex financial institutions

Increasing capital requirements and instituting leverage and liquidity rules are the most important steps being taken to make the financial system safer, complementing many other regulatory actions being taken to enhance systemic safety. But the new rules cannot guarantee against the failure of a large institution, an event that could potentially disrupt the entire financial sector and trigger a recession. We are not persuaded that a financial system where a large fraction of the assets are in large institutions is any less safe than a system with only smaller institutions. But nonetheless, it is important that the large institutions that make bad decisions and get into difficulties be allowed to fail, with the owners and managers of such companies bearing the costs rather than taxpayers.

Before Dodd-Frank, the failure resolution strategy applicable to these large banking organizations was bifurcated: the holding company was subject to the bankruptcy code and the failures in bank subsidiaries were handled by the FDIC. Large bank holding companies that also owned securities broker-dealers or insurance companies were subject to further failure resolution complexity with a specialized strategy for the broker-dealer administered by the Securities Investor Protection Corporation or for the insurance company by state insurance regulators. While a number of countries have special resolution regimes or arrangements for banks and other financial institutions (including Brazil, Canada, Hong Kong, Italy, Japan, South Korea, Singapore, Turkey, and the United Kingdom), no country has yet established effective means of resolving a large diverse financial group. In fact, the large financial institutions in many countries are widely viewed as being "too big to fail," in that their governments would provide whatever support were needed to avoid failure.

Bifurcated failure resolution regimes have worked well for particular institutions and particular failures (the failures of depository institutions of the 1980s and 1990s come to mind). But in most cases where such a regime has been successful, the failure itself was pretty straightforward: the failed depository institution was often the sole or most significant asset of the holding company, the balance sheet was simple, and the resolution was aided by a bank willing to acquire and take on the assets and liabilities of the failed bank, with limited help from the FDIC and its deposit insurance fund.

However, as the crisis of 2008 revealed, the FDIC's limited tools were only applicable to depository institutions, with no jurisdiction over holding companies or nonbanking subsidiaries. So, when the institution in question is a large, complex bank holding company with many nonbanking subsidiaries, a bifurcated regime has been less effective, especially since failures outside the bank subsidiary itself can cause a run on the bank. Moreover, in periods of systemic risk, the bankruptcy code was the only means of addressing the bank holding company and other nonbank subsidiaries, and the code proved to be inadequate and slow. Additionally, the bankruptcy courts themselves have no special expertise in dealing with the complicated problems of large financial institution failures. While the traditional failure resolution regime can be sufficient for certain institutions during normal circumstances, 2008 proved that such a regime is limited in stressful circumstances, ones involving systemic risk and multifaceted financial institutions.

To create a framework in which large, complex institutions could fail, Congress approved the creation of the Orderly Liquidation Authority (OLA) in Title II of the Dodd-Frank Act. This failure resolution framework imposes losses suffered by financial institutions on their shareholders and creditors and prohibits taxpayer payments for losses. It sets up a process that is intended to provide an orderly, organized system of resolution. The conditions for the use of the Title II option of Dodd-Frank are restricted. It can only be enacted when officials from the Treasury Department, the Federal Reserve, and the FDIC agree that normal failure resolution mechanisms would cause instability. If such a consensus is not created, failure is addressed under pre-Dodd-Frank frameworks: the Federal Deposit Insurance Act handles failures in the banks and the bankruptcy code is used for the bank holding company. The new Title II strategy acknowledges the reality that large, diversified US financial institutions usually consist of a holding company that owns various subsidiaries such as a bank, a broker-dealer, and even an insurance company. The issues that can topple this sort of institution often begin with losses or stress at one or many of the operating subsidiaries.

There has been considerable skepticism about the OLA provision of Dodd-Frank, however, and its creation has been a flash point for those who wish to repeal Dodd-Frank. A key objection is that it is said to enshrine bailouts of large institutions and worsen the "too-big-to-fail" problem and the associated moral hazard. That concern does have legitimacy. In a financial crisis, bank regulators, the Treasury, and the Federal Reserve are facing great uncertainty and fear a financial meltdown. The pressure is very high to step in and prevent bank failures by injecting taxpayer funds into troubled institutions. In our judgment, however, substantial progress has been made in developing a strategy to resolve large institutions safely and avoid moral hazard, either through the OLA or through a bankruptcy process. Work remains to be done, but the fundamentals are now being put into place.

The single point of entry approach

A new strategy has been developed for the failure resolution of systemically important financial institutions: the single point of entry (SPOE) approach that could provide a means of resolving SIFIs without triggering a panic or relying on taxpayer-funded bailouts. The SPOE approach has been developed largely at the FDIC.

The SPOE approach provides a predictable, pre-announced strategy for the private sector recapitalization of a failing SIFI. The holding company absorbs all of the organization's losses, including those of its operating subsidiaries. SPOE is designed to impose losses on shareholders and long-term unsecured debt holders of the parent holding company. The holding company would be put into FDIC receivership under the Orderly Liquidation Authority. (It could alternatively be placed into bankruptcy with the FDIC as a party to the proceeding.) The holding company's entire required cushion of long-term unsecured debt and equity would be available to bear the losses of the group, regardless of the legal entity in which the losses occurred. In order for SPOE to work and for the holding company to be recapitalized by converting its debt to equity, the company would need to have sufficient capital and unsecured long-term debt to absorb the losses. The post-recession increases in required capital and long-term debt levels of large US bank holding companies should be enough to provide this absorption capacity, something that can be verified using the mandated stress tests.

Shareholders of the holding company would absorb the first losses. If the losses were large enough, the value of the holding company shares would be eliminated and the unsecured creditors in the company would bear further losses. The holding company creditors would have their left-over claims transformed to equity and become new owners of the financial institution (much as in a regular Chapter 11 proceeding). Thus, long-term debt holders of the parent holder would become equity holders of the new bridge company. The management responsible for the financial institutions' losses would be replaced with the caveat that a core of senior staff would be retained, at least for a period, to ensure the continued operations of the subsidiaries. While the holding company would be in receivership, the retail and investment banks, broker-dealer, and other under-stress subsidiaries would continue to operate, meeting the obligations of their customers and avoiding disruption of the economy.

Under this recapitalization strategy, the holding company's assets (including stock of its operating subsidiaries) are down-streamed and transferred to a bridge company established by the FDIC (or a bankruptcy judge). Provided the debt and equity cushion of the original holding company had been set at an adequate level, the bridge company would be solvent; with its liabilities lifted off of it, it would be operational. Assets at the holding company are likely to be a combination of cash and receivables from the various subsidiaries. Cash can arise from issuing long-term unsecured debt at the holding company, which the FDIC is encouraging as a condition for the SPOE strategy. Particularly in times of stress, that cash would be down-streamed from the holding company to the subsidiaries in order to protect their solvency. Receivables would be created back to the holding company—and most holding company assets would be such receivables. In times of stress, the holding company would convert this intercompany debt to equity in the subsidiaries, thereby protecting the solvency of the subsidiaries at the expense of the holders of the holding company debt who would be either wiped out or end up holding equity of questionable value. This cash from the holding company down to the subsidiaries and receivables back is an intercompany loan.

If the bridge holding company or any of the operating subsidiaries were unable to secure enough liquidity to keep their business running smoothly (a likely outcome), the FDIC would use the orderly liquidation fund established under Title II of Dodd-Frank. The OLF allows the FDIC to borrow funds from the Treasury Department to lend fully secured liquidity to failing financial institutions. This provision of liquidity funding will only be available if private market funding is unavailable. The OLF is intended solely to provide fully secured liquidity and is forbidden from providing capital. The distinction between providing capital to a failing company and providing temporary, secured liquidity may seem overly technical. But in reality the distinction between the two is the distinction between taxpayer-funded bailouts reminiscent of 2008 and acceptable government-funded, fully secured, short-term solutions. It is important to recognize that this temporary funding does not represent a bailout. Instead, this liquidity would be lent at above-normal market rates and only until the market stabilized and the bridge and its subsidiaries would be able to pay back the FDIC in full. This is not a bailout and is, instead, essentially lender-of-last-resort lending. A failed institution needs liquidity funding in order to maintain value and continue operations until it can be sold, recapitalized, or liquidated. Historically, central banks have acted as the lender of last resort by providing liquidity. The provision of liquidity funding under Title II is simply an extension of these same principles, allowing for funding to be available to failing institutions on an expedited basis. Liquidity funding could also be provided to the bridge bank if a bankruptcy proceeding is the vehicle for resolving the failing bank holding company.

The removal of the financial holding company of the troubled institution, together with its debt and equity liabilities, would provide immediate recapitalization of the new bridge holding company. It would still have troubled subsidiaries on its books. But since it has been relieved of substantial liabilities, the new entity is solvent. The transfer could be accomplished over a weekend or even overnight. Moreover, deposits and short-term obligations are almost always issued by the operating subsidiaries, not by holding companies. Therefore, as is the case under SPOE, if only the holding company fails, uninsured depositors or short-term creditors of the operating subsidiaries would have no reason to run because their obligations would still be satisfied. Even creditors of the holding company would benefit from a SPOE recapitalization as this strategy would keep subsidiaries open and therefore preserve the holding company's franchise value. So creditors are likely to suffer lower losses than if the operating subsidiaries had been liquidated. The SPOE approach offers an organized means of allowing shareholders and long-term creditors (who cannot run in a crisis) to absorb losses; allowing operating businesses of the organization to remain open and continue serving the economy; putting new management in place; and avoiding runs and potential financial panics.

Properly designed, the SPOE strategy can stave off a couple of special problems that other recapitalization strategies could trigger, such as the potential problems derivatives pose during times of failure resolutions. Swaps and other derivative instruments typically allow a party to end a derivative contract if the counterparty is failing, or sometimes even if an affiliate of a counterparty defaults. So when a financial institution with a large derivatives business fails, it could easily trigger an entire wave of derivative terminations, a wave that could destabilize the economy. Derivatives are almost exclusively issued by the operating subsidiaries of financial institutions (not by holding companies). Therefore, if only the holding company fails, then there would likely be no defaults on the derivatives issued by the bank or any other of the operating subsidiaries. Additionally, Title II has specific provisions to protect against derivative terminations that are relevant to SPOE-style recapitalizations. The FDIC, under Title II of Dodd-Frank, has clarified that, for example, if a holding company fails and is placed into receivership under Title II but its operating subsidiary has not failed, a derivatives counterparty to the operating subsidiary cannot end a derivatives contract solely because of the failure of the parent company.

Cross-border resolution issues
The SPOE recapitalization strategy does not solve the problems of resolving a global bank with foreign subsidiaries, but it makes that problem much easier to deal with. Many systemically important financial groups operate on a global scale, making an uncoordinated set of national resolution systems extremely problematic. Indeed, the most complex SIFI has 2,435 majority-owned subsidiaries, with 50 percent of them operating abroad. A complicated international corporate structure makes an orderly unwinding extremely difficult as resolution is subject to national legal frameworks.

For decades, there have been discussions on how to best supervise cross-border banking groups. In fact, in 1975 the Basel Committee on Banking Supervision first issued a statement of principles, or concordat, regarding how to regulate banks spanning various territories. The basic principles in the concordat have been further strengthened by statements from the committee specifically addressing cross-border supervision and home-host supervisor relationships. In practice, however, when a financial institution is faltering or exhibiting signs of a potential failure, there is a risk that foreign regulators will "ring-fence" the assets of that company in a particular country. Indeed, when regulatory authorities are faced with the possible failure of a financial institution within their territory, they tend to prioritize the interests of the creditors and depositors to branches or subsidiaries located within their jurisdiction and of the local taxpayers. The ring-fencing of assets by host jurisdictions can hamper an effective resolution.

The SPOE approach helps a great deal because only the financial holding company located in the United States is put into resolution or bankruptcy. The subsidiaries remain operational so that, for example, the retail banking subsidiary in South America of a US-based institution going through resolution would open its doors on Monday morning and be able to give depositors access to their funds.

One further challenge to the resolution of a US-based financial firm is that certain OLA stabilization mechanisms detailed in Title II of Dodd-Frank, including the one-day stay provision with respect to over-the-counter derivatives and other financial contracts, may not apply beyond the United States. Therefore, counterparties to financial contracts with the foreign subsidiaries of a US firm may have contractual rights and incentives to end their transactions as soon as the US parent holding company begins the resolution process. Regulators are focused on addressing this problem through modifying the contractual cross-default and netting practices.

At this point there is not a broad understanding of the SPOE approach internationally. However, Paul Tucker, then at the Bank of England, voiced support for this approach, offering hope that other foreign regulators will echo that sentiment in the future.

Ensuring an adequate cushion in financial holding companies

Key to the SPOE approach is the availability of sufficient debt at the parent holding company of the failed firm, as mentioned earlier. In light of this, the Federal Reserve (while working with the FDIC) is considering a regulatory requirement that the largest, most complex US banking groups maintain a minimum amount of outstanding long-term unsecured debt at their holding companies, beyond their regulatory capital requirements. This requirement would increase the chances of an orderly resolution under OLA by ensuring that shareholders and long-term debt holders of a SIFI can bear potential losses and capitalize a bridge holding company. Switzerland, the United Kingdom, and the European Commission are also looking into similar requirements. For example, Swiss banks have introduced contingent convertible bonds (CoCos) and Barclays Bank has issued long-term bonds that automatically suffer 100 percent default if the capital of the bank falls below a certain level. (The Barclays bonds were oversubscribed at an 8 percent coupon.) To help encourage cross-border cooperation, it might be helpful to consider an international agreement on minimum total loss absorbency requirements for globally systemic firms.

Earlier in this chapter we describe the proposals to make institutions safer by increasing capital requirements and other measures. And of course this additional capital is also part of the cushion that would protect taxpayers against taking losses in a resolution process. There is, though, a question about whether adding the additional requirement of a large amount of unsecured debt at the holding company would end up raising the cost of capital, pushing up lending rates and discouraging investment and economic growth. The public debate on this issue has become extremely politicized, with strong populist pressure to clamp down on the banks and make them smaller. The claim is made that the financial sector became too large in the United States and must have its sails trimmed. The financial industry is pushing back, of course, and arguing that it must compete globally and that raising capital and debt requirements too high will stifle growth. We have argued elsewhere that a balance must be struck between fostering lending and growth, on the one hand, and making the system safer, on the other. We do not know the optimal size of the financial sector, but note that bank assets are twice as high in Germany as in the United States in relation to GDP. The United States does not have a particularly large banking sector.

Aligning Titles I and II of Dodd-Frank

Many economists and policymakers strongly support the use of legal bankruptcy proceedings to deal with failing financial institutions. John B. Taylor, with several co-authors, has published extensively on the importance of using bankruptcy and has led a group that is committed to improving the bankruptcy code (creating Chapter 14) to make sure there are no more bailouts.[5] A key argument is that any government-supervised

---

5. See Kenneth E. Scott, George P. Schultz, and John B. Taylor, eds., *Ending Government Bailouts as We Know Them* (Stanford, CA: Hoover Institution Press, 2009) and Kenneth E. Scott and John B. Taylor, eds., *Bankruptcy Not Bailout: A Special Chapter 14* (Stanford, CA: Hoover Institution Press, 2012).

resolution regime will inevitably lead to bailouts in which taxpayer funds are at risk. We will not take a stance in this paper on the relative merits of bankruptcy and resolution for large financial institutions nor try to determine the circumstances under which each of the two approaches should be used. We do make a judgment that Titles I and II of Dodd-Frank have not been aligned, creating some confusion and an unnecessary compliance burden for companies.

The Dodd-Frank legislation in Title I addresses the liquidation or reorganization of large institutions under the bankruptcy code. An important provision of this title is that living wills are required as a means of facilitating bankruptcy by providing the court with a blueprint for resolution of the parent company and the disposition of the subsidiaries, either by shutting them down or by selling them to other institutions. The living wills are also intended to reduce moral hazard and increase market efficiency by making clear to creditors their exposure to losses in the event of failure. It is also believed that the process of preparing a living will would encourage institutions to simplify their corporate structures. As a point of reference, the administrators of the Lehman Brothers bankruptcy estimated that at least $75 billion was wasted due to lack of any preparation for bankruptcy. Finally, greater awareness by the board of directors and more in-depth analysis of the institution's activities are likely to result in greater discipline and risk avoidance.

As Richard Herring has pointed out in *Ending Government Bailouts as We Know Them,* creating a really effective living will under Title I rules in a large complex institution is a very substantial undertaking. At the same time, large institutions must also comply with Title II of Dodd-Frank, which gives a mandate to the FDIC as the regulator responsible for resolving large complex institutions under the terms of an Orderly Liquidation Authority. As things stand at present, FDIC's SPOE approach is completely different from the bankruptcy process described in Title I. Large complex institutions, therefore, currently face dual and conflicting rules for how they must prepare for potential failure. Having these two parallel tracks of potential resolution makes no sense in policy terms and places an unnecessary regulatory burden on the institutions.

As a result, we support a convergence of the Title I and Title II resolution processes for global and/or complex SIFIs. Given the advantages of the SPOE approach, we suggest that institutions be required under Title I to prepare living wills that describe a resolution plan based on SPOE that can be applied under a modified bankruptcy law or, in extreme cases, by the FDIC Orderly Liquidation Authority.

We have noted the importance of making liquidity available in a resolution process and this remains the case for court-supervised bankruptcy. Debtor-in-possession (DIP) financing is needed if the going-concern value of any bankrupt organization is to be preserved. Often such funds are available from the private sector, but that may not be the case for a large, complex financial institution whose assets are hard to value. Thus, liquidity funding, perhaps on a large scale, must be available under either Title I or Title II resolution. This should and can be done without cost to taxpayers by lending against collateral at a penalty rate. In the event that the collateralized assets turn out to be inadequate, the net cost of the resolution would be recovered by a levy on other financial firms, as described in Dodd-Frank.

Beginning of macroprudential oversight

We believe that another improvement in the safety of the financial system will come from the increasing adoption of a macroprudential approach to the financial system. This involves viewing the safety of the financial system as being more than just the sum of the individual levels of safety of different financial institutions, and instead considering the risks that arise from the interactions of all the different participants in the financial system. For example, liquidity risks were underweighted in earlier regulatory considerations in part because any individual bank that got into trouble would have had a relatively easy time selling off financial instruments in the absence of a larger crisis. However, the effect of many institutions looking to sell at the same time, under conditions of widespread crisis, was to freeze markets and create very large fire sale discounts for those transactions that did occur.

Contagion effects were similarly given too little weight. That is, concerns about one financial institution, such as Lehman Brothers, ended up having widespread impacts on other firms. This was partly out of concern for direct exposures these firms might have to Lehman and partly out of a fear that the problems at Lehman would prove to be replicated in other firms, whether those were poor risk management, excessive exposure to housing markets, or some other problem.

Macroprudential policy refers to using regulatory tools to attempt to lower the level of systemic risk in the financial sector.[6] It falls between monetary policy, which operates at the level of the entire economy, and traditional safety and soundness regulation of individual financial institutions, now referred to as "microprudential" to distinguish it. There are two broad categories of macroprudential policy. One is "cyclical" or "time-varying," which refers to efforts to damp down booms and mitigate busts in the financial system. The other is "structural," meaning that the policies are intended to increase safety by making the financial system less vulnerable at all times.

Many of the regulatory changes coming out of Dodd-Frank and Basel III can be considered, at least in part, to be of a structural macroprudential nature. For example, moving standardized derivatives onto exchanges and increasing collateral requirements for other derivatives are intended to reduce the probability of excessive risk building up in the system, particularly through counterparty exposures. Most of the reforms are also intended to improve the safety of each individual financial institution, which is largely the context in which we have discussed these reforms elsewhere in this chapter.

The innovation, as compared to recent times, is that US authorities are also considering the potential for regulatory moves to dampen potential bubbles as they develop and to increase safety margins in those times in order to reduce the damage if a bubble develops and then, inevitably, bursts. The United States has a long history of macroprudential actions of this nature, going back to at least 1913, as shown by Douglas J. Elliott, Greg Feldberg, and Andreas Lehnert.[7] However, such activities largely ceased in the 1980s and there were virtually no attempts of this nature to counter the developing bubble that led to the recent financial crisis.

---

6. Douglas J. Elliott, "An Overview of Macroprudential Policy and Counter-cyclical Capital Requirements," The Brookings Institution, March 10, 2011, http://www.brookings.edu/~/media/research/files/papers/2011/3/11 capital elliott/0311_capital_elliott.pdf. Douglas J. Elliott, "Choosing among Macroprudential Tools," The Brookings Institution, June 7, 2011, http://www.brookings.edu/research/papers/2011/06/07-macroprudential-tools-elliott. Douglas J. Elliott, Greg Feldberg, and Andreas Lehnert, "The History of Cyclical Macroprudential Policy in the United States," The Brookings Institution, May 15, 2013, http://www.brookings.edu/research/papers/2013/05/15-history-cyclical-macroprudential-policy-elliott.

7. Elliott, Feldberg, and Lehnert, "The History of Cyclical Macroprudential Policy."

There are three main ways in which the new US macroprudential approach should decrease systemic risk and, indirectly, reduce risk at the individual banks in the system. First, the new consensus on examining systemic risks and not just looking firm by firm for weaknesses should significantly aid in catching and acting upon the buildup of excessive systemic risks. This change in attitude is pervasive and should show up in multiple ways. Second, Dodd-Frank created an Office of Financial Research (OFR) within the Treasury Department with the missions of gathering the data necessary to monitor the financial system as a whole and of watching for systemic risks and reporting on them to Congress and the regulatory agencies. Third, Dodd-Frank set up a new Financial Stability Oversight Council (FSOC) to coordinate actions among the regulators and to promote any necessary steps to deal with the buildup of systemic risks. The OFR is mandated to assist the FSOC in its monitoring actions.

Should the FSOC spot rising systemic risks, the authorities now have a wide range of powers for intervention. Dodd-Frank allows the regulators to order the cessation, restructuring, or reduction of activities by SIFIs that create excessive systemic risk. Regulators also have the power, as they did under earlier legislation, to increase capital requirements to build bigger safety buffers. Symmetrically, they would be able to reduce the requirements to counter the credit contraction triggered by a financial bust, as long as the levels stay at or above certain statutory minimums. Once liquidity rules are in place, there will similarly be an ability to tighten or loosen them in response to changing financial conditions. Regulators can also influence or set minimum levels of collateral to be required for various securities transactions, such as repurchase agreements. Overall, the range of potential macroprudential tools is wide and US authorities have the ability to use most of them, although not to set credit quotas or take some other interventionist measures that are used in certain developing nations such as China.

There is a limit to how effective macroprudential policy can be. We start with technical limitations because we still lack a great deal of historical data that would be useful in comparing future conditions to past ones. We also are still in the process of developing accepted conceptual and quantitative models of the financial system and its cycles. On top of this, there will always be a need for subjective judgments, which can be flawed, and there are certainly political pressures against taking steps to dampen a bubble or to build safety margins against its eventual bursting. Even with these limitations, however, we believe that the new macroprudential approach and tools should reduce the volatility of financial cycles and better prepare us to deal with the credit busts that follow the booms. Not using such an approach is tantamount to leaving macroprudential policy at the same setting at all times, which the recent financial crisis demonstrates can be very dangerous.

Conclusions

This paper has set out the ways in which the financial system has become safer since the crisis because of higher capital requirements, the development of leverage and liquidity rules, and progress in the effort to resolve large institutions through the SPOE approach. It is important to document these changes because they have not been sufficiently appreciated by policymakers or the public. Better shock absorbers are in place or are being put in place to make the financial system more resilient to the next shock.

There are of course many additional regulatory issues where more progress is needed. There is a perception that the whole regulatory reform process is a mess with regulators fighting with each other, with the financial industry, and with the populist effort to break up the banks. While this perception has some truth, it neglects the progress that has been made. Moreover, an important reason more progress has not been made in rule-making is that it is very hard to formulate some of the rules, particularly those around derivatives trading. Amendments that were added to Dodd-Frank in order to secure enough votes to pass the bill (the Volcker Rule and the Collins, Lincoln, and Franken amendments) have proven very difficult to implement. (Some or all of these amendments were not needed, but we leave that discussion for another time.) Since the time of the conference at which this paper was presented, the regulatory agencies have been able to agree, finally, on the implementation of the Volcker Rule, although the proposed rules specify that recalibration will surely be needed to apply the rules to both high turnover markets and low turnover markets. Metrics will have to be developed and this process will take time to get right. In addition, progress has been made in improving transparency, raising margins, and moving trading onto clearing houses.

One important question we have not tackled here is the trade-off between safety and cost. There are two lines of argument taken by those who favor ignoring the cost of higher capital requirements or other rules. The first argument is that the cost of the crisis was so large that any improvement in safety is worthwhile. The second is that there actually is no cost to higher capital requirements because of the Modigliani-Miller theorem.[8] We disagree. There were several contributors to the crisis and the persistent recession that has followed. And we are concerned about the negative effect on growth of reduced lending from banks and other financial institutions if capital levels and other rules are set too tight. Setting the right level for financial regulation is very hard to do. It will be important to monitor the economic impact of the changes in regulations being put into place.

---

8. There is a spirited debate about the applicability of Modigliani-Miller. See Anat Admati and Martin Hellwig, *The Bankers' New Clothes: What's Wrong with Banking and What to Do about It* (Princeton, NJ: Princeton University Press, 2013) and Harry DeAngelo and René M. Stultz, "Why High Leverage is Optimal for Banks," working paper, Ohio State University, August 2013.

CHAPTER 10

Toward a Run-free Financial System

John H. Cochrane

Introduction and overview

At its core, our financial crisis was a systemic run. The run started in the shadow banking system of overnight repurchase agreements, asset-backed securities, broker-dealer relationships, and investment banks. Arguably, it was about to spread to the large commercial banks when the Treasury Department and the Federal Reserve Board stepped in with a blanket debt guarantee and TARP (Troubled Asset Relief Program) recapitalization. But the basic economic structure of our financial crisis was the same as that of the panics and runs on demand deposits that we have seen many times before.

The run defines the event as a crisis. People lost a lot of money in the 2000 tech stock bust. But there was no run, there was no crisis, and only a mild recession. Our financial system and economy could easily have handled the decline in home values and mortgage-backed security (MBS) values—which might also have been a lot smaller—had there not been a run.

The central task for a regulatory response, then, should be to eliminate runs.

Runs are a pathology of specific contracts, such as deposits and overnight debt, issued by specific kinds of intermediaries. Among other features, run-prone contracts promise fixed values and first-come first-served payment. There was no run in the tech stock bust because tech companies were funded by stock, and stock does not have these run-prone features.

The central regulatory response to our crisis should therefore be to repair, where possible, run-prone contracts and to curtail severely those contracts that cannot be repaired. "Financial crises are everywhere and always due to problems of short-term debt" is a famous Doug Diamond (2008) aphorism, which we might amend to "and its modern cousins." Well, then, let us purge short-term debt from the system and base regulation on its remaining truly necessary uses.

I thank the CRSP and the Guggenheim Foundation for research support, and I thank participants at the October 1, 2013, Brookings/Hoover Financial Crisis Conference for helpful comments.

When they failed, Bear Stearns and Lehman Brothers were financing portfolios of mortgage-backed securities with overnight debt at 30:1 leverage. For every thirty dollars of investment, every single day, they had to borrow a new twenty-nine dollars to pay back yesterday's lenders. It is not a surprise that this scheme fell apart. It *is* a surprise that our policy response consists of enhanced timid increases in bank capital ratios, fancier risk-weighting, macroprudential risk regulation, security-price manipulation, a new resolution process in place of bankruptcy, tens of thousands of pages of regulations, and tens of thousands of new regulators. Wouldn't it be simpler and more effective to sharply reduce run-prone funding, at least by intermediaries likely to spark runs?

In this vision, demand deposits, fixed-value money-market funds, or overnight debt must be backed entirely by short-term Treasuries. Investors who want higher returns must bear price risk. Intermediaries must raise the vast bulk of their funds for risky investments from run-proof securities. For banks, that means mostly common equity, though some long-term or other non-runnable debt can exist as well. For funds, or in the absence of substantial equity, that means shares whose values float and, ideally, are tradable.

Banks can still mediate transactions, of course. For example, a bank-owned ATM machine can deliver cash by selling your shares in a Treasury-backed money market fund, stock index fund shares, or even the bank's own shares. A bank can originate and sell mortgages, if it does not want to finance those mortgages with equity or long-term debt. Banks can still be broker-dealers, custodians, derivative and swap counterparties and market makers, and providers of a wide range of financial services, credit cards, and so forth. They simply may not fund themselves by issuing large amounts of run-prone debt.

If a demand for separate bank debt really exists, the equity of 100 percent equity-financed banks can be held by a downstream institution or pass-through vehicle that issues equity and debt tranches. That vehicle can fail and be resolved in an hour, without disrupting any of the operations or claims against the bank, and the government can credibly commit not to bail it out.

I argue that Pigouvian taxes[1] provide a better structure for controlling debt than capital ratios or intensive discretionary supervision, as in stress

---

1. Pigouvian taxes are designed to discourage undesirable activities, especially externalities such as pollution. Kocherlakota (2010), Jeanne and Korinek (2011),

tests. For each dollar of run-prone short-term debt issued, the bank or other intermediary must pay, say, five cents tax. Pigouvian taxes are more efficient than quantitative limits in addressing air pollution externalities, and that lesson applies to financial pollution. By taxing run-prone liabilities, those liabilities can continue to exist where and if they are truly economically important. Issuers will economize on them endogenously rather than play endless cat-and-mouse games with regulators.

Technology

The essence of this vision is not novel. Proposals for narrow banking or equity-based banking have been with us about as long as runs and crashes have been with us. The "Chicago Plan," discarded in the 1930s, is only one of many such milestones.[2]

Here a second theme emerges: *Modern financial, computational, and communication technology allows us to overcome the long-standing objections to narrow banking.*

Most deeply, "liquidity" no longer requires that people hold a large inventory of fixed-value, pay-on-demand, and hence run-prone securities. With today's technology, you could buy a cup of coffee by swiping a card or tapping a cell phone, selling two dollars and fifty cents of an S&P 500 fund, and crediting the coffee seller's two dollars and fifty cents mortgage-backed security fund. If money (reserves) are involved at all—if the transaction is not simply netted among intermediaries—reserves are held for milliseconds. In the 1930s, this was not possible. We could not instantly look up the value of the S&P 500 (communication). There was no such thing as an index fund, so stock sales faced informational illiquidity and large bid-ask spreads (financial innovation). And transactions costs would have ruled out the whole project (computation, financial innovation). Closer to current institutions, electronic transactions can easily be made with Treasury-backed or floating-value money-market fund shares, in which the vast majority of transactions are simply netted by the intermediary. When you buy something, your account loses an electronic dollar and the seller's account gains one, and no security actually changes hands.

---

and Perotti and Suarez (2011) suggest Pigouvian taxes to limit debt. Stein (2012) explores their equivalence to a cap-and-trade proposal.

2. My discussion has much in common with Kotlikoff (2010), Chamley, Kotlikoff, and Polemarchakis (2012), and Admati and Hellwig (2012). It also builds on Cochrane (2010, 2011). The larger points in this essay build on Cochrane (2013b).

On the supply end, $18 trillion of government debt is enough to back any conceivable remaining need for fixed-value default-free assets. Three trillion dollars of interest-paying reserves can easily be $6 trillion of reserves. We can live Milton Friedman's (1969) optimal quantity of money, in which the economy is awash in liquidity. This optimal quantity will have financial stability benefit far beyond its traditional elimination of shoe-leather costs. Again, technology has fundamentally changed the game: instant communication means that interest-paying money is now a reality, so we can have the optimal quantity without deflation. Our government should take over its natural monopoly position in supplying interest-paying money, just as it took over a monopoly position in supplying nineteenth-century bank notes, and for the same reason: to eliminate crises, which have the same fundamental source.

The quantification of credit risk, the invention of securitized debt, long-only floating-value mutual funds, and the size and liquidity of today's markets mean that financial flows needed to finance home and business investment can come from everyday saver/investors who bear risk rather than hold traditional deposits.

So, the most fundamental objection is met: that society "needs" a large stock of money-like assets, more than can be supplied by other means, so banks must try to "transform" maturity, liquidity, and risk, both to supply adequate assets for transaction-type needs and to provide adequate credit for real investment. I treat a wide range of additional common objections below.

Current policy

Our current regulatory response to financial crises is based on a different basic vision, which evolved piecemeal over more than a century. In order to stop runs, our government guarantees debts, implicitly or explicitly, and often ex-post, with credit guarantees, bailouts, last-resort lending, and other crisis-fighting efforts. But guaranteeing debts gives the borrowers (banks and similar institutions) an incentive to take on too much asset risk, and it gives them an incentive to fund those risks by too much debt. It gives depositors an incentive to ignore bank risks when lending to the banks. So our government tries to regulate the riskiness of bank assets and imposes capital requirements to limit banks' debt funding. Then banks game their way around regulations, take on more risk, and skirt capital requirements; shadow banks grow up around regulations; and another crisis happens. The government guarantees more debts, expands its regulatory reach, and intensifies asset regulation.

Less heralded, but no less important, this regulatory approach demands strong limits on competition and innovation, even before banks try to capture it. If regulators let new institutions circumvent regulated ones, the problems erupt again. Too big to fail means too big to lose money, and too big to lose money means too big to compete.

Thus, Dodd-Frank regulation and its international cousins are not a radical new approach. They are just a natural expansion of a longstanding philosophy. Each new step follows naturally to clean up the unintended consequences of the last one. The expansion is nonetheless breathtaking. Beyond massively ramping up the intensity, scope, and detail of financial institutions and markets regulation, central banks are now trying to control the underlying market prices of assets, to keep banks from losing money in the first place.

The little old lady swallowed a fly, then a spider to catch the fly, a bird to catch the spider, and so on. Horse is on the menu. Will we eat?

Comparison

The insight that the crisis was a systemic run, that we can fix runs by fixing and removing run-prone financial contracts, and that new financial and communication technology addresses the classic objections, liberates us from this Rube Goldbergian (or Orwellian?) regulatory project.

We do not have to fix every actual and perceived fault of the financial system in order to protect against future crises. We do not have to diagnose and correct the sources of the crisis, Fannie Mae and Freddie Mac, the community reinvestment act, so-called predatory lending, no-documentation loans, perceived global imbalances or savings gluts, Wall Street "greed," executive compensation, perceived bubbles (whether thought to be caused by irrational speculation or too-low interest rates), and so on. We do not have to fix credit card fees, disparate-impact analysis, student loans, or hedge fund fees. We don't need to micromanage over-the-counter versus exchange-traded derivatives, swap margins, position limits, the bloated Basel bank regulation mess, the definition of risk-weighted assets, the internal process and regulatory designation of S&P and Moody ratings, the treatment of off-balance-sheet credit guarantees, and on and on and on. The thousand pages of the Volker rule alone can start a nice bonfire. If a crisis is a run, and we can remove or fix run-prone securities, none of these steps is either necessary (whew) or sufficient (ouch) to stop a future crisis. A narrower regulatory approach that can stop runs, and hence crises, without requiring these Herculean (or Sisyphean?) tasks, no matter how desirable each one might be, is much more likely to succeed.

If financial institutions' *liabilities* no longer can cause runs and crises, we don't have to try to micromanage institutions' *asset* choices or the market prices of those assets. Nor do we have to stop entry by new and innovative institutions. Rather than dream up a financial system so tightly controlled that no important institution ever loses money in the first place, we can simply ensure that inevitable booms and busts, losses and failures, transfer seamlessly to final investors without producing runs.

Zero cost is not the standard. The financial crisis was, by most accounts, a hugely expensive event. Dodd-Frank regulation and its international cousins are not cheap, either. The challenge is only to show that my vision, which narrowly focuses on eliminating the poison in the well— run-prone assets—stops crises more effectively and costs less than these alternatives.

Runs and run-prone assets

Demand deposits offer the paradigmatic example of a run-prone contract. If I suspect trouble at the bank, I have an incentive to get my money out before you do so. You, seeing me run, have an incentive to get your money out before someone else. Based on this simple description, we can sketch the essential characteristics of a run-prone security. [Obviously, I'm building on Diamond and Dybvig (1983) here.]:

- The contract promises a fixed value, payable in full on demand or on very short notice.
- Failure to pay triggers bankruptcy.

Fixed-value short-maturity promises, like "lend me five dollars, I'll pay you tomorrow," invoices, trade credit, and so forth are not run-prone contracts, because one cannot force the firm into bankruptcy for failure to pay immediately. If the firm has the right to delay payment, suspend convertibility, or pay in part, it is much harder for a run to develop.

Runs also require specific types of issuers. A run can't develop if the issuing institution can easily sell assets to meet creditor demands or get money elsewhere:

- Runs require that the assets of the issuing institution are illiquid and cannot quickly be sold to meet redemption demands.
- Runs require that the issuing institution cannot borrow or issue equity to meet redemptions.

These assumptions are bandied about all the time as facts. But as we think about reforming the financial system, it's important to question them. Really? Why? There are a vast number of unleveraged, deep-pocket investors around sniffing for bargains, including endowments, Warren Buffets, sovereign wealth funds, hedge funds, and so on. If a bank is really "illiquid" but not "insolvent," then just why will these investors not lend or buy equity, especially at a nice discount?

Debt overhang is a common story. When a firm's value falls, the market value of its long-term debt falls, so new equity in the first instance just raises the market value of long-term debt. But banks routinely manage to issue equity after losses, and many companies with outstanding long-term debt are able to issue equity. The deals by which the entire firm is sold to new owners over a weekend are really just equity infusions, in which presumably the new owner's overpayment to rescue debt is matched by the greater profitability of a better-managed or combined company.

Equity issues—especially on terms that force current equity to restore bondholders—also dilute current equity's option value for the firm's recovery and dilute the value of prospective bailouts and debt guarantees. Banks were paying dividends and big bonuses in fall 2008. Why, if they were undercapitalized? Observers suggested that the banks had to signal strength and retain talent. Lack of desire to issue new equity, and bet the farm instead, rather than the impossibility of obtaining new equity, is a distinct possibility. Bear Stearns' existing equity holders were the ones to object to the deal, not the prospective equity buyers.

Similarly, why can't banks sell assets? Well, they are said to face "fire sales" of unwilling buyers. Again, just why are the deep-pocket investors and market-timers, usually facing the buying opportunity of a lifetime, so unwilling?

Here, too, banks are often unwilling rather than unable to sell. Assets booked as "hold to maturity" can be counted at cost, not market value.

Selling them forces the bank to acknowledge the loss. Selling illiquid assets can force the bank to acknowledge that actual prices are in fact less than even mark-to-market values, so selling one asset can depress the declared value of others. None of these are genuine economic impediments to asset sales, and could be fixed by changes in accounting and regulation.

I will not pursue this line, but it certainly is worth asking just why markets for new equity or bank assets are so bad and what can be done to improve them. There is a tendency to allude to frictions, to take them as gospel without really examining whether they exist in reality, without questioning their source, and then to design policies around them, or to exploit them, rather than questioning whether we could fix the frictions instead.

A key characteristic:

- A run requires that if one investor pulls out, the firm is closer to bankruptcy, giving a second investor greater incentive to pull out.

This is the core externality of run-prone debt. My action to pull out alters your incentives. Externalities do suggest a need for regulation, even once all the unintended disincentives and subsidies have been fixed.

If bankruptcy were costless, consisting of a smooth recapitalization in which debt becomes equity the moment firm value is one cent below debt's promises, there would be little incentive to run. Therefore,

- Runs require significant bankruptcy costs.

Without bankruptcy costs, runs would also incur little social cost. If an institution shuts down and a bunch of investors lose money, that's just a transfer unless something real is affected. For runs to be a social problem, Diamond and Dybvig (1983) assume that real projects are abandoned after a run.

- Runs are more likely if the institution's assets are nebulous and hard to value.

Not for nothing have most runs been sparked by an accounting scandal or fraud. If we knew exactly what the bank's assets were worth at all times, there would be little incentive to run. Even if the assets were illiquid, lenders could always know when the bank was insolvent. The fact that illiquidity and insolvency are essentially indistinguishable in a crisis is a key component of runs.

- Runs require that a substantial fraction of the firm is funded by run-prone securities.

If an institution is 95 percent financed by equity, there is little chance of bankruptcy, and thus little chance of a run. That's why capital ratios are popular. Alas, the measurement of capital, the measurement of the risk and illiquidity of a bank's asset portfolio, and the effort to find an exact number—one side of which is safe and the other side of which is risky—has not proved successful.

Shadow-banking runs

The concept that the financial crisis was, centrally, a run in the "shadow banking system," and the features of the financial contracts that suffered runs, are well described by Darrell Duffie (2010a, 2010b) and Gary Gorton and Andrew Metrick (2012).

Duffie shows how the contract structures of the shadow banking system have the same run-inducing features as conventional uninsured bank deposits. (See also French et al. (2010b).) As Duffie describes, leaving securities with your broker-dealer is not like leaving your car in the repair shop, where the car transparently belongs to you if the dealer goes bankrupt. The broker-dealer may have used your securities as collateral for borrowing to fund the dealer's proprietary trading, so you cannot seamlessly retrieve them after the dealer's bankruptcy. In turn, if you do retrieve your securities from the dealer, the dealer no longer has that collateral, and may have to unwind his proprietary trades at a loss. Thus, if you remove your securities from a broker-dealer, the dealer is closer to bankruptcy, and that fact raises the incentives for me to remove my securities from the same broker-dealer. Derivatives contracts, though senior in bankruptcy, also cause problems for lenders and are a source of cash for the dealer. Most of all, though overnight repurchase agreements would seem exquisitely engineered to protect the lender in case of default, their protection is not in fact perfect. Some jurisdictions treat repurchases as collateralized lending, putting the borrower in line during bankruptcy. Many lenders are not legally eligible to hold the posted collateral, so those lenders may have to dump the collateral immediately upon receipt. Having to unload a large portfolio of securities on the Monday afternoon of Lehman's bankruptcy is not a picnic. Better to refuse rolling over the loan on Friday.

As one reads through Duffie's analysis, an insistent voice springs up, "I can fix that!" Does rehypothecation of securities make broker-dealer relations a run-prone contract? Then hold securities with a custodian. Yes, that may cost a few basis points, but those basis points are, in the end, coming from taxpayers. Being able to use client securities as collateral for proprietary trading is not such a huge social gain that it's worth going through another financial crisis.

Systemic Runs

A run on an individual institution is not a crisis, however. To be a crisis, the run has to affect the financial system and, ultimately, the real economy. We need to understand what makes for "contagion" or a "systemic" run.

Gorton and Metrick (2012) fill in this part of the picture. Seeing a run on institution A, investors in institution B question its finances, and are sparked to run there as well. The system as a whole promises more cash than is available, so a simultaneous run threatens systemic insolvency.

In Gorton and Metrick's vision, short-term debt is normally an "information-insensitive" security. When the bank is far from default, the value of its debt, especially short-term debt, is essentially the same for a wide range of values for the bank's assets. Debt holders therefore don't need to investigate the company's finances. In turn, this feature means that the short-term debt of companies and banks far from bankruptcy is highly liquid. If I offer to sell you such debt, you don't have to worry that I know something you don't know, because nobody can really have much information about the value of such debt. As a result, bid-ask spreads, which derive from asymmetric information, are tiny. Such debt can circulate as easily as money. But it pays interest, a crucial advantage until the era of interest-paying reserves.

This is the point of highly-rated and, especially, short-term debt. It is designed to be information-insensitive and therefore liquid, bought and sold easily with little investigation of underlying value.

Once a bank is closer to bankruptcy, however, its debt becomes information-sensitive. Information about the bank's prospects changes the value of its debt substantially. Now, anyone selling the bank's debt is suspected of having information about the bank's prospects. Buyers are unwilling to take such debt without a lot of due diligence, a steep price discount, and a large bid-ask spread. Traditional buyers may not be willing to buy it at all. Traders and institutions that are not set up to do information-sensitive market-making just bow out. The sudden illiquidity of the bank's debt can lead to a rollover crisis and run long before actual next-morning insolvency-driven bankruptcy fears become an issue.

This process provides a central mechanism of perceived contagion: how trouble at one bank turns into a systemic run. Creditors, learning that one bank's or mortgage-backed security's assets are suddenly revealed to be bad, start worrying about other similar banks and securities. This shift of attitudes would not make sense if we thought of all active investors as constantly monitoring and forming opinions about the value of a bank, as we think of stock investors. But investors in short-term highly rated debt are not paying attention. That's the whole point. Until they do.

Gorton (2010) tells a nice story. We usually assemble ingredients from a salad bar without investigating their individual safety. If somebody says she read a news story about E. coli in some vegetable, rather than investigate just which ingredient is risky and avoid it, it's easier to shun them all and have a hamburger instead. Chamley, Kotlikoff, and Polemarchakis (2012) tell an even more vivid story. "Eight bottles of Tylenol laced with cyanide, sold in a Chicago drugstore, instantly transformed 31 million bottles of Tylenol located in stores all over the globe into toxic assets that could find no buyers." It's just not worth investigating each bottle.

The information-sensitivity story applies to securities as well as to bank debt. Long-lived securities, including highly-rated tranches of mortgage-backed securities, collateralized debt obligations, and corporate bonds, are information-insensitive and therefore liquid. Cash-like liabilities of special-purpose vehicles, auction-rate securities, or other structures that issue short-term debt to hold long-lived or illiquid securities and thus emulate banks are information-insensitive and therefore liquid as well. As long as the assets are complex, illiquid, hard to value, or subject to large price shifts (important qualifications), securities of this sort can suddenly become information-sensitive and much less liquid.

This process leads to the systemic "run on repo" that Gorton and Metrick (2012) document. A bank may have used information-insensitive securities, such as AAA tranches, as collateral to finance borrowing. People who want collateral only want liquid, information-insensitive securities, and they suddenly will not take the previously liquid securities as collateral, or they require a large "haircut," i.e., much more collateral than the loan is worth. Now the bank is in a bind. With inadequate collateral (and inadequate equity, and all the above-cited restraints on finding new equity or new sources of borrowing), the bank must sell some of the assets it has financed at just the worst possible moment. The repo haircut works analogously to reserve requirements in generating a collateral multiplier. If the haircut rises substantially, a whole chain of debts must be unwound.

The sudden illiquidity leads to a second mechanism of contagion. Suppose Bank B was holding a lot of Bank A debt, or A-type securities. When that debt or those securities suddenly become illiquid, Bank B can no longer count on selling those securities to raise cash to pay its creditors in case of a run. So bank or security A's problems can spark bank B's run.

The sudden illiquidity means that the run-prone characteristics I listed above are heavily state-contingent. Assets that are liquid and willing equity investors can disappear quickly, so a reasonable plan to pay creditors falls apart when it is most needed.

In short, when a systemic run breaks out—when one institution's or asset class's troubles bring into question many others—we see events that are colorfully, if confusingly, described as flight to quality, fire sales, frozen markets, and illiquidity. There is a dramatic shift in total demand toward government debt and money and away from private debt.

Real effects

Not only must a run be systemic to be a crisis, a crisis only matters if the systemic run has real effects.

As the tech bust example made clear, and as much macroeconomic research confirms,[3] simple wealth effects from a decline in asset values have limited macroeconomic repercussions. In part, declines in values of existing assets are mostly redistributional: if home values fall by half, those planning to sell large houses and downsize lose, but young people can spend half as much on housing, and thus a lot more on other things. Houses are only durable goods, after all, and a decline in value by half is a different event than half of the houses in the country being washed away by a tsunami. We would cheer car prices dropping by half, despite the loss to prospective used-car sellers. Why not houses?

There are two central competing stories for why the systemic run of the financial crisis had, apparently, such a large macroeconomic effect.

One view thinks it's "financial constraints." The central story here is that banks in the fall of 2008 lost asset values and so were undercapitalized: The decline in asset value lowers the value of equity, so the ratio of equity capital to debt is now too low. In this story, banks could not raise new capital, they could not lower capital-draining dividend and bonus payments or acquisitions, they could not sell lending operations to better

---

3. For example, see Ludvigson, Steindel, and Lettau (2002).

capitalized investors, all for various complex reasons. And despite their claims to meet regulatory requirements, they were undercapitalized by internal metrics. As a result, in this story, they resorted to asset sales and certainly were not making additional loans. But individual banks do not matter. The banking and financial *system* matters. This view answers that criticism by asserting that better-capitalized banks or other financial institutions could not come in and take the new-lending business that existing troubled banks were abandoning, and that borrowers could not switch to other markets.

In short, this theory goes, banks *wanted* to keep lending at the same rate, people and businesses *wanted* to keep borrowing at the same rate, but internal or regulatory capital ratios forced banks to stop lending. Other banks and institutions could not fill the gap, so the otherwise healthy economy (healthy demand for investment) was starved of funds.[4]

Bernanke (1983) fleshed out the modern credit constraints view. In his analysis, banks in the Great Depression failed, and then the human and organizational capital that knew how to make relationship loans vanished as well. The result was a great wedge between savers and borrowers. However, perhaps partly due to the same Bernanke's actions, there simply was not a wave of bankruptcies at large commercial relationship-lending banks in 2008. There was a large wave of Federal Deposit Insurance Corporation (FDIC)-run failures at smaller banks, but the lending operations were preserved and transferred to new owners. However powerful in the Great Depression, this mechanism is not really a candidate for 2008–2009.

Another view focuses on "aggregate demand." The run provoked a massive shift in demand away from private securities corresponding to physical investment and toward government debt, including money (cash and reserves) but also toward longer-maturity government debt. But someone has to hold the existing assets, so this demand shift ends up simply changing prices. Government bond prices rose (interest rates declined) while prices on private securities dropped (risky interest rates, including low-grade bonds and commercial paper, rose dramatically). This rise in interest rates, along with a similar decline in stock prices (a rise in the equity premium), a rise in risk-aversion, and economic forecasts of poor conditions ahead led to a sharp drop in consumption and investment demand.

---

4. Bernanke and Gertler (1989, 1995) are two classic examples of this view. Bernanke, Gertler, and Gilchrist (1999) and Gertler and Kiyotaki (2011) are two good summaries. Gambacorta and Marques-Ibanez (2011) is an excellent survey of the lending channel view of the 2008 crisis.

Tying these ideas together, the aggregate budget constraint says that aggregate nominal demand for goods and services must add up to demand for nominal government debt. The only way to consume less and invest less is to pile up government debt. So a "flight to quality" and a "decline in aggregate demand" are the same thing. The rise in demand for money and short-term government debt, perfect substitutes at zero interest rates, is deflationary, and we saw a short, sharp deflation. Sufficient deflation might provide the real value of government debt people want to hold, but add some sticky prices and you have a theory of a real recession.

The "frictions" and "aggregate demand" mechanisms are more different than they appear. Fundamentally, the question is whether "institutional finance" or fundamental investor-based finance matters for the connection of asset prices to business cycles. In the former view, fundamental investors and borrowers such as homeowners and firms didn't change views or behavior, and wanted to borrow and invest as much as before, but the machinery connecting them broke down. In the latter view, the run fundamentally happened across the economy. Completely unlevered final investors—including endowments, pension funds, sovereign wealth funds, family offices, and so forth—panicked every bit as much as leveraged intermediaries, which is why the former were not there when the latter wanted to sell assets. Firms and households didn't want to borrow as much as before.

The controversy over these questions continues, in part because the glass is surely neither completely empty nor full. Many models mix both ingredients—for example, Bernanke, Gertler, and Gilchrist (1996). There is compelling cross-sectional evidence that some businesses and people were credit-constrained in the chaos of fall 2008. But is that the key causal mechanism for the economy as a whole, or was it a distributional sideshow to a recession that would have happened anyway? Many unconstrained businesses contracted dramatically as well—and, moreover, did not expand to take over the business of the unfortunate constrained businesses. A small taste: Chari, Christiano, and Kehoe (2008) document that bank lending overall did not decline early in the crisis—it declined later, when the recession was well under way. Highly rated nonfinancial companies were able to issue lots of commercial paper at low rates. They remind us that most investment comes from retained earnings and that 80 percent of corporate debt does not come from banks anyway. Ivashina and Scharfstein (2010) counter, however, that much new lending was simply borrowers drawing down credit lines and that banks in worse shape cut lending more than banks in better shape. But this is a long way from showing that the financial system as a whole refused to lend to clearly profitable *new* investments. Dell'Ariccia, Detragiache, and Rajan (2008) show that sectors more dependent on external finance fell more during the recession following a financial crisis. But sectors not at all so dependent also fell, and external financial dependency is endogenous, which one can never fully control for. Cochrane (2011) argues for the view that a coordinated rise in risk premiums, even in completely un-intermediated markets and even after intermediation frictions washed away, was a major characteristic of financial markets in the fall of 2008.

All of this matters, for several reasons. Again, if crises do not cause recessions or other real economic damage, we don't care. Well, crises do cause real damage, but *why* they cause economic damage illuminates what a crisis is in the first place, what steps we might take to avoid crises, how costly crises really are, and thus how much cost we should tolerate from anti-crisis policies, which put-out-the-fire policies are important to contain economic damage, and what structural reforms we might undertake to limit economic damage.

If the essential link from run to macroeconomy is undercapitalized intermediaries, then the final form of the TARP—recapitalizing intermediaries—should have solved the macroeconomic problem. That it did not do so is one piece of evidence in my mind against this view, but one can always argue that even more capital was needed.

If the essential link from run to macroeconomy is a flight to quality, then lender-of-last-resort institutions and massive exchanges of government debt for private debt are more promising fire extinguishers. The lender-of-last-resort theory has always preached to accommodate shifts in money demand versus other assets, with the traditional limitations of "against good collateral" and "at a penalty rate" open to question and usually ignored. One can argue that, in our crisis, the government should simply have exchanged trillions (more) of government debt for trillions of private securities that people did not want to hold. Of course, the question of "good collateral" and the moral hazard of this extreme central-banker's put option will limit the idea.

Both views, I think, pose an unresolved challenge to the project of an expensive regulatory response. If, as Keynesians believe, aggregate demand is the only link from anything to recessions, and it can easily be managed with sufficient fiscal and monetary stimulus, then in fact we only need to fix macro policy and leave the banks alone; crises really are not by themselves a social problem. (I don't see any Keynesians advocating this position, but it is a logical consequence of belief in aggregate demand and stimulus.)

If the main link from crisis to real activity is a sort of clogging of the arteries of existing banks, with layers and layers of additional frictions required to keep still-optimistic investors from getting money to still-optimistic firms, then one could suffer runs far more easily with faster and more effective recapitalization.

In both views, we should be paying a lot more attention to the hazily-described "frictions." If price stickiness is the bottom of recessions, then why are economists who write such models not outraged at the government's efforts to make prices and wages stickier, and why are they not campaigning to fix price stickiness? If inadequate capital and frictions in the way of private recapitalization are the key problem, fixing capital-raising frictions would seem to be at the top of the agenda, rather than amassing larger options for ex-post bailouts and government-funded recapitalizations.

Aside from that weakness, however, both views point to large macroeconomic effects and important benefits from stopping systemic runs in the first place. Those who think undercapitalized banks led us to five years of GDP falling $1 trillion below potential should be in the front of the queue demanding much, much more capital to begin with.

Stock again

Common equity is the paradigmatic example of a corporate liability that is immune from runs. When an equity-funded company is in trouble, you can try to sell stock, and stock values can crash. But you cannot run to the company and demand your money back and you cannot drive the company into bankruptcy should it fail to pay. When you sell stock, you do not do anything to push the company closer to insolvency. Seeing your investment crash, your neighbor, invested in another company, can't demand his money back and cause that company to fail either.

One might feel that stock price crashes represent fire sales, irrational fads, or otherwise socially suboptimal phenomena. Stock market crashes can come with important shifts in investment and other economic outcomes. But stock market crashes are not runs and they are not crises. Investors bear risk for their returns directly and inescapably. My decision to sell—even if unwise, even if it provokes a price decline—does not pose an externality to you. If anything, the opposite is true: my fire sale is your buying opportunity.

An exchange-traded fund (ETF) is a paradigmatic example of a run-proof intermediary. When asset values fall, the liability values of an exchange-traded fund fall automatically and the fund itself cannot go bankrupt.

For this reason, the tech boom and bust of the late 1990s is a good comparison. The decline in tech stock value was similar to the decline in subprime mortgage-backed security value by September 2008. But there was no crisis and only a mild recession in the early 2000s. Why? Because tech losses were held in stock, and when stock falls you can't run. Housing losses were held in fragile, run-prone securities.

Yes, the Great Depression was heralded by a stock market crash. But financial turmoil came from defaults by intermediaries who had borrowed to invest in stock and by the subsequent bank runs and bank failures. These are failures of debt, not of equity.

Long-term debt occupies an intermediate spot. It does make fixed promises, but only at periodic intervals. On suspecting bad news, like equity, there is nothing you can do immediately to avoid losses. Long-term debt leads to crises when it isn't quite long enough, when it needs to be refinanced in large chunks. The Greek debt crisis came when Greece needed to refinance long-term debt, not when it could not borrow for one year's spending.

Things that don't matter

The view that the financial crisis was, at heart, a systemic run is as—or more—important for clarifying things that are *not* important in the quest to avoid another crisis as it is for clarifying what is important.

The source of losses does not matter. So fixing the (deplorable, in my view) federal interventions in housing finance, or fixing the various abuses, predations, and irrational behavior others see in housing, is neither necessary nor sufficient to stop crises. The next panic may start with losses on sovereign debts: perhaps a new European crisis or a US state debt and pension crisis. The whole long argument over whether supposed global imbalances can fuel a savings glut, and whether policymakers are wise enough to detect and prevent such things, is pointless. If such events exist but savings are held in floating-value non-runnable assets, then, yes, big price drops (buying opportunities!) and exchange rate changes can happen—but not a crisis.

The "dominoes" or "interconnectedness" theory is a popular alternative view of a crisis: A defaults on its debts to B, so B defaults on its debts to

C, and so forth. Much regulation is written against the dominoes theory—for example, the new limits on single-party exposures. But dominoes were not a major factor in our crisis or in previous crises. Companies build buffers against dominoes. If A's default is to cause B, C, and D to default, A's loss of value must exceed the combined capital and borrowing capacity of A, B, C, and D. But what happened to us was that seeing A fail, investors ran on B, C, and D, who had little unhedged direct exposure to A. The systemic run view argues that lots of "interconnectedness" regulation is fairly pointless.

Stopping Runs

An end to run-prone financing

If the problem is runs, and runs are identifiable features of certain kinds of contracts issued by certain kinds of intermediaries, then the focus of regulation should rather naturally be to fix run-prone contracts where possible and to strongly discourage their use when they can't be fixed.

For commercial banks, the answer is pretty simple: equity, lots more equity. How much? Well, more is better, and "enough so that it doesn't matter" or "enough that we never, ever hear again the call 'recapitalize the banks'" are good answers. One hundred percent is perfectly workable.

More is obviously better, because more capital puts banks further from bankruptcy and further from a run to begin with. Less obviously, all of the dynamic problems sparking runs are ameliorated by capital. If a bank has 2 percent equity capital, loses 1 percent of the value of its assets, and (as the story goes) cannot quickly issue more equity to rebuild capital, then it has to sell half of its assets to restore its capital ratio. If the bank has instead 50 percent equity capital and loses 1 percent of the value of its assets, it only needs to sell 2 percent of its assets to get back to a 50 percent capital ratio. And if the bank is 100 percent equity-financed, it doesn't have to sell anything. If you worry about fire sales, you should like equity.

Similarly, if a bank has 2 percent equity capital and loses 1 percent of the value of its assets, it is one more such loss away from bankruptcy. Debt overhang will surely loom over any equity issues, recapitalization, or effort to sell the company. If a bank has 50 percent equity capital and loses 1 percent of the value of its assets, it is so far from bankruptcy that issuing more equity involves essentially no transfers to debt holders and can be accomplished seamlessly. If a bank is 100 percent equity-financed, it doesn't have to issue any more equity at all in response to losses. If you worry about the difficulty of issuing or hanging on to equity, you should like more equity to start with.

Many recent proposals specify debt that converts to equity under some circumstances. Examples include French et al. (2010a) and Hart and Zingales (2011). Some convertible debt has been issued. More simply, banks could be required to buy put options, giving them the right to issue new equity at predetermined prices. However, critics such as Admati and Hellwig (2012) point out, why bother? Why bother with the fig leaf that the convertible security is debt rather than equity or really an equity option? The answers mostly do not come from fundamental economic problems: to keep the tax-deductibility of interest payments, for example, or to address accounting rules. Well, if these are why we have runs, they're not that hard to fix. In addition, rumors that a conversion option might be triggered may induce turmoil as investors who really want debt and not equity try to sell in advance of the conversion. In turn, such rumors would make the convertible debt suddenly information-sensitive and its liquidity would dry up just when it is needed.

For the purpose of stopping runs, what really matters is that the value of investors' claims floats freely and the investors have no claim on the company which could send it into bankruptcy. Common equity has a variety of other rights, such as voting. Nonvoting equity or any similar floating value claim would do for this purpose. I use equity only because it is the most familiar form of non-runnable bank liability.

Long-term bank debt occupies a more nuanced middle ground. If bankruptcy-remote, it can become information-insensitive and hence potentially more liquid than equity. But current long-term debt is not long-term enough for either purpose. By having fixed maturities rather than perpetual coupons, it raises a rollover risk. By issuing many different securities across maturity dates, it lowers liquidity. If banks issued perpetual debt, it would be exactly the same security; one "bond" could be delivered in a short position that had borrowed a different "bond." In any event, the vast amount of equity trading and the uniformity of that security means that equity bid-ask spreads and liquidity are hardly a first-order social problem.

Part of the business of being a bank, of course, involves making some fixed-value promises in the natural process of buying and selling on behalf of customers, market-making, and over-the-counter securities transactions. One may also object that banks will try to financial-engineer their way around restrictions on short-term debt issue, as they engineered their way around capital regulation. For example, a bank can synthesize borrowing by put-call parity in options markets.

However, there is a fundamental distinction between *financing* a large portion of bank assets by rolling over short-term debt and the sort of short-term promises to pay, in a matched book, that market-making, loan origination, and other bank-like activities imply. Detecting hidden run-prone financing will require a few regulators, but the project is an order of magnitude easier than current asset regulation, capital regulation, and stress testing. Detecting a dangerous deviation from 0 leverage is a lot easier than detecting a dangerous deviation from 25:1 leverage.

Capital regulation

Though my main focus is describing the financial system we should strive for, rather than regulations on how to get there, this is an important exception. *How* should we increase bank capital?

The first step, of course, is to remove distortions subsidizing debt, especially short-term debt. Subsidizing debt and simultaneously trying to regulate against its use is about as smart as, oh, subsidizing energy prices and trying to regulate against energy use.

The tax-deductibility of interest payments versus dividends is an obvious target. However, nonfinancial corporations do not lever to the immense degree that large banks do, so this tax shield cannot be the entire answer. A second subsidy comes from the regulatory preference for (apparently) high-rated short-term debt as an asset of institutions that buy such debt. Intermediaries such as money market funds are required to hold short-term debt, and short-term debt carries lower risk weights for banks who hold it. This augmentation of the demand for run-prone assets encourages their supply. If the regulatory system looked uniformly at short-term debt as poison in the well, we might not have such trouble convincing banks not to issue so much of it.

The major subsidies to debt, however, are the implicit (deposit insurance) and explicit (bailouts) guarantees. These are not likely to end. Our government is not likely to eliminate deposit insurance, or want to or be able to credibly pre-commit against bailouts of other short-term creditors. In addition, though unregulated banks in the nineteenth and early twentieth centuries issued as much as 40 percent equity, in order to reassure creditors, nonetheless they failed on occasion as well.

There is a genuine externality with run-prone debt, and thus a genuine tendency for banks to issue too much and people to hold too much. So even most dedicated free-market economists must countenance some form of regulation. Not many observers want to return to bank notes issued by private banks, recognizing the incentives for banks to over-issue notes. Short-term debt is the modern equivalent.

PIGOUVIAN TAXES

Capital regulation should, I think, take the form of Pigouvian taxes rather than a regulatory ratio. For every dollar of short-term debt that a bank or other intermediary issues, it has to pay, say, five cents tax per year. That tax could, in principle, decline smoothly with maturity, be larger depending on capital ratios and other measures of how run-prone the institution is (providing a nudge rather than a brick wall at a specific ratio), could be larger for "systemically important" institutions, and could be varied over time as macroprudential policymakers sniff trouble. On the other hand, the hard lessons of complexity, regulatory capture, regulators' human inability to see crises ahead of time, and their likely desire to prop up troubled institutions rather than pile on higher taxes (or capital ratios) suggest the simplest and most uniform tax.

Pigouvian taxes are better than quantity controls in many areas of regulation, from import tariffs versus quotas to pollution taxes versus direct emission regulation, especially when, as in this case, precise costs and benefits are hard to measure.

Quantitative capital ratio regulations quickly lead to arguments and games. Should the denominator be "risk-weighted" assets or total assets, or should the capital requirement be based on a full-value-at-risk model? The total-assets approach has a satisfying simplicity. But, as Duffie (2014) emphasizes, a binding ratio of debt to total assets leaves banks with awful incentives. It is easy to construct assets whose value is low but whose risks (betas) are large. Risk-weighting individual assets sounds better, but then we argue about risk weights. Furthermore, a first-year MBA student understands that the riskiness (chance of default) of a portfolio of assets depends on the correlations between the assets as much as on the individual riskiness, but risk weights ignore correlations. A full-value-at-risk model including correlation between assets is the economically satisfying answer—but it relies on a big black box that few trust.

Most of all, where is the bright line of what capital ratio makes a bank safe? The answer "enough so it doesn't matter" is correct but unsatisfying. The fact is, there is no bright line. The top of a hill is flat. More is always safer. Why not have a regulation that says as much and that rewards banks that are safer than the minimum?

A Pigouvian tax will also allay critics who champion the economic necessity of short-term debt financing. In places where short-term debt financing is really vital, it will survive paying a run-prone externality tax. On the other hand, if a small tax leads banks to shift toward equity finance, then those arguments will quickly be resolved.

Pigouvian taxes set a price, and maybe a wrong price, but at least then we know the shadow value of the constraint. A quantity constraint may actually have a small shadow value, especially to society or to an industry as a whole if not to an individual bank, but it's still worth the bank's lobbyists whining about it constantly. A quantity constraint may have a very large shadow value that nobody knows about and do far more damage than its advocates realize. With a Pigouvian tax we will at least learn something about the necessity of run-prone contracts. With quantity constraints, we don't learn.

Who should be regulated?

One can argue that only certain financial intermediaries should be restricted from issuing run-prone liabilities, including very short-term debt. Only systemic runs really matter, so only runs at institutions likely to spark runs at others—and at times when such sparks are likely to catch fires—really matter. Runs are a feature of institutions, as well as contracts, as I listed above. One might argue that if, say, Kraft Foods wants to issue a small amount of overnight commercial paper, why not let it do so. One might argue that such restrictions are only needed in times of systemic danger, so restrictions should vary macroprudentially. MF Global failed with no crisis.

There are strong counterarguments. If any class of institution is allowed to issue runnable debt, then surely those institutions will grow up and become systemically dangerous. We had capital requirements supposedly limiting debt issue to safe levels, but the requirements were gamed and the institutions failed. Our regulators did not fail to notice systemic dangers from a lack of wisdom. The nature of a crisis is that if anyone can see it coming, it either won't happen or it already has happened. And the nature of regulators is that they are not going to get tough when they are trying to paper things over and prop things up.

An optimal-policy trade-off balances costs and benefits. I will argue below that vast amounts of privately issued runnable debt and other run-prone contracts confer few social benefits. If that is true, then we do little damage by taxing in such a way that not enough debt emerges. I also am suspicious of overly complex regulations requiring lots of discretion. I acknowledge, however, that if Kraft Foods wants to finance 5 percent of its assets with market issues of short-term debt, that won't be a disaster.

Banks, quasi-banks and nonbanks

Commercial banks are a small part of the financial system. The run started in the shadow banking system, and only a sense of their greater "systemic importance" caused so much regulatory attention to big commercial banks.

Money market funds

Money market funds promise fixed values and first-come first-served redemption. "Prime" funds invest in illiquid or low-grade paper to generate higher yields than available in Treasuries. The Reserve Fund, heavily invested in Lehman Brothers debt, "broke the buck" in 2008. Subsequently, the Treasury guaranteed money market fund debts.

Such funds are "banks" with no equity. The closest to equity that many funds have is a guarantee from a sponsor, which makes those funds one more sudden drain of cash in a crisis and one more way for banks to take on credit risk and get around asset regulation and capital ratios.

The answers are pretty simple: fixed-value money market funds must invest in short-term Treasuries. Those funds that want to offer higher yields by investing in anything else can grow a substantial equity or liquidity cushion. In my view, that cushion should be 100 percent. Or, fund values can float freely, which is equivalent to equity financing.

Now, even floating NAV (net asset value) is not a complete guarantee against problems. A floating NAV fund establishes its best guess of security values at the end of the day, and the fund allows investors to buy or sell at that price, creating liquidity by a sort of internal market. However, the fund may not be able actually to liquidate large volumes of securities at the set price, so floating NAV is dangerous if all investors want to leave at once. Thus, it is even safer if the fund's shares themselves are tradable in a reasonably liquid market. Then, in a crisis, investors wanting cash quickly can sell their shares to others rather than make a claim on the company.

Funds could also have the right to suspend convertibility, redeem in kind, or switch from fixed to floating NAV. However, any structure in which the fund exercises an option risks generating a run as people try to get out before the fund exercises its option.

Examining all these options, the simplest one seems the best to me: any fund not entirely invested in Treasuries must have floating values and, ideally, also tradable shares. This is all-equity financing without the control rights, which are not needed for a pass-through structure invested entirely in marketable securities. See French et al. (2011) for more analysis of these and other options.

Any of these proposals would substantially reduce the possibility that money market funds contribute to financial crises. Yet, in six years since the crisis, the Securities and Exchange Commission has not enacted any of these reforms. The Federal Reserve openly kept interest rates above zero so that money market funds would not have to charge customers to keep their money. Money market funds only came into existence in the 1980s as a response to the failure of Regulation Q, which stopped banks from paying interest on deposits. The regulatory system cannot bring itself to reform or put out of business a very simple structure, invented to avoid unintended consequences of previous regulation, that failed. This is perhaps a good warning of the political obstacles facing genuine reform of any set of institutions.

AUCTION-RATE SECURITIES AND SPECIAL-PURPOSE VEHICLES

Auction-rate securities and special-purpose vehicles have a similar structure. They invest in illiquid securities, typically with longer maturity than would be allowed in a money market mutual fund, such as mortgage-backed securities. They fund these purchases by rolling over short-term debt, which allows investors effectively to run at each rollover point. They issue no equity, but typically have a guarantee from a sponsoring institution. That credit exposure, which did not trigger a capital charge, again makes the structure a simple way for banks to avoid capital regulation.

These structures are banks in an economic sense of the word, except that they hold marketable (if illiquid) securities rather than relationship loans. Like overnight repurchase agreements, they offer institutional investors a high-yielding form of "cash." They also failed in the crisis, suffering runs and failures to roll over debt. In turn, these runs triggered guarantees from sponsoring banks, revealing the banks' credit exposure.

Obviously, this game needs to end. Funds or pools of mortgage-backed securities are a great idea—if they are funded by floating-value liabilities.

The story of how banks evaded risk regulation and capital regulation through all three sets of securities is a good warning against putting too much faith in longer and more detailed asset and capital regulation in the future.

Objections

The most natural objection is that we need banks to "transform" maturity and risk—borrow short and safe, lend long and risky—and to "create" liquidity. Without this function, it is claimed, there will not be an adequate supply of "safe" assets for people and businesses to hold and there will not be an adequate supply of risky credit to fund housing for people and business investment.

But risk and maturity "transformation" are fallacies. Maturity and credit risk can be sliced and diced, pooled and tranched, but they cannot be removed. Still, just how vital is bank creation of a run-prone short-term debt tranche? Is it worth the costs we have just paid in occasional crises, and the cost we are starting to pay in massive regulation, to preserve this attempted transformation?

Technology and the demand for "safe" assets

The quantity of short-term debt and run-prone securities is large in our economy. For example, Krishnamurthy and Vissing-Jorgensen (2013) measure all short-term debt as averaging 66 percent of GDP, with a peak of 99 percent in 2007.

It is easy to label this equilibrium outcome as a "demand" and to assume that it is inviolable—that the economy simply cannot function without a large quantity of privately-provided runnable assets, backed by risky investments. For example, Gorton, Lewellen, and Metrick (2012) state " . . . regulators and policymakers must adroitly balance the need to improve financial stability with the simultaneous need to maintain enough liquid, safe debt in the economy to meet the demand for such debt." Krishnamurthy and Vissing-Jorgensen (2013) go on:

> " . . . investors have a large demand for safe and liquid investments, and that short-term debt satisfies this demand . . . The financial sector supplies such debt by holding positions in other risky assets (loans, securities, etc.) that is funded by short-term debt. The corporate sector, particularly the high-grade segment, also satisfies this demand by issuing commercial paper. Our evidence supports standard theories of banking that emphasize the special role of banks in

transforming risky, illiquid assets into safe and liquid assets . . . the shadow banking system played an important role in the production of safe and liquid assets over the last decade."

But an observed equilibrium quantity does not measure what demand would be under alternative arrangements or how easily investors can substitute, given an incentive to do so. Our tough job, in thinking about a regulatory regime, is to understand how much of this observed quantity is really economically necessary and what the finite costs would be of a different arrangement. If Treasuries offer 2 percent, large corporations will happily declare a "need" for overnight repurchase agreements paying 2.5 percent, especially if they think they're all smart enough to run the day before bankruptcy or if they know the government will support the market in a run. The question is: if the only way to get 2.5 percent were to hold a floating-value fund, shoulder some price risk, and give up the right to run, would this "need" for higher-yielding fixed-value securities evaporate?

Why do people need liquid, fixed-value assets, money, or money-like securities? Well, to make transactions, you might say. And that once was true. To pay for something, you have to offer in return a security whose value the seller knows exactly and which can be transferred at minimal cost. You need to hold an inventory of such assets in your portfolio in order to make transactions and other unscheduled payments in between times that you access floating-value or illiquid assets held for portfolio purposes.

But, as I argued in the introduction, technology renders this "need" obsolete. We can now know exactly the prices of floating-value securities. Index funds, money market funds, mutual funds, exchange-traded funds, and long-term securitized debt have created floating-value securities that are nonetheless information-insensitive and thus extremely liquid.

Consumers already routinely make most transactions via credit cards and debit cards linked to interest-paying accounts, which are in the end largely netted without anyone needing to hold inventories of runnable securities and despite the artificially large (4 percent) fees charged by credit card companies. Allowing more competition in electronic transactions could increase that quantity.

The inventory is the real point. Even if we transfer fixed-value securities such as bank reserves to finalize a transaction, we no longer need to hold a large inventory of such securities. Business and financial actors really do not need to hold more than a day or two's worth of actual fixed-value transferable securities, because floating-value securities can be so easily bought and sold. Does this inventory demand constitute 66 percent of GDP? Not even close. People can easily pay credit card charges at the end of the month from floating-value funds.

I have used "fundamental economic need" as a qualifier because not all the discussion in the literature on the "need" or "demand" for safe assets spells out exactly where such demand comes from. Much of the remaining "demand for safe assets" gets psychological—infinite risk-aversion—or almost mystical and axiomatic. I find that a pretty dubious basis for policy.

Yes, we observe a large quantity of short-term debt. That observation does not prove it must be so.

Supply of safe assets

Even if the *demand* for run-prone securities is large, that does not mean that we must insist on a private *supply* of such securities, backed by risky assets and prone to runs.

There is a bright side to our government's fiscal profligacy: $18 trillion of federal government debt is enough to 100 percent back any imaginable fundamental economic need for run-prone assets. Reserve balances at the Fed corresponding to purchases of agency debts add to the total. If we need more still, the government can buy additional assets and issue more debt. Agency debts, student loan debts, and other debts already guaranteed by the government are a good place to start, given the government's choice to issue those guarantees. One worries about our government buying additional assets, but foreign sovereign wealth funds such as the Norwegian oil fund are transparently managed and avoid crony investments. And any such purchases are an order of magnitude more transparent than the possibilities for cronyism and directed lending posed by our current large-scale discretionary bank regulation.

Demand deposits are only about $1.5 trillion (Federal Reserve Money Stock Measures Release H.6). Money market funds are another $2 trillion, although some of those funds are already invested in Treasuries. Savings and time deposits are large at $8 trillion, but most of those could presumably be easily held as floating value, or at least not immediate-service and hence run-prone securities. Even all of Krishnamurthy and Vissing-Jorgensen's (2013) 66 percent of GDP in short-term debt is only about $10 trillion.

Small changes in the structure of government debt and a concerted effort by the government to displace private money with run-free public interest-paying money could speed the process.

As of Spring 2014, the Federal Reserve holds about $3.5 trillion of assets, corresponding to about $1 trillion in cash and $2.5 trillion in interest-paying reserves as the Fed's liabilities. The Fed should keep the large balance sheet and pay market interest on reserves. A corresponding $2.5 trillion in bank liabilities are now run-free. The Federal Reserve's intention to open the interest-paying reserve market to nonbanks via reverse repurchase agreements is a good step in the right direction.

The Treasury can issue more short-term debt. Ideally, the Treasury should issue fixed-value, floating-rate, electronically transferable debt, divisible to the cent, and let the rest of us have the same reserves that banks get at the Federal Reserve.

Now, long-term Treasury debt is also desirable as it insulates the Treasury from the fiscal consequences of interest rate changes. The Treasury can issue remaining debt in longer form—perpetuities are ideal—or engage in swap contracts to reduce that interest rate risk. The Treasury can separate the maturity and liquidity structure of its liabilities from its interest-risk exposure via swaps just like any bank.

TREASURY DEBT AS MONEY

There is a deeper point here. For most of the corporate and financial system, cash is irrelevant. Short-term debt *is* money. Technology and communications mean we now have interest-paying money for all legal transactions.

Since it's denominated in dollars, US federal debt is the most default-free and run-proof security we have. The government can always print dollars to pay off debts. It might inflate, but it need not default. The underlying claim to future taxation is a safer backing for short-term debt than any claim the private sector can securitize. These features give the government a natural monopoly in producing run-proof interest-paying money.

We have used private intermediation to create a multiplier, to create a larger volume of interest-paying claims that promise payment of a limited amount of government short-term debt. The vast volume of government debt, together with the much lower fundamental economic demand for run-prone assets, means we no longer need this multiplier.

In the nineteenth century, we realized the government had a similar natural monopoly in the production of bank notes. Now that electronic transfers and instant communication make interest-paying money possible, the government should extend its natural monopoly to interest-paying electronic money as well.

ACCOUNTING AND TAXES

There are some genuine accounting and legal roadblocks to what I have just written. Floating-value funds generate a capital-gains tax record-keeping nightmare. Fixed-value funds appear as cash on balance sheets. Both facts are part of the implicit subsidies given to run-prone securities by many laws and regulations.

Rather obviously, those accounting and legal restrictions need to be changed. Expensive and difficult, you may say, but nothing like the expense and difficulty of implementing the Dodd-Frank Act!

Credit supply

A second broad objection is that run-prone bank financing is necessary not so much to create "safe" assets for people and businesses to *hold*, but in order to create an adequate supply of loans for households and businesses to *borrow*.

A MONITORING NEED FOR RUN-PRONE LIABILITIES

Diamond and Rajan (2001) propose a theory of the need for run-prone liabilities that is diametrically opposite to the Gorton-Metrick view of short term debt as information-insensitive and hence money-like. In Diamond and Rajan's view, short-term investors monitor intensively and discipline management with the threat of a run. Therefore, "stabilization policies, such as capital requirements, narrow banking, and suspension of convertibility, may reduce liquidity creation," and thereby reduce the banking system's ability to make loans.

I am less convinced of the quantitative significance of this story. First, it simply does not ring true. Overnight repo is not held by institutions which closely monitor management; repo is a form of corporate cash management. Second, if so, Diamond and Rajan ought to add deposit insurance to the list of stabilization policies that reduce lending. For deposit insurance cures runs, and insured depositors no longer monitor. If government monitoring were a sufficient substitute, it could monitor equity-financed banks just as well. At least, if Diamond and Rajan are right, I get to convert all insured deposits to floating value or 100 percent backed form. Third, their theory starts, "Loans are illiquid when a lender needs relationship-specific skills to collect them." In their view, the special character of relationship lending versus, say, operating a tech startup or a car company, needs monitoring by run-prone debt rather than the usual monitoring by corporate equity holders. But what relationship lending remains is done by small commercial banks, not the bureaucratic behemoths at the center of the storm. Originate-to-sell activities, proprietary trading, investments in marketable securities, shadow banking, repurchase agreements, and so forth invest in marketable, if somewhat illiquid, securities, not relationship banking. Fourth, in fact, our banks have a substantial equity cushion in line before a run by short-term creditors, and equity is presumed to monitor management as in other corporations.

A GOOD WORD FOR SECURITIZATION

If banks are "special," it is centrally their ability to make relationship loans based on "soft information." Once again, information, communication, and financial technology have dramatically reduced the underlying need for soft-information lending, as the quantification of everything is replacing soft information by hard information and big data.

Mortgages, student loans, credit card loans, and many others are now routinely securitized. Technical innovation underlies that fact: quantifiable information such as credit scores, income, location, and so forth can, if allowed, do as good a job (or a good enough job) of assessing credit risk as the supposed soft information of loan officers. The big data revolution, if allowed, will only improve matters. Google and Facebook could probably predict defaults with great accuracy—which might or might not be regarded as a good thing.

Securitized debt, with a secondary market, does not have to be financed by run-prone assets. If, for some reason, equity-funded banks do not supply adequate credit, then long-term commercial paper, corporate bonds, and mortgage-backed securities held directly or at floating value in exchange-traded or mutual funds can do so.

Financial innovation has helped this holding end as well. The fundamental savers in our economy—people, pension funds, endowments, etc.—can easily hold (slightly) floating-value long-only funds invested in mortgage-backed securities or other securitized debt. Liquidity is now provided by the liquid markets for these securities, not by banks' run-prone redemption promises.

Relationship-lending banks, if they do need to be financed by run-prone securities, simply do not have to be a large part of finance, commingled with other activities, and at the center of systemic runs.

EXPENSIVE CAPITAL AND MODIGLIANI-MILLER

A second line of criticism is that equity capital is "expensive." If banks have to fund their loans by issuing equity, long-term debt, or other floating-value run-proof claims, they will have to pay higher returns, and will in turn have to pass those higher costs on to borrowers in the form of higher interest rates. Admati and Hellwig (2012) [see also my review, Cochrane (2013a)] skewer this view and lucidly address much of the basic confusion on the issue of bank equity. No, banks do not "hold" equity as reserves and a use of funds. Banks issue equity and equity is a source of funds. If banks issue more stock and less debt, the stock becomes less risky. That much is just accounting and inarguable. The argument is whether the expected return on that stock, which is the bank's cost of equity capital, will decline in proportion to the risk, as the Modigliani-Miller (MM) theorem asserts.

There is, in fact, one good reason for the MM pricing result to fail: the government guarantees and subsidizes bank debt. So, by switching to equity financing, the bank gives up that subsidy and the bank's total value falls. But taxpayers are equally better off, so the experience of individual banks[5] does not tell us anything about the *social* MM theorem. To argue that debt-financed banking provides lower social-cost loans than equity-financed banking, we must count the costs of debt guarantees and subsidies, of financial regulation, and of occasional crises to the bill.

It might well be that equity-financed banks charge fifty basis points (bp) more in mortgages because they lose the subsidy associated with government debt guarantees and the tax shield. If the fifty bp subsidy is an important social goal, let the government subsidize the lending directly, and on budget, without creating a run-prone intermediary in the way.

To argue beyond this resolution, one needs to imagine something deeply important, and often psychologically rather than economically important, about the difference between "equity" and "debt." One has to argue why a bundle of 90 percent debt and 10 percent equity is much more palatable to investors than the same security, with the same risk profile, sold as equity.

---

5. For example, Baker and Wurgler (2013) argue that lower-beta, and hence presumably less-leveraged, bank stocks give the same average return as higher-beta bank stocks.

CREATING "BANKS" THAT CAN FAIL

If there truly is a deep need for debt rather than equity, as an asset, there is no reason the bank itself must provide it. Banks could issue 100 percent equity. That equity could be purchased by a second institution, structured investment vehicle, or similar pass-through entity that tranches bank equity into short-term debt, long-term debt, and remaining risky equity.

But this vehicle very clearly is not too big to fail and has no government guarantees. Because, who cares if it goes bankrupt?

We fear the bankruptcy of banks because they are complex and might take years to unwind. Most of all, we fear the disruption of their operations. The failure of a special-purpose vehicle that holds bank equity, by contrast, can be handled in a morning. Short-term debt gets paid first, long-term debt gets the bank equity, equity is wiped out. The equity-issuing bank itself never fails, so there is no issue at all of sorting out thousands of claims in thousands of jurisdictions, clearing out huge derivatives books, or closing down the lending operations while they are sold to a new owner.

Even short-term debt of such a pass-through entity poses little systemic risk. The assets—bank equity—are liquid and tradable. The assets' value is known to within a bid-ask spread every few seconds. The illiquidity and obscurity of run-prone institutions' assets are not present.

Alternatively, if indeed the Modigliani-Miller theorem fails and the value of bank equity is less than an equivalent package of debt and equity, leveraged not-too-big-to-fail hedge funds will step in and do the unbundling, as long as the demand for debt was not really a demand for government guarantees.

Fixing bankruptcy

The trope following the financial crisis is: "bankruptcy can't work for large financial institutions." But it is not often explained exactly why. Especially with hundreds of billions of dollars of resources spent in fighting the financial crisis, a small amount of resources spent diagnosing and fixing bankruptcy ought to be a key part of the reform effort.[6]

The Lehman bankruptcy was a bit chaotic. But once you ask just what went wrong, specifically, rather than just accept "Lehman was a mess,

---

6. Scott and Taylor (2012) is a prime source for this view. Summe (2010), Fleming and Sarkar (2014), and Duffie (2010a, 2010b) are excellent summaries of some details of what went wrong in 2008.

we can't do that again," the problems do not seem beyond the fixing capacities of a small army of lawyers. And we have a large army of lawyers trying to implement Dodd-Frank. Collateral was commingled and hard to retrieve. OK, segregate capital better. United Kingdom bankruptcy law did not fully recognize that repo collateral belonged to those who owned it. OK, we can fix that. Under US bankruptcy law, the assets are drained to pay the (large) bid-ask spread on the entire derivatives book, so each counterparty is made whole. OK, we can fix that by, for example, assigning long positions directly to short positions, with a novation in between, or selling the whole book. Too many jurisdictions? Living wills are a fine idea, along with exactly which claims will be adjudicated where. And so on and so forth. Bankruptcy law was built up over centuries of experience by just such patient tinkering.

Remember, bankruptcy does not leave a crater behind, as in the popular imagination. Bankruptcy is a reorganization, with preservation of the good parts of a business. Bankruptcy is also a recapitalization. Too many analysts write "banks must be recapitalized" and jump to the conclusion that taxpayers must provide the capital. In bankruptcy, existing equity claims are written off, existing debt is written down and becomes the new equity, and valuable operations are sold to new owners. Bankruptcy wipes out the debt overhang and marries operations to a sufficient capital base (new owners, debt holders who now own equity) and ready to function with a new sign on the door. The question is the sand in the gears of that desirable process.

People are capable of thinking ahead of time about how things will be resolved in bankruptcy. Much of the page after page of legalese in financial contracts that critics so bemoan really comes down to exactly that planning.

If indeed bankruptcy can't work for large financial institutions, so creditor's bankruptcy protections are invalid, why did creditors lend to, or deal with, such institutions in the first place? The only sensible answer: creditors don't think it will happen. Having seen bailout after bailout, they think the bank is too big to fail, so there is no point in spending a lot of time sorting out bankruptcy procedures. Government fear of bankruptcy creates the fragility that reinforces the fear.

If bankruptcy is necessary—if for some reason equity-funded banks can't exist, even with equity tranched out by an easy-to-fail downstream institution—a little effort in fixing bankruptcy, or fixing institutions so they can survive bankruptcy, seems worthwhile!

BERNANKE, INNOVATION, AND BANKRUPTCY

Bernanke (1983) described the loss of human and organizational capital in bankruptcy. Legal and financial innovation has fundamentally changed that scenario. In 1933, interstate banking was prohibited, branch banking was prohibited, remote ownership was prohibited, and certainly international ownership was prohibited. In bankruptcy, the people and organizational capital of a bank simply could not, by regulation, be married to new capital. If the (fictitious) first bank of Omaha went bankrupt in 1933, it could not sell—or even give—the deposit-taking and loan-making operations to JP Morgan, receive an equity infusion from a sovereign wealth fund, or even be sold to a private equity fund. Now it can, so the special loan-making human capital Bernanke pointed to need not be lost. Canada's federal banking system, with nationwide branches, has long been held up as a model that did not suffer the United States' historical crises. Now we essentially have such a system.

The economy needs a *banking system*. Rather than save existing individual banks, their management, their equity holders, or their creditors, saving the banking system should be the priority. New banks, new management, new equity holders, and new debt holders can and should quickly take over failing ones. But the process is not perfect, and it can still be made much easier for investors to quickly take over bank assets.

This lesson remains important for Europe, in which many small national banks, stuffed with sovereign debt, remain, and it is hard for large, well-capitalized, international competitors to swoop in and get bankrupt pieces moving again.

Current policy

Runs and panics have been with us for centuries. The policy and regulatory response in the United States and around the world has evolved following a different model than the one I have sketched. Each intervention made some sense but had unintended consequences. New "reforms" patched up unintended consequences of past regulations with somewhat sensible new ones. But then those had unintended consequences as well. Each time, the size and scope of regulation expanded. The Dodd-Frank Act is not at all a new or radical set of ideas. Its core—credit guarantees, risk and capital regulation, and a big kit of lender-of-last-resort and resolution fire hoses—simply builds on and dramatically expands the same ideas that have been tried for over a hundred years in the United States and United Kingdom.

This set of ideas has run its course. It's pretty clear that the Dodd-Frank regulation is a stifling monster. *The Economist*'s review (2012) captures beautifully Dodd-Frank's mind-boggling complexity, inevitable politicization, and dysfunction. Basel bank regulation, even to regulators such as Andrew Haldane (2012), appears a hopelessly complex Rube Goldberg contraption. Most observers do not really expect either structure to stop financial institutions from once again undermining the regulations or to stop, rather than institutionalize, too-big-to-fail bailouts. And the scale of the bailouts and credit guarantees approached last time, and will likely exceed next time, governments' finite ability to provide guarantees and bailouts.

It is important to sketch and understand this evolution. All too often, fairly radical ideas (a class to which I freely admit this essay belongs) portray conventional wisdom as simply silly or misguided. That portrayal undermines the new ideas, I think. It is better to understand how the current ideas evolved as reasonable solutions to problems as they occurred, and then somewhat reasonable patches to the system as undesired consequences emerged. That understanding, a clear picture of just how many (and much larger) undesired consequences the current framework will have, and a recognition of how technology has changed basic assumptions, should help sensible people of all backgrounds, even those who participated in the last few rounds of patchwork, to see it's time to go back to the beginning rather than patch more.

Deposit guarantees and regulation

The United States responded to the bank runs of the 1930s with federal deposit insurance. Deposit insurance stops runs by removing the need to get your money out before bankruptcy, or before the other guy.

However, deposit insurance and the Fed's lender-of-last-resort function give rise to moral hazard. Bank management is now playing with a free option, artificially cheap debt, and a source of crisis financing. Bank depositors no longer have an incentive to monitor the quality of the bank's assets or to care about capital buffers. So, the US enhanced risk regulation and capital requirements to try to offset this induced moral hazard.

But regulatory supervision is a poor substitute for market discipline, with both bank and depositor now having even stronger incentives to undermine it. So, time after time, crises erupted anyway. Each time, credit guarantees grew and the scale and intrusiveness of asset and capital regulation grew. The government bailed out unsecured debt-holders in the Continental Illinois failure, when the term "too big to fail" came into common use. The savings and loan crisis and bailout of the 1980s, the various Latin American crises, the collapse of Long-Term Capital Management and the Russian default crisis, the Asian currency crises of the late 1990s—each provoked larger and larger creditor guarantees. All paved the way for Bear Stearns, opening the discount window to broker-dealers, Fannie and Freddie, the Lehman exception that proved the rule, the TARP bailouts, the (more important in my view) October 2008 blanket guarantee of all bank debt, and finally the massive expansion of regulation under Dodd-Frank.

Rules and discretion

"Regulation" can mean laws, with clear rights, recourse, and judicial arbitration. It can mean rules written by regulatory agencies, where the regulated have at least administrative, if not judicial, recourse. Or it can mean that regulators use discretion to approve plans ahead of time, oversee moment-by-moment business decisions, or deny actions after the fact.

Financial regulation largely conforms to the latter mold. There are rules, mountains of rules. But the rules are so complex and overlapping that there is little chance of simply reading them and complying. Each large bank has hundreds of regulators sitting inside, approving every deal. Lucchetti and Steinberg (2013) quote John J. Mack, Morgan Stanley's chairman and chief executive from 2005 to 2009: "Your No. 1 client is the government." They report that current CEO James Gorman "phones Washington before making major decisions," and note: "About 50 full-time government regulators are now stationed at Morgan Stanley."

The stress tests give a good example. One might think that the Fed would write down rules for the stress test. But no, the Fed changes the rules and scenarios each time. And for good reasons. Fed staffers know that if they announce the rules ahead of time, the banks will cleverly cook the books to pass the tests. So the staff finds fun, new, and innovative tests each time.

The newspaper reports on Citigroup failing stress tests in March 2014 are revealing. The *Financial Times* wrote:[7] "One senior executive said that

---

7. Tom Braithwaite, Camilla Hall, Gina Chon, and Martin Arnold, "Citi Stress Test Hit by Audit Lapses," *Financial Times,* March 28 2014, http://www.ft.com/intl /cms/s/0/06ba38f2-b69b-11e3-905b-00144feabdc0.html.

[Citi CEO Michael] Mr. Corbat had shown himself to be 'overconfident' that he had repaired the bank's rickety relationship with regulators and had mistaken a 'not bad' relationship for a 'good relationship.'" The *Wall Street Journal*[8] wrote: "Mr. Corbat had met on multiple occasions with senior officials at the Federal Reserve and the New York Fed and believed Citigroup was on track to meet the Fed's demands." More revealingly still, the *Journal* article continues:

> "[The] so-called qualitative part [of stress tests] has become increasingly important. It includes subjective factors such as how the bank manages the stress-test process and incorporates past lessons and concerns. It also takes into account how a bank handles costly litigation [brought by the government!] and manages its technology systems. Regulators have been saying for some time that they are placing more emphasis on the so-called subjective aspects of the test and not just capital levels, leverage ratios and other quantitative measures."

You don't need a "relationship" to pass a driver's license test. "Subjective aspects" mean pretty much anything the regulator wants them to mean. A system more ripe for capture and a revolving door would be hard to design. A system more ripe for political control would be hard to design. No banker would dare to speak out against regulators who can "subjectively" do pretty much anything the regulator wants.

Innovation cat and mouse

Many of the structures of the shadow banking system were clear end-runs around this regulatory system. Regulation Q limited the interest banks could pay on deposits, to keep banks from exploiting deposit insurance by offering higher interest rates to invest in riskier projects. Money market funds evolved in the 1980s to circumvent Regulation Q. Banks and savings and loans were forbidden to buy stock, obviously risky. Junk bonds were invented in the late 1980s, and they gave savings and loans risky assets that behaved like stocks but were regulated like bonds. Prime money market funds, financial commercial paper, special-purpose vehicles with

---

8. Suzanne Kapner, Stephanie Armour, and Julie Steinberg, "'Stress Test' Failure Sparked Scramble at Citigroup," *Wall Street Journal*, March 27, 2014, http://online.wsj.com/news/articles/SB10001424052702304688104579465851513193722.

off-balance-sheet credit guarantees, and overnight repo financing were the tricks that led to our financial crisis. It's an old game. The Medici bank used offsetting foreign exchange forward contracts to synthesize interest-paying debt against the church's prohibition of usury.

Yet it is time for some sympathy. Huge complex rules that lead to armies of discretionary regulators doing what they please do not occur for some dark conspiratorial reason. The minute we write down rules, banks game their way around the rules. If we're going to subsidize and guarantee debt and then regulate that horrendously complex too-big-to-fail banks will not then lever up and exploit the guarantee, then an army of discretionary regulators, with all its unsavory consequences, is a logical necessity. This system cannot be cleaned up, reformed, or made more rule-based. But it would be a triumph of hope over a century worth of experience that regulators will finally, this time, put a stop to the clever tricks that banks use to get around the regulations. The only alternative is to undo the "if."

Innovation and competition
Not all of financial innovation involves clever tricks to undermine regulation. In fact, most financial innovations serve good purposes, even the innovations that are also used to undermine regulation. The first money market funds invested in Treasuries, providing run-free access to Treasury yields to small investors who had been locked out of those yields by Regulation Q. Junk bonds were a key innovation in the productivity-improving buyout wave of the 1980s. Repo financing is an effective way for risk-averse investors to lend out the collateral value of their securities and for corporations to synthesize interest-paying money that is safer than deposits substantially larger than the limit for federal insurance.

Financial regulation by its nature limits competition and innovation. It was clear already in the 1930s that competition and innovation would undermine the regulatory package of deposit insurance, asset and capital regulation, and the lender-of-last-resort function, so the Glass-Steagall Act put in a sharp distinction between commercial and investment banking. Commercial banks were granted a near-monopoly on issuance of demand deposit-like securities. Regulation Q, with an explicit goal of enhancing the profitability of the banking industry, capped interest rates to stop competition for depositors. Barriers to entry kept too many banks from trying to divvy up the spoils. And bankers played a lot of golf. Investment banks and other financial institutions couldn't issue demand deposits—but they were pretty lightly regulated and free to fail.

But Glass-Steagall fell apart, financial innovation did the rest, and the Dodd-Frank Act breaks the remains of the wall surrounding regulated finance. Essentially the entire financial system is now subject to detailed federal control. Already the Financial Stability Oversight Council (FSOC) has designated[9] as systemically important two insurance companies (AIG and Prudential Financial) and GE Capital as "non-bank financial companies" along with a long list of financial market "utilities." The Treasury's Office of Financial Research (2013), in an official report to the FSOC, now worries that "reaching for yield" and "herding" by asset managers will provoke fire sales, thus making run-proof equity mutual funds systemically important. The council is, as I write,[10] therefore considering whether to extend systemically important designation to such funds.

Pretty much every market, contract, and financial institution receives much more regulation under Dodd-Frank. As part of our new effort to avoid crises, the Consumer Financial Protection Bureau will regulate the font on your credit card disclosures. (Well, nearly!)

This dramatic expansion is a natural result of the basic philosophy. Having seen money-market funds, savings and loans, junk bonds, special-purpose vehicles, auction-rate securities, and overnight repo turn "systemically important," having seen investment banks and hedge funds (in regulator's eyes) turn "systemically important," there is no way to tell what new idea or institution might cause trouble. So, give an army of discretionary regulators authority to regulate it all as they see fit.

To stop potential regulatory arbitrage, the Dodd-Frank Act pretty much puts every action of every large institution under discretionary control of regulators, and every institution potentially under such scrutiny. Nowhere does the Dodd-Frank Act even *define* systemic importance. It is pretty much whatever the regulator thinks it is. The legal power to *determine* systemic importance is, by contrast, well-defined. Conversely, there is no safe harbor, no definition of any activity that is *not*, and cannot be deemed ex-post, systemically important, "could pose a threat to US financial stability," in the regulator's judgement, and be subject to detailed regulation. There is no standard one could use to appeal that decision.

---

9. Financial Stability Oversight Council, US Department of the Treasury, http://www.treasury.gov/initiatives/fsoc/designations/Pages/default.aspx.

10. Mark Schoeff Jr., "SEC commissioners push back against systemic designation for mutual funds," *Investment News*, April 3, 2014, http://www.investmentnews.com/article/20140403/FREE/140409958.

Every element of Dodd-Frank regulation is thus anathema to innovation, competition, and (above all) entry. Simply the need for an immense compliance department and relationships with regulators puts a prohibitive barrier to entry in place.

More deeply, the basic idea in Dodd-Frank is to designate specific *institutions* as systemically important rather than isolate *contracts* that pose systemic risks as I have suggested. If an institution is "systemically important," that means, almost by definition, that it cannot be allowed to fail, and that in turn means that it cannot be allowed to lose money or be driven out by upstart competitors who threaten its profits.

All this stifling of competition and innovation is a consequence of the regulation even if the regulation works exactly as benevolently intended. Regulatory capture adds additional barriers. Regulatory capture is one of the most classic unintended consequences of discretionary regulation: the regulatory structure becomes an instrument for incumbents to protect themselves from competition, especially competition by innovative new companies. This is not just theory. Centuries of bitter experience taught us to be a nation of laws and rules, not to place our faith in a benevolent aristocracy. Discretionary regulators, no matter how well-intentioned, are much more subject to the political pressure that institutions with hundreds of billions of dollars at stake can bring to bear.

Thus, under Dodd-Frank we will likely have a financial system dominated by the same six large banks thirty years from now that we do today, protected from innovation and competition, subsidized by the government to remain profitable, though occasionally penalized by showy prosecutions when they step out of political line, and engaged in a constant battle of wits with discretionary regulators. Financial market participants will focus on currying favor with regulators and politicians. Stress tests and official pronouncements will continue to be awaited with the solemnity once reserved for a change of pope.

Putting out fires

Firefighting is the second major component of our current financial regulation scheme. The Bank of England started acting as a lender of last resort in the late 1870s. Following the 1907 panic, the United States created the Federal Reserve in 1914, largely to be a lender of last resort. Runs happened anyway in 1933.

Firefighting in the 2008 crisis extended to lending to banks and broker-dealers, debt guarantees, FDIC resolution, bailouts, shotgun marriages, asset purchases, and many other measures. The European Central

Bank (ECB) guarantee to "do what it takes" to stop sovereign debt crises could ratchet up the quantities even further.

"Bailout" is a misnomer. We should call it a "creditor bailout," because that is what matters. It does not matter much if management keeps their jobs, if equity is wiped out, and so forth. It's hard to say that Greece or Ireland was bailed out. They're suffering pretty badly. Greece's creditors were bailed out.

Ex-post creditor bailouts are irresistibly tempting, because they are about the only way to stop a run once it has started. Deposit insurance was originally limited in scope, because the government wanted large depositors to exercise the sort of discipline and caution that they had before. For the same reason, the government shrinks from ex-ante guarantees of overnight repurchase agreements, prime money market funds, and so forth. But any runnable debt can run, and when the government wants to stop runs, ends up guaranteeing debts. The attempt, I think, is to pretend ex-ante that the government won't bail out ex-post, to get the moral hazard right, and then bail out ex-post to stop the run. But markets see through the game.

Conversely, the anti-bailout language in Dodd-Frank might actually be strong enough to put us in the worst possible world: markets expect too-big-to-fail but the government can't or won't do it. Prevailing sentiment in the markets is that law and regulation don't seem to constrain executive action that much, so the government find a way to bail out creditors. Prevailing sentiment among government officials seems to be that Dodd-Frank restrictions really do prevent bailouts. Everyone's sentiment seems to be that Lehman's failure was a catastrophe. The result of these contradictory expectations will be interesting to see.

Politicians and regulators are also tempted to bail out failing companies and countries in order to paper over difficulties and stop their perception of domino-like contagion. But this strategy is fairly pointless. In a systemic run, news that bank A is insolvent will spread to a run in bank B whether or not the government bails out bank A creditors. It's the news that matters.

To the extent that such bailouts work, they mainly demonstrate the regulators' commitment to bailing out. Bailing out Bear Stearns sent an unintended "don't' worry" message to Lehman Brothers creditors. (Summe (2010, p. 87) gathers considerable evidence on this point.) Greece didn't owe Italy any money, and news about Greek finances has little information about Italy's. By bailing out Greek creditors, the European Union, ECB, and International Monetary Fund let creditors know an Italian bailout was more likely, easing Italy's crisis.

PROPPING UP PRICES

In the 2008 financial crisis, a new—or, at least, vastly expanded—fire-fighting tool emerged: directly manipulating asset prices. The original TARP idea, as presented by Treasury Secretary Henry Paulson, was to use $700 billion to buy mortgage-backed securities on the open market in order to prop up their prices and thus make banks look more solvent. That announcement coincided with a ban on short-selling bank stocks, a clear attempt to boost bank-stock prices. Europe also banned short sales during the sovereign crises. In fall 2008, the Federal Reserve lowered interest rates to zero, equivalently doing everything in its power to raise the price of Treasury debt and any other debt related to Treasury. The Fed, together with Treasury, also successfully intervened in financial commercial paper markets, buying up large quantities and driving up their prices.

This asset-price manipulation impulse has continued in the Fed's quantitative easing (QE) program and in the macroprudential policies which other central banks are following and the Fed is considering. QE2 and QE3 were explicitly aimed at raising the prices of long-term Treasury and mortgage-backed securities. Macroprudential policy elsewhere targets house prices, exchange rates, credit spreads, and stock prices. Many observers blame the Fed for holding interest rates too low before the crisis in an apparently all-too-successful effort to inflate housing values, and the same after the crisis in a transparent attempt to do the same again. Stein (2014) is a thoughtful review of the Fed's ideas to target risk premiums, including corporate bond spreads.

The idea is, in general, for central banks to keep prices from rising "too fast" in a boom and then to prop prices up in a bust. Central banks will use regulatory tools including leverage and capital ratios and mortgage-loan-to-value ratios, along with interest rate policy, to diagnose and correct perceived bubbles, imbalances, savings gluts and so forth. Governments will also, with grand international coordination, undertake policies to manipulate exchange rates, force other countries to push consumption versus exports, and so on.

In short, policy should now fight runs by manipulating prices and economies so that banks don't ever lose money in the first place. This is truly a grand expansion of regulation. What did the old lady eat after the horse?

RESOLUTION AUTHORITY

The Dodd-Frank Act adds a new "resolution authority" to handle failing so-designated systemically important institutions. This is at least an attempt to think through firefighting bailouts ahead of time. The authority comes in place of bankruptcy court, laws, and procedures. The authority is supposed to follow the order of precedence specified in bankruptcy law. But those are more what you'd call guidelines than actual rules, as the authority has broad powers to pay creditors in whatever order it deems appropriate, particularly to address perceived systemic problems and to invest government money. That's the whole point. If we were going to follow or fix bankruptcy law, or any set of rules, we would write the rules and follow the law. The point of a "resolution authority" is to hand discretionary power to the officials who will run it, to address "systemic risks" as those officials perceive them.

Given that necessary discretion, it seems likely that the resolution authority will induce runs rather than calm them, so the net result will be a government guarantee of every claimant in a crisis.

Imagine markets are nervous, as in September 2008, with a few high-profile failures in the background. You are a claimant to a large, designated systemically important financial institution, or one that might get designated systemically important. You have some certainty about where you stand with bankruptcy law. Perhaps you have repo collateral or a collateralized derivatives contract that is supposed to be subject to automatic stay. You haven't run yet. But now you suspect that your creditor might be "resolved" by politically appointed government officials—officials who have wide powers, a clear mandate to bail out systemically important creditors, no definition of what that means, and strong political pressures being brought to bear. You know that big banks with the Treasury secretary's private cellphone number will soon be screaming their own systemic importance and the disasters that will befall the republic should they not get paid back. You remember how Goldman Sachs got its collateral from AIG and how the General Motors bankruptcy trampled creditor rights. What do you do? Run.

So the prospect of resolution, rather than calming the waters, seems doomed to start its own run. Now take one more step back. What will officials do? They don't want to liquidate commercial banks unnecessarily, especially in the middle of a crisis. They need to stop the emerging run of the last paragraph. Guaranteeing all debts to avoid resolution seems like their only possible course—just as the Fed and Treasury guaranteed all of the TARP banks' debts in October 2008.

Keep in mind the crucial difference between a looming crisis and normal times. MF Global's failure was a lot different from Lehman's failure. We could well see a successful resolution in "calm" markets, where the troubles of a single bank have little information content about its competitors. And that success could lull us into a false sense of confidence. It all works differently when political appointees are trying to "instill confidence," "stop contagion," and so forth.

Resolution authority fails on a simple elemental contradiction. Its premise is that large financial institutions are too complex to be resolved by bankruptcy law, with its centuries of law, precedent, and experience, and with acres of fine print in contracts specifying just who gets what and when. But if that is too complex, how is a team of appointed officials going to figure out who gets how many billions of dollars out of hundreds of thousands of complex contracts, over a weekend?

Making markets more fragile

Deposit insurance, explicit and implicit guarantees, ex-post creditor bailouts, a lender of last resort, asset price manipulation, and other firefighting measures all have the unintended effect of making markets more fragile and thus becoming more dependent on regulatory intervention.

Before the lender-of-last-resort function, banks had developed a clearinghouse system to deal with runs. With the lender of last resort, the clearinghouse ceased to function, so when the Fed arguably fell short as lender of last resort in the 1930s, the banking crisis was worse than it would have been. The shadow banking system was arguably more fragile than an unregulated banking system.

Similarly, the array of firefighting tools invites people to hold fewer fire extinguishers. With a resolution authority in place, a creditor's incentives now are to be as systemically important as possible in the authority's eyes, to ensure getting paid first, and to invest heavily in political connections with the appointees in charge.

All of asset pricing relies, in the end, on deep-pocket long-term investors who are willing to swing in with ready cash and buy. Your fire sale is their buying opportunity. But when the Fed "stabilizes" prices in a crash, the rewards to bottom-feeders evaporate. They learn to "ride the bubble" on the upside next time rather than keep some cash around ready to pounce. Similarly, if the Fed starts limiting upside price movements, then the returns to buying in the bottom of the recession are limited.

Where was the smart money in 2008–2009? If limits to arbitrage, leveraged intermediaries, and so forth in fact cause fire sales to break out, where are the long-only, multi-strategy funds, endowments, sovereign wealth funds, pension funds, family offices, and uber-wealthy 0.01 percent? Nothing institutional stopped them from participating in what turned out to be the buying opportunity of a lifetime in junk bonds, stock indices, commercial paper, and mortgage-backed securities. It isn't hard, there are Vanguard funds and ETFs for each of the asset classes! To some extent, these investors may simply have panicked like everyone else, rationally or irrationally. If true, that event denies the importance of the institutional-finance paradigm. Alternatively, being a multi-strategy investor, understanding many markets, waiting to take advantage of transient opportunities, and, in doing so, providing liquidity and countering volatility in those markets takes a big up-front investment while forgoing narrower and more specialized opportunities. The less the rewards to such fast-moving capital, the more frequent the central bank put, the fewer such investors there will be.

When bailouts and market interventions rule the day, then financial market participants spend their efforts divining and influencing the will of government officials rather than understanding the value of companies and assets. In turn, their extra influence means officials are as likely to cause trouble as to repair it. By showing up in front of Congress with three pages of notes, asking for $700 billion, with no clear idea of what he wanted to do with it except a transparently hopeless plan to float the MBS market, Secretary Paulson is as likely to have started a run as to have stopped one. Taylor (2009) argues persuasively for this view based on detailed analysis of the timing. Add that performance to a short-sale ban on banks, and information-insensitive investors got the word they should look really hard, right now. The ebb and flow of the European debt crisis tracked changing sentiments about the bailout-will of government officials, not from any news or even rumors about Greece and the other countries' fundamental solvency.

In the end, if you have a big firehouse, then people start to store gas in the basement and don't keep their fire extinguishers ready. Sending an army of regulators around to make really sure nobody ever lights a match is not that effective. This moral hazard is well-known, but it is perhaps not so well-appreciated just how much more fragile markets are as a result of a century of crisis management.

Comparison

I hope this little review shows how the current state of regulation evolved naturally. But it has now grown to a size where the collateral damage—unintended, or understood but accepted—is enormous, and current regulation is not likely actually to stop another crisis. Those costs and limitations are important, because drastically limiting run-prone liabilities will bear some costs and require some regulation. But with the current state of affairs in front of us, you can see that an approach based on limiting run-prone liabilities is orders of magnitude simpler, clearer, and more open to rule-based rather than discretionary regulation.

There are some fundamental differences between my approach and the development of our current regulatory system. I started with a defined view of the problem—we had a systemic run—and an economic analysis of the incentives that led to that problem. I analyze the nature of regulation, not its quantity. That's how we're supposed to approach economic regulation: understand the crucial market failure, then craft a minimal intervention to solve it. Regulation is effective or ineffective, smart or dumb, not more or less. That approach leads me to a focused set of changes that should stop runs while leaving untouched a whole panoply of real or imagined ills and complaints about the financial system that, in that analysis, have nothing to do with stopping runs.

The Dodd-Frank regulatory package, by contrast, really never decided what the problem was. The financial system failed, so add "regulation" to anything smacking of finance, as if regulation were like fertilizer one can simply throw on a field. The law is, in fact, mostly authorization for agencies to go figure out what to do. The Dodd-Frank Act does not define "systemic" or "contagion" or "interconnection" or even what "pose a danger" means. Without such a framework, under the guise of stopping crises, every complaint about the financial system got thrown in one bill.

Again, we can have some sympathy. The ideas I summarize in this essay evolved by a long conversation among academics and policymakers in the years since Dodd-Frank was enacted. At the time, the systemic-run view was not as common, nor was the view that lots of bank equity would be cheap. Chasing down "causes of the crisis" or, all too commonly, a witch hunt for the villains of the crisis, seemed more plausible. Since the crisis was associated with the failure of large companies, efforts to keep large financial firms from failing seemed more plausible. Legislators' view that "finance failed" so it needed "more regulation," given the cacophony of experts before those legislators, might be pardonable. Such sympathy does not mean, however, that now, later and wiser, we must continue to pursue that hastily-enacted framework.

Despite its huge increase in contemplated regulation, the Dodd-Frank apparatus does very little in the directions I have suggested actually to stop run-prone financing. Yes, Basel rules and Federal Reserve policy include modest rises in capital ratios, but these are modest, a very small part of the overall policy response, and subject to the same games as the last round of capital ratios, especially given the huge increase in the complexity of capital-ratio regulation. One can see the Federal Reserve already giving up on formal ratios and relying on its own discretionary stress tests instead.

In fact, some recent regulation goes in the opposite direction. For example, the SEC decided that money market funds should hold shorter maturity debt, to make the funds safer. But this step, of course, gives an added incentive for intermediaries to manufacture shorter-maturity debt, pushing the run one step up the ladder. So much for the systemic rather than institution-specific regulatory approach the FSOC was supposed to inculcate.

Focusing on run-prone contracts frees us from the need, and the adverse consequences, of the rest of this regulatory effort. If the liabilities can't run, banks can do what they want with assets. Equity-financed banks need not shed assets to pay off debt, so there can't be fire sales.

Current regulation focuses on *assets*, tightly regulating their risk and nature, and now their market prices. I focus on *liabilities*. Equity-financed banks would require next to no asset risk regulation. Bank asset risk regulation is strange on first principles. Bank assets, largely loans or fixed income securities, are much safer than the assets or profit streams of other corporations. They are certainly much safer than the assets of an equity mutual fund. Why put so much effort into regulation of such extraordinarily safe assets? Because the *liabilities* are prone to runs. Equity-financed banks would be more boring than regulated utility stocks. Boring is good.

Dodd-Frank focuses on systemically dangerous *institutions*. I focus on systemically dangerous *contracts*, and an institution is only dangerous if it issues such contracts. Regulation should be based on behavior, not identity.

Dodd-Frank resolution and the following trend to so-called macroprudential regulation focuses on fighting fires, giving regulators bigger and bigger tool kits to fight crises. I focus on clearing out the underbrush, making the system less prone to catching fire in the first place.

The current regulatory approach relies more than ever on regulatory prescience to spot trouble ahead. A financial system that can't have runs in the first place needs no great men or women guiding the ship. If you still have any trust in regulatory prescience—or the ability of prescient individual regulators to take unpopular actions while trying to "bolster confidence" and prop up weak institutions—consider the astonishing fact that, with the financial crisis just behind them, European bank regulators still treated sovereign debt as a risk-free asset to banks.

Concluding comments

Regulation and deregulation

I have focused on describing what a run-free financial system can look like in the context of modern communications and financial technology. I have tried to answer the standard objections and I have shown how much better it would be than our current path. I have focused less on what kinds of regulation are needed to prod the market to that point. There are several reasons, in addition to the limits of space and reader patience.

First, there are lots of ways to achieve the same goal. We have to agree on the vision of where we want to go before we decide on the best way to get there. This vision is radical enough and sketchy enough that it makes sense to work on that agreement first. Even once we agree on the principles, a lot of details of the vision need to be worked out before we start playing central planner and writing regulations.

Second, much of the pathology of markets, during the crisis and now, derives from the ill effects of existing regulations. A detailed plan is as much a disassembly as it is the construction of regulations needed to avoid the difficulties of a hypothetical completely free market.

Third, there is an interesting inverse correlation between complexity and cost. For example, a simple, clear regulation is this: nobody but the Treasury may issue short-term, fixed-value, first-come-first-served, I'm-bankrupt-if-I-can't-pay debt. Now, one might object that goes too far and is too costly. Surely it does and surely it is. So, one tries to get more complex to try to economize on perceived costs. Maybe some kinds of firms can issue a little short-term debt? Who? How do we define what kinds of debt? What are the costs, really? That delicate trade-off is beyond my scope. Since the costs in any case are orders of magnitude less than what we are seeing in the current regulatory regime, and with a distrust of complex regulation, I favor a simpler but somewhat more costly approach. But a bad job of a difficult problem does not advance the overall vision.

Fourth, actual regulatory plans must consider political constraints that are better left out while still working out the vision.

Most of all, and especially given how much discretion and agency rule-writing dominate the process, accepting the vision itself is half the battle.

If every agency writing rules, implementing rules, approving plans, subjectively evaluating stress tests, and so on, even under Dodd-Frank, had firmly in mind that run-prone short-term debt is poison in the well, is the central systemic danger, and needs to be purged wherever possible, you and I would not need to do a lot of fancy optimal-policy work.

In sum, let us first agree on the vision and philosophy. If by some miracle that happens, a regulatory plan will be easy. Conversely, a detailed regulatory plan is of no use until we agree on the vision and philosophy.

I have phrased the ideas in this essay as an alternative to Dodd-Frank-style regulation and its international cousins because I see those falling apart at the seams. However, dismantling Dodd-Frank is not a logical necessity. The core complaint about Dodd-Frank regulation, from all sides, is that it does little actually to prevent another crisis, just as its milder ancestors did little to prevent this one. My core complaint is that it fails to do much about run-prone liabilities. If you think all the other things in Dodd-Frank are great, and address other alleged faults of the financial system, then the liability-focused structure I advocate here can be added to, rather than substitute for, the current system.

Sovereign debt disclaimer

I built the monetary side of my proposal on sovereign debt, by a sovereign such as the United States that issues debt in its own currency. The resulting stability guarantee presumes a fiscally healthy sovereign in the background. Narrow banking backed by Treasuries is only perfectly safe so long as Treasuries themselves are perfectly safe. What happens if the sovereign defaults or severe inflation looms so there is effectively a run on government debt? Sovereign default, inflation, or currency devaluation are different kinds of crises altogether from a run or panic in the private financial system.

One should at least consider the possibility of such crises, especially in a moment of emerging low secular growth, ballooning public debt, and vast hidden liabilities.

Government and private default are a bit intertwined: the last crisis cost the US government about $1 trillion per year for several years. Another crisis will cost trillions more in bailouts, propping up markets, credit guarantees, transfers, and fiscal stimulus efforts. These guarantees may well exceed the government's ability to credibly pledge future tax revenues, and thus to borrow. These guarantees may thus spark a sovereign crisis as well. So, creating a run-free financial system reduces the chance that a private crisis will spill over and become a sovereign crisis.

Constructing a financial and monetary system which is immune both to private and to public default is an interesting question. Rather than pursue a fundamentally different monetary standard—substitute bitcoins, gold, or SDR (special drawing rights) for short-term nominal Treasury debt—I think fairly simple innovations in government debt would suffice. If the government were to issue long-term, ideally perpetual, debt that comes with an option to temporarily lower or eliminate coupons, without triggering a legal or formal default, then government financial problems could be transferred to bondholders without crisis or inflation. Reputation and a desire to issue future debt at good prices would lead governments voluntarily to pay coupons when they can. Really, this is no more than a modern version of the institution by which the British government suspended convertibility to gold during wars and then voluntarily reestablished convertibility at par after the war in order to preserve its ability to borrow the next time.

For now, though, I simply note that banking crises against the background of a solvent sovereign are a separate issue from sovereign crises. This essay has really only considered the former. The latter is potentially just as important, especially looking forward.

References

Admati, Anat, and Martin Hellwig. 2012. *The Bankers' New Clothes: What's Wrong with Banking and What to Do about It.* Princeton NJ: Princeton University Press.

Baker, Malcolm, and Jeffrey Wurgler. 2013. "Would Stricter Capital Requirements Raise the Cost of Capital? Bank Capital Regulation and the Low Risk Anomaly." NBER Working Paper No. 19018, May 2013

Bernanke, Ben. 1983. "Non-monetary Effects of the Financial Crisis in the Propagation of the Great Depression." *American Economic Review* 73 (3): 257–276.

Bernanke, Ben, and Mark Gertler. 1989. "Agency Costs, Net Worth, and Business Fluctuations." *American Economic Review* 79 (1): 14–31.

Bernanke, Ben, and Mark Gertler. 1995. "Inside the Black Box: The Credit Channel of Monetary Policy Transmission." *Journal of Economic Perspectives* 9 (4): 27–48.

Bernanke, Ben, Mark Gertler, and Simon Gilchrist. 1996. "The Financial Accelerator and the Flight to Quality." *The Review of Economics and Statistics* 78 (1): 1–15.

Bernanke, Ben, Mark Gertler, and Simon Gilchrist. 1999. "The Financial Accelerator in a Quantitative Business Cycle Framework." In *Handbook of Macroeconomics*, edited by John Taylor and Michael Woodford. Amsterdam: Elsevier.

Chamley, Christophe, Laurence J. Kotlikoff, and Herakles Polemarchakis. 2012. "Limited Purpose Banking—Moving from 'Trust Me' to 'Show Me' Banking." *American Economic Review* 102 (3): 113–119, http://dx.doi.org/10.1257/aer.102.3.113.

Chari, V. V., Lawrence J. Christiano, and Patrick J. Kehoe. 2008. "Facts and Myths about the Financial Crisis of 2008." Federal Reserve Bank of Minneapolis Working Paper 666, http://www.minneapolisfed.org/research/pub_display.cfm?id=4062.

Cochrane, John H. 2010. "Lessons from the Financial Crisis." *Regulation* 32 (4): 34–37.

Cochrane, John H. 2011. "Discount Rates." *Journal of Finance* 66 (4): 1047–1108.

Cochrane, John H. 2013a. "Running on Empty: Review of 'The Banker's New Clothes' by Anat Admati and Martin Hellwig." *Wall Street Journal,* March 1.

Cochrane, John H. 2013b. "Stopping Bank Crises Before They Start." *Wall Street Journal*, June 24.

Dell'Ariccia, Giovanni, Enrica Detragiache, and Raghuram Rajan. 2008. "The Real Effect of Banking Crises." *Journal of Financial Intermediation* 17 (1): 89–112.

Diamond, Douglas W. 2008. "The Current Financial Crisis, Other Recent Crises, and the Role of Short-term Debt." Slides at http://research.chicagobooth.edu/igm/docs/ChicagoCrisistalk.pdf.

Diamond, Douglas W., and Phillip H. Dybvig. 1983. "Bank Runs, Deposit Insurance, and Liquidity." *Journal of Political Economy* 91 (3): 401–419, http://www.jstor.org/stable/1837095.

Diamond, Douglas W., and Raghuram G. Rajan. 2001. "Liquidity Risk, Liquidity Creation, and Financial Fragility: A Theory of Banking." *Journal of Political Economy* 109 (2): 287–327.

Duffie, Darrell. 2010a. "The Failure Mechanics of Dealer Banks." *Journal of Economic Perspectives* 24: 51–72.

Duffie, Darrell. 2010b. *How Big Banks Fail and What to Do about It.* Princeton NJ: Princeton University Press.

Duffie, Darrell. 2014. "Is Keeping It Simple for Banks Stupid?" *Bloomberg View,* January 7, http://www.bloombergview.com/articles/2014-01-07/is-keeping-it-simple-for-banks-stupid-.

The Economist. 2012. "The Dodd-Frank act: Too big not to fail," February 18, http://www.economist.com/node/21547784.

Fleming, Michael J., and Asani Sarkar. 2014. "The Failure Resolution of Lehman Brothers." *Economic Policy Review* 20 (2), http://www.newyorkfed.org/research/epr/2014/1403flem.html.

French, Kenneth, et al. 2010a. "An Expedited Resolution Mechanism for Distressed Financial Firms: Regulatory Hybrid Securities." In *The Squam Lake Report: Fixing the Financial System.* Princeton NJ: Princeton University Press.

French, Kenneth, et al. 2010b. "Prime Brokers, Derivatives Dealers, and Runs." In *The Squam Lake Report: Fixing the Financial System.* Princeton NJ: Princeton University Press.

French, Kenneth, et al. 2011. "Reforming Money Market Funds." Manuscript, http://www.squamlakegroup.org/Squam%20Lake%20MMF%20January%2014%20Final.pdf.

Friedman, Milton. 1969. *The Optimum Quantity of Money and Other Essays.* Chicago: Aldine.

Gambacorta, Leonardo, and David Marques-Ibanez. 2011. "The bank lending channel: Lessons from the crisis." BIS Working Paper no. 345, http://www.bis.org/publ/work345.pdf.

Gertler, Mark, and Nobu Kiyotaki. 2011. "Financial Intermediation and Credit Policy in Business Cycle Analysis." In *Handbook of Monetary Economics.* Edited by Ben Friedman and Michael Woodford. Amsterdam: Elsevier.

Gorton, Gary. 2010. "E-coli, Repo Madness, and the Financial Crisis." *Business Economics* 45: 164–173.

Gorton, Gary, and Andrew Metrick. 2012. "Securitized Banking and the Run on Repo." *Journal of Financial Economics* 104: 425–451, http://dx.doi.org/10.1016/j.jfineco.2011.03.016.

Gorton, Gary, Stefan Lewellen, and Andrew Metrick. 2012. "The Safe-Asset Share." Manuscript.

Haldane, Andrew G. 2012. "The Dog and the Frisbee." Speech given at the Federal Reserve Bank of Kansas City's 36th economic policy symposium, "The Changing Policy Landscape," Jackson Hole, Wyoming, http://www.bankofengland.co.uk/publications/Documents/speeches/2012/speech596.pdf.

Hart, Oliver, and Luigi Zingales. 2011. "A New Capital Regulation for Large Financial Institutions." *American Law and Economics Review* 13: 453–490.

Ivashina, Victoria, and David S. Scharfstein. 2010. "Bank Lending During the Financial Crisis of 2008." *Journal of Financial Economics* 97: 319–338.

Jeanne, Olivier, and Anton Korinek. 2011. "Managing Credit Booms and Busts: A Pigouvian Taxation Approach." Working Paper, University of Maryland.

Kocherlakota, Narayana. 2010. "Taxing Risk and the Optimal Regulation of Financial Institutions." Economic Policy Paper 10–3, Federal Reserve Bank of Minneapolis.

Kotlikoff, Laurence J. 2010. *Jimmy Stewart Is Dead: Ending the World's Ongoing Financial Plague with Limited Purpose Banking*. New York: John Wiley & Sons.

Krishnamurthy, Arvind, and Annette Vissing-Jorgensen. 2013. "Short-term Debt and Financial Crises: What We Can Learn from U.S. Treasury Supply." Manuscript.

Lucchetti, Aaron, and Julie Steinberg. 2013. "Life on Wall Street Grows Less Risky." *Wall Street Journal*, September 9, http://online.wsj.com/news/articles /SB10001424127887324324404579044503704364242.

Ludvigson, Sydney, Charles Steindel, and Martin Lettau. 2002, "Monetary Policy Transmission through the Consumption-Wealth Channel." Federal Reserve Bank of New York *Economic Policy Review* (May): 117–133.

Office of Financial Research, US Department of the Treasury. 2013. "Asset Management and Financial Stability," http://www.treasury.gov/initiatives/ofr /research/Documents/OFR_AMFS_FINAL.pdf.

Perotti, Enrico, and Javier Suarez. 2011. "A Pigovian Approach to Liquidity Regulation." *International Journal of Central Banking* 7: 3–41.

Scott, Kenneth E., and John B. Taylor, eds. 2012. *Bankruptcy Not Bailout: A Special Chapter 14*. Stanford CA: Hoover Institution Press.

Summe, Kimberly Anne. 2010. "Lessons Learned from the Lehman Bankruptcy." In *Ending Government Bailouts as We Know Them*. Edited by Kenneth E. Scott, John B. Taylor, and George P. Shultz. Stanford CA: Hoover Institution Press.

Stein, Jeremy. 2012. "Monetary Policy as Financial Stability Regulation." *Quarterly Journal of Economics* 127 (1): 57–95, doi:10.1093/qje/qjr054.

Stein, Jeremy. 2014. "Incorporating Financial Stability Considerations into a Monetary Policy Framework." Speech, March 21, http://www.federalreserve .gov/newsevents/speech/stein20140321a.htm.

Taylor, John B. 2009. *Getting Off Track: How Government Actions and Interventions Caused, Prolonged, and Worsened the Financial Crisis*. Stanford CA: Hoover Institution Press.

CHAPTER 11

Financial Market Infrastructure
Too Important to Fail

Darrell Duffie

A major focus of this book is the development of failure resolution methods, including bankruptcy and administrative forms of insolvency management, that reduce to a manageable level the damage to the economy caused by any financial firm's failure. The alternative is the moral hazard of allowing a financial firm to believe that its failure would be dangerous to the financial system and that it would therefore likely receive significant government assistance when its solvency is suddenly threatened.

While orderly failure resolution is a desirable principle, I do not believe that it currently applies to all financial firms. In this chapter, I argue that failure resolution could not yet be safely applied to certain firms that operate key financial market infrastructures (FMIs) used for clearing over-the-counter derivatives or tri-party repurchase agreements (repos). The failure of key FMIs could indeed be dangerous to the financial system, even with the best available approaches to failure resolution.

By implication, a financial institution should not operate key financial market infrastructure backed by the same capital that supports much more discretionary forms of risk-taking, such as speculative trading or general lending. Not only would such a combination of activities expose a key FMI to losses caused elsewhere in the same financial institution, it would raise the firm's moral hazard based on the importance to the economy of the survival of the FMI and, thus, the entire firm.

Later in this chapter I will focus special attention on tri-party repo clearing, because this key FMI is currently operated in the United States by two large, complex banks that have significant latitude for risk-taking in their other lines of business. The failure of these banks could sharply

I am grateful for comments from many. All errors and opinions are my own, exclusively. For potential conflicts of interest, please see my web page at www.stanford.edu/~duffie/. E-mail remarks to duffie@stanford.edu

reduce access by the largest US broker-dealers to tri-party repo financing for their securities inventories. This would be dangerous to the financial system, possibly through the impact of fire sales of large quantities of securities. Every day, each of the larger US broker-dealers receives $100 billion or more in overnight financing that depends from an operational perspective on one of these two tri-party repo clearing banks.

Central clearing parties

Central clearing parties (CCPs) for derivatives are FMIs that guarantee derivatives payments to surviving clearing members of a CCP in the event of the failure of other clearing members. The potential loss exposures of some CCPs are extremely large in practice. These losses are intended to be covered by a "waterfall" of default management resources, including the initial margins and default guarantee funds of clearing members and the capital of the CCP.[1]

The failure of a CCP cannot be safely and effectively treated by currently available forms of bankruptcy or by the Dodd-Frank Act's Title II administrative failure resolution.

For treating the failure of a systemically important bank holding company (BHC), the Federal Deposit Insurance Corporation (FDIC 2013) has suggested that it would exercise its authority under Title II of the Dodd-Frank Act by using a "single point of entry" approach by which the BHC can in principle be quickly recapitalized through a conversion of some of its debt to equity. This single-point-of-entry approach does not apply to a CCP, which has almost no debt relative to the largest plausible losses that could arise through the failure of its clearing members. Once the capital of a CCP is wiped out, the tail risk is held by clearing members, who are generally themselves systemically important firms. Whether Title II failure resolution authority applies to CCPs is argued by DeCarlo and Steigerwald (2013). If Title II does apply, it is also uncertain whether the FDIC is prepared to use this authority for resolving a failing CCP.[2] No other avail-

---

1. For details, see the appendix of Duffie (2010), ISDA (2013), and Elliott (2013).

2. To my knowledge, the FDIC has not declared its intent in this area, for example in any response to a letter of November 10, 2010, from the general counsel of the CME Group Inc., Kathleen Cronin, to Ronald Feldman, executive secretary of the FDIC, requesting clarification regarding whether the CME is subject to the FDIC's Orderly Liquidation Authority under Title II of the Dodd-Frank Act.

able form of administrative failure resolution authority is evident. The US bankruptcy code is not currently adapted to safely resolve a failing CCP. Even a proposed new Chapter 14 of the code that is designed to treat a range of systemically important non-bank financial companies, as outlined by Jackson (2012), would be poorly adapted to the special case of CCPs.

Altogether, this absence of systemically effective failure resolution methods for US CCPs is an unsatisfactory situation and is contrary to recommendations by the Committee on Payment and Settlement Systems, Technical Committee of the International Organization of Securities Commissions (CPSS-IOSCO 2013), as well as official-sector guidance from the European Commission (2012) and the Financial Stability Board (2013).

A mitigating factor here is the restricted scope of risk-taking actions by a CCP, which cannot make general loans and has limited discretion over the manner in which it invests collateral. Lower discretion in risk-taking implies lower scope for moral hazard. Given the systemic importance and relatively limited scope for risk-taking of large CCPs, it is reasonable to treat them as "too important to fail." That said, CCPs do fail from time to time. For example, in October 1987 the clearing house of the Hong Kong Stock and Futures Exchange had a disorderly failure described by the Hong Kong Securities Review Committee (1988). Careful regulation, supervision, and failure planning should be used to reduce to the greatest possible extent the adverse impact of CCPs' failures. There is room for significant improvement in this area. For now, CCPs are too important to fail, as key regulators have acknowledged.[3]

---

3. In testimony provided in October 2013 to the Treasury Select Committee of the UK Parliament, Bank of England Deputy Governor Paul Tucker stated that "central counterparties have almost been mandated by the G20 leaders to be too important to fail. We need to make sure these institutions are sound and well-regulated and could recover in distress." http://www.telegraph.co.uk/finance/newsbysector/banksandfinance/10363688/Clearing-houses-are-the-biggest-risk-says-Tucker.html

In Dudley (2012), the president of the Federal Reserve Bank of New York, William C. Dudley, stated that "for the system to be safer it is not sufficient to ensure that trades are standardized and that they are mandated to be cleared through CCPs, but also it is necessary that CCPs be 'bullet proof.' They have to have the ability to perform and meet their obligations regardless of the degree of stress in the financial system and even if one or more of their participants were to fail in a disorderly manner." See http://www.newyorkfed.org/newsevents/speeches/2012/dud120322.html.

Tri-party repo clearing

A repurchase agreement, or repo, is the sale of a portfolio of securities combined with an agreement to repurchase that portfolio on a specific future date at a pre-arranged price. Abstracting from some legal distinctions concerning their bankruptcy treatment, repos are essentially collateralized loans. The cash provided at the purchase leg of a repo is effectively the proceeds of the loan; the repurchase price is the effective loan repayment amount; and the underlying securities are the loan collateral. Repos are normally over-collateralized in order to protect the cash provider from exposure to loss associated with a decline in the value of the collateral before the repo matures.

Broker-dealers finance substantial amounts of their securities inventories with tri-party repos (TPRs). The three parties involved in a TPR are the borrowing dealer, the cash lender, and an agent that assists with trade confirmations, settlements of the cash and securities transfers, the allocation of each dealer's collateral to its various lenders, and other forms of operational assistance. Copeland, Duffie, Martin, and McLaughlin (2012) provide details on the operation and systemic importance of the tri-party repo market. In the United States, two large banks, JPMorgan Chase and The Bank of New York Mellon, act as the agents for the vast majority of tri-party repos. Currently, a total of roughly $1.5 trillion of tri-party repos is handled by these two banks every day.

There is nothing in principle that requires a TPR agent bank to be exposed to losses on the repurchase agreements that it handles for borrowers and lenders, nor to expose repo counterparties to its own failure. In US practice, however, both directions of loss exposure exist and represent systemic risk.

The two large clearing banks offer intraday credit to a securities dealer between the times at which its previously arranged repos mature and the times at which new repos are funded by new cash investors. Until recently, this intraday credit provided by the two TPR agent banks was extensive, covering essentially all repos for a substantial part of each day. The Federal Reserve Bank of New York (2010) has encouraged a financial industry task force to dramatically reduce the extent of this intraday credit. Significant progress has been made toward this goal. But for now the TPR agent banks could nevertheless suffer significant losses in the most extreme plausible scenarios.

The other direction of exposure, of the repo borrower and lender to a potential failure of the TPR agent bank, is the main focus of my remarks here. If one of the two large TPR agent banks were to become illiquid or insolvent due to losses in some other line of business such as trading or general lending, a systemic crisis could be triggered by the potential discontinuation of its TPR clearing function.

First, the dealers who rely on the TPR agent bank for handling their repos could find themselves without the means to quickly obtain financing from other sources. They may not have operationally feasible backups, given their dependence on the specific infrastructure of their TPR agent banks. A fire sale of a large quantity of securities could follow. This could depress the prices of the securities, causing other levered investors to add to the aggregate magnitude of the fire sale, further reducing the securities prices, and possibly creating a general financial crisis. Begalle, Martin, McAndrews, and McLaughlin (2013) have examined the potential size of the fire sales relative to typical daily trade volumes, pointing to some large asset classes that could be heavily affected.

Second, in US practice, cash borrowers and lenders settle their TPR cash transfers in the form of deposits in the TPR agent banks. This exposes repo counterparties to a potential failure of their TPR agent bank, for example through losses to the TPR agent bank that stem from its unrelated lines of business. Even a perceived threat to the liquidity or solvency of an agent bank could provide a sufficient incentive for cash investors to fail to renew tri-party repos with dealers using that agent bank. This in turn could cause extreme stress to those dealers and possibly the earlier mentioned risk of fire sales.

The settlement of FMI transactions in commercial bank deposits is contrary to clear and well-justified principles set down by CPSS-IOSCO (2012), whose Principle 9 for FMI states:

An FMI should conduct its money settlements in central bank money where practical and available. If central bank money is not used, an FMI should minimize and strictly control the credit and liquidity risk arising from the use of commercial bank money.

CPSS-IOSCO (2012) continues by stating, "One way an FMI could minimize these risks is to limit its activities and operations to clearing and settlement and closely related processes." Applying the CPSS-IOSCO principles to US tri-party repo clearing practice, either a TPR agent bank should have no other significant lines of business or the agent bank should arrange for cash settlement in central bank deposits or in a separate "narrow bank" that is not exposed to losses from unrelated lines of business. While the current US practice of settling TPRs in the agents' commercial bank deposits may offer operational efficiencies, this benefit is trumped by the imperative to insulate system-critical FMIs and systemically important FMI users from unnecessary exposures.

When a large multi-line financial institution operates a systemically important FMI, as is current practice in the US tri-party repo market, its government and central bank are under pressure to forestall the failure of the financial institution in order to assure continuity of services provided by the FMI. In some cases, a government official should not stand rigidly on the principle that no such financial institution should receive extra assistance to avoid failure. By this point, it would be too late to prevent the too-important-to-fail moral hazard with a better design of the tri-party repo market architecture. The exigencies of preventing a significant financial crisis would take priority.

References

Begalle, Brian, Antoine Martin, James McAndrews, and Susan McLaughlin. 2013. "The Risk of Fire Sales in the Tri-Party Repo Market." Federal Reserve Bank of New York staff report 616. http://www.newyorkfed.org/research/staff_reports/sr616.html.

CPSS-IOSCO (Committee on Payment and Settlement Systems, Technical Committee of the International Organization of Securities Commissions). 2012. "Principles for Financial Market Infrastructures." Madrid: IOSCO. http://www.bis.org/publ/cpss101a.pdf.

CPSS-IOSCO. 2013. "Recovery of Financial Market Infrastructures." Consultative report. Madrid: IOSCO. http://www.bis.org/publ/cpss109.pdf. Comments: http://www.bis.org/publ/cpss103/comments.htm.

Copeland, Adam, Darrell Duffie, Antoine Martin, and Susan McLaughlin. 2012. "Key Mechanics of the U.S. Tri-Party Repo Market." *Economic Policy Review,* Federal Reserve Bank of New York. http://www.newyorkfed.org/research/epr/2012/1210cope.html.

DeCarlo, David, and Robert Steigerwald. 2013. "Orderly Liquidation under Title II of Dodd-Frank. Part I: Do Financial Market Utilities Qualify as 'Financial Companies'?" Draft working paper, Federal Reserve Bank of Chicago.

Dudley, William. 2012. "Reforming the OTC Derivatives Market." Remarks at the Harvard Law School's Symposium on Building the Financial System of the 21st Century, Armonk, New York, March. http://www.newyorkfed.org /newsevents/speeches/2012/dud120322.html.

Duffie, Darrell. 2010. *How Big Banks Fail and What to Do about It.* Princeton, NJ: Princeton University Press.

Elliott, David. 2013. "Central counterparty loss-allocation rules." Financial Stability Paper No. 20, Bank of England.

European Commission. 2012. "Consultation on a Possible Recovery and Resolution Framework for Financial Institutions other than Banks." Directorate General Internal Market and Services. Brussels: DG Internal Market and Services. http://ec.europa.eu/internal_market/consultations/2012/nonbanks /consultation-document_en.pdf.

FDIC. 2013. "The Resolution of Systemically Important Financial Institutions: The Single Point of Entry Strategy." Washington, DC: FDIC. http://www.fdic .gov/news/board/2013/2013-12-10_notice_dis-b_fr.pdf.

Federal Reserve Bank of New York. 2010. "Tri-Party Repo Infrastructure Reform." New York: Federal Reserve Bank of New York. http://www.newyork fed.org/banking/tpr_infr_reform.html.

Financial Stability Board. 2013. "Application of the Key Attributes of Effective Resolution Regimes to Non-Bank Financial Institutions." Consultative document. Basel, Switzerland: FSB.

Hong Kong Securities Review Committee. 1988. "The Operation and Regulation of the Hong Kong Securities Industry." Hong Kong: Securities Review Committee.

ISDA (International Swaps and Derivatives Association). 2013. "CCP Loss Allocation at the end of the Waterfall." New York: ISDA.

Jackson, Thomas. 2012. "Bankruptcy Code Chapter 14: A Proposal." In *Bankrucpty Not Bailout, A Special Chapter 14,* edited by Kenneth Scott and John Taylor, 25–72. Stanford CA: Hoover Institution Press.

CHAPTER 12

"Too Big to Fail" from an Economic Perspective

Steve Strongin

Strengthening the resilience of TBTF banks

In assessing the resiliency today of the biggest US banks, the G-SIFIs[1]—those that are often considered "too big to fail" (TBTF)—it is important to disentangle the progress that has been made in shoring up their safety and soundness since 2008 from the lingering concerns and prejudices regarding their riskiness. As a community, we have required more and better capital and have implemented more conservative risk-management practices at the biggest banks, while we have at the same time reduced our belief in the power of markets and incentives to manage any remaining risk. We have increased supervisory oversight of the biggest banks even as we have continued to assume the likely failure of this supervision. We have better harmonized international information flows, communication, and approaches to critical safety measures beyond any historical expectation. But we have simultaneously become fixated on the remaining areas of imperfect cross-border coordination. Our attention, in short, has been drawn to the points of maximum difficulty, rather than to those of greatest economic importance.

We should instead view improvements to the safety and soundness of the US G-SIFIs through the prism of economic importance. In our view, doing so demonstrates that they are far more resilient to economic shocks

---

This paper was co-authored by Amanda Hindlian, Sandra Lawson, Jorge Murillo, Koby Sadan, and Balakrishna Subramanian, all of Goldman Sachs. The authors would like to thank Richard Ramsden, Charlie Himmelberg, Louise Pitt, Conor Fitzgerald, Jehan Mahmood, Daniel Paris, and Ron Perrotta for their significant contributions to this paper.

1. The Financial Stability Board identifies annually a list of Global Systemically Important Financial Institutions (G-SIFIs) that are subject to capital surcharges because of their size and interconnectedness. There are eight US G-SIFIs as of November 2013: Bank of America, Bank of New York Mellon, Citigroup, Goldman Sachs, JPMorgan Chase, Morgan Stanley, State Street, and Wells Fargo.

today than is widely believed. This is particularly easy to see once we make two subtle modifications to the prevailing narrative.

First, a change in perspective: rather than focusing on the most challenging remaining obstacles to the resolution of US G-SIFIs—like derivatives and liquidity—we should emphasize instead the multiple lines of defense that have been strengthened or newly created to protect against their failure in the first place. We examine the resilience of the banks across each line of defense in sequential order. This is relevant because it is far more economically meaningful to fix the first and second lines of defense than to fix the fifth, unless the first few lines of defense are systematically ineffective. As we show, the improvements already made to the first two lines of defense—equity capital and the incentives it creates—have in fact been significant and robust. This makes the next lines of defense—the "debt shield" and the incentives it creates—unlikely to be used in the "normal" course. Instead, these additional lines of defense would only be necessary in inherently low-probability states characterized by unusual events and extreme conditions. We think they should be evaluated in this light, rather than as part of the "normal" resolution process.

Second, a shift in terminology: rather than using standard statistical notions like confidence intervals to measure resilience, we focus instead on the more easily interpreted notion of "mean time between failures." This concept enables us to assess the likely frequency of failures at US G-SIFIs—measured in years—across each line of defense. Using a measure of years makes it clear that increasing the mean time between failures from twenty years to seventy years, for example, is more economically important and less theoretical than extending the mean time between failures from seventy years to 120 years. Thus we believe the concept of mean time between failures lends itself to easy assessments of the cumulative impact of various regulatory measures, and their relative economic importance, in ways that other frameworks don't.

When US G-SIFIs are viewed within this framework, we believe it is possible to demonstrate—using a model based on assumptions that conform to standard market assessments and normal pricing—that the likely frequency of their failure has shifted from years (frighteningly few before the crisis for banks with weaker capital positions) to several decades under the new capital rules. Additionally, the likely frequency of failure has moved even further—from several decades to centuries—when the new improvements in incentives and supervision that drive voluntary recapitalization are taken into account.[2] Our work shows that the anticipated "debt shield" (long-term debt that can be forcibly converted to equity in a crisis) would also maintain mean time between failures at centuries rather than decades. Unlike incentives, the debt shield would only come into play in the case of a massive firm-specific failure or a historically severe macro-stress event. Either would require extraordinary—not normal course—regulatory responses. Also unlike incentives (which some distrust), the debt shield has the added benefit of protecting the government by ensuring that there are sufficient private-sector resources available to absorb losses even in such unusual circumstances.

Distrust of figures like centuries between failures is natural, but the statistical frameworks we use to model bank failures incorporate the notion that models do fail. Of course our methods may not prove sufficient, as prior statistical analyses have sometimes failed to anticipate the potential scope and size of unanticipated events. But the failure of the model would

2. By providing regulators with a readily available source of private-sector capital that can be used to recapitalize a failed bank, the debt shield reduces the cost of regulatory intervention and thus increases incentives for banks to manage their capital conservatively. In theory, the managerial incentives created by the existence of "bail-in" debt are sufficiently strong that the risk of a gradual deterioration into severe distress is essentially reduced to zero. This is because a bank faced with losses would, whenever feasible, respond by reducing debt or raising equity to maintain a target leverage ratio. Thus, as a practical matter, the only losses that would be large enough to push a bank into severe distress would be losses arising from "jump risk." This intuition can be formalized in a model designed for the pricing of contingent capital bonds that convert to equity on highly dilutive terms for existing shareholders (see, for example, "Pricing Contingent Capital Bonds: Incentives Matter," October 2012, working paper, Charles P. Himmelberg and Sergey Tsyplakov). This line of reasoning suggests that the risks that need to be considered when evaluating the default risk of well-incentivized financial institutions are those that result in large, discontinuous "jump" events. Moreover, like well-structured contingent capital securities, the debt shield creates incentives for shareholders of a failing bank to recapitalize the bank during the early signs of distress. Well-structured contingent capital also creates these incentives by "triggering" early, at a point when significant intrinsic value in the bank remains, and by imposing extremely high dilution rates for existing shareholders (e.g., 90 percent or more). Although the debt shield may trigger later than well-structured contingent capital might, it creates similarly strong incentives for shareholders to recapitalize because it threatens to fully dilute existing shareholders. This intuition is also discussed in "Pricing Contingent Capital Bonds: Incentives Matter," http://www.efmaefm.org/0EFMAMEETINGS/EFMA%20ANNUAL%20MEETINGS/2012-Barcelona/papers/EFMA2012_0599_fullpaper.pdf.

of necessity be part of a sequence of extraordinary events. The regulatory progress made to date suggests that even such extreme events could be better addressed than critics would suspect, although it is of course true that unprecedented events can only be anticipated to a limited extent. But to assume that all frameworks fail no matter how they are designed, simply because some models do fail, leaves little hope and even less guidance as to how to proceed.

First things first: getting the first line of defense right

The first line of defense is the most important in our view, yet the least discussed: the regulatory changes that have already been implemented to require more and better capital. Capital provides a buffer to absorb unexpected or exceptional losses on a going-concern basis. Accordingly, appropriate capital buffers should be sufficient to prevent banks from failing even when losses are at the tail end of a "normal" probability distribution. We believe the combination of regulatory reforms, market pressures, and industry efforts have significantly improved the capital positions of the US G-SIFIs since the 2008 crisis.

In 2007, the six largest US banks (excluding Goldman Sachs and Morgan Stanley, which as broker-dealers at the time were not required to disclose risk-weighted assets) had loss-absorbing capital (common equity, preferred, and trust preferred) of only 6.2 percent of aggregate risk-weighted assets (RWA). Of this, just 4.6 percent was tangible common equity, which was the sole part of the capital structure that could truly absorb losses without extraordinary action. Other classes of capital that were considered loss-absorbing at the time, including preferred and trust preferred shares, turned out not to be: in reality they could only absorb losses through special actions that required significant stress and time to execute and which would massively dilute the common equity shareholders whose interests the bank management represented.[3] A low effective common equity base created lags in the recapitalization process as well as poor incentives for common equity shareholders.

Today, even before Basel III is fully implemented, the eight US G-SIFIs (including Goldman Sachs and Morgan Stanley, which are now banks)

---

3. See "Trust Preferred Securities and the Capital Strength of Banking Organizations," *Supervisory Insights*, Winter 2010, FDIC, http://www.fdic.gov /regulations/examinations/supervisory/insights/siwin10/trust.html.

have on average aggregate loss-absorbing capital worth 13.1 percent of RWA, as we show in figure 12.1. Of this, 11.6 percent is tangible common equity—more than twice the pre-crisis figure. Risk weights are also significantly higher under Basel III, which makes risk-weighted capital measures more robust today and thus further improves banks' ability to absorb losses. This level of capital is more than adequate even for a stress scenario as severe as the one embedded in the Federal Reserve's 2012 Comprehensive Capital Analysis and Review (CCAR) exam. Our banking analysts estimate that the US G-SIFIs could withstand a CCAR-like shock today and still remain above—in many cases well above—a 7 percent tier 1 common equity minimum.

While capital ratios are clearly a useful and important metric, they do not translate easily into a measure of the likely frequency of bank failures. As a more accessible alternative, we examine banks' improved resiliency through the lens of "mean time between failures." The appendix describes our methodology in detail. Our analysis suggests that the US G-SIFIs' current capital position should be sufficient to cover losses even in a "once-in-every-several-decades" shock. This is a vast improvement over the "once-in-less-than-a-single-decade" frequency that prevailed prior to 2008 for banks that maintained weaker capital positions (see figure 12.2).

Equity-driven incentives: a stronger second line of defense

The second line of defense also involves capital—not the quantum or quality itself but the incentives it creates for banks' shareholders and management to recapitalize early in a stressed situation, before losses can spiral into outright failure and the bank is put into resolution.

Under the old rules, it was possible for shareholders of an "adequately" capitalized bank to have virtually no remaining intrinsic equity value even relatively early in a stressed situation. This is because starting equity levels simply weren't sufficiently high or of sufficiently robust quality to absorb significant losses. Faced with severe stress, the incentives for both bank management and shareholders (who are the primary source of discipline on the bank's behavior) were to increase risk in hopes of recovering value—because if the only value you have left is option value, the best way to maximize that value is to increase volatility. Moreover, shareholders were not at risk of losing their equity stakes and the optionality that equity entailed until the point of bankruptcy itself—which would only occur if the bank's attempt to "earn its way out of trouble" failed. Bank

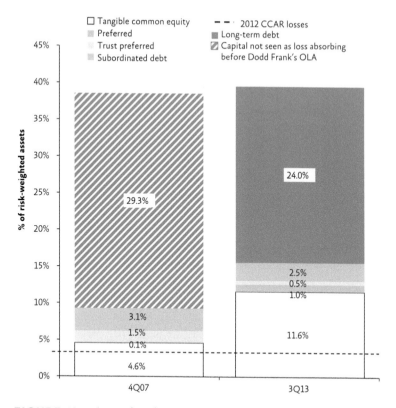

FIGURE 12.1 Loss-absorbency among US G-SIFI banks has risen sharply since the crisis

Note: Aggregate regulatory financial data is based on Basel I definitions. Long-term debt is defined as all other borrowed money, which is largely senior debt. US G-SIFI banks are Bank of America, Bank of New York Mellon, Citigroup, Goldman Sachs, JP Morgan Chase, Morgan Stanley, State Street, and Wells Fargo. As broker-dealers before the crisis, Goldman Sachs and Morgan Stanley were not required to disclose risk-weighted assets. They are therefore excluded from the 4Q2007 data but, because they are banks today, are included in the 3Q2013 data. Excluding Goldman Sachs and Morgan Stanley from 3Q2013 would result in tangible common equity of 11.2 percent, preferred equity of 0.9 percent, trust preferred of 0.4 percent, subordinated debt of 2.4 percent, and long-term debt of 20.5 percent. The CCAR loss calculation includes results from Goldman Sachs and Morgan Stanley.
Source: Federal Reserve, SNL Financial, Goldman Sachs Global Investment Research.

Pre-crisis expected frequency of undercapitalization	# of years
Frequency of falling below 4% tier 1 capital for well capitalized banks in 4Q2007	41
Frequency of falling below 4% tier 1 capital for less well capitalized banks in 4Q2007	7
Post-crisis expected frequency of failure	**# of years**
Frequency of falling below 5.5% tier 1 capital	39
Frequency of falling below 4% tier 1 capital	56
Frequency of wiping out equity	86
Frequency of wiping out equity and long-term debt worth 12% of RWA	358
Frequency of wiping out equity and long-term debt worth 16% of RWA	563

FIGURE 12.2 Bank failures have become far less likely after the crisis

Note: We use a decline in tier 1 common equity below 4 percent as a threshold for regulatory action, reflecting market expectations prior to the crisis. We also include a 5.5 percent threshold for the post-crisis period because we believe market expectations have shifted in the wake of Dodd-Frank's Orderly Liquidation Authority, putting the expected threshold closer to 5.5 percent. In 4Q2007, the relatively better-capitalized banks had 6.6 percent tier 1 common equity, on average, while the relatively less-well-capitalized banks had 5.1 percent tier 1 common equity, on average. We assume a tier 1 common equity starting point of 8 percent in the post-crisis analysis. Our post-crisis base-case assumptions are in the appendix.
Source: Goldman Sachs Global Investment Research.

management faced another troubling incentive: taking a public action like cutting dividends to strengthen the balance sheet would likely have been seen as a signal that an already tenuous capital position was weakening further.

This dynamic played out in big banks' behavior during the 2008 financial crisis. Banks that entered the financial crisis in a position of relative capital weakness—the very banks that should have acted promptly to strengthen their balance sheets—in fact delayed taking steps to do so until their capital positions had deteriorated even more significantly. In contrast, banks that entered the crisis in a position of relative capital strength did not delay; they improved their balance sheets while their capital ratios were still relatively robust.

Specifically, as we show in figure 12.3, banks that entered the crisis in a weaker capital position recapitalized only when their capital ratios were roughly 150 basis points lower, on average, than those of their better-capitalized peers. And the less-well-capitalized banks cut dividends only when their capital ratios were roughly 120 basis points lower, on average, than those of their better-capitalized peers.

Company name	Capital ratio during the financial crisis (Tier 1 common / RWA)									Capital ratio prior to first capital raise	Capital ratio prior to first dividend cut
	4Q07	1Q08	2Q08	3Q08	4Q08	1Q09	2Q09	3Q09	4Q09		
Citigroup	4.9%	4.2%	4.4%	3.7%	2.3%	2.2%	2.8%	9.1%	9.7%	4.2%	2.3%
Bank of America	4.9%	4.6%	4.8%	4.2%	4.6%	4.5%	6.9%	7.2%	6.6%	4.8%	4.6%
National City	5.1%	4.9%	4.7%	9.0%	–	–	–	–	–	4.7%	4.9%
Wachovia	5.3%	4.8%	4.8%	4.1%	–	–	–	–	–	4.8%	4.8%
PNC	5.4%	5.7%	5.7%	5.7%	4.8%	4.9%	5.3%	5.5%	6.0%	4.9%	4.9%
U.S. Bancorp	5.6%	5.7%	5.6%	5.7%	5.1%	5.4%	6.7%	6.8%	6.8%	5.4%	5.1%
Wells Fargo	6.5%	6.5%	6.3%	6.3%	3.1%	3.1%	4.5%	5.1%	6.4%	6.3%	3.1%
JPMorgan Chase	7.0%	6.9%	6.3%	6.3%	6.5%	6.9%	7.7%	8.2%	8.8%	6.3%	6.5%
Washington Mutual	7.2%	6.9%	8.5%		–					6.9%	7.2%
Less capital at start of crisis	5.1%	4.9%	4.9%	5.4%	3.9%	3.9%	5.0%	8.2%	7.4%	4.7%	4.3%
More capital at start of crisis	6.6%	6.5%	6.7%	6.1%	4.9%	5.1%	6.3%	6.7%	7.3%	6.2%	5.5%

Commercial banks & thrifts — Less capital / More capital

= common dividend cut   = common equity raised   = bank sold or failed

FIGURE 12.3 During the crisis the better capitalized banks were more aggressive in strengthening their capital than the less well capitalized banks

Note: Common dividend cut defined as a quarterly dividend reduced to $0.00–$0.10.

Source: Company data, SNL Financial, FactSet, Goldman Sachs Global Investment Research

Although stand-alone broker-dealers were not required to disclose risk-weighted measures of capital during this period, their leverage (defined as tangible assets over tangible common equity) tells a similar story, as we show in figure 12.4.

The aggregate economic impact of these incentives is telling. Compare the economic losses sustained by banks that failed or received special assistance during the crisis to the impact of their capital actions, like share buybacks and dividends. As we show in figure 12.5, the depletion of capital from voluntary capital actions was nearly twice as large as the impact of net economic losses—even during the worst economic downturn in decades. Merrill Lynch looks like an exception, with outsized net economic losses. However, it should be noted that Merrill Lynch posted a significant portion of these losses in its last quarter as an independent company, likely in anticipation of its announced acquisition by Bank of America. If Merrill Lynch is excluded from the analysis, the ratio of capital depletion from voluntary actions to net economic losses is far higher—at fourteen times.

The new capital rules ensure that all banks have strong incentives to behave like the better-capitalized banks did during the last crisis. With higher and more robust common equity levels as a starting point, equity holders should still maintain significant intrinsic value even in a highly stressed environment. This gives them incentives to protect that value by forcing management to quickly and aggressively strengthen their balance sheets. Their ability to exercise market discipline is reinforced by the ongoing CCAR process, which makes it far easier for equity holders to detect incipient problems than was possible in the past. The CCAR process also makes it notably easier for regulators to force actions should these incentives prove insufficient to motivate the private sector. As we noted earlier, these incentives should only strengthen our finding that the biggest US banks are far more resilient today, moving the mean time between failures from several decades under the new capital rules alone to centuries under the combination of these capital rules and their associated incentives.

The likely effectiveness of these incentives may be easy to dismiss in the current environment of extreme skepticism about the effectiveness of market discipline without strong regulatory oversight. But even the incentives that existed before the crisis were sufficient for the biggest US banks to recapitalize in 2008, as long as they had a reasonable (albeit relatively low by today's standards) level of common equity. Well-capitalized banks

Leverage during the financial crisis (tangible assets / tangible common equity)

Company name	4Q07	1Q08	2Q08	3Q08	4Q08	1Q09	2Q09	3Q09	4Q09	Leverage prior to first dividend cut	Leverage prior to first capital raise
Stand-alone broker dealers											
Merrill Lynch (More levered)	45.0z	50.4x	59.6x	35.5x	77.0x	–	–	–	–	–	37.0x
Lehman Brothers (More levered)	38.8x	43.0x	40.7x	37.8x	–	–	–	–	–	–	43.0x
Morgan Stanley (Less levered)	38.4x	37.3x	33.8x	31.1x	24.7x	23.0x	22.1x	25.5x	25.4x	24.7x	23.0x
Bear Stearns (Less levered)	37.6x	37.5x	–	–	–	–	–	–	–	–	–
Goldman Sachs (Less levered)	30.7x	32.9x	28.4x	27.7x	20.6x	22.0x	17.3x	16.4x	14.3x	–	27.7x
More levered to start the crisis	40.7x	43.6x	44.7x	34.7x	50.8x	23.0x	22.1x	25.5x	25.4x	34.4x	34.4x
Less levered to start the crisis	34.1x	35.2x	28.4x	27.7x	20.6x	22.0x	17.3x	16.4x	14.3x	27.7x	27.7x
Commercial banks & thrifts											
Citigroup (More levered)	29.6x	33.1x	30.9x	34.1x	43.6x	41.5x	34.8x	16.2x	14.4x	43.6x	33.1x
Bank of America (More levered)	25.3x	27.1x	27.0x	31.7x	30.2x	28.2x	19.7x	19.3x	19.9x	30.2x	27.0x
Wachovia (More levered)	23.5x	26.3x	27.4x	34.2x	–	–	–	–	–	27.4x	26.3x
Washington Mutual (More levered)	23.1x	26.5x	19.6x	–	–	–	–	–	–	26.5x	26.5x
JPMorgan Chase (Less levered)	19.5x	20.0x	21.3x	24.1x	24.5x	22.6x	20.1x	18.8x	18.2x	24.5x	21.3x
PNC (Less levered)	18.7x	20.1x	19.9x	23.4x	29.3x	27.1x	24.5x	20.7x	19.1x	27.1x	27.1x
U.S. Bancorp (Less levered)	18.5x	18.9x	19.1x	19.4x	26.3x	23.5x	18.1x	17.0x	17.6x	26.3x	23.5x
National City (Less levered)	18.1x	19.6x	21.0x	11.1x	–	–	–	–	–	19.6x	21.0x
Wells Fargo (Less levered)	16.3x	16.6x	17.1x	18.2x	28.2x	27.7x	21.4x	18.0x	15.4x	27.7x	18.2x
More levered to start the crisis	24.2x	26.6x	25.2x	31.0x	32.8x	30.7x	24.9x	18.1x	17.5x	30.4x	26.8x
Less levered to start the crisis	17.9x	18.8x	19.3x	18.0x	27.9x	26.1x	21.3x	18.6x	17.4x	25.1x	22.4x

Legend:
⬭ = common dividend cut ▢ = common equity raised ▰ = bank sold or failed

FIGURE 12.4 During the crisis, less-levered firms strengthened their capital more aggressively than more-highly-levered peers did

Note: Common dividend cut defined as a quarterly dividend reduced to $0.00–$0.10.

Source: Company data, SNL Financial, FactSet, Goldman Sachs Global Investment Research

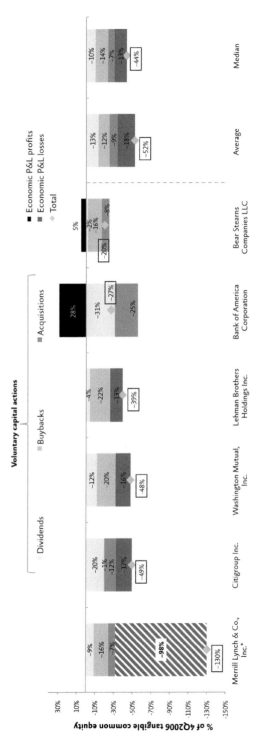

FIGURE 12.5 The depletion of capital from voluntary capital actions was nearly twice as large as the impact of economic losses during the crisis

*Merrill Lynch posted outsized net economic losses in 4Q2008, likely in anticipation of its acquisition by Bank of America in the following quarter.

Note: calculated as dividends, buybacks and net income (ex goodwill writedowns which is not a capital event) from 2007 through the time of failure or receiving special assistance

Source: SNL Financial, FactSet, Goldman Sachs Global Investment Research

did recapitalize in 2008, despite poor and inconsistent public disclosures along with fragmented and relatively modest regulatory oversight. With today's far stronger capital standards, better disclosures, more rigorous supervisory practices, and the public nature of the CCAR process, these incentives should be thought of as highly robust despite any (quite natural) lingering skepticism.

Using plain English to assess the need for the debt shield

Before discussing the next line of defense—the debt shield—it is important to understand the math behind the bond pricing models that we use to assess bank resiliency. Doing so enables us to get a better sense of the actual level of uncertainty surrounding bank failures and associated losses. This is important because, as our mean time between failures assessment shows, the debt shield should only be needed in the most extreme situations, which makes mathematical assessments inherently imprecise.

Bond models rely on a variety of highly technical approaches and jargon, and they sometimes seem designed to appear more scientific and precise than is possible given the underlying level of uncertainty. To pierce this veil, we translate a bit of the jargon back into everyday English.

These models typically begin by assuming that prices move up and down according to the observable data. As long as banks are well-capitalized at the start, are correctly incentivized to recapitalize when capital deteriorates, and are subject to price movements that are in line with these models, nothing interesting should ever happen! And if banks don't default, no special resolution powers are needed.

But reality is different. Banks do fail, and bond markets do price the possibility of failure. Models address this fact by introducing a second mathematical concept called "jump-to-default." Jump-to-default is essentially the assumption that at times models fail and the totally unexpected happens: in an instant the bank and its investors find themselves in a state they would never have reached in the normal course. The jump-to-default scenario is necessarily marked by limited data and extreme outcomes.

The first two lines of defense against bank failure—stronger common equity capital and the associated incentives for early recapitalization—should be sufficiently robust to address the ordinary "once-in-several-decades" events. Thus the only time the resolution apparatus should be used is in the jump-to-default scenario. The idea that the resolution process for US G-SIFIs will almost certainly never be used in the "normal course," and that it should instead be understood as part of an "extraordinary" process, appears to have been lost in the broader discussion, as regulators and others have sought to make every possible type of failure addressable in the normal course.

The extraordinary shocks that could drive a jump-to-default can be split into two categories: idiosyncratic or bank-specific and macroeconomic.

The idiosyncratic or bank-specific failure requires a massive failure of control, akin to fraud, that goes undetected for an extended period. Because US G-SIFIs are highly regulated and supervised today in ways that aren't comparable to the past, relevant historical examples of this sort of failure are hard to come by. AIG and Enron provide a flavor, but they too fall short of a direct comparison to today's US G-SIFIs given the lack of regulation and supervision to which those firms were subject at the time.

Bank-specific failures by their very nature typically cannot be prevented by things like capital buffers and liquidity ratios. Such failures are characterized either by a complete misunderstanding of the underlying risk being taken or by significant fraud. Perversely, more capital and liquidity may only provide additional fuel that enables the problem to grow larger for longer. This could make unwinding it that much more difficult, and the economic and market damage that much harder to offset, once the failure is finally identified. This type of failure can only be addressed by robust supervision; the good news is that this is one of the areas of particular improvement since the crisis.

In the context of resolution, it is critical to understand how regulators would likely address such a failure. While certain parts of the bank may need to be spun out and liquidation may ultimately be required, orderly resolution of the firm itself wouldn't necessarily be regulators' first concern. Instead, the risk associated with the failure of the bank would likely lie in the broader markets. This is because banks that fail under these idiosyncratic circumstances tend to have large net market positions—and the unwinding of these positions tends to be highly destabilizing to markets. Thus regulators would likely shift their focus to maintaining market stability, which might require extraordinary steps that aren't strictly resolution-related.

The second possible path to jump-to-default is an extreme macroeconomic shock. Under the changes to the capital rules that are already in place—Basel III and the US CCAR process—today's US G-SIFIs have sufficient capital to weather any historical macroeconomic shock, and with a significant margin of error. This means that a macroeconomic crisis severe enough to generate a resolution requiring use of the debt shield—rather than a voluntary recapitalization—would need to be unprecedented: a shock significantly larger than either 2008 or the Great Depression. This in turn makes it all the more likely that this would be a severe systemic crisis.

Calculating the probability of such an extreme macroeconomic shock is clearly subject to a high degree of uncertainty, especially because there is necessarily no appropriate historical data. While we make a more technical assessment in the appendix, our estimates suggest that the probability is less than "once in every few hundred years." Such estimates should be viewed as inherently imprecise, as there is clearly insufficient data to have tremendous confidence in any data-based estimation (this is the typical problem in assessing highly unlikely events for which there is no observable history, but for which risk analysis is needed). Regardless, it is clear that the type of macroeconomic shock that would trigger use of the debt shield, given the new capital and supervisory structures, would be unprecedented. As such, central banks as well as governments would need to respond in an extreme fashion, invoking their extraordinary powers as part of an extraordinary process.

The debt shield: a new third line of defense

We believe the new third line of defense—the debt shield—needs to be thought of in this context, as a tool to be used in extraordinary circumstances rather than in the "normal course." The first two lines of defense—common equity and the associated incentives for recapitalization—would be used in the normal course and the debt shield would be invoked only if those failed, whether due to a bank-specific failure or to a macroeconomic shock. Even in extreme circumstances, the debt shield is designed to provide the added benefit of sufficient private-sector financial resources to protect the government from losses.

The debt shield is an integral part of the Single Point of Entry (SPOE) approach to resolution, which provides regulators with a robust and systemically safer answer to the question of "what next?" in extraordinary circumstances. It makes a critical distinction between "capital liabilities," which are principally long-term unsecured debt issued by the bank holding company, and "operating liabilities," which include short-term funding and derivatives contracts and are overwhelmingly transactions of the operating companies rather than of the holding company. SPOE effectively makes operating liabilities senior to capital liabilities by allowing regulators to put a troubled bank's holding company, but not its operating entities, into resolution. Equity would be written to zero and some or all of the holding company's long-term unsecured debt would be converted to equity in a bridge bank; the bridge would use this new equity to recapitalize its material operating subsidiaries. Shareholders and bondholders of the holding company would bear losses—not taxpayers—but counterparties of the operating companies would not, and customers of the bank's systemically important functions (payments processing, clearing, etc.) would not be affected.

SPOE requires banks to have a thick tranche of loss-absorbing debt—a debt shield—to make the recapitalization work. The Federal Reserve has indicated its intention to propose a rule requiring the holding companies of US G-SIFIs to issue long-term debt that is explicitly subject to "bail-in." (While commonly referred to as the debt shield, it is possible that the buffer may include equity above the regulatory minimum.) The debt shield requirement is anticipated to be worth at least 12 percent of RWA, although some estimate this figure at closer to 16 percent (we use both figures in our mean-time-between-failures analysis but assume a base case of 12 percent).

Like today's common equity position, the debt shield also improves incentives—especially for regulators. SPOE sets up a system by which a stressed bank can be recapitalized even under the difficult market conditions that would be associated with an extreme event, without disrupting fragile short-term funding markets or the bank's systemically important operating functions. This incentivizes regulators to act early and decisively rather than wait to see whether problems can be resolved in time. The debt shield also makes it easier for regulators to provide emergency liquidity to operating subsidiaries by providing an extraordinarily strong cushion of capital between the holding company and operating subs. This in turn allows the FDIC to use all available collateral at the operating subsidiary for collateral at the Federal Reserve's discount window, as the FDIC will not need to worry about the need for additional loss absorbency. It should also make it much easier to maintain access to private-sector liquidity. The key in both cases is that the FDIC does not encumber or threaten to encumber operating-company assets.

Along with these new regulatory incentives come even more incentives for shareholders: if they don't voluntarily recapitalize the bank, regulators can forcibly do so. In doing so, they would eliminate shareholders' equity while significant value remains (given the expectation that regulators will trigger resolution well before equity reaches zero—though some of this value might be partially recouped through the grant of warrants). This threat should bolster the discipline equity holders will already exert over banks as a result of the stronger capital structure.

Again looking through the lens of mean time between failures, our analysis suggests that the debt shield requirement, on top of today's common equity, would reduce the frequency of failures—or the point at which both the full equity and the entire debt shield are depleted—to centuries. How many centuries is at best a guess, but it is clear that additional measures to protect against extraordinary failures would only add a marginal measure of safety, potentially at significant cost.

Conclusion: maintaining economic perspective

When the resilience of US G-SIFIs is viewed from the perspective of the lines of defense that have been enhanced or newly created since 2008 to protect against their failure, it is easy to see that the US financial system is far safer today than it was in the past. And while there are clearly some substantive issues that need to be solved for resolution to work well in practice, such as derivatives and liquidity, these remaining problems should be put in appropriate economic perspective.

As our analysis shows, the likelihood of resolution—rather than voluntary recapitalization—is low in the "normal course." It is instead only likely to be employed in extraordinary circumstances. Thus we believe any solutions that enable resolution to work better but that are costly to implement should be carefully and skeptically evaluated relative to their associated benefits. Doing otherwise would weigh on the ability of the banking system to provide the services that are vital to economic growth over the next several decades, in exchange for preventing the chance that a "once-in-several-centuries" storm emerges.

Appendix: modeling the frequency of bank failures

To demonstrate how the improved equity capital position, the debt shield, and their related incentives are likely to reduce the frequency of bank failures, we have constructed a model that calculates mean time between failures under various scenarios. This model uses assumptions that conform to standard market expectations and normal pricing and we demonstrate sensitivity analyses around these assumptions where appropriate.

Our model uses a probability distribution approach because the estimated frequency of failures is a function of the probability of different levels of losses. The higher the probability of losses that are severe enough to deplete equity and loss-absorbing debt, the more frequent the failures; conversely, the lower the probability of such losses, the less frequent the failures. In normal times, the probability distribution should be akin to a log-normal distribution. In times of systemic financial distress, the probability distribution should provide for more extreme results, such as a log-T distribution with "fat tails," as we show in figure 12.6.

We consider these two distributions equivalent to two economic states. The first is a "normal" or "non-crisis" state, in which financial markets have low to medium volatility. The second is a "systemic financial crisis" environment, in which several financial institutions are under stress simultaneously and financial markets experience high volatility. We assume that for any given period of time, a bank will have some probability of being in either environment; it must always be in either one or the other.

Our base case assumes that a theoretical bank has tier 1 common equity of 8 percent of RWA and a debt shield of 12 percent of RWA, for total loss-absorbing capital of 20 percent of RWA. We assume that the bank's bonds default when regulators put the holding company into resolution, modeled in our base case as the point at which tier 1 common equity falls below 5.5 percent of RWA. We also examine a decline in tier 1 common equity below 4 percent of RWA as a less conservative point at which regulators might put the holding company into resolution. Because assets are sold over time in a SPOE resolution, the implied losses do not include any liquidation costs. We assume that a systemic financial crisis environment occurs every twenty years, given historical experience since 1900 that suggests systemic financial crises have occurred in the United States every few decades.[4]

To model the "normal" or non-crisis environment, our base case assumes a log-normal probability distribution with a mean of zero, asset volatility of 1 percent, and expected losses on bonds given default of

---

4. For a discussion of historical banking crises, see Carmen M. Reinhart and Kenneth S. Rogoff, *This Time Is Different: Eight Centuries of Financial Folly* (Princeton, NJ: Princeton University Press, 2009).

Probability densities used for the crisis and non-crisis economic environments

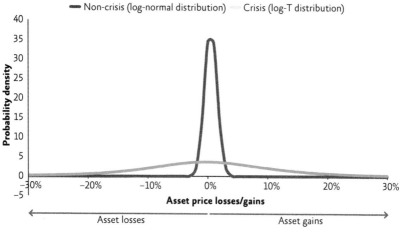

Magnified probability desnity for asset losses greater than 2% (the "tail")

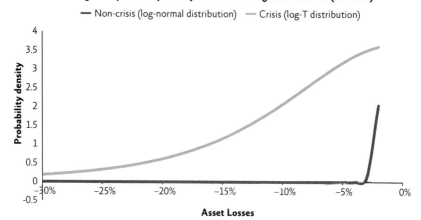

FIGURE 12.6 The log-T distribution better accounts for extreme losses than does the log-normal distribution

Source: Goldman Sachs Global Investment Research.

10 percent. To model the "systemic financial crisis" environment, our base case assumes a T-distribution with three degrees of freedom ("fat tails"), a mean of zero, and expected losses on bonds given default of 30 percent, which translates to maximum asset volatility of 10 percent.

We also validate our results using CDS pricing. Because investors use CDS as protection on bond instruments, the CDS price represents the cost of insurance and thus the market's expectation of both the likelihood of default and the associated losses. And because the full price of CDS also reflects characteristics of the CDS instrument itself, such as liquidity, our assumption that the price of CDS reflects in its entirety the market's expected loss on the bonds is inherently conservative. We incorporate CDS information by confirming that expected maximum losses are no greater than 100 basis points (average CDS prices for the six largest US banks over the past three months). In our base case scenario, expected maximum losses do not breach 100 basis points and are thus validated.

We model how frequently losses would be expected to deplete certain levels of loss-absorbing capital under these base-case assumptions, using the following thresholds:

- A loss of 2.5 percent of RWA (when tier 1 common equity falls below 5.5 percent and regulators put the bank into resolution)
- A loss of 4 percent of RWA (when tier 1 common equity falls below 4 percent)
- A loss of 8 percent of RWA (when equity is fully depleted)
- A loss of 20 percent of RWA (when equity and a 12 percent debt shield are both fully depleted)
- A loss of 24 percent of RWA (when equity and a 16 percent debt shield are both fully depleted)

The results of our base-case analysis can be seen in figure 12.7, which also shows the results of sensitivity analyses for these base-case assumptions. These sensitivity analyses show that the results do not vary significantly when we modify the inputs. We sensitize our model to:

- A threshold for bond default of 4 percent of RWA, rather than 5.5 percent
- A maximum expected loss using CDS spreads of 50 and 150 basis points
- Different degrees of freedom of the log-T distribution

| | Base case scenario | Sensitivity Test 1 - Varying the equity level at which bonds default | Sensitivity Test 2 - Varying the maximum expected loss on bonds (reflected by CDS prices) | | Sensitivity Test 3 - Varying the degrees of freedom in the log-T distribution | |
		Bonds default when equity reaches 4.0% (vs. 5.5% base case)	Maximum expected loss on bonds: 50bps (vs. 100bps base case)	Maximum expected loss on bonds: 150bps (vs. 100bps base case)	Log-T distribution with 1 degree of freedom (vs. 3 DOF base case)	Log-T distribution with 25 degrees of freedom (vs. 3 DOF base case)
Frequency of falling below 5.5% tier 1 capital	39	39	49	39	45	38
Frequency of falling below 4% tier 1 capital	56	58	98	56	75	54
Frequency of wiping out equity	86	92	275	86	127	78
Frequency of wiping out equity and long-term debt worth 12% of RWA	358	422	2,954	358	316	463
Frequency of wiping out equity and long-term debt worth 16% of RWA	563	675	5,274	563	387	1,063

FIGURE 12.7 Sensitivity analyses do not significantly vary the results of the base case scenario

Note: Base case assumes the following parameters: Bonds default when equity breaches 5.5%; maximum expected loss on bonds is 100bps; crisis distribution has 3 degrees of freedom. All scenarios assume the following: synthetic bank with 8% equity to RWA ratio; 12% long-term debt to RWA ratio; normal probability distribution volatility is 1%; normal loss given default on bonds is 10%; crisis loss given default on bonds is 30%; frequency of crisis environment is 20 years
Source: Bloomberg, Goldman Sachs Global Investment Research

PART IV

Bankruptcy, Bailout, Resolution

CHAPTER 13

Framing the TBTF Problem
The Path to a Solution

Randall D. Guynn

his essay will first discuss the development, status, and momentum of the single-point-of-entry (SPOE) strategy for solving the "too-big-to-fail" (TBTF) problem.[1] It will then describe the resiliency of the SPOE strategy in the face of criticism of the strategy itself or the statute under which it is implemented. It will next describe the nature of the problem it is trying to solve and the key to a solution. Then it will describe the statute under which the strategy has been developed. It will then describe the basic elements of the SPOE strategy. Finally, it will discuss how the strategy can be implemented under the Bankruptcy Code and what amend-

I would like to thank Bradley Schecter and Reena Agrawal Sahni for their superb assistance in preparing this essay, portions of which are based on "Too Big to Fail: The Path to a Solution," a report of the Failure Resolution Task Force of the Financial Regulatory Reform Initiative of the Bipartisan Policy Center, May 2013, pp. 18–20. That report, which I co-authored, gives a more complete description of some of the concepts discussed in this essay.

1. For a good description of the TBTF problem and why it arises, see "Too Big to Fail: The Path to a Solution," a report of the Failure Resolution Task Force of the Financial Regulatory Reform Initiative of the Bipartisan Policy Center, May 2013, pp. 18–20. Several people have questioned whether the TBTF problem is really only—or even primarily—a question of size, rather than some combination of size, complexity, interconnectedness, maturity mismatches between assets and liabilities, or some other factors that make it likely that the failure of one or more of a particular type of financial institution is likely to trigger the sort of contagious panic throughout the financial system that can destabilize or even bring down the financial system, at least under certain severely adverse economic conditions when some sort of unexpected common shock occurs. Being persuaded by the latter view, I tried to redefine the problem as the too-systemic-to-fail (TSTF) problem in a previous publication: Randall D. Guynn, "Are Bailouts Inevitable?" Yale Journal on Regulation 29, no. 2 (Winter 2012), pp. 121–22. That and similar efforts by others proved to be futile, and it is clear that the TBTF label is here to stay. As a result, I have used that more common term throughout this essay even though I do not believe size is the only—or even the predominant—factor defining the TBTF problem.

ments might be useful to make it more likely to be successful under the Bankruptcy Code under the broadest range of economic scenarios.

Development, status, and momentum of the SPOE strategy

The SPOE strategy has taken the world by storm as the most promising solution to the TBTF problem since the strategy was first publicly announced by then-acting FDIC Chairman Martin Gruenberg in May 2012.[2] The speed with which it has been endorsed—or at least acknowledged—as a promising solution to the TBTF problem by a wide range of key US regulators, financial industry groups, think tanks, rating agencies, and other stakeholders has been nothing short of phenomenal.[3] Federal Reserve Board governors and other senior Federal Reserve officials have endorsed or praised it as innovative, promising, or even a "visionary breakthrough idea";[4] former FDIC Chairman Sheila Bair has called it a "viable

---

2. Martin J. Gruenberg, acting chairman, FDIC, remarks to the Federal Reserve Bank of Chicago Bank Structure Conference, May 10, 2012.

3. In addition, Paul Tucker, then deputy governor for financial stability at the Bank of England and chairman of the Resolution Steering Committee of the Financial Stability Board, said, "US authorities have the technology—via Title II of Dodd-Frank" and the bank holding company structure to use the SPOE strategy to resolve a US G-SIB today. "I don't mean it would be completely smooth right now; it would be smoother in a year or so as more progress is made. But in extremis, it could be done now." Paul Tucker, "Solving too big to fail: where do things stand on resolution?" speech given at the Institute of International Finance 2013 annual membership meeting, Washington, D.C., October 12, 2013, p. 2.

4. Daniel K. Tarullo, member of the Board of Governors of the Federal Reserve System, "Toward Building a More Effective Resolution Regime: Progress and Challenges," remarks at the Federal Reserve Board and Federal Reserve Bank of Richmond Conference, "Planning for the Orderly Resolution of a Globally Systemically Important Bank," Washington, D.C.. October 18, 2013, p. 8 (SPOE offers the "best potential for the orderly resolution of a systemic financial firm under Title II"); testimony of Janet Yellen, *Hearing on the Nomination of Janet L. Yellen, of California, to be Chairman of the Board of Governors of the Federal Reserve System, before the Senate Committee on Banking, Housing, & Urban Affairs*, 113th Cong., November 14, 2013 (calling SPOE "very promising"); Jerome Powell, member of the Board of Governors of the Federal Reserve System, "Ending 'Too Big to Fail,'" remarks at the Institute of International Bankers 2013 Washington Conference, Washington, D.C., March 4, 2013, p. 6 (calling SPOE strategy an "innovative" mind changer, a "classic simplifier, making theoretically possible something that seemed impossibly complex"); William C. Dudley, president of the Federal Reserve Bank

strategy";[5] Moody's Investors Service cited it as the reason for eliminating "all uplift from US government support in the ratings for bank holding company [BHC] debt,"[6] which had previously existed for certain large US BHCs because Moody's had assumed they would be bailed out rather than being allowed to fail; various trade associations and think tanks have concluded that it would be a viable solution to the TBTF problem, if properly implemented;[7] University of Rochester Professor Thomas Jackson, one of the leading bankruptcy scholars in the country and the principal author of the original Chapter 14 proposal,[8] called the SPOE strategy a breakthrough and suggested how the proposed new Chapter 14 might be revised to facilitate the successful use of the SPOE strategy under the Bankruptcy Code;[9] and a bill that would enact a version of the proposed Chapter 14 to facilitate a SPOE strategy under the Bankruptcy Code has been proposed by senators John Cornyn (R-TX) and Pat Toomey (R-PA).[10]

---

of New York, "Ending Too Big to Fail," Remarks at the Global Economic Policy Forum, New York City, November 7, 2013, p. 4 ("I very much endorse the FDIC's single point of entry framework for resolution. I think it is the best plan for implementing Title II . . ."); Thomas C. Baxter, executive vice president and general counsel of the Federal Reserve Bank of New York, "Resolving the Unresolvable: The Alternative Pathways to Ending Too Big to Fail," Remarks at the International Insolvency Institute, 13th Annual Conference, Columbia University Law School, New York City, June 17, 2013, p. 4 (calling SPOE a "visionary breakthrough idea").

5. Mike Konczal, "Sheila Bair: Dodd-Frank really did end taxpayer bailouts," *Washington Post,* May 18, 2013.

6. Moody's Investors Service, "Rating Action: Moody's concludes review of eight large US banks," November 14, 2013, p. 1.

7. See, e.g., The Clearing House, "Ending 'Too-Big-to-Fail': Title II of the Dodd-Frank Act and the Approach of 'Single Point of Entry' Private Sector Recapitalization of a Failed Financial Company," Banking Brief White Paper Series, January 2013; The Clearing House, "Report on the Orderly Liquidation Authority Resolution Symposium and Simulation," January 2013; Bipartisan Policy Center report, "Too Big to Fail," p. 2.

8. Thomas H. Jackson, "Bankruptcy Code Chapter 14: A Proposal," in *Bankruptcy Not Bailout: A Special Chapter 14,* eds. Kenneth E. Scott and John B. Taylor (Stanford: Hoover Institution Press, 2012), p. 14.

9. See Bipartisan Policy Center report, "Too Big to Fail." Jackson made the comment during the process of researching the BPC report, which he co-authored. See especially pp. 82–89. Among his many contributions to the BPC report were suggestions about how the original Chapter 14 proposal could be revised to facilitate a SPOE strategy under the Bankruptcy Code. See pp. 11–14.

10. Taxpayer Protection and Responsible Resolution Act of 2013, S. 1861, 113th Cong., 2013.

The speed with which SPOE has been accepted outside the United States has been no less astonishing. Shortly after the first public elaboration of the strategy by the Federal Deposit Insurance Corporation (FDIC), the Bank of England signaled its agreement.[11] Indeed, the Bank of England had already been discussing bail-in within resolution[12] as a possible solution to the TBTF problem. Those discussions had grown out of proposals to use contingent convertible securities, bail-in bonds, or even statutory bail-in as recovery tools to recapitalize a troubled firm before any insolvency or resolution proceedings need to be invoked.[13] The Bank

---

11. Martin J. Gruenberg, chairman of the FDIC, remarks at the Volcker Alliance Program, Washington, D.C., October 13, 2013, p. 9.

12. The Financial Stability Board subsequently defined "bail-in within resolution" as "restructuring mechanisms to recapitalise a firm in resolution or effectively capitalise a bridge institution, under specified conditions, through the write-down, conversion or exchange of debt instruments and other senior or subordinated unsecured liabilities of the firm in resolution into, or for, equity or other instruments in that firm, the parent company of that firm or a newly formed bridge institution, as appropriate to legal frameworks and market capacity." Financial Stability Board, "Thematic Review on Resolution Regimes," Peer Review Report, April 11, 2013, p. 2.

13. The most visible early advocates of bail-in as a recovery tool were Wilson Ervin, Credit Suisse special adviser to the chairman; Thomas F. Huertas, then UK Financial Services Authority director; and the Institute of International Finance (IIF). See, e.g., Wilson Ervin and Paul Calello, "From bail-out to bail-in," *The Economist*, January 28, 2010; Thomas F. Huertas, "The Road to Better Resolution: From Bail Out to Bail In," LSE Financial Markets Group Paper Series, Special Paper 195, December 2010; IIF, "Preserving value in failing firms," September 9, 2010. See also Lisa Curran and Jaap Willeumier, "Report of the International Bar Association in Connection with Legal Issues Arising in Relation to Proposals for Bank 'Bail-in' Measures," November 29, 2010, submitted on behalf of the Financial Crisis Task Force of the Legal Practice Division. The idea that bail-in could be used as a resolution strategy under Title II of Dodd-Frank was first publicly suggested by the author during the question and answer period after a debate ("Resolving large and complex financial institutions: Making it work," organized by the IIF and hosted by the Federal Reserve Bank of New York on January 31, 2011) as to whether bail-in, as a recovery tool, was a superior method of resolving failing firms than orderly liquidation proceedings under Title II of the Dodd-Frank Act. The idea had been jointly developed with Davis Polk bankruptcy partner Donald Bernstein and former FDIC general counsel John Douglas after a meeting with the U.S. Treasury on November 9, 2009 in which bail-in as a recovery tool had been discussed. See also "Are Bailouts Inevitable?" a debate between Paul Mahoney, dean of the University of Virginia School of Law, and

of England subsequently published a joint paper with the FDIC endorsing the SPOE strategy.[14] Paul Tucker, then deputy governor for financial stability at the Bank of England and chairman of the Resolution Steering Committee of the Financial Stability Board, co-authored an Op-Ed in the *Financial Times* with then-acting FDIC Chairman Martin Gruenberg on the promise of the SPOE strategy in providing a viable solution to the TBTF problem.[15] Germany and Switzerland subsequently endorsed the strategy as their preferred method of resolving systemically important

---

Randall D. Guynn, head of the Financial Institutions Group, Davis Polk & Wardwell, February 28, 2011. The debate, on whether allowing large, complex financial firms to fail under the Bankruptcy Code in all circumstances (Mahoney) or invoking Title II of Dodd-Frank to resolve them using a bail-in-within-resolution strategy during financial emergencies (Guynn) was more likely to end bailouts, is available at http://www.youtube.com/watch?v=yiOvMR5rvMY. The bail-in-within-resolution idea germinated into a joint comment letter submitted to the FDIC on May 23, 2011, by the Securities Industry and Financial Markets Association (SIFMA) and The Clearing House Association (TCH), urging the FDIC to develop a recapitalization-within-resolution strategy for resolving firms under Title II of Dodd-Frank. The FDIC described the comment letter as "an example of the value generated by constructive dialogue between the private financial markets and the federal government on topics such as this one." See "Certain Orderly Liquidation Authority Provisions under Title II of the Dodd-Frank Wall Street Reform and Consumer Protection Act (Final Rule)," 76 Fed. Reg. 41626, 41634–41635 (July 15, 2011). See also Financial Stability Board, "Key Attributes of Effective Resolution Regimes for Financial Institutions," October 2011 (endorsing "bail-in-within resolution" as a preferred resolution strategy). The FDIC developed the SPOE strategy in the process of adapting the recapitalization (bail-in) within resolution model to the U.S. bank holding company structure. James Wigand, director of the FDIC's Office of Complex Financial Institutions, first described it publicly in January 2012. "Resolution Strategy Overview," presentation of James Wigand, director of the Office of Complex Financial Institutions, to the FDIC's Systemic Resolution Advisory Committee (January 25, 2012). Gregory Baer of JPMorgan Chase (JPMC) subsequently illustrated the strategy using JPMC's balance sheet at December 31, 2012. Gregory Baer, managing director and general counsel for corporate law and global regulatory affairs, JP Morgan Chase & Co., "Orderly Liquidation of a Failed SIFI," presentation at the "Harvard Symposium on Building the Financial System of the 21st Century: An Agenda for Europe and the United States," March 24, 2012.

14. FDIC and Bank of England, "Resolving Globally Active, Systemically Important, Financial Institutions," joint paper, December 10, 2012.

15. Martin J. Gruenberg and Paul Tucker, "Global Banks Need Global Solutions When They Fail," Op-Ed, *Financial Times*, December 10, 2012.

banking groups with global operations (G-SIBs).[16] The UK government proposed legislation that would authorize the use of a SPOE strategy.[17] And the European Union added language in its proposed Bank Recovery and Resolution Directive (BRRD) authorizing resolution authorities at both the member state and union levels to resolve European banking and other financial organizations using the SPOE strategy.[18]

In short, in less than two years after the strategy was first announced by the FDIC, it has gained such wide acceptance and momentum, at least among government officials and other thought leaders throughout the United States and around the world, that it is fair to say that the SPOE strategy is the leading strategy for solving the TBTF problem for G-SIBs with centralized structures and a sufficient amount of combined capital, long-term unsecured debt, and other loss-absorbing resources at the top-tier parent.[19]

---

16. See, e.g., FINMA (Swiss Financial Market Supervisory Authority) Position Paper, "Resolution of Globally Systemically Important Banks," August 7, 2013; and Martin J. Gruenberg, remarks at the Volcker Alliance Program, pp. 9–10.

17. Financial Services (Banking Reform) Act 2013, Schedule 2, pp. 121–123 (adding a "bail-in" tool and amending the "bridge-bank" tool contained in the UK Banking Act 2009).

18. Council of the European Union, Proposal for a Directive of the European Parliament and of the Council establishing a framework for the recovery and resolution of credit institutions and investment firms (final compromise text), document 17958/13, December 18, 2013; see also Freshfields Bruckhaus Deringer, "European Bank Recovery and Resolution Directive," January 2014.

19. It is generally acknowledged, however, that SPOE is not the best solution for all banking or other financial groups. A multiple-point-of-entry (MPOE) strategy may be more promising for G-SIBs with decentralized or "archipelago" structures where loss-absorbing resources are generally pre-positioned at operating subsidiaries instead of being concentrated at a top-tier parent company. See Institute of International Finance, "Making Resolution Robust—Completing the Legal and Institutional Frameworks for Effective Cross-Border Resolution of Financial Companies," June 2012, pp. 19, 54. Nor is it necessarily the most efficient strategy for resolving smaller US banking groups in which depository institution subsidiaries account for the vast majority of the group's assets, short-term deposits and other short-term liabilities account for the vast majority of liabilities, and cross-border operations are not material. More traditional strategies such as putting the depository institution subsidiaries into one or more FDIC receiverships under Section 11 of the Federal Deposit Insurance Act and selling their assets and liabilities to a healthy third party through a purchase and assumption agreement, with or without loss-sharing, or transferring their businesses to a bridge bank to be sold in pieces over time may be more efficient and just as effective.

Resiliency of the SPOE strategy

The SPOE strategy, or at least Title II of the Dodd-Frank Wall Street Reform and Consumer Protection Act (Dodd-Frank Act), the law under which the strategy was developed, has not been without its detractors. For example, the Hoover Institution originally proposed a new Chapter 14 of the Bankruptcy Code as a substitute for Title II, not as a supplement to it.[20] The principal criticism against Title II was that it gave the FDIC too much discretion to resolve a systemically important financial institution (SIFI) without meaningful judicial review and was therefore unpredictable, inconsistent with traditional notions of due process and the rule of law, and possibly unconstitutional.[21] Others have warned that once the market understands that the long-term unsecured debt holders at the top-tier parent will bear the first losses of the group under a SPOE strategy after the group has suffered losses that render it critically undercapitalized or illiquid, investors will shift from holding long-term unsecured debt at the top-tier parent to holding short-term unsecured debt at the operating subsidiary level.[22] Still others have argued that the orderly liquidation fund (OLF), which Title II permits the FDIC to use to provide liquidity to a bridge financial company, is a form of taxpayer-funded bailout.[23] Finally, others have suggested that the FDIC's SPOE strategy may be inconsistent with its statutory duty to liquidate a financial company that is put into a Title II receivership[24] because the strategy is more like a corporate reorganization that preserves the going concern value of the group's operating subsidiaries than a traditional liquidation as contemplated by the statute.[25]

---

20. Kenneth E. Scott, "A Guide to Resolution of Failed Financial Institutions: Dodd-Frank Title II and Proposed Chapter 14," in *Bankruptcy Not Bailout*.

21. See, e.g., Kenneth E. Scott, "Dodd-Frank: Resolution or Expropriation?" in *Bankruptcy Not Bailout*; and David A. Skeel Jr., *The New Financial Deal: Understanding the Dodd-Frank Act and its (Unintended) Consequences* (Hoboken, NJ: John Wiley & Sons, 2011).

22. Tarullo, "Toward Building a More Effective Resolution Regime," pp. 11–12.

23. Peter J. Wallison, "Too big to ignore: The future of bailouts and Dodd-Frank after the 2012 election," American Enterprise Institute, October 24, 2012, pp. 3–4.

24. Dodd-Frank Act, Sect. 214(a).

25. See, e.g., comments of Paul Volcker and Simon Johnson at the FDIC's meeting on December 11, 2013, with its Systemic Resolution Advisory Committee, https://fdic.primetime.mediaplatform.com/#/channel/1384300429544 /Advisory+Committee+on+Systemic+Resolution

Rather than defeat SPOE, these criticisms have tended to reveal the fundamental resiliency of the strategy by showing how easy it is to make refinements to address these criticisms. For example, in order to address the criticism that Title II provides the FDIC with too much discretion and is therefore unpredictable and inconsistent with the rule of law, the Bipartisan Policy Center (BPC) report urged the FDIC to "announce a strong presumption in favor of using SPOE recapitalization to resolve all G-SIFIs."[26] The FDIC subsequently issued a proposed notice that went a long way toward making such a public statement,[27] although it did not include as strong a public commitment to use its SPOE strategy as would be necessary to entirely address these predictability and rule-of-law concerns. The fundamental point, however, is that these concerns could be fully addressed with a strong enough public commitment, such as in a statement of policy or regulation or by a statutory mandate.

In response to the criticism that the FDIC's discretion to discriminate among similarly situated creditors under Title II could result in a subsidy of favored creditors by disfavored creditors if the differential treatment is unexpected because the market will misprice the risk,[28] the BPC report recommended that the FDIC "confirm that it will not use its general discretion to discriminate among similarly situated creditors."[29] Such discretion is not needed for financial stability reasons in a SPOE resolution of a US G-SIB. The only legitimate reason for using that discretion for financial stability reasons would be to favor short-term unsecured debt over long-term unsecured debt to deter runs by the holders of short-term debt, since contagious runs can destabilize the financial system. But US

---

26. BPC report, "Too Big to Fail," p. 8.

27. "Notice and Request for Comments, Resolution of Systemically Important Financial Institutions: The Single Point of Entry Strategy," 78 Fed. Reg. 76614 (Dec. 18, 2013) (SPOE notice).

28. Professor Scott had rightly defined such an unexpected transfer of wealth as a bailout of the favored creditors by the disfavored creditors. See Scott, "A Guide to Resolution," *Bankruptcy Not Bailout*, pp. 9–10.

29. BPC report, "Too Big to Fail," p. 8. The BPC report probably should have included an exception for differential treatment that would maximize the recovery of all creditors, such as the differential treatment in favor of critical vendors permitted under the Bankruptcy Code. See Douglas G. Baird, *The Elements of Bankruptcy, 5th ed.* (New York: Foundation Press, 2010), pp. 225–26, in which he describes the availability under Chapter 11 of so-called critical vendor orders and other immediate payments to certain unsecured creditors where such payments are "in the interests of the estate as a whole."

G-SIBs typically have substantial amounts of long-term unsecured debt at the top-tier parent levels and almost no short-term unsecured debt at those levels; virtually all of their short-term unsecured debt is located at the operating subsidiary level. Because parent unsecured debt is structurally subordinate to unsecured debt at the operating subsidiary level, the long-term unsecured debt at the parent level is already subordinate to the short-term unsecured debt at the operating subsidiary level, so there is no reason for the FDIC to preserve any of its disparate treatment discretion. Moreover, if the long-term unsecured debt that will be used to absorb first losses is structurally subordinate to the short-term debt at the operating subsidiary level, the market will price the two types of debt efficiently and eliminate any subsidy that might otherwise arise.

The FDIC confirmed in its proposed notice that it has severely limited its own discretion to discriminate among similarly situated creditors,[30] although it did not make the sort of categorical limitation as would be necessary to entirely address this subsidy risk. The fundamental point, however, is that this subsidy risk could be fully addressed with a strong enough limitation on this power, such as in a statement of policy or regulation or by statutory amendment.

The concern that a SPOE strategy would create an incentive for investors to shift out of long-term unsecured debt at the parent level and into short-term unsecured debt at the subsidiary level is addressed in two ways. First, if this dynamic started to occur, the price (rate) the parent would have to pay to investors for long-term unsecured debt would rise, making it relatively more attractive to investors. At the same time, the price (rate) the subsidiaries would be required to pay to investors for short-term unsecured debt would drop, making it relatively less attractive to investors. Presumably, the market would settle upon an efficient risk-adjusted price for the long-term unsecured debt at the parent level and an efficient risk-adjusted price for the short-term debt at the subsidiary level. This market dynamic would reduce much of the incentive for investors to shift out of long-term unsecured debt at the parent level and into short-term debt at the subsidiary level. The same analysis would apply to long-term unsecured debt at both levels.

Second, just in case the market does not result in enough long-term unsecured debt at the parent level, the Federal Reserve has indicated that it intends to issue a regulation requiring US G-SIBs to maintain enough

---

30. 78 Fed. Reg. 76622.

combined equity, long-term unsecured debt, and other loss-absorbing resources to ensure that the SPOE strategy would be feasible under severely adverse economic circumstances.[31] This regulatory mandate will obligate US G-SIBs to raise additional long-term unsecured debt at the top-tier parent level if investors shifted too much unsecured debt from the parent to its operating subsidiaries.

In response to the argument that the OLF is a form of bailout if it is used to provide capital or other financial assistance to the bridge financial company, the FDIC has responded by publicly stating that it will only use the OLF to provide liquidity to a bridge financial company on a fully secured basis. It has also stated that it will never use the OLF to provide capital to a covered company in receivership or a bridge financial company. The BPC report recommended that the FDIC go a step further and confirm that it will only use the OLF to provide liquidity to a bridge financial company in a manner that complies with the classic principles for central bank lender-of-last-resort facilities—that the liquidity would only be available to bridge financial companies and operating subsidiaries that are both solvent and sufficiently capitalized, on a fully secured basis at above-market rates.[32] The BPC report argued that if the OLF is only used to provide temporary fully secured liquidity in accordance with these classic principles, it would not amount to a bailout because taxpayers would not face any material prospect of losses and would be fully compensated for any risk assumed.[33]

Finally, the argument that the FDIC's SPOE strategy is inconsistent with its statutory duty to liquidate any US G-SIB put into a Title II receivership—because it is more like a value-maximizing reorganization under the Bankruptcy Code than a traditional liquidation as contemplated by the statute—is incorrect. The duty to liquidate does not imply a duty to minimize value. Indeed, Title II imposes a statutory duty on the FDIC to carry out a Title II receivership in a manner that maximizes the return on the covered company's assets and minimizes its losses.[34] It is also required to minimize moral hazard and mitigate any risk to financial stability.[35]

---

31. Tarullo, "Toward Building a More Effective Resolution Regime," pp. 11–12.

32. BPC report, "Too Big to Fail," p. 9. See also Walter Bagehot, *Lombard Street: A Description of the Money Market* (London: Henry S. King & Co., 1873), establishing classic central bank lender-of-last-resort principles.

33. Ibid., p. 32.

34. Dodd-Frank, Sect. 210(a)(9)(E).

35. Ibid., Sect. 204(a)

Moreover, the duty to liquidate only applies to the financial company that is actually put into a Title II receivership.[36] Under the SPOE strategy, only the parent would be put into such a receivership. There is nothing in the letter or spirit of Title II that requires a US G-SIB's operating subsidiaries to be put into a Title II receivership if the parent is put into such a receivership. As a result, the FDIC's SPOE strategy is clearly consistent with its duties to liquidate the covered company, maximize the value of the covered company's assets, minimize its losses, minimize moral hazard, and mitigate any risk to financial stability.

Nature of the TBTF problem

What is the TBTF problem?

The TBTF problem is essentially the Hobson's choice between a taxpayer-funded bailout, on the one hand, and the destabilization or collapse of the financial system, on the other. It arises when the failure of one or more financial institutions creates a contagious panic characterized by fire-sale liquidations and value-destroying reorganizations that can severely destabilize or even cause a collapse of the financial system.[37] All indications from history suggest that when public policymakers, and even the public, are faced with the choice between bailout and collapse or destabilization, they typically choose bailouts rather than risk a collapse of the system.

Why does it arise?

The TBTF problem arises because banks and other non-bank financial institutions engage in the socially useful activity of maturity transformation—the process by which financial institutions fund themselves with short-term borrowing and use those funds to make loans or investments in other illiquid assets. Engaging in maturity transformation renders financial institutions vulnerable to liquidity runs during a financial crisis. If concern about the solvency or liquidity of one of these institutions forces it to sell its illiquid (but valuable) assets at fire-sale prices, that concern can turn into a contagious panic throughout the financial system that causes otherwise solvent financial institutions to become insolvent. It could be said that the TBTF problem would be resolved by doing away with maturity transformation. Most people, however, believe that maturity

---

36. Dodd-Frank, Sect. 214(a).
37. BPC Report, "Too Big to Fail," pp. 18–19.

transformation is a valuable social good—having money and credit from banks is a positive thing. Without maturity transformation the modern economy would grind to a halt. The question is really not whether to ban maturity transformation or to allow it without any limitations, but rather what the right balance is in terms of capital and liquidity requirements on the maturity transformation process.[38]

Key to a solution

The key to solving the TBTF problem without taxpayer-funded bailouts is a high-speed recapitalization of the failed financial group that imposes losses on shareholders and other stakeholders but avoids unnecessary value destruction and preserves the group's going-concern value.[39]

This sort of strategy needs certain characteristics. It has to be predictable and viable, so that the market will know how to price the risks. There must be a sharp distinction between capital and liquidity. Losses should be borne by the holders of capital structure liabilities—the equity holders, the long-term debt holders—not avoided by taxpayer or public injections of capital. The group needs to have enough loss-absorbing resources—including long-term debt on the right side of the parent's balance sheet and enough assets on the left side of its balance sheet—to recapitalize subsidiaries to the extent necessary. Long-term debt must be legally or structurally subordinate to short-term debt, which is vulnerable to runs in a financial crisis. This subordination must be clear in advance of a crisis. Finally, the recapitalized business must have access to a temporary secured liquidity facility from the public or private sector that is sufficiently large to make the process work.[40]

Orderly Liquidation Authority of Title II of Dodd-Frank

The Orderly Liquidation Authority (OLA) established under Title II of the Dodd-Frank Act was designed to provide an *ex post* solution to the TBTF problem if *ex ante* requirements like enhanced capital, liquidity, and other enhanced prudential regulations did not prevent failure. The best way of looking at Title II is as a last-resort option for reorganizing, liquidating, or otherwise resolving (to use the FDIC's terminology)

---

38. BPC Report, pp. 16–18.
39. Ibid., p. 3.
40. Ibid., pp. 3–4.

a SIFI without destabilizing the financial system and without resorting to a taxpayer-funded bailout. OLA was designed to supplement the Bankruptcy Code, which remains the preferred law to govern most financial institution insolvencies or failures. OLA remains a last-resort option because its administrative system is considered less transparent, more discretionary, and less well-understood than the judicially administered bankruptcy process.

It is very important to recognize that Title II is not available for use unless certain determinations are made. The two most important ones are, first, that procedures under the Bankruptcy Code would be unable to reorganize, recapitalize, liquidate, or otherwise resolve the SIFI without destabilizing the financial system or resorting to a taxpayer funded bailout; and, second, that OLA would more successfully achieve that goal.[41] If either of those conditions is not satisfied, OLA cannot be legally invoked.

OLA was modeled on the bank insolvency provisions of the Federal Deposit Insurance Act,[42] but it was actually harmonized in many respects with the rules that define creditors' rights in the Bankruptcy Code. Such harmonization is necessary because a holding company would be resolved under either the Bankruptcy Code or the OLA, and it would be highly undesirable to suddenly change any material rules that define creditors' rights upon making a determination that OLA would be used.

OLA can only be legally invoked if an institution is found to be a "financial company"[43] and certain financial distress findings are made. One key finding relates to whether the financial institution is in default or in danger of default. This can be based on a finding either that an institution is balance-sheet insolvent or that it is facing a liquidity run, such

---

41. Dodd-Frank Act, Sect. 203(b)(2), (5).

42. The bank insolvency provisions are principally contained in Sections 11 and 13 of the Federal Deposit Insurance Act.

43. It is important to note that OLA can be invoked for *any* financial company that is not a bank or other excluded company if the financial distress and other conditions are satisfied. OLA is *not* limited to bank holding companies with assets of $50 billion or greater or non-bank financial companies that have been designated as systemically important or subject to the enhanced prudential supervision of the Federal Reserve. Thus, for example, it could be invoked for bank holding companies with less than $50 billion in assets if their resolution under the Bankruptcy Code would result in serious adverse effects to financial stability such as if several of them failed at the same time. That being said, the conditions for legally invoking OLA are most likely to be satisfied only with respect to systemically important financial groups under the most extreme economic conditions.

that it is unable or unlikely to pay debts as they come due in the ordinary course of business.[44]

Two other key findings, discussed above, are that reorganization or liquidation of the company under the Bankruptcy Code would result in serious adverse effects on financial stability in the United States—whether alone or with other financial companies that fail at the same time—and that the use of OLA would avoid or mitigate those effects.

In addition, OLA can be invoked through the use of the so-called three keys process. The treasury secretary, in consultation with the president, must make the financial distress findings listed above (danger of default, serious adverse effects on the financial stability of the United States, and an avoidance or mitigation effect of using OLA). Action must then be recommended by two-thirds of the FDIC Board of Directors and two-thirds of the Federal Reserve Board. For broker-dealers, the approval requirement is two-thirds of the Securities and Exchange Commission and two-thirds of the Federal Reserve Board, with the consultation of the FDIC. For insurance companies, the director of the Federal Insurance Office and two-thirds of the Federal Reserve Board must agree to invoke OLA, with the consultation of the FDIC.

These determinations are subject to judicial review only of the "default" and "financial company" determinations. This judicial review will be triggered only if the board of directors of the company refuses to consent to the FDIC's receivership. If there is no consent, confidential court review takes place within twenty-four hours and applies an arbitrary and capricious standard of review to the two determinations. The board is insulated from liability for consenting.[45]

Special rules apply under OLA for broker-dealers and for insurance companies. For broker-dealers, Securities Investor Protection Act-like provisions apply for the protection of customer securities.[46] For insurance companies, state insurance law insolvency codes apply in place of the substantive provisions of OLA.[47] The FDIC may only be appointed receiver if the state insurance commissioner refuses to take action. Problems may arise in application of these insurance rules because state insurance insolvency codes are typically not very comprehensive—many

---

44. Dodd-Frank Act, Sect. 203(b)(1), (c)(4).
45. Ibid., Sect. 202(a)(1)(A), (e).
46. Ibid., Sect. 205.
47. Ibid., Sect. 203(e).

are not much more than general grants of discretion to state insurance commissioners. Since the FDIC is directed to apply those rules in receivership of an insurance company, it could have even more open-ended discretion to resolve insurance companies than other non-bank financial companies.

SPOE Strategy

G-SIFIs (including G-SIBs) are often discussed as if they are legal entities or institutions. Instead, they are legal groups. The classic structure of a US G-SIB is a holding company at the top, a bank subsidiary, a broker-dealer, perhaps a foreign broker-dealer, and a series of other foreign and domestic operations.

Under SPOE, after being appointed as receiver, the FDIC transfers all the assets of the failed financial company in receivership, including its operating subsidiaries, to a newly formed bridge financial company. The FDIC leaves the failed company's equity and long-term debt behind in the receivership, resulting in the business transferred to the bridge being recapitalized.

The company then uses assets available at the bridge financial company level, including the forgiveness or contribution of intercompany receivables, to recapitalize the operating subsidiaries and keep them out of insolvency proceedings. The claimants left behind in the receivership are entitled to the residual value of the bridge financial company and any assets left behind in the receivership, to be distributed to them in satisfaction of their claims in accordance with the priority of their claims.

In the final step, the old bridge company becomes a new financial holding company, fully in the private sector. It no longer has access to the OLF secured liquidity, but instead receives liquidity exclusively from the private sector. The BPC report contains a graphical step-by-step description of the SPOE strategy.[48]

The overarching benefit of the SPOE method is that only the holding company is put into a receivership and the operating subsidiaries remain going concerns. This is important for several reasons. If the SIFI in question has cross-border operations, including foreign branches, the transfer of any assets of the branches is generally unenforceable or prohibited

---

48. BPC report, "Too Big to Fail," pp. 23–31.

without the consent of foreign counterparties, foreign regulators, or foreign courts. SPOE avoids the need for those consents. SPOE reduces or eliminates the incentive to ring-fence foreign operations and reduces the need to rely on cooperation from foreign authorities.

Another benefit is that, by taking advantage of the structural subordination of long-term unsecured debt (most of which is held by US financial groups at the parent holding company level) to short-term unsecured debt and derivatives contracts (most of which is held at the operating subsidiary level), the SPOE strategy reduces or eliminates the incentive of short-term creditors to run and the right of derivatives counterparties to terminate. This in turn reduces or eliminates the likelihood of contagious panic throughout the financial system. The statute overrides cross-defaults based on the failure of the parent company in financial contracts at the operating subsidiary level, except for foreign contracts that are outside the territorial reach of the statute.

Meanwhile, the OLF ensures that the bridge financial company will have access to sufficient secured liquidity to preserve going-concern value and prevent value destruction of valuable but illiquid assets.

SPOE strategy and the Bankruptcy Code

Prerequisites
Whether it is possible to execute a SPOE recapitalization under the Bankruptcy Code was once an open question. It is now understood to be possible. Such a recapitalization would require the same prerequisites as under OLA: sufficient loss-absorbing resources at the parent company level in the form of equity, long-term unsecured debt, and assets available to recapitalize operating subsidiaries, and structural subordination of long-term debt at the parent level to short-term debt at the operating subsidiary level. It also requires a few extra prerequisites. For instance, a shell company may need to be established in advance to serve as the bridge financial company. Bankruptcy judges may need to be educated about this in advance, so that no difficulties arise in the execution of the strategy.[49] A new Chapter 14 of the Bankruptcy Code, which could clarify these issues, would be a valuable addition to the statute.

---

49. The living will process under Title I of Dodd-Frank is designed to, among other things, have contingency plans to identify and begin to implement items such as this.

Mechanics

After filing for bankruptcy, the debtor transfers all of its assets, including its operating subsidiaries, to a debt-free bridge financial company under Section 363 of the Bankruptcy Code, to be held by a private trustee for the benefit of the bankruptcy estate. The bankruptcy court should be willing to approve this transfer because the assets are not being transferred away from the bankruptcy estate, but instead are held for its benefit.

The debtor leaves its equity and long-term debt behind in its bankruptcy estate, resulting in the business transferred to the bridge being recapitalized. Assets available at the parent or bridge financial company level, including intercompany receivables, are used to recapitalize the operating subsidiaries and keep them out of insolvency proceedings.

The claimants left behind in the bankruptcy estate are entitled to the residual value of the bridge financial company and any assets left behind in the bankruptcy estate, to be distributed to them in satisfaction of their claims in accordance with the priority of their claims.

Key benefits

By keeping the operating subsidiaries out of insolvency proceedings, the SPOE strategy avoids the most significant impediments that otherwise apply to the resolution of a SIFI with cross-border operations. It reduces or eliminates the incentive to ring-fence foreign operations and reduces the need to rely on cooperation from foreign authorities.

By taking advantage of the structural subordination of long-term unsecured debt (most of which is held by US financial groups at the parent holding company level) to short-term unsecured debt (most of which is held at the operating subsidiary level), the SPOE strategy reduces the incentive of short-term creditors to run and cause contagious panic throughout the financial system.

Missing benefits

The major drawback to SPOE under the Bankruptcy Code, as opposed to under OLA, is that there is no provision analogous to the OLF that ensures that the bridge financial company would have access to sufficient liquidity, even on a fully secured basis, to preserve going-concern value and prevent value destruction of valuable but illiquid assets. In the severely adverse scenario under which SPOE recapitalization is likely, private sector DIP (debtor-in-possession) financing may not be available to the parent company or its non-bank subsidiaries in sufficient amounts.

Unless the relevant SIFIs have access to sufficient liquidity resources in addition to loss-absorbing resources, this would leave few clear sources of liquidity. The Fed's discount window can provide secured liquidity to the subsidiary bank, but Section 23A of the Federal Reserve Act limits the bank's ability to provide secured liquidity to non-bank affiliates. Section 13(3) of the Federal Reserve Act could be invoked to provide such liquidity in extreme circumstances. But such liquidity must be part of a program or facility with broad-based eligibility, which creates uncertainty as to its use.

Another issue is that the Bankruptcy Code does not have a provision analogous to OLA's provision that overrides cross-defaults in financial contracts at the operating subsidiary level based on the failure of the parent company.

If Congress and the public find that using the Bankruptcy Code would be superior to Title II (because it is rule-based, better-understood, more transparent, and more predictable), then finding some way to provide a secure liquidity facility to facilitate a SPOE recapitalization under bankruptcy would make the Bankruptcy Code more effective and useful in a greater range of circumstances.

Proposal for secured liquidity provision under Chapter 14

A new Chapter 14 would be more effective in limiting the need for OLA under severely adverse economic circumstances when ordinary financial markets break down if it contained a provision that authorized the Federal Reserve to provide secured liquidity to a bridge financial company. This would be a genuine liquidity facility, and not a bailout, if three conditions were met:

- The liquidity would only be available if the bridge financial company and its operating subsidiaries were well capitalized because of an effective SPOE recapitalization.
- The liquidity is fully secured.
- The liquidity is provided at above-market rates.[50]

A bridge holding company and its operating subsidiaries that are fully recapitalized should be able to pledge or sell, subject to a repurchase agreement, illiquid assets to the private sector if three conditions are satisfied:

---

50. Bagehot, *Lombard Street.*

(1) the private sector is confident that they are sufficiently recapitalized; (2) ordinary financial markets are not dysfunctional; and (3) private sector institutions are not prohibited from providing the necessary amount of secured liquidity by the proposed new limits on counterparty credit exposures.

But sufficient private sector liquidity may not be available if any of these conditions are not satisfied, especially if the market is dysfunctional. Therefore, unless the relevant SIFIs have access to sufficient liquidity resources, the only reliable source of secured liquidity under those circumstances may be the government—likely the Federal Reserve Board.

If sufficient secured liquidity is not available, even a well-capitalized bridge financial company will be forced to sell illiquid assets at fire-sale prices, causing it to become insolvent. These fire sales are likely to be contagious throughout the system to other financial institutions engaged in maturity transformation, thereby threatening a collapse of the system. This would mean Chapter 14 would not be a useful alternative to bailouts in severely adverse economic scenarios when ordinary financial markets are dysfunctional. If OLA is not repealed, this state of affairs will justify invoking Title II to give access to the OLF; if OLA *is* repealed, the lack of secured liquidity under the Bankruptcy Code could result in irresistible pressure for capital injections—bailouts—to prevent the financial system from collapsing.

Several objections have been leveled against such a secured liquidity provision. First, although the vast majority of people who have considered whether a government-provided secured liquidity facilities are a form of bailout have concluded that they are not,[51] at least one commentator has argued that they are simply another form of bailout.[52] From this perspective, enacting the secured liquidity provision would be authorizing one type of bailout to avoid another, and the only real solution is to completely eliminate the availability of government assistance.

A more political objection is that, if such a liquidity source were included in Chapter 14, it would undermine the narrative that Title II and OLF are really just institutionalized government bailouts; a secured

---

51. See, e.g., Joint Economic Committee of the Senate and House of Representatives, "Lender of Last Resort in the Modern Financial System," November 29, 2012; BPC Report, "Too Big to Fail," pp. 46–53.

52. Stephen J. Lubben, "Why Federal Reserve Support is Really a Bailout," *New York Times,* December 9, 2013.

liquidity provision under Chapter 14 would serve a similar role to the OLF under OLA.

Finally, it could be argued that the Federal Reserve is justified to provide discount window secured liquidity to insured banks and the uninsured branches of foreign banks but not to uninsured but recapitalized bridge financial companies or to their uninsured non-bank operating facilities, such as broker-dealers, that are also engaged in maturity transformation.

I agree with those who argue that a government-provided secured liquidity facility that satisfies Bagehot's classic conditions—borrower must be solvent, the liquidity must be fully secured, and the credit must be provided at above-market interest rates—is not a form of bailout.[53] Such facilities protect governments against loss and compensate them for the risks they take. It is noteworthy that such reliable free-market economists as Milton Friedman have never considered the Federal Reserve's discount window to be a form of bailout or to be inconsistent with free market principles or the goals of minimizing moral hazard and maximizing market discipline. This is because the discount window is only available when the free market is dysfunctional. The borrower must be solvent and liquidity must be fully secured and priced at an above-market rate. A bailout involves capital injections or loss- or uncompensated risk-shifting from private sector to government; if the discount window conditions are satisfied, there is no loss- or uncompensated risk-shifting to the government.

A secured liquidity provision in Chapter 14 of the sort recommended by the BPC would be subject to the same conditions as the current discount window.[54] All losses would be borne by the group's shareholders and debt holders, with no material risk of loss to the Federal Reserve if it sets proper haircuts for collateral, and the Federal Reserve would be compensated for the risk it would take.

If such a secure liquidity facility is not available and a SPOE recapitalization under the Bankruptcy Code takes place, even a well-capitalized bridge financial company may be forced to sell illiquid assets at fire sale prices, causing it to become insolvent, unless it otherwise has access to sufficient liquidity. This would mean that a Bankruptcy Code SPOE would not be a useful alternative to either bailout or a potential destabilization or collapse of the financial system. If that were the case, then the TBTF problem will not have been solved—at least not with the Bankruptcy

---

53. See, e.g., Joint Economic Committee, "Lender of Last Resort."
54. BPC Report, "Too Big to Fail," p. 12.

Code. This would just lead to Title II being invoked in a greater number of circumstances.

Bankruptcy Code and Title II

The Bankruptcy Code and Title II should coexist. The Bankruptcy Code should be made as effective as it possibly can be in order to reduce the need to use Title II to the smallest possible number of circumstances. But Title II must be preserved for those extreme circumstances where the discretion afforded by its administrative process, and the secured liquidity available through the OLF, are absolutely needed.

Conclusion

In conclusion, the FDIC's SPOE strategy has taken the world by storm. It is now widely considered to be the dominant strategy for solving the TBTF problem for G-SIBs with centralized structures, like US bank holding company groups. The TBTF problem arises primarily because large, inter-connected banking groups are engaged in the socially beneficial activity of maturity transformation. The key to a solution to the TBTF problem without taxpayer-funded bailouts is a high-speed recapitalization of the failed financial group that maximizes value. OLA can be invoked only if the resolution of a particular financial company under the Bankruptcy Code would result in severe adverse effects to financial stability in the United States and if OLA would avoid or mitigate those adverse effects. The SPOE strategy would avoid or mitigate such effects if they arise. The SPOE strategy can be implemented under the existing Bankruptcy Code, although a new Chapter 14 could increase the likelihood of its success, particularly if it were coupled with a secured liquidity facility from the government that would be able to provide such liquidity under the most severe economic conditions.

CHAPTER 14

Designing a Better Bankruptcy Resolution

Kenneth E. Scott

To begin, I will offer some background on the origin and activities of the Resolution Project which has been spearheading research and development on a new chapter in the bankruptcy code: Chapter 14. The Resolution Project was formed in 2009, in the aftermath of the September 2008 financial panic, under the aegis of George Shultz and John B. Taylor. It has consisted (apart from John and myself and originally Andrew Crockett) of two finance professors, two former regulators, two bankruptcy professors, two industry participants, and two United Kingdom experts. It has produced thus far several conferences and two books: *Ending Government Bailouts As We Know Them* in 2010 and *Bankruptcy Not Bailout: A Special Chapter 14* in 2012 (both published by Hoover Institution Press). The objectives have been to respond to the crisis situation and to the perceived shortcomings of both the current bankruptcy code and, after it was enacted, the Dodd-Frank Act.

On the bankruptcy code, of course, numerous criticisms have related to the Lehman Brothers failure. As for Dodd-Frank—in theory, if you're an optimist, then you believe the problem has been rendered moot by Title I: there will no longer be failures of "too-big-to-fail" institutions or any need for bailouts. But there is a certain amount of skepticism about whether failure has really been abolished and bailouts made extinct. With regard to bailouts, should such a failure reoccur, some of the skepticism may come from the fact that the statute in Title II creates a receiver with an explicit pipeline to the Treasury. There are a lot of provisions about how it is to be used (only for short term liquidity, and there should be a repayment plan) and how the resolution should be conducted. Section 214, for example, mandates that the failed firm is to be liquidated and tax-payer losses are prohibited. The Federal Deposit Insurance Corporation (FDIC) as receiver is given extensive authority and discretion, and various instructions and determinations are specified to govern how it is used. But there is no way of legally enforcing them, and everything is taking place internally within the agency.

How is it supposed to work? Title II—assuming Title I hasn't ended all failures—creates an Orderly Liquidation Authority (OLA), as has been described by Randy Guynn.[1] The political slogan in passing Dodd-Frank was that it would end bailouts of Wall Street, but what that meant was limited to taxpayer-funded bailouts. To understand the problem, you have first to define what constitutes a bailout in the event of a failure, a term often used loosely. We define the bailout of a stakeholder as the receipt of more than what would be received in a normal bankruptcy.

But who is being bailed out, exactly? Is it a bailout of "the firm"? What would that mean—a bailout of the stockholders of a large financial company, so they suffer little or no loss? In point of fact, that has been a rare—if not nonexistent—event. Usually in a financial resolution the stockholders have been completely wiped out or nearly so—completely in Lehman, largely so in Citigroup.

The concern really is—and should be—more over bailouts of major creditors. Why is that the important group to focus on? Because what's at stake is the preservation of effective market discipline on management. Historically, it's usually been actions by creditors that have led to the failure or restructuring of large financial institutions, often ahead of—and forcing—regulatory intervention.

So in these OLA receiverships, how are they supposed to work and what perceived flaws are there that we have been concerned to try to deal with? The procedures currently contemplated involve the receiver using a "single point of entry" to take over the failed institution and transfer its business to a new "bridge" company, as outlined by Guynn. The place where I think we have problems comes with the extent and use of the discretionary powers that are vested in the receiver in this process:

- Discretion over what liabilities are transferred to the bridge institution, which means that those creditors will be fully protected, as opposed to the liabilities that are not transferred and are left behind in the debtor's estate, so that those creditors will take large losses.
- Discretion with respect to the valuation of the assets that are being transferred to the bridge.

1. See chapter 13 in this volume.

- Discretion with respect to allocation of losses—not only as between one creditor and another at the level of the parent holding company but also with respect to the subsidiaries.

There have been assertions or expectations that the receiver could simply take assets, shuffle them around, and bestow them upon certain subsidiaries that have incurred losses, thus keeping those subsidiaries in full operation with their creditors fully paid. When it's a foreign subsidiary, this has been a point (to which we will return) of considerable concern for foreign regulators: whether that would actually take place and how and why.

Procedural fairness is an issue in this discretionary environment because the decisions are made by internal agency processes that are closed to outside participation. That brings us to the question: what kind of judicial oversight or role is there in OLA? This has two levels. One is the original decision by the secretary of the treasury, *ex ante,* to take over a particular financial institution and put it through this OLA process. To do that, he has to file a petition in the District of Columbia district court in which the judge is asked to determine whether or not certain statutory conditions are met. (There are seven determinations the secretary has to make, but only two of them may be reviewed by the court.) That starts a twenty-four-hour statutory deadline for the judge to hold a hearing, get all the relevant evidence, hear arguments, make findings of fact, reach a conclusion, and write an opinion. If the petition was filed at the close of business on one day, than the deadline is five o'clock the next day. Should the judge decline to play his truncated role so superficially, the petition is deemed granted by operation of law. This treatment of judicial oversight reduces it to an empty formality.

The second level of judicial oversight takes place *ex post,* after the institution has been put into receivership. The financial company apparently can file an appeal from the district court to the court of appeals, and perhaps further. But stays are prohibited during appeal, and the firm is supposedly being altered and sold off during this receivership process. So if at the end of the day, months later, you actually got a ruling in your favor from a court that had an opportunity to consider the grounds and the evidence more fully, what would be the remedy? The answer is: it's very unclear that there is any. The firm no longer exists and the statute gives no authorization for a damage remedy by shareholders.

From the standpoint of the creditors who went through this process, some of whom were fully paid off and many of whom were not, there is an express prohibition of any judicial review of those decisions by the receiver in its conduct of the receivership. Substantial constitutional issues are embedded in all of this—certainly debatable ones. And if the debate were ever actually undertaken in a legal action and pursued to a decision, one might find that it had invalidated the whole mechanism of Title II.

To address some of these problems, the Resolution Project has been drafting a proposal for a new chapter in the bankruptcy code: Chapter 14. Let me give a brief overview of its structure and of some issues still under discussion.

The coverage is of financial institutions with total consolidated assets greater than $50 billion. This simply tracks the Dodd-Frank definition of the institutions to which it applies, and includes a lot of financial institutions that are very far from being systemically important.

There are special provisions for systemically important financial institutions (SIFIs), including mechanisms to facilitate (through a section 363 sale) the single-point-of-entry bridge mechanism advocated by FDIC as a means of resolution. Proceedings can be commenced voluntarily by management, as is true under the bankruptcy code now, or by a supervisor, which is not a provision in the current code. Filing serves as a pathway to reorganization under Chapter 11 or liquidation under Chapter 7. In the case of SIFIs, where the concern is to continue operations so as to reduce systemic risk, the choice would of course normally be reorganization rather than liquidation (a point that was lost on California Senator Barbara Boxer's section 214 amendment requiring liquidation under Dodd-Frank).

The relationship of Chapter 14 to Title II is that bankruptcy is stated to be the preferred mode of resolution. SIFIs are supposed to prepare resolution plans ("living wills") that are designed to be effectuated under the bankruptcy code; to invoke a Title II receivership there first has to be a determination that a bankruptcy resolution would have serious adverse effects on financial stability.

If a Chapter 14 bankruptcy case has begun, Dodd-Frank would still give the secretary of the treasury power to put the institution into an OLA receivership under Title II. How would that be accomplished? One way would be to provide that the secretary would simply file an ex parte transfer motion in the bankruptcy district court that would be automatically granted. A preferable provision might be to require that the motion be accompanied by a statement of the reasons for the secretary's determination that there is otherwise a substantial possibility of the systemic risk consequences necessary for invocation of jurisdiction under Title II.

Under Chapter 14, a main difference is in the treatment of creditors. There is adherence to core bankruptcy code principles, strict priority, and equal treatment. In other words, the selection and treatment of claims is a great deal less discretionary. The reason is that creditors are the source of the most timely and best-informed discipline on management risk-taking, through the terms of credit extension—or its denial. That is the key function that we're trying to preserve and, indeed, strengthen.

In terms of judicial oversight, under the bankruptcy code, the procedures both permit and require the involvement of creditors. They participate in the decisions being made about asset sales and loss allocations. The whole proceeding takes place with court hearings and with decisions and authorizations that occur in public and not in secret or in closed internal agency processes. In that way, creditor concerns and valuation issues are addressed more openly and predictably, in accord with constitutional standards.

The actions taken in the crisis, and the driving forces behind the enactment of Dodd-Frank, were motivated by fears of a systemic financial collapse. That is a consideration in some, but certainly not most, failures of financial institutions. In most financial institution failures, reorganization in the normal Chapter 11 fashion would be the way to proceed. But when it comes to SIFIs, and if there is a justifiably great concern with continuing operations to minimize systemic spillover consequences, then the current view is that there ought to be a transfer of the business (as intact as possible) to a new bridge company, whether in Title II or Chapter 14.

There are problems in doing so that must be conceded and addressed. Some are problems that we can try to deal with in the bankruptcy code. For others, the only way to handle them will be outside the bankruptcy code, including:

- Blocking runs by short-term creditors, involving matters like QFCs (qualified financial contracts), termination rights, and stay durations. This is something that David Skeel will address in more detail.[2]
- Assuring the bridge company has "adequate capital." How much do you have to have? Are there special concessions for bridge

---

2. See chapter 15 in this volume.

companies? What form does it take—common equity, bail-in debt, other instruments? Is it based on risk-weighted assets or a leverage ratio? These requirements and their details, which obviously must come from the regulators and supervisors, are still being debated. How they can be met in a resolution is a case-specific empirical question, depending on the magnitude of losses and on where in the firm group the losses are located.

- Liquidity requirements. If the bridge company is strongly capitalized, short-term funding should be available from the market. If need be, there could be a provision for the kind of "administrative expense" priority given DIP (debtor-in-possession) financing for companies reorganizing under Chapter 11. If the market did not have such confidence in the new company's capital strength, as a fallback the supervisor participating in a Chapter 14 case could be authorized to make use of the OLF (orderly liquidation fund) mechanism of Title II.

These are all important aspects of the evolution of financial regulation now taking place and they will have to be accommodated in a Chapter 14 reorganization. But the specifics won't be available until we see what Basel III (which provides global banking standards) or the Fed or the Financial Stability Oversight Council (FSOC) ultimately comes up with.

In addition, there are the problems of cross-border operations and cross-border resolution. These are dealt with to some extent by Chapter 15 of the bankruptcy code, which we think can be modified to work somewhat better in this context—for example, through adoption of a reciprocity provision for recognition of foreign home countries' stay orders. Meanwhile, a great deal of international conferring is going on.

Further analysis of the status of insolvent foreign subsidiaries is a really important issue. Are you going to recapitalize them? Foreign regulators certainly would like to see that happen. But if that's a big black hole, how is it going to take place? The options are basically three. Is it going to be a judgment on the part of the management of the old or the new firm as to whether this is an expenditure of funds that is warranted from a business standpoint? Is it going to be because we've now moved to an organizational form in which, fundamentally, there is an established legal obligation on the part of the parent to meet all debts in subsidiaries (in effect turning a legal entity structure into a consolidated single firm)? Or is it going to be a matter of regulatory discretion, which is the way it seems to be looking at the moment when we try to interpret what FDIC and the Fed have said on the subject (although their authority for this under the statute is far from clear). If it's a matter left to regulatory discretion then, again, the market doesn't know what's going to take place and there are uncertainty costs as well as impairment of market discipline.

So the Resolution Project is ongoing. Our discussions and work are not finished. We are trying to refine bridge procedures, to figure out the best way to accommodate different capital and bail-in debt proposals, and to adapt to different organizational structures that may be required. Where will all this end up? We are trying to bring our part of it to at least an interim conclusion and hope that soon a more complete version 2.0 of Chapter 14 will be ready for release.

CHAPTER 15

Single Point of Entry and the Bankruptcy Alternative

David A. Skeel Jr.

Introduction

Viewed at a high level of abstraction, the Dodd-Frank Act has two main objectives. The first is to limit the risk of the banking system by more carefully regulating the key instruments and institutions of contemporary finance: the instruments being derivatives and other financial contracts and the institutions being the giant, systemically important financial firms like JP Morgan Chase, Citigroup, or AIG. The principal strategies for achieving the first objective are (1) requirements that most derivatives be cleared and traded on an exchange or similar platform and (2) the designation of systemically important financial institutions and the subjection of these institutions to, among other things, more stringent capital regulation.[1]

The Dodd-Frank Act's second objective is to limit the damage in the event one of these giant institutions nevertheless fails. To achieve the second objective, the Dodd-Frank Act gave bank regulators sweeping new authority to take over a struggling financial institution whose failure might pose systemic risk to the economy. Prior to the enactment of the Dodd-Frank Act, bank regulators had extensive resolution powers with commercial bank subsidiaries but did not have resolution authority over the bank holding company or nonbank affiliates, each of which was subject to the ordinary bankruptcy process.[2] Although bankruptcy remains the strategy of choice for resolving even the largest financial institutions,

---

Thanks to Randall Guynn and Thomas Jackson for helpful comments on an earlier draft of this chapter.

1. Each of these issues is discussed in detail in David Skeel, *The New Financial Deal: Understanding the Dodd-Frank Act and its (Unintended) Consequences* (Hoboken, NJ: John Wiley & Sons, 2011).

2. The Bankruptcy Code excludes commercial banks and insurance companies but not their holding company (11 USC Sec. 109[b]). Brokerages can file for Chapter 7, which provides for liquidation, but not Chapter 11, which governs reorganization (11 USC Sec. 109[d]).

the Dodd-Frank Act gives bank regulators an extensive new set of resolution tools.

This chapter focuses on the new resolution tools and, more generally, on the Dodd-Frank Act's second objective of containing systemic risk and more effectively resolving the failure of a systemically important financial institution. Housed in Title II of the Dodd-Frank Act—the Orderly Liquidation Authority, or OLA—the resolution rules were characterized by advocates as an extension of the powers the Federal Deposit Insurance Corporation has for resolving the financial distress of ordinary commercial banks. If the US Treasury, Federal Reserve, and FDIC agree, they are authorized to file a secret petition in a federal court in Washington, D.C. The court must approve the intervention so long as the troubled institution is engaged primarily in financial activities and is in default or in danger of default.[3] In most cases, the FDIC then takes over as receiver.[4] Title II instructs the FDIC to replace any managers who were "substantially responsible" for the financial institution's predicament, to impose losses on shareholders and creditors, and to liquidate (rather than reorganize) the troubled institution.[5] Although Title II contains an elaborate framework of rules, the rules provide only a sketchy picture of what a resolution might actually look like.

Over the past several years, the FDIC has attempted to fill in the picture with a remarkable new strategy it calls single point of entry.[6] In a single-point-of-entry resolution, bank regulators would put the financial institution's holding company into resolution, then transfer its assets, any short-term liabilities, and any secured obligations to a new bridge institution while leaving its stock and long-term unsecured debt (primarily bonds) behind in the old institution. The transfer would create a well-capitalized new institution and the FDIC would have access to large

---

3. Dodd-Frank Act, Sec. 202(a).

4. If the institution is primarily a brokerage, the Securities Investor Protection Corporation shares responsibility for customer accounts.

5. Dodd-Frank Act, Sec. 206 (shareholders recover last); Sec. 214 (liquidation).

6. The best current overview of single point of entry and the bankruptcy alternative is John F. Bovenzi, Randall D. Guynn, and Thomas H. Jackson, "Too Big To Fail: The Path to a Solution" (Washington, DC: Bipartisan Policy Center, May 2013). The FDIC has recently outlined the SPOE strategy in a call for comments. Federal Deposit Insurance Corporation, "Notice and Request for Comments, Resolution of Systemically Important Financial Institutions: The Single Point of Entry Strategy," 77 Fed. Reg. 76614 (December 18, 2013).

amounts of liquidity from the US Treasury as needed for the holding company or subsidiaries. The FDIC would eventually distribute some or all of the equity of the new institution to the old long-term debt holders, while most likely wiping out the old stock.

The single-point-of-entry strategy is made possible by the unusual structure of large US financial institutions. Unlike their European counterparts, US financial institution groups generally have a top-level holding company whose capital structure includes substantial amounts of bonds and other long-term unsecured debt but relatively few derivatives and other short-term debt. Short-term debt and much of the group's operations are in subsidiaries. With bank holding companies especially, this structure is in large part a historical accident, caused by restrictions on banks' ability to branch across state lines and other regulatory obstacles. If it works, single point of entry will thus be a rare illustration of a happy unintended consequence.

Single point of entry has generated so much enthusiasm among regulators that the original working title of this chapter was "The Single-Point-of-Entry Silver Bullet." The title was only partly ironic. The single-point-of-entry approach does appear to be quite promising, and considerably more plausible than the process envisioned by the drafters of Title II. It would impose fewer demands on regulators than putting the entire holding company framework into resolution and could reduce the risk that foreign subsidiaries would face liquidity crises or other problems at the outset of the resolution, as they did when Lehman Brothers filed for bankruptcy in 2008. Although the virtues of single point of entry are real, the technique also has important vulnerabilities, and some of the claims made on its behalf are quite exaggerated. It does not end "too big to fail," for instance, as some advocates have claimed, and regulators may be reluctant to invoke it if multiple financial institutions face default at the same time or if resolution would expose particularly messy problems at one or more subsidiaries. It also reinforces problematic incentives for financial institutions to rely on short-term financing.

This chapter begins with a brief overview of concerns raised by the Lehman Brothers bankruptcy about the adequacy of our existing architecture for resolving the financial distress of systemically important financial institutions. The principal takeaway of the first section is that Title II as enacted left most of these issues unanswered. By contrast, the FDIC's single point of entry, which is introduced in the second section, can be seen as addressing nearly all of them. The third and fourth sections point out some of the limitations of single point of entry, first by highlighting potential pitfalls and distortions and then by explaining that single point of entry does not end the too-big-to-fail problem and would not reduce worrisome concentration in the financial services industry. The final section turns to bankruptcy, which remains the strategy of choice for resolving even systemically important financial institutions and considers how a single-point-of-entry-style strategy could be used in bankruptcy. Indeed, the strategy harkens back to the original procedure used to reorganize American railroads well over a century ago.

The Lehman challenge

It would be difficult to identify an aspect of the Lehman Brothers default in 2008 that is not subject to at least some controversy and debate. This includes, of course, the accepted wisdom that Lehman's bankruptcy triggered the market chaos of 2008.[7] Even those who interpret the significance of Lehman's collapse in diametrically opposed ways tend to agree, however, on many of the shortcomings Lehman exposed in the existing architecture for handling the financial distress of a systemically important financial institution. (By architecture, I mean both the formal options in place for handling financial distress and regulators' use of those options.) In this section, I briefly describe five challenges Lehman posed for the current architecture and show how the Dodd-Frank Act addressed several of these challenges but left most of them unresolved. In the next section, I will turn to the FDIC's innovative single-point-of-entry strategy and will explain how it theoretically could address many or all of the issues left open by the Dodd-Frank Act.

Five issues from Lehman

The first issue posed by Lehman was what tools are necessary for regulators to adequately address the financial distress of a systemically important institution. As of fall 2008, the Federal Reserve had the authority to make emergency loans under section 13(3) of the Federal Reserve Act so long as the loans were fully collateralized, but it and other bank regulators did not otherwise have direct authority to resolve the financial distress of a bank holding company or nonbank financial institution.

---

7. For criticism of the accepted wisdom, see, e.g., Kenneth Ayotte and David A. Skeel Jr., "Bankruptcy or Bailouts?" *Journal of Corporation Law* 35 (2010): 469.

After Lehman defaulted and the failure to bail out Lehman was widely criticized, Treasury Secretary Henry Paulson and Fed Chairman Ben Bernanke both asserted that the restrictions prevented them from providing rescue funding. Because Lehman did not have adequate collateral, the reasoning went, the Federal Reserve could not make an emergency loan and therefore was forced to let Lehman default.[8] Although their claim that the Fed could not have made an emergency loan seems implausible, especially given the creativity the Fed used in its other rescue operations during the crisis, Lehman did highlight the limitations of bank regulators' authority in the event a systemically important financial institution failed. Bankruptcy was available, but bank regulators have limited authority in bankruptcy and did not have other resolution options.

A second issue raised by Lehman concerns the predictability of regulators' intervention in the event of a crisis. Prior to the crisis, some commentators advocated an intervention strategy known as "constructive ambiguity."[9] In a system characterized by constructive ambiguity, regulators do not signal in advance whether they will provide rescue financing in the event a systemically important financial institution or other entity falls into financial distress. The uncertainty theoretically could create an equilibrium in which the managers and creditors of a large financial institution don't count on a bailout, which removes the moral hazard created by the expectation of a bailout, but regulators can provide a bailout if this proves to be necessary to prevent systemic harm.[10] The events of 2008, especially Lehman's collapse, cast serious doubt on the efficacy of constructive ambiguity. Although regulators insisted that large financial institutions should not expect to be bailed out, Lehman CEO Richard Fuld believed, almost up to the moment of Lehman's default, that rescue financing would be available if necessary. Similarly, faced with uncertainty as to whether they would be bailed out, AIG's managers spent considerable

---

8. For the retrospective of another Treasury official, see Philip Swagel, "Why Lehman Wasn't Rescued," *New York Times*, September 13, 2013, http://economix .blogs.nytimes.com/2013/09/13/why-lehman-wasnt-rescued/?_r=0.

9. See, e.g., *Statement of E. Gerald Corrigan Before the United States Senate Committee on Banking, Housing, and Urban Affairs*, Washington DC, February 4, 2010.

10. For a critical assessment of constructive ambiguity after the crisis, see Jeffrey M. Lacker, "Reflections on Economics, Policy, and the Financial Crisis," speech before the Federal Bank of Richmond, September 24, 2010, http://www .richmondfed.org/press_room/speeches/president_jeff_lacker/2010/lacker_speech _20100924.cfm.

energy in the weeks before the government stepped in preparing a report that was designed to persuade regulators that a failure to bail out AIG could be disastrous.

One very destructive consequence of Lehman's assumption it would be bailed out was that Lehman made almost no efforts to prepare for the possibility of bankruptcy. Lehman has speculated that up to $75 billion of value was destroyed due to the absence of pre-bankruptcy planning.[11] Whatever the precise costs, the failure of constructive ambiguity suggests the need to devise clearer signals whether and how regulators are likely to intervene. As with the prompt corrective rules that apply to ordinary banks, the ideal framework would provide clarity as to when regulators will intervene and how they will resolve financial distress. It also would encourage the parties to prepare for the possibility of financial distress.

A third issue raised by Lehman relates to the trade-off between speed, on the one hand, and information and rule-of-law virtues, on the other, when a financial institution's distress is resolved very quickly. Ordinary bank resolution offers speed and regulators generally are well informed, but it sacrifices rule-of-law virtues, since regulators have nearly complete discretion in resolving a bank.[12] Ordinary bankruptcy better honors the rule of law and is designed to produce considerable information, but it is more time-consuming than bank regulation. The Lehman case was an odd hybrid of the two approaches. Although the case has remained in bankruptcy for five more years, Lehman sold its core brokerage operations to Barclays four days after it filed for bankruptcy. The speed came at the cost, however, of information and rule-of-law virtues. In approving the sale motion, the bankruptcy judge emphasized that the process had been rushed, with little time to digest the relevant information, and made clear that the case should not be viewed as precedential for future transactions.[13] Lehman hewed more closely to rule-of-law virtues than

---

11. See, e.g., Jeffrey McCracken, "Lehman's Chaotic Bankruptcy Filing Destroyed Billions in Value," *Wall Street Journal*, December 29, 2008, http://online.wsj.com/news/articles/SB123050916770038267.

12. For an analysis of the benefits and shortcomings of administrative resolution and bankruptcy, see Thomas H. Jackson and David A. Skeel Jr., "Dynamic Resolution of Financial Institutions," *Harvard Business Law Review* 2 (2012): 435.

13. See, e.g., Emily Chasan, "Judge Approves Lehman, Barclays Pact," *Reuters*, September 21, 2008, http://www.reuters.com/article/2008/09/21/us-lehman-barclays-idUSN1932554220080921. (Article quotes Judge James Peck as

the bailouts of Bear Stearns and AIG did, but Lehman—like the two bailouts—raised the question whether the rule of law can be honored more fully without sacrificing the need for speed.

The fourth concern that emerged from Lehman is the susceptibility of derivatives and short-term credit to run, creating a risk that value will be destroyed due to premature liquidation, as well as concerns about larger systemic consequences. With Lehman, the principal concerns related to its repo financing and J.P. Morgan's grabbing of collateral as uncertainties about Lehman grew.[14] Although Lehman's derivatives portfolio was unwound without major incident, a run on AIG's credit default swaps—and AIG's inability to halt the run even temporarily—was a major factor in AIG's collapse.[15] These incidents raised the question whether the risk that short-term credit will run, and that these runs will have destructive effects, can be contained in the event a systemically important financial institution threatens to collapse.

The final issue arises from the global reach of systemically important financial institutions like Lehman. Some of the most destructive consequences of Lehman's failure came outside the United States. Due to their loss of immediate access to funds in Lehman's cash management system, several Asian subsidiaries failed. Several hedge funds failed after Lehman's London subsidiary was placed in administration. The worldwide ripple effects of Lehman's default underscored the fact that an effective resolution strategy needs to consider not only the domestic effects of financial institution distress but the potential for worldwide consequences. The question here is how best to minimize the global disruption caused by the default of a systemically important financial institution.

The regulatory response in Dodd-Frank

How well does Dodd-Frank address these issues? To answer this question, I will briefly describe Dodd-Frank's strategy for resolving financial distress, highlighting a handful of provisions of particular relevance. I then will consider how fully this strategy addresses the Lehman questions.

---

saying, "It can never be deemed precedent for future cases. It's hard for me to imagine a similar emergency.")

14. These concerns are discussed in David A. Skeel Jr. and Thomas H. Jackson, "Transaction Consistency and the New Finance in Bankruptcy," *Columbia Law Review* 112 (2012): 152, 163–66.

15. Ibid., 165–66.

Dodd-Frank's core strategy for resolving troubled financial institutions is to funnel them into formal bankruptcy or resolution proceedings.[16] The principal mechanisms for achieving this are two key financing provisions. The first restricts the Federal Reserve's section 13(3) power—its power to make emergency loans—by prohibiting the Fed from providing rescue funding to a single financial institution.[17] In theory, this restriction will sharply constrain regulators' capacity to bail out troubled financial institutions as they did with Bear Stearns and AIG. If regulators invoke the resolution rules, by contrast, they have access to large amounts of funding from the US Treasury. As receiver of a troubled financial institution, the FDIC is entitled to borrow up to 10 percent of the institution's pre-resolution book value and 90 percent of the fair value of its assets once it has been placed in resolution.[18]

Although the financing provisions reflect a preference for resolution rather than bailouts, the legislation signals that resolution should be used only if the other major alternative—bankruptcy—is likely to be unavailing. When a systemically important financial institution prepares a living will ("resolution plan" is the term used), as Dodd-Frank now requires it to do, the living will must explain how a bankruptcy would unfold, rather than resolution under Dodd-Frank.[19] Similarly, Dodd-Frank ostensibly precludes regulators from invoking the resolution rules unless they first determine that alternatives such as bankruptcy are not feasible or would create a risk of adverse systemic effects.[20]

The drafters of Dodd-Frank seem to have envisioned that regulators would look to bankruptcy as the option of choice, and then Dodd-Frank resolution if bankruptcy did not appear to be adequate. If regulators do

---

16. There is an interesting echo here of the funneling strategy used for ordinary corporations in the New Deal. In the Trust Indenture Act of 1939, Congress prohibited voting provisions that had previously been included in an increasing number of bond indentures to facilitate restructuring of bonds outside of bankruptcy. The provision was designed to force troubled companies to use bankruptcy instead. See, for example, Mark J. Roe, "The Voting Prohibition in Bond Workouts," *Yale Law Journal* 97 (1987): 232, 234, 251.

17. Dodd-Frank Act, Sec. 1101(a).

18. Dodd-Frank Act, Sec. 210(n).

19. Dodd-Frank Act, Sec. 165(d)(4). (This section requires the Federal Reserve and FDIC to assess whether the living will is credible and would facilitate an orderly resolution under the bankruptcy laws.)

20. One of the systemic risk findings bank regulators must make before initiating a resolution is "an evaluation of why a case under the Bankruptcy Code is not appropriate for the financial company." Dodd-Frank Act Sec. 203(a)(2)(F).

put the institution into receivership under the resolution rules, they will have access to copious funding. Under the other resolution provisions, they also would have extensive flexibility in deciding how to resolve the financial distress, subject only to the proviso that the resolution rules require that the institution be liquidated.[21]

Also of particular note for assessing how fully the Dodd-Frank framework addresses the questions raised by Lehman is Dodd-Frank's new requirement that most derivatives be cleared and presented to an exchange.[22] Under the new rules, a clearinghouse will guarantee the performance of both parties to a cleared derivative, entering into agreements with both the buyer and the seller, thus shifting counterparty risk to the clearinghouse. It remains to be seen how much of the derivatives markets will be cleared, but already roughly 65 percent of interest rate swaps and 40 percent of all credit derivatives are migrating to the clearinghouses.[23]

Under the Dodd-Frank resolution rules, derivatives and other financial contracts are subject to a one-plus day stay after the receivership of a systemically important financial institution begins.[24] Counterparties are prohibited from terminating their contracts during this period and cross-default provisions—provisions that make the receivership of one entity an event of default for contracts with an affiliate—are invalidated. Regulators are required to continue making margin payments on the derivatives, and they must either assume or reject all of the contracts with any given counterparty—they cannot keep some and terminate others.

If we map this framework onto the questions raised by Lehman, Dodd-Frank clearly responds to the first of the five issues. Under the new resolution rules, regulators have sweeping authority to intervene if a systemically important financial institution totters, with almost no judicial second-guessing of a decision to intervene. Although regulators are required to make a list of findings, their petition can only be rejected if the institution in question is not a financial company or is not in default or in danger of default.[25] The resolution rules give the FDIC enormous

---

21. Dodd-Frank Act, Sec. 214.

22. The new derivatives requirements are set forth in Title VII of the Dodd-Frank Act. For an overview, see Skeel, *The New Financial Deal,* 59–75.

23. See Financial Stability Board, "OTC Derivatives Market Reforms: Sixth Progress Report on Implementation," September 2, 2013, 27.

24. Dodd-Frank Act, Sec. 210(c)(8)(F).

25. For extensive discussion of the petition requirements and limited judicial oversight, see Kenneth E. Scott, "Dodd-Frank: Resolution or Expropriation?" in

discretion as receiver. No longer need regulators worry that they lack sufficient authority to intervene.

Although Dodd-Frank clearly addresses the first of the five issues, on each of the others the framework as enacted is at best incomplete. The framework does not increase the mystery as to whether and how regulators will intervene, but neither does it remove the uncertainty. Although struggling financial institutions are funneled to bankruptcy or resolution, the funnel is quite leaky. As discussed in more detail below, regulators still can bail out the financial institution, despite the restrictions on the Fed's emergency lending powers. And the top managers of the institution have strong incentives to resist Dodd-Frank resolution, since they are likely to be ousted.

With the third issue, Dodd-Frank appears at first to have made significant strides in incorporating rule-of-law virtues into an administrative resolution process. The resolution rules include a priority scheme that instructs regulators to impose losses on shareholders and junior creditors; promises that every creditor will be given at least the liquidation value of its claim and that excess payments can be clawed back; and borrows preference, fraudulent conveyance, and setoff provisions from the bankruptcy laws.[26] These provisions give the OLA a patina of regularity. But the rule-of-law protections are more illusory than real. The FDIC can ignore the priorities if it deems an alternative approach necessary to financial stability; and the promise of liquidation value has little content, since the FDIC can take the position that there would be little or no value available to any creditors if it had not intervened. Considerable uncertainty remains under the Dodd-Frank framework as enacted.

In one very important respect, the risk of runs on short term funding—the fourth issue—has been reduced by the Dodd-Frank Act. Counterparties of derivatives that are now cleared have much less incentive to run in the event the other party threatens to collapse. Even here, however, the solution is incomplete. Many derivatives are likely to remain uncleared—especially those that cannot easily be standardized.[27] The

---

Bankruptcy Not *Bailout: A Special Chapter 14,* eds. Kenneth E. Scott and John B. Taylor (Stanford CA: Hoover Institution Press 2012), 199.

26. For a more detailed discussion, see Skeel, *The New Financial Deal,* 142–48.

27. As of September 2013, roughly 65 percent of US interest rate swaps and 40 percent of credit derivatives were being cleared, as noted earlier, but the percentages are much lower with commodity-based and other derivatives. See Financial Stability Board, "OTC Derivatives Market Reforms," 27.

counterparties to these derivatives still have reason to run in a crisis. Moreover, the Dodd-Frank Act did almost nothing to address the fragility of the short term repo market, which figured prominently in the Lehman and Bear Stearns collapses.

Finally, Dodd-Frank did not address the international dimensions of a systemically important financial institution's collapse. Presumably, regulators have taken these concerns into account in implementing Dodd-Frank's living will requirement. Other than with living wills, almost the only references in Dodd-Frank to the global dimensions of a financial institution default are a handful of exhortations of US regulators to coordinate with their foreign counterparts.

As this brief overview makes clear, the Dodd-Frank framework as enacted leaves many of the most important issues raised by Lehman unaddressed or, at the least, under-addressed.

The single-point-of-entry strategy

In the discussion thus far, I have referred on occasion to the Dodd-Frank framework "as enacted." I have used this language to distinguish the bare statutory rules from the quite remarkable strategy for implementing the resolution rules that the FDIC has developed and promoted over the past several years. In this section, I briefly describe the single-point-of-entry approach. I then map the strategy against the question we considered in the previous part. A signal selling point of the new strategy is that it far more effectively answers nearly all of the Lehman questions than does the framework as enacted.

The new approach is called single point of entry because the holding company atop a financial institution's corporate structure would be put into receivership but most or all of the affiliated entities would not.[28] The restructuring would occur primarily at the holding company level, with liquidity down-streamed to affiliates as necessary. In a single-point-of-entry resolution, the FDIC would transfer all of the holding company's assets, any short-term unsecured debt, and any secured debt to a newly created bridge institution. The holding company's stock and long-term unsecured debt would be left behind, leaving the bridge institution with a more sustainable capital structure. At some point thereafter, the FDIC

---

28. Bovenzi, Guynn, and Jackson, "Too Big To Fail: The Path to a Solution," 26–27.

would (probably) wipe out the old stock and would convert at least some of the long-term debt to stock in the bridge entity. If one or more subsidiaries were facing a solvency issue, the holding company could inject capital by converting obligations owed by the subsidiary to the bridge entity into stock or by contributing other holding company assets (including receivables from other subsidiaries) to the needy subsidiary.[29]

Much more than the Dodd-Frank Act as enacted, which seems to contemplate a wind-down of the troubled institution, single point of entry addresses the issues posed by Lehman. The approach is far from foolproof, and I will consider some of its limitations in the next two sections. But single point of entry is considerably more promising than the structure envisioned by the rules as enacted.

Start with the second issue, the uncertainty whether and how regulators will intervene. With a well-defined single-point-of-entry strategy in place, it is at least possible that regulators would invoke the resolution rules if a systemically important financial institution threatened to fail. The uncertainty would not be dispelled altogether, but it is more plausible that regulators would use Title II to effect a single-point-of-entry restructuring than it is that they would take over a giant financial institution and wind it down.

On the third issue, too—the tension between speed and rule-of-law virtues—single point of entry is more promising than the rules as enacted. By fully protecting one group of unsecured creditors (derivatives and other short-term debt) while restructuring another (long-term debt), the single-point-of-entry strategy alters ordinary priorities. But if the FDIC commits to using single point of entry, the treatment is known in advance and in this sense honors rule-of-law virtues. While codification of these principles would be clearer still, single point of entry could couple a relatively clear set of rules with the speed of administrative resolution.[30]

Fourth, because single point of entry promises that the financial institution's derivatives and other short-term debt will be fully protected,

---

29. Ibid., 27. If one or more subsidiaries continued to face a liquidity crisis after being recapitalized, the bridge entity theoretically could make a secured loan to the needy subsidiary and re-pledge the collateral received from the subsidiary to the FDIC in return for a matching secured loan from the FDIC's orderly liquidation fund (which is borrowed from the US Treasury).

30. Thus far, the FDIC unfortunately has continued to insist on retaining the discretion to alter claimants' treatment on an ad hoc basis in the event of a resolution. See FDIC, "Notice and Request for Comments."

it diminishes the likelihood of runs in the event a financial institution threatens to default. The risk of runs will not disappear altogether; repo lenders may still refuse to roll over their repo loans, for instance. But single point of entry reduces the downside consequences of failure for a financial institution's short-term creditors and as a result should reduce the risk of runs.

Finally, if the single-point-of-entry plan works as intended, it addresses the global consequences of a failure by limiting the consequences of default to the US holding company. Foreign subsidiaries theoretically will be insulated from the failure and will continue to operate on normal terms. So long as the crisis is limited to the US holding company, or to the holding company and one or more US subsidiaries, the effects of a financial institution's default outside the United States will be much less serious than with Lehman.[31]

In the next two sections of this chapter I will explore some of the problems with, and concerns about, the single-point-of-entry strategy. But it should by now be evident that single point of entry is a far more promising approach to financial institution failure than the Dodd-Frank resolution rules as enacted.

What could go wrong?

The single greatest threat to single point of entry is simply that regulators won't take the weapon out of its holster when a troubled financial institution stumbles. In the past, regulators have rarely if ever intervened in a timely fashion. The prompt corrective action rules enacted after the savings and loan crisis of the 1980s were designed to respond to precisely this problem. Even these rules, which instruct the FDIC to intervene before a bank becomes insolvent, do not always assure a timely regulatory response. The decision when to intervene under Dodd-Frank is entirely discretionary. Because it is a plausible mechanism for resolving the financial distress of a systemically important financial institution, single point of entry will make regulators more comfortable intervening. But

---

31. US and UK regulators have attempted to signal their confidence in the likely effectiveness of this approach through a joint statement endorsing the general framework. See Martin J. Gruenberg (chairman, FDIC) and Paul Tucker (deputy governor, financial stability, Bank of England), "Global Banks Need Global Solutions When They Fail," *Financial Times,* Op-Ed, December 10, 2012.

regulators will still be tempted to delay. The longer the time lag between the last crisis and the next one, the greater the temptation may be. The Fed and FDIC have scaled up significantly in the wake of the crisis and enactment of Dodd-Frank and might well intervene if a large financial institution were to stumble in the near future. But the state of readiness will inevitably erode with time.

Regulators' natural reluctance to intervene will be still greater if there is a potentially messy crisis at a major subsidiary. Single point of entry is designed for financial distress that can be resolved with the financial equivalent of arthroscopic surgery—a narrowly targeted intervention. Although the FDIC has considered ways of down-streaming capital and liquidity to troubled subsidiaries, capital and liquidity alone may not be enough to solve the problems. If this is the case, regulators may be particularly hesitant to invoke their resolution powers. If they do attempt to stanch the crisis through a single-point-of-entry restructuring, the restructuring could fail or it could leave the troubled institution in government hands for years, rather than the much shorter period the FDIC contemplates.

The risk of subsidiary-level complications could be particularly acute if there are problems with a non-US subsidiary. Although British regulators have endorsed the single-point-of-entry approach, as noted earlier, they worry about whether US regulators will act as vigorously to recapitalize a troubled UK subsidiary as with a troubled US subsidiary.[32] Uncertainties abound for US regulators as well. Although they can be confident that the United Kingdom will welcome direct injections of capital, US regulators would not have any control over the restructuring or liquidation of a non-US subsidiary.

JP Morgan Chase poses another version of the messy subsidiary problem. J.P. Morgan, a subsidiary of JPMorgan Chase, and Bank of New York Mellon handle the vast majority of tri-party repo transactions in the United States. Although tri-party repo is not nearly as important a profit center for J.P. Morgan as it is for Bank of New York, a J.P. Morgan failure could entangle a large portion of the tri-party repo market.[33] Although regulators theoretically could use single point of entry to resolve

---

32. The general issue is discussed in Thomas F. Huertas, "Safe to Fail," LSE Financial Markets Group Paper, Series 21 (May 2013).

33. For related reasons, Darrell Duffie has argued that tri-party repo clearing services should operate through a regulated utility. See Darrell Duffie, "Replumbing Our Financial System: Uneven Progress," *International Journal of Central Banking,* January 2013: 251, 253.

a J.P. Morgan default without interfering with tri-party repo clearing, they might be very reluctant to take the risk. As a practical matter, J.P. Morgan's centrality to the tri-party repo market could function as a poison pill that will prevent regulators from invoking the Dodd-Frank resolution rules.

Thus far, I have focused on the problems that could arise if a single financial institution fell into distress. Historically, financial crises have often engulfed multiple banks rather than just one. The 2008 crisis was of course a vivid illustration, bringing the collapse of two investment banks and bailouts of other struggling banks as well. It is quite unlikely that regulators would seriously consider attempting single-point-of-entry resolutions of more than one systemically important institution at the same time. Even after their post-Dodd-Frank expansion, regulators probably do not have the capacity to handle multiple resolutions simultaneously; and their capacity is likely to erode as memories of the last crisis recede. Moreover, broader crisis conditions make it much less likely that systemically important financial institutions can be restructured and released from FDIC oversight quickly to resume normal operations in the marketplace.

With each of the concerns I have discussed—regulators' general reluctance to intervene, the messy subsidiary problem, and simultaneous failures—single point of entry may not work at all, either because regulators are unwilling to use it or because the resolution process may not function as intended. Several collateral consequences of the single-point-of-entry strategy also warrant mention. First, bank regulators recognize that they will need to impose mandatory bondholding requirements, lest banks shift to other, protected forms of financing, leaving insufficient bond funding to facilitate a single-point-of-entry restructuring.[34] In addition, because

---

34. See Federal Reserve Governor Daniel K. Tarullo, "Toward Building a More Effective Resolution Regime—Progress and Challenges," Speech at the Federal Reserve Board and Federal Reserve Bank of Richmond Conference, "Planning for the Orderly Resolution of a Global Systemically Important Bank" (October 18, 2013). (Tarullo states that an important "way to enhance the credibility of the FDIC's approach is to require adequate loss-absorbing capacity within large financial firms"); Federal Reserve Governor Daniel K. Tarullo, *Dodd-Frank Implementation: Testimony Before the Committee on Banking, Housing, and Urban Affairs*, US Senate, July 11, 2013. (Tarullo states that "in consultation with the FDIC, the Federal Reserve is working on a regulatory proposal that requires the largest, most complex US banking firms to maintain a minimum amount of outstanding long-term unsecured debt on top of their regulatory capital requirement.")

the FDIC has not specified how or when it will determine the magnitude of the haircuts to bondholders in the event of a single-point-of-entry restructuring, bondholders may put even more pressure on regulators to avoid a default than they did in 2008. The uncertainty as to how bondholder haircuts will be determined is not likely to prevent single point of entry from working, but it is a potential problem that the FDIC would do well to fix by providing more guidance about the process it plans to use.

The second concern is the implications to the derivatives market of a commitment to single point of entry. By committing to fully protect derivatives in the event of a resolution, single point of entry diminishes the monitoring incentives of derivatives counterparties, who will often be the first to recognize that a systemically important financial institution is in financial distress; and it strengthens incentives to use derivatives and other short-term financing. Given the problems with these financial contracts in 2008, the added incentive to use fragile forms of financing could have dangerous unintended consequences. To be sure, the risks are mitigated somewhat by the increased clearing and exchange trading of derivatives. But a substantial percentage of derivatives still is not cleared; and with cleared derivatives, the protection may have a dampening effort on the clearinghouses' monitoring incentives.

Is "too big to fail" over?

When President Obama signed the Dodd-Frank Act in July 2010, he proclaimed that it would end the too-big-to-fail problem. "Because of this law," the president said, "the American people will never again be asked to foot the bill for Wall Street's mistakes. There will be no more taxpayer-funded bailouts. Period."[35] Although these words can perhaps be construed as the hyperbole that attends the enactment of once-in-a-generation legislation, other enthusiasts have continued to make similar claims. In a recent book and in public appearances, Sheila Bair, the former head of the FDIC, also has expressed optimism that Dodd-Frank has ended taxpayer bailouts and the too-big-to-fail problem.[36]

---

35. See, e.g., Annalyn Censky, "Obama on new law: 'No more taxpayer bailouts,'" *CNN Money*, July 21, 2010, http://money.cnn.com/2010/07/21/news /economy/obama_signs_wall_street_reform_bill/.

36. Sheila Bair, "Why taxpayers may now be off the hook when a big bank fails," *Fortune*, April 11, 2013.

The basis for this claim is two key parts of the Dodd-Frank Act. The first is the provision in the law that limits the ability of the Federal Reserve to make the kind of extraordinary bailout loans that it gave Bear Stearns and AIG during the crisis in 2008.[37] Under the new provision, which amends the Fed's emergency lending powers under section 13(3) of the Federal Reserve Act, the Fed cannot make an extraordinary loan to a single institution. Only industry-wide programs are permitted. The second part of the answer is Dodd-Frank's resolution rules, as supplemented by the single-point-of entry resolution strategy. These provisions may have reduced the likelihood of bailouts in some circumstances. But by no stretch of the imagination can they be said to have eliminated bailouts or the too-big-to-fail problem.

The most obvious limitation of the restrictions on the Federal Reserve is that they can only work if the Federal Reserve adheres both to the spirit and to the letter of the restriction on its section 13(3) powers, which is highly unlikely in a crisis. The Fed still has the power to make emergency loans to an entire industry, and if the Fed really only wanted to bail out one institution, it isn't hard to create a program that purports to be for the entire industry but really has one institution in mind. In fact, if the Fed wanted to, it could simply ignore the law and make a loan directly to one bank, because no one would be in a position to bring suit against it. Still another option is for regulators to go to Congress to ask for a new source of bailout funding, as they did with the TARP (Troubled Asset Relief Program) legislation in 2008. If there is a will, bank regulators will have ways to bail out systemically important financial institutions in the next crisis, as they did in the last.

Suppose, however, that this time really is different and regulators take their chances with Dodd-Frank's resolution rules rather than bailing out the troubled institution. Even here, it would not be accurate to say that bailouts will be avoided and too-big-to-fail and related concerns will be fully addressed. The generous financing provisions provided by Title II, which allow the FDIC to borrow up to 10 percent of the financial institution's pre-resolution book value and 90 percent of its fair value in resolution,[38] have several important leaks. One potential leak is hidden in a provision governing the interest rate to be paid for the financing. Title II instructs regulators to base the interest rate on the average interest rate for

---

37. Dodd-Frank Act, Sec. 1101(a).
38. Dodd-Frank Act, Sec. 210(n)(6).

a basket of corporate bonds.[39] The corporate bond rate may well be less than the appropriate rate for the resolution of a troubled financial institution (even one that has been recapitalized through a transfer of assets and liabilities to a bridge) and it will almost certainly be less than the penalty rate of interest called for in traditional lender-of-last-resort lending. Moreover, regulators can ensure an even lower interest rate through strategic selection of the term or category of bonds they use as a bench mark. The implicit costs of below-market lending will of course be costs that are borne by taxpayers.

A second leak comes with the tax status of the bridge institution. The bridge institution is exempt from nearly all taxes while it remains in Title II.[40] The longer the Title II process takes, the greater the magnitude of this tax break. Although the FDIC envisions a comparatively short resolution process, there is no guaranty that this will be the case. The FDIC can keep the bridge institution in place for up to five years. The cost to taxpayers could therefore be considerable.

The final leak arises in the event the bridge institution is not able to repay its loans in full. Under these conditions, Title II requires bank regulators to make an assessment on other systemically important institutions to cover the shortfall.[41] Because the assessment is directed to other financial institutions, Title II advocates can claim that under no circumstances will taxpayers be responsible for the difference. But the costs of any assessment are likely to be passed on to the financial institutions' customers. As a result, although the costs are not a tax on taxpayers, they may have a somewhat similar effect.

In addition to the potential for a partial bailout even within Title II, the FDIC's single-point-of-entry strategy has another, related limitation: it is not designed to reduce concentration in the banking industry. The principal objective of single point of entry is to quickly restructure and recapitalize a troubled bank. If it works as intended, the troubled financial

---

39. Dodd-Frank Act, Sec. 210(n)(5)(C) (interest rate based on difference between Treasury bill rate and interest rate for corporate securities of comparable term).

40. Dodd-Frank Act, Sec. 210(h)(10) states that: "Notwithstanding any other provision of Federal or State law, a bridge financial company, its franchise, property, and income shall be exempt from all taxation now or hereafter imposed by the United States, by any territory, dependency, or possession thereof, or by any State, county, municipality, or local taxing authority."

41. Dodd-Frank Act, Sec. 210(o).

institution will emerge from the restructuring nearly as large and domi-nant as it was before the crisis. If it is one of the six dominant bank holding companies before the crisis, it will almost certainly retain that status after its single-point-of-entry resolution.

This last point is not necessarily a criticism of the single-point-of-entry approach so much as a corrective to suggestions that single point of entry is a comprehensive solution to "too big to fail" and related problems. If the banking industry is too concentrated, as many believe, single point of entry is not the solution. Other correctives are necessary.

The bankruptcy alternative

Although the exact genealogy of the single-point-of-entry strategy is unclear,[42] it bears a striking resemblance to the transactions that were used to bail out and restructure Chrysler and General Motors in 2009. In each case, the company filed for bankruptcy at the behest of the US govern-ment and promptly transferred nearly all of its assets and many (but not all) of its liabilities to a newly created entity. The claims that were trans-ferred, such as employee health care obligations and the companies' trade debt, were paid in full, while many of the creditors left behind received only a fraction of what they were owed. To finance the transactions, the US Treasury made substantial loans to each company.[43]

Whether the car bailouts honored or abused the bankruptcy process is the subject of an extensive debate that we need not enter into here. The important point for my purposes is that bankruptcy can be used in this fashion if the transactions are structured properly. Indeed, a bankruptcy "sale" to an entity set up by the debtor itself—the bankruptcy equivalent of what hipsters call a "selfie"—is precisely the form that the railroad reorga-nizations of the late nineteenth century, the precursors of Chapter 11, took. This suggests that the single-point-of-entry strategy for resolving system-ically important financial institutions could potentially be employed in bankruptcy. In the discussion that follows, I briefly describe a handful of reforms that would need to be made for the strategy to be effective,

---

42. Randy Guynn appears to deserve considerable credit as author of a SIFMA (Securities Industry and Financial Markets Association) memo and a law review article that contain some of the earliest outlines of the approach. See Randall D. Guynn, "Are Bailouts Inevitable?" *Yale Journal on Regulation* 121 (2012):29.

43. For more detailed discussion, see Mark J. Roe and David Skeel, "Assessing the Chrysler Bankruptcy," *Michigan Law Review* 108 (2010): 727.

focusing in most detail on the two biggest concerns: the timing of the initial sale and the funding.[44]

In order to facilitate the transfer of any derivatives and short-term debt to the newly created entity, the Bankruptcy Code would need to be amended to alter the special status of derivatives.[45] Under current law, the stay that prevents creditors from terminating their contracts and seizing or selling collateral and the bankruptcy rules that invalidate provisions that deem bankruptcy to be an event of default do not apply to derivatives. At the least, derivatives would need to be subject to at least a one- or two-day stay to facilitate the transfer to a new entity. As noted earlier, Dodd-Frank's resolution rules provide a one-plus day stay.

Second, and more importantly (given that the holding company itself is unlikely to have significant amounts of derivatives), the bankruptcy laws would need to invalidate so-called cross-default provisions—that is, provisions in contracts that have been entered into by the debtor's affiliates that make the debtor's bankruptcy a default under the affiliate contract. The invalidation of cross-defaults is somewhat trickier because a US law to this effect would bind US counterparties but not counterparties in another country such as the UK. This issue would need to be addressed either in the standard ISDA (International Swaps and Derivatives Association) contract or through a treaty or other arrangement with the United Kingdom. US and European regulators are at work on this issue as it applies to Dodd-Frank resolution.[46] Including bankruptcy in any solution

---

44. For an excellent new analysis of the bankruptcy alternative, see Thomas H. Jackson, "Resolving Financial Institutions: A Proposed Bankruptcy Code Alternative," *Banking Perspective,* March 2014.

45. For much fuller discussions of these issues, see Skeel and Jackson, "Transaction Consistency"; and Darrell Duffie and David A. Skeel, "A Dialogue on the Costs and Benefits of Automatic Stays for Derivatives and Repurchase Agreements," University of Pennsylvania Institute for Law and Economic Research paper 12–02. See also Mark J. Roe, "The Derivatives Market's Payments Priorities as Financial Crisis Accelerator," *Stanford Law Review* 63 (2011): 539; and Stephen J. Lubben, "Repeal the Safe Harbors," *American Bankruptcy Institute Law Review* 18 (2010): 319.

46. The FDIC, the Bank of England, the German Federal Financial Supervisory Authority, and the Swiss Financial Market Supervisory Authority recently sent a letter to ISDA calling for ISDA to include a "short-term suspension of early termination rights" in its contracts. See FDIC Press Release, "Federal Deposit Insurance Corporation, Bank of England, German Federal Financial Supervisory Authority and Swiss Financial Market Supervisory Authority Call for Uniform Derivatives

that emerges would facilitate the use of quick sales in bankruptcy as an alternative to single point of entry under Title II.

The third adjustment that would be needed is a provision assuring that any licenses that are transferred in the initial sale would continue to be valid, so that the company did not risk a disruption in its ability to do business as a result of the sale.

This brings us to the two most difficult issues with achieving a quick sale in bankruptcy: the need for speed and the need for liquidity funding. Although bankruptcy courts routinely oversee prompt sales of debtors' assets under Section 363, the transfer of a systemically important financial institution's assets would need to be much faster than the ordinary thirty- or sixty-day auction period used in bankruptcy, given the fragility of bank assets and liabilities. Timing is less of an issue with single point of entry under Title II because, with the exception of an extremely limited, secret, initial hearing, the Dodd-Frank Act gives bank regulators discretion to transfer a financial institution's assets as quickly as they choose. Bankruptcy's rule-of-law protections make a quick sale more difficult. The most obvious solution to the timing issue is to provide for a much quicker sale than is usually the case, with notice given to regulators and a group of the largest creditors. Under one current proposal, the notice and sale would take place within twenty-four hours of the bankruptcy filing.[47]

The other major issue is funding. As discussed earlier, Title II makes huge amounts of funding available from the US Treasury for a Dodd-Frank resolution. Although the financing provisions of US bankruptcy law are extremely generous by international standards, they rely on financing by private lenders.[48] There are serious questions whether private

---

Contracts Language," November 5, 2013. Relatedly, the EU has included a provision in the final compromise language of its proposed Recovery and Resolution Directive that would override cross-default provisions in ISDA contracts with European counterparties. Council of the European Union, "Proposal for a Directive establishing a framework for the recovery and resolution of credit institutions and investment firms," December 18, 2013 (includes as Article 60a "Exclusion of certain contractual terms in early intervention and resolution").

47. The Hoover Institution working group that developed the proposed new Chapter 14 is currently developing a quick sale procedure along the lines discussed in this chapter. The quick sale provisions would be included as part of Chapter 14 or could be adopted separately. A stand-alone version of the quick sale procedure was introduced by Senators John Cornyn and Pat Toomey in December 2013 as S. 1861.

48. The rules for debtor-in-possession financing are set forth in 11 USC Sec. 364.

financing could be raised quickly enough in the midst of a systemically important financial institution's distress to satisfy its liquidity needs. Most commentators who have followed the bank resolution discussions believe that it could not be. Although I generally share this view, it may be useful to begin by considering some of the arguments in favor of private funding. Perhaps the most important is that the new entity created for the purposes of a quick sale will be extremely well-capitalized. It will have left its long-term debt behind, with the expectation that much or all of the debt will be converted into equity in the new entity. It is possible that this cleansing of its capital structure would enable the new entity to very quickly arrange funding from private lenders.[49]

It is also worth noting that, if there were a system-wide liquidity crisis affecting multiple financial institutions, the Federal Reserve might implement an emergency lending program under its section 13(3) powers, as revised by the Dodd-Frank Act. A new entity created for the purposes of a quick bankruptcy sale presumably would have access to this funding.

If one were to conclude that an additional form of funding is necessary due to the uncertainty of private-market funding, what form should that funding take? One obvious alternative would be to replicate the funding terms of Dodd-Frank. A troubled financial institution could be given access to Treasury funding in the same or similar amounts. The principal concern with this approach is that it seems to put too much funding at the new entity's disposal. In theory, this need not have distortive effects, but it is impossible to avoid the suspicion that it would. In my view, these concerns counsel in favor of a more carefully calibrated approach, such as limited access to the Federal Reserve's discount window. If the new entity were temporarily permitted to borrow on a fully collateralized basis, as ordinary banks do, the danger of excessively generous access to liquidity would be reduced.

One important benefit of a quick sale in bankruptcy, as compared to single point of entry under Dodd-Frank, is that the new entity would be outside of bankruptcy from the moment the sale was completed. Indeed, if lawmakers wished, they could move the process outside of bankruptcy altogether by enacting legislation authorizing a restructuring of the existing financial institution along the lines I have discussed, as a bail-in

---

49. It also would be possible to develop more ambitious forms of private funding, such as pre-committed lines of credit, or a public-private facility in which private loans were supported with government guarantees.

arrangement that did not require the pretense of a sale. Because the new entity would not be subject to bankruptcy, it would be subject to normal market forces from the beginning. Unlike with single point of entry under Dodd-Frank, regulators would not be in a position to prolong the period in which the institution is a ward of regulators. There would be no risk of an ongoing state of limbo, as has been the case with the government-sponsored enterprises Fannie Mae and Freddie Mac.

Conclusion

Single point of entry is one of the most important innovations to emerge in the implementation of the Dodd-Frank Act. In this chapter, I have described how single point of entry has addressed many of the issues that were raised by the Lehman case and which were curiously neglected by the Dodd-Frank Act itself. I have also pointed out that some of the claims surrounding single point of entry, such as the claim that it has eliminated the too-big-to-fail problem, are exaggerated. Even when coupled with the single-point-of-entry strategy, the Dodd-Frank Act does not prevent bailouts; and single point of entry is not a plausible strategy under all circumstances. It is unlikely to be attempted if more than one systemically important financial institution were to fall into financial distress, for instance, and may not work with an institution that has one or more significant and troubled foreign subsidiaries. Single point of entry is quite promising, but it is important to be realistic about its limitations.

The chapter concluded by discussing how a similar strategy could be achieved in bankruptcy. The bankruptcy alternative is subject to similar concerns as single point of entry and needs to address concerns about speed and access to liquidity. Addressing these concerns would further buttress bankruptcy as the resolution forum of choice in all but the most extreme cases of bank holding company and nonbank financial institution distress.

CHAPTER 16

We Need Chapter 14— *And* We Need Title II

Michael S. Helfer

A number of thoughtful commentators have proposed that Congress amend the Bankruptcy Code to add a new chapter—generally referred to as Chapter 14—that would apply in the event of the failure of a systemically important financial institution (SIFI). Chapter 14 would remedy a number of perceived inadequacies in the current version of the Bankruptcy Code as it would apply to the failure of a SIFI, including speed of the process, role of the regulators, close-out of derivatives, and possibly liquidity facilities. Some of the proponents of a Chapter 14, or their allies in Congress, say that upon, or in connection with, the adoption of Chapter 14, the Orderly Liquidation Authority (OLA) of Title II of Dodd-Frank should be repealed. Improving the Bankruptcy Code with a new Chapter 14 is a good idea. Repealing Title II, whether or not Chapter 14 is enacted, is a bad idea.

It is worth starting with some basic principles. A sensible and effective resolution process for large financial institutions—in bankruptcy or otherwise—ought to include at least the following particularly important elements in order to prevent adverse systemic consequences and to end "too big to fail" (TBTF):

- Assuring that liquidity is available—and, if it comes from the public sector, assuring that it is fully secured and at a penalty rate. Note that fully secured liquidity is not the same as capital—capital, which can absorb losses, should come only from the private sector and is key to preventing contagion.
- Dealing with qualified financial contracts like derivatives.
- Making sure the authority responsible for overseeing the resolution proceedings has the expertise and resources to move quickly and fairly.
- Providing for the continuation of critical services for customers and clients so as to minimize the adverse impact of the failure on

the economy as a whole, consistent with the public interest and the legitimate interests of creditors.

* Making sure that losses are imposed on stockholders, creditors, and responsible management of the failed institution, and are not borne by taxpayers.

In most important respects, Title II addresses these issues, and it does so in a way that is consistent with the Financial Stability Board (FSB) Key Attributes, which is important for international credibility. These alone are pretty good reasons not to repeal Title II. So is the fact—as shown by the list of ways in which the proponents of Chapter 14 say it would improve the bankruptcy process—that a large part of what Chapter 14 would do is address these exact issues, often in ways that are similar to the ways that Title II addresses them.

But no matter what Chapter 14 eventually looks like, when and if enacted, it would be a bad idea to repeal Title II because Title II provides the government with a set of tools that may work better than bankruptcy in the next crisis.

What is particularly important about Title II in this regard is the Title II single point of entry (SPOE) approach developed by the Federal Deposit Insurance Corporation (FDIC). Under the SPOE approach, in the event of a SIFI failure, the operating subsidiaries of the institution—the bank, the broker-dealer, the insurance company, as the case may be—will remain open and operating, providing essential services to customers and clients and to the market as a whole. Meanwhile, the loss will be imposed, as it should be, on the stockholders and long-term unsecured creditors of the holding company and on responsible management. This is accomplished under the FDIC SPOE plan by having a holding company convert holding company advances to the subsidiary into equity or by "downstreaming" other holding company assets, thereby recapitalizing the subsidiary and keeping it solvent and operating, even though the holding company fails and is resolved through an FDIC-administered bridge holding company. While there is more to be done by the regulators to implement the SPOE plan—particularly, requiring holding companies to have sufficient loss-absorbing capital (equity and long-term unsecured debt) as well as assets that can recapitalize the bank and other operating subsidiaries in the event of failure, and issuing a clear "presumptive path" telling the market how the regulators expect to implement Title II—the basic plan is clear and it will work.

And, of critical importance, a Title II SPOE resolution will assure foreign governments that the operating subsidiaries of the failed SIFI, particularly the ones that are important to the economy of the host country, will remain open and provide services locally and internationally. With sufficient assurance, foreign governments will have no incentive to "ring-fence" or take other actions that would threaten global flows and world-wide economic activity. Given the uncertainty about what will work best in the circumstances we may face, it makes no sense to take away a very important tool like Title II—a tool that ends TBTF by making the shareholders and creditors of the failed institution bear the losses of the enterprise, assuring the dismissal of responsible management, and protecting taxpayers from any risk of loss.

An opponent of Title II might say that a properly drafted and comprehensive Chapter 14 could also result in the operating subsidiaries of the SIFI remaining open and operating. It is true that a single point of entry approach is not necessarily exclusive to Title II. It may well be possible to achieve a SPOE result, in whole or in part, for certain institutions, depending on their structure and financial condition, under existing Chapter 11 of the Bankruptcy Code and under Chapter 14, depending on what it ultimately contains.

But the fact that you could get to some form of SPOE through bankruptcy does not mean Title II is not needed. In fact, for various reasons, Title II is likely to work better than bankruptcy in certain circumstances.

Most importantly, under Title II foreign regulators can reach agreements with US regulators now, in advance of the next crisis, outlining how each will act if the cross-border resolution of a SIFI is required. The joint FDIC-Bank of England paper[1] issued in December 2012 was a step in this direction. And the FDIC announced in 2012 that it had entered into a bilateral resolution memorandum of understanding with at least four jurisdictions—including the United Kingdom—and had many others in discussion or planned.

It is obviously not feasible for the foreign regulators to develop these kinds of agreements with bankruptcy judges. Without at all suggesting that Chapter 11 and Chapter 14 are not useful tools or that suitable resolution plans cannot be developed under those provisions, one can

---

1. Federal Deposit Insurance Corporation and Bank of England, "Resolving Globally Active, Systemically Important, Financial Institutions," Joint White Paper, December 10, 2012.

easily imagine why a plan of action, constructed well before the crisis and agreed-upon by regulators who know and have worked with each other in the crisis management groups or otherwise, would facilitate the rapid cross-border resolution of a SIFI once a crisis hits in a way that cannot be replicated when the US decision-maker is an unknown bankruptcy judge.

Since Title II has these desirable characteristics, there would have to be extremely persuasive reasons to repeal it. The reasons in support of repeal are not, however, persuasive.

The most common arguments for the repeal of Title II are that it gives the regulators too much discretion; that it puts taxpayers at risk; and that its very existence has immediate adverse economic impacts. A full response is beyond the scope of this note, but a few quick points show that these arguments are unpersuasive.

The "too much discretion" argument focuses particularly on the contention that Title II provides insufficient clarity about the order of priority of claims because it allows the FDIC under certain circumstances to pay some creditors more than others, which, it is said, would not be permissible in bankruptcy. Putting aside whether this argument fairly describes the supposed clarity of the bankruptcy process, there are three responses:

- First, Dodd-Frank contains a "no worse off than under Chapter 7 of the Bankruptcy Code" provision to protect creditors, so no matter what the FDIC does, the bankruptcy rules provide a floor for all creditors.
- Second, the range of discretion that the FDIC would have in a Title II resolution is fundamentally the same as the range of discretion it has had for many years in resolving failed banks, without evidence of the kind of abuse imagined by opponents of Title II.
- Third, Title II can be used in place of bankruptcy only if resolution under the Bankruptcy Code would result in severe adverse effects on US financial stability. In other words, the FDIC gets to use its discretion only when the alternative would be worse for the country.

The argument that taxpayers are put at financial risk by Title II is based on the provision that allows the FDIC, with the approval of the secretary of the treasury, to draw on the orderly liquidation fund to provide interim liquidity to a holding company that the FDIC has taken over. But Title II requires that OLA advances be fully secured by a first priority lien on the assets of the failed institution; and if these prove to be insufficient to repay the government in full, Title II requires that any shortfall be paid by other large financial institutions. Dodd-Frank categorically provides that "taxpayers shall bear no losses from the exercise of any authority" granted by Title II. One would have to believe that the regulators and the Treasury Department would knowingly violate the express requirements of the law to believe that taxpayers will lose money if OLA is invoked. That is an unfair and unjustified insult to dedicated and hard-working government employees who are charged with administering Dodd-Frank.

The most important argument against Title II is that, despite what Title II was designed to do and what it says it does, Title II actually preserves "too big to fail." Because of Title II, the argument runs, creditors of large financial institutions do not believe they are at risk; instead, they believe they will be protected—"bailed out"—by the government in the event of a failure. Therefore, it is said, creditors do not provide market discipline for SIFIs, as shown by their willingness to lend to SIFIs at lower rates than they offer to smaller institutions.

The problem with this argument is that the facts undermine it. As the September 2013 Treasury paper[2] on the financial crisis shows, "senior unsecured borrowing costs for large bank holding companies have risen more than for small, regional bank holding companies." Specifically, Fifth Third, KeyCorp, PNC, and SunTrust all have lower spreads over Treasury yields than do Bank of America, Citigroup, Goldman, J.P. Morgan, and Morgan Stanley.

In addition, and just as telling, the Treasury paper shows that spreads vary widely among the largest six financial institutions. This is completely inconsistent with the notion that creditors of these institutions expect to be bailed out. If they did, all of the large institutions would have the same or very similar spreads, and they would be very small—neither of which is true post-Dodd-Frank. So there is ample evidence that long-term unsecured creditors of large bank holding companies understand they are at risk—and will not be bailed out by the government—in the event of a failure and the use of Title II.

---

2. Anthony Reyes, "The Financial Crisis Five Years Later: Response, Reform, and Progress," US Department of the Treasury, September 2013.

The ratings agencies, always slow post-crisis to change their views, have caught up to the reality that holding company creditors are at risk under the FDIC's Title II SPOE plan. In mid-November 2013, Moody's eliminated the ratings "uplift" based on assumed government support for the eight large bank holding companies, noting that Title II SPOE "is designed to allow regulators to restore the solvency of a distressed entity without using public funds." Moody's went on (emphasis added), "As envisioned by US regulators, *the [SPOE] approach would impose losses on US bank holding company creditors* to recapitalize and preserve the operations of the group's systemically important subsidiaries in a stress scenario. As a result, *the holding company creditors are unlikely to receive government support, signaling a higher risk of default.*"

And some key policymakers outside the United States understand the point. Paul Tucker of the Bank of England is reported to have said recently that US regulators are "basically equipped to resolve" US SIFIs and that a US government bailout would not be needed.

For all these reasons, which are summarized here only at a very high level, Title II is a useful and important tool. It is a tool which can only be invoked with approval of independent banking regulators and highest executive branch officials, and only if a financial institution's failure and resolution under the Bankruptcy Code would result in severe adverse effects on US financial stability. If Title II is invoked, US taxpayers will not bear the cost, which will be imposed, as it should be, on stockholders, creditors, and responsible senior management of the institution's holding company.

Improving the bankruptcy process for dealing with the failure of a large financial institution is highly desirable. Indeed, no set of institutions has a greater stake in making sure that the bankruptcy process works as effectively as possible for the failure of large financial institutions than large financial institutions themselves. The reason is simple. Large financial institutions are required by Title I of Dodd-Frank to submit resolution plans (living wills in common parlance). These plans must be based on the assumption that the Orderly Liquidation Authority granted to the FDIC by Title II of Dodd-Frank is not available and that the institution is resolved under the Bankruptcy Code. The more effectively the bankruptcy system can handle the failure of a SIFI, the more likely it is that that the living wills of SIFIs will be deemed satisfactory. And satisfactory resolution plans are plainly a good thing—good for the country, good for the regulators, and good for the institutions themselves. So improving the bankruptcy process through some form of Chapter 14 is a good idea.

But when and if Congress adopts a Chapter 14, it should reject any attempt to take Title II authority away from the regulators who may someday need it. The country needs to have more tools in the toolbox when a large financial institution fails, not fewer.

Remarks on Key Issues Facing Financial Institutions

Paul Saltzman

All too often, the debate surrounding the lessons learned from the subprime mortgage crisis, and the regulatory framework needed to mitigate against future crises, is filled with distractions, populist rhetoric, revisionist history, and a reliance on false narratives. Much like Grover Cleveland's non-existent illegitimate child, there are too many untested and unchallenged foundational assertions that are repeated over and over and taken as truths by the media, by politicians, and even by regulators. Events such as the October 1, 2013, Brookings-Hoover conference on the financial crisis allow us to close that awareness gap, to debate and challenge each other respectfully, and to share thoughts regarding how best to achieve what we all want to achieve, which is to create a stable financial system without inhibiting the critical role that banks, and large banks in particular, play in facilitating economic recovery.

In this chapter, I'd like to share three things. First, I'll describe The Clearing House, which I lead. Second, I will endeavor to dispel some misunderstandings and mischaracterizations of the industry's position on certain key macroprudential rules. And last, I'll offer some recommendations and observations about how to improve both the pace and the quality of Dodd-Frank rulemaking.

Not too many institutions actually can lay claim to a direct connection to our nation's Founding Fathers. In 1841, eight years before his passing, Albert Gallatin, the treasury secretary under presidents Jefferson and Madison, proposed the idea of New York banks getting together to solve large payment flows. The idea was the establishment of a consortium of private banks, where each bank would place funds proportionate to its capital, and through which their books would be debited and credited in relation to all member banks. Gallatin's idea was based on the structure at the time of the Bank of England and was a model for how private participants can work together to solve systemic crises. Twelve years later, in 1853, the New York Clearing House was incorporated, becoming the nation's first banking association, the largest payment processor in the world, and the oldest payments company in the United States.

The Clearing House (TCH) recently sponsored a conference with Columbia University focused on the role of private market participants in promoting stability in the banking system from 1853 to 1913. Fast forward 160 years, and The Clearing House now operates under a dual corporate structure: The Clearing House Payments Company and the Association. The Clearing House Payments Company owns and operates the critical infrastructure of our nation's payment system, along with the Federal Reserve. It operates three core products and clears almost $2 trillion a day. It's not a central counterparty—it is a payments processor, despite the name. It owns and operates CHIPS (Clearing House Interbank Payments System), a large-value payment system, the ACH (Automated Clearing House) small-value payment system, and a check imaging business.

Recently, The Clearing House was designated as a systemically important financial market utility (SIFMU) by the Financial Stability Oversight Council (FSOC)—interestingly enough, only in its capacity as owner and operator of CHIPS. The FSOC avoided the characterization of The Clearing House Payments Company in its entirety because of issues associated with the small-value payments system.

Leveraging that infrastructure, The Clearing House is working on a number of groundbreaking initiatives involving mobile payments, medical payments, and P2P (person-to-person) payments and recently launched a transformational initiative to deal with the safety and soundness of the mobile payments architecture.

In addition to its role serving the nation's payments infrastructure, The Clearing House Association provides thought leadership on the most important issues facing the banking industry today. Its membership consists of eighteen large and diverse commercial banks, ranging from large, systemically important globally diverse firms to super-regionals, regionals, and seven foreign banking organizations. It operates on a strong consensus basis. Although not every issue affects every particular member, there is an undeniable commonality of interests among the membership when it comes to finalization and implementation of all financial rules and regulations, especially macroprudential rules, which affect markets and products beyond the firms that are particularly targeted.

A few words about macroprudential regulation. It's clear that an evolution in the approach to banking regulation is occurring. Every major rule that comes out of the Fed cites macroprudential and systemic goals as its underlying motivation. This approach, shifting from a microprudential focus, which is concerned with the safety and soundness of individual banks, to focusing more on systemic risks, is understandable. But it is striking that, as Kevin Warsh has pointed out,[1] there is so little debate and even less quantitative and empirical analysis about the risks of this paradigm shift. Simply put, macroprudential regulation comes with macroeconomic risks. Unlike microprudential mistakes, macroprudential mistakes are likely to involve macroeconomic consequences.

Moreover, there is real risk that macroprudential regulation can quickly transform, either explicitly or implicitly, into a form of industrial policy that favors certain markets, businesses, or products. In that regard, I commend to your attention an op-ed by Professor John Cochrane on this very point.[2]

And last, by definition, macroprudential regulation suffers from an inherent flaw. It focuses on the tail risk and the lowest common denominator. By definition, it embraces a one-size-fits-all regulatory methodology. This is especially interesting because most of the macroprudential rules deal with regulation of a bank's balance sheet, which, by definition, is inherently idiosyncratic. No individual G-SIB (global systemically important bank) or D-SIB (domestic systemically important bank) is like any other. And this tension probably explains why the rulemaking process has been a challenging endeavor. Fitting square pegs into round holes is never an easy task.

Because this new macroprudential agenda is so important, and because the industry's position on individual macroprudential rules is so often mischaracterized, I'd like to set the record straight with regard to certain key issues on which The Clearing House lobbies.

First up is capital. The Clearing House banks have consistently supported increasing the quantity and quality of capital, certainly relative to pre-crisis levels. On balance, the current approach to capital regulation is comprised of four legs of a table: risk-weighted assets (RWA)-based capital methodologies; the Collins Amendment,[3] which sets minimum overall capital requirements on depository institutions; a leverage ratio

---

1. See chapter 4 in this volume.

2. John Cochrane, "The Danger of an All-Powerful Federal Reserve," *Wall Street Journal*, August 26, 2013.

3. Section 171, Dodd-Frank Act (Wall Street Reform and Consumer Protection Act of 2010).

as a backstop; and stress testing. Currently, this approach is robust and is headed in the right direction. The Clearing House will continue to offer technical comments or suggestions to improve the regulatory framework, for example, by recognizing the value of mortgage servicing rights and deferred tax assets and by making policymakers aware of the volatility associated with the removal of the accumulated other comprehensive income (AOCI) filter. But these are areas where empirical analysis and scrutiny are critical. And no one should mistake overall constructive suggestions as somehow negating the industry's support for higher and better capital.

Notwithstanding that support, the question of capital and the appropriate levels of capital involves a fundamental trade-off. TCH wholeheartedly rejects the notion, offered by some, that the theoretical framework of Modigliani and Miller applies to real-world bank balance-sheet decisions. The ratio between debt and equity matters. The economic impact is real. And the appropriate capital level needs to be empirically and historically analyzed. Those who present the issue of ever-higher capital levels as a one-sided free option, with no acknowledgment of the economic downsides, are doing a disservice to the debate.

Long-term debt is another issue that is critically important. To be clear, TCH banks support a long-term debt requirement at the holding company level for those banks that, because of their complexity and structure, would likely be recapitalized under the single-point-of-entry approach of Title II. The critical question here is the amount of loss absorbency. To date, empirical research undertaken by The Clearing House suggests that two times tier 1 capital plus a G-SIB surcharge is a reasonable amount to cover all historical losses, including analyses of stress-testing results and a return variability analysis. Based on those three empirical approaches, that is the appropriate level that TCH believes should be implemented.

Regulatory policymakers will soon present two other key questions to the public. One is the question of pre-positioning of assets to facilitate a holding company recapitalization and the other is what to do with the right side of the balance sheet. However constructed, the objective of long-term debt should be to facilitate such a holding company recapitalization and to work in concert with existing capital and liquidity regulations—and not to be a supplemental instrument of regulatory capital.

Another key issue on the macroprudential agenda is the leverage ratio, which is currently the subject of significant proposals in both the United States and Basel. Again, TCH banks support an enhanced supplementary leverage ratio. But it is critical that the leverage ratio function as a backstop measure and neither be the primary source of capital regulation nor act as the binding constraint. A leverage ratio that acts as a binding constraint will inject perverse incentives for the banking industry to hold riskier assets. The regulatory architecture should continue to embrace risk weightings, notwithstanding their shortcomings.

It is also crucial that the denominator in any leverage ratio calculation be calibrated appropriately. In that respect, the most recent Basel proposals fail to reflect netting and recognize the benefit of collateral. It's critical to get the calibration right. Research from The Clearing House has found that the Basel proposal, combined with a minimum leverage ratio of 5 to 6 percent for US G-SIBs, would make the leverage ratio the binding constraint for approximately 67 percent of US G-SIB assets. TCH's study also found that under a combined US numerator and Basel denominator, the distance to compliance would require $202 billion of additional tier 1 capital or an exposure reduction of $3.7 trillion, equal to 19.6 percent of covered industry exposures. It's difficult to imagine how that amount of deleveraging could have anything but a negative impact on the economy.

It's important to have an effective resolution framework to resolve a systemically important bank without taxpayer-funded support, and for that reason The Clearing House banks strongly support Title II of the Dodd-Frank Act.

Paul Tucker, former deputy governor of the Bank of England, made some very comforting remarks to a question by Gillian Tett of the *Financial Times* at a recent conference.[4] He indicated he firmly believes that if a large, systemically important financial institution in the United States were to fail, it could successfully be resolved under Title II. It wouldn't be pretty, but it could be successfully resolved without any taxpayer-funded support. Although some are calling for a legislative repeal of Title II, and there is a legislative debate about the appropriateness of Title II, we remain steadfastly supportive of it as an effective resolution framework.

At the same time, TCH is also supportive of other efforts, including the efforts by Hoover and the resolution working group, whether they be legislative or regulatory, to improve the Title I process.[5]

---

4. Speech by Paul Tucker, deputy governor for financial stability at the Bank of England, at the INSOL (International Association of Restructuring, Insolvency & Bankruptcy Professionals) International World Congress, The Hague, Netherlands, May 20, 2013.

5. See Michael Helfer's remarks, chapter 16 in this volume.

Next to last is liquidity. Another key pillar of a macroprudential agenda is strengthening liquidity requirements, in particular the liquidity coverage ratio (LCR) and net stable funding ratio (NSFR). Here, again, is another positive, constructive story. The Clearing House has consistently supported prescriptive regulations around liquidity. Its research has shown that large banks are more liquid than ever. Since 2010, US commercial banks have reduced their reliance on short-term wholesale funding by almost $250 billion and have increased demand deposits accordingly.

The LCR, generally speaking, is appropriately calibrated, although the failure to treat GSE (government-sponsored enterprise) securities and the Federal Home Loan Bank borrowings should be reconsidered. TCH research has shown that the US banking industry average LCR changed from 59 percent in 2010 to 81 percent at the end of 2012.

On the NSFR, it's critical that the calibrations reflect empirical data and actual experience of liquidity, as well as management actions likely to be taken in the event of a liquidity crisis. Currently, they do not. TCH's recently-released NSFR white paper revealed that the industry-wide NSFR shortfall in the numerator ranges from approximately $1.4 trillion to $2.4 trillion, depending on whether banks are assumed to manage to a 100 percent or a 110 percent NSFR compliance level. Something's not right there, and a Basel Committee re-proposal of the NSFR was certainly called for.

Last, another key macroprudential initiative both in the United States and abroad is the establishment of single counterparty credit limits, which, again, The Clearing House supports. Such a requirement can serve as an important prudential tool to limit contagion and mitigate the effects of a crisis. But it is critically important that single counterparty limits reflect true economic risk. TCH had serious concerns about the approach proposed. It produced a quantitative analysis that demonstrated the flaws and prompted the Federal Reserve to step back and commence an effort to study the impact.

The Clearing House, notwithstanding its brand and approach, makes no apologies for representing the views of its membership to regulators and other policymakers. Some have suggested this is a form of cognitive capture, a derivation of regulatory capture. On the contrary, TCH has offered our support constructively on a host of macroprudential rules and will continue to do the same, and TCH will continue to interact with thought leaders like Brookings and Hoover, and with academics and other professionals, to get it right.

Clearly, both industry and regulators want to get it right, and getting it right will take some time. But there are two points that need to be made in this regard. First, the marketplace has already accelerated the pace of rule implementation, and in many instances firms have already implemented changes, notwithstanding the pace of implementation of Dodd-Frank rules. In other words, much of the "delay" in rulemaking is what some people would call a false negative.

In addition, there are improvements that can be made to enhance the rulemaking process, which The Clearing House and its members would assuredly support. And it's all based on the simple notion that good is better than perfect when perfect takes too much time. The following are a few short recommendations in that regard.

Number one: greater use of advanced notice of proposed rulemakings. There's no reason that these issues should be debated in an opaque way. Regulators should be issuing more Advanced Notice of Proposed Rulemakings, much like the SEC issues concept releases. Let's get the proposals out there, get all the ideas out there, and flesh out the issues.

Second, shorter comment periods. This is something that some TCH members might not necessarily support. But it's clear that during the comment process, work expands to fill the time allotted. Whether it's a 60-day period, a 90-day period, or a 180-day period, the industry will get it done. And if it means enacting rules in a more accelerated pace, TCH and its owner banks will support a shorter comment period.

Third, and perhaps most important: staged implementation. Instead of trying to adopt the perfect rule—whether it be single counterparty credit limits or the Volcker Rule, for example—rules can be implemented in stages, recognizing that the work is not yet finished. Despite the best intentions of the Federal Reserve and all the other dedicated public servants, this is very, very difficult and complex stuff. At times, unfortunately, it appears that politics may be inhibiting free thinking because people are afraid to throw ideas out there.

And last, more transparent empirical analysis. It sounds like a delay tactic, but the fact of the matter is that each of the initiatives that have been described can and should be subject to detailed and rigorous quantitative impact analysis.

Concluding Remarks

George P. Shultz

I have a few reflections. The first one: what a sensational job Martin Baily and John Taylor have done in putting together such a riveting conference. The quality of the discussion has been very high. The people who are here are impressive. And it gives you a good feeling that somehow or other there's an ability here to grapple with some very difficult problems.

I had a hard time keeping up with a lot of the things we've discussed, and this confirms a decision I made a long time ago. When I was secretary of state, I was in the midst of ending the Cold War, and I was really interested in the work I was doing. When I was offered the job of chairman of the Fed, I declined. I see now that I would have been out of my depth if I had taken that job. It was too far ahead of me. But it does raise one question about most of our discussion. That is, we haven't reflected very much on the international implications of what goes on here and what goes on over there. For example, when our Federal Reserve creates massive liquidity, it doesn't necessarily stay here. I suppose some might say that the Federal Reserve is a massive currency manipulator that causes all kinds of problems elsewhere. Somehow, it seems to me—maybe it's just because I have my foreign policy hat on—that these problems need to be taken into consideration.

I thought there was more agreement here than people may have expected at the beginning of the meeting, and it wasn't simply on the idea of going to zero interest rate on reserves. Who could pass a bill in the Congress saying that we want to give banks *x* billion dollars a year? But that's what the Fed is doing, so going to zero is good on many grounds.

I think there also was agreement, as we looked at the financial crisis, that the regulatory system failed. There was probably quite a lot of disagreement, however, on why and what to do about it. At least as I see it, this was a classic case of over-the-shoulder-type regulation. As George Stigler taught us long ago, it simply doesn't work; it's captured. When the head of Citibank says, "As long as the music is playing, you've got to get up and dance," you would think the New York Fed, which was the regulator, would say, "Wait a minute, we want to find out about that music. What's going on here?" But nothing was done—nothing.

So as we try to design a different regulatory system, over-the-shoulder regulation is not the way to go about it. We need to devise something that is simple and easy for anyone to spot so you don't need a regulator. Capital requirements can be spotted, types of trading can be spotted, and leverage can be spotted. So there's a certain automaticity in a regulatory regime that's simple and easy to understand so that anyone can see if you're out of line.

We had a conference here recently on nuclear security, and John Taylor took part in it. We had participants who worked on warheads, on the power industry, and on regulation. We also had some press people. In the nuclear industry in the United States, there is a really effective kind of regulation because all the people who own nuclear power plants recognize that if any one plant goes down, they all will suffer. So they have created their own regulatory mechanism where they visit each other's plants. If they spot something wrong, they say so and it gets fixed. This mechanism is knowledge-based, and those being regulated have a stake in seeing that the regulations work, not only for them but for everybody. It seems to me that's a principle to use when designing regulations.

During the conference, there was also emphasis on the importance of long-term, strategic thinking. When that isn't done, it's easy to get off the track. That's the importance of something like the Taylor Rule, or having clarity in what your procedures are going to be. For example, this is a long-term proposition that we're talking about here: we have a plan, we're going to stick to that plan, and it's going to work.

Legitimate questions were raised about what the Fed has done in an institutional way. I worked closely with the Fed in my role as secretary of the treasury and in other positions, and I've always thought of the Fed as a limited purpose organization, not a general purpose organization. If you say to yourself, "I've got to solve all the problems," then you're opening yourself up to overstepping and you'll wind up getting your wings clipped if you aren't careful. In the national security field, we call that mission creep. You sit in the situation room, you hear something you want to do, and a mission gets designed carefully. The military says, "This is what we can do." Then you succeed and all of a sudden the mission changes. That's when you get in trouble. Mission creep is something to watch out for.

We had quite a lot of discussion about the very important question of intervention. I had several brushes with it that made an impact on me. I recognize this incident is simple compared with the issues you've been struggling with, but when I became director of the budget in 1970, I discovered that a major financial company, the Penn Central, had badly mismanaged its affairs and was about to go bankrupt. My friend, Arthur Burns, who was chairman of the Fed, was a very strong personality and he knew a lot about financial markets. He had been my mentor when he was chairman of the Council of Economic Advisers and I was on the council staff. He thought that if the Penn Central went bankrupt, it would be a huge negative event for the financial system, and he had somehow worked out a bailout with a reluctant David Packard in the Defense Department.

I thought it was a bad idea, and I used all the arguments you could easily imagine for why it was a bad idea. Half of me was convinced that I was right, but the other half of me was saying, "What am I doing arguing with Arthur Burns?" Then, all of a sudden, Bryce Harlow, a savvy political counselor to both Eisenhower and Nixon, walked into the room. He said, "Mr. President, in its infinite wisdom, the Penn Central has just hired your old law firm to represent them in this matter. Under the circumstances, you can't touch this with a ten-foot pole." So there was no bailout, and guess what? No dominoes fell. Arthur Burns had thought a lot about what the repercussions would be and he flooded the system with liquidity, among other things. In other words, he addressed the system as distinct from the company. Not only did no dominoes fall, the whole event was a very healthy development from the standpoint of the financial community because everybody had to realize that "apparently we're not going to get bailed out even if we're very big, so maybe we should run things better." So it was a healthy development.

I think it is important to recognize—and I think we all instinctively do realize—that once there are bailouts, people's behavior changes, and the change in behavior is very undesirable. So it's important to figure out how to arrange things so that people who have the decision to make on bankruptcy can stand up to it. It is not easy to stand up to it if you are there. I've seen this in a number of cases. I've just finished reading a biography of President Eisenhower. Obviously, he had to stand up to a lot, mostly in the national security field. In 1945, General Eisenhower was the only one at Potsdam who opposed dropping the atom bomb. On at least two occasions when he was president, all of his advisers—civilian and military, state and defense—said, "Mr. President, you've got to use the nuclear weapon on this crisis." But he declined. He was very skillful at working on something in a strategic sense. He said, "The hard part is to have the courage to be patient." It's essential to have a strategy. But then to carry out the strategy, you will be confronted with a lot of difficult situations and you will need to have the guts to stand up to them.

When President Reagan took office, inflation was in the 'teens, the economy was going nowhere, and the Soviet Union was running wild. Paul Volcker at the Fed realized what needed to be done to get inflation under control, and President Reagan knew it, too. All who were advising him knew that you can't have a decent economy with that kind of inflation. So Paul went ahead and acted. My belief is that he could not have done so if President Reagan had not put a political umbrella over him. Paul has told me on a number of occasions that there were a lot of press conferences where the press served up questions inviting Reagan to criticize Paul, but he never did. People would run into the Oval Office and say, "Mr. President, he'll create unemployment. You're going to lose seats in the midterm election." And he said, "Well, if not now, when? If not us, who? Volcker is doing the right thing and we've got to support him."

What I'm saying here is that in order for all of the fascinating and important issues you have been talking about in this conference to work, there have to be some people at the top with guts who are willing to look at these things and see them through. It isn't easy.

I will finish by going back to the very interesting remarks by Larry Summers. Basically, he said that the financial side of the economy was badly mismanaged. Remarkably, even though that was going on, the real economy kept going, but finally the financial mismanagement knocked it down. Then the rescue came along, and fundamentally it focused on getting the financial community straightened around, and it more or less has worked. But the real economy is still down, and the huge amount of stimulus from the Fed and from fiscal policy has not succeeded in rejuvenating the real side. So it seems to me that the lesson of this story is that we should stop focusing on the financial community and think about what it takes to get the real economy moving. Then, Allan Meltzer was saying, you reduce the uncertainty and get a regulatory system in place that is constant and that people understand. Everybody knows the personal and corporate income tax system needs to be reformed—that's not even controversial—so why don't we do it? We have the template of the 1986 tax act that passed the Senate 97–3. Some of these things could be done, and they're the kinds of things that would get the real economy going—accommodated, of course, by access to capital and so on.

Let me once again turn to John Taylor and Martin Baily to thank them for putting together a really stimulating day. I want to say again how impressed I am with the quality of the people who have spoken to us and answered questions and with the high caliber of the conversation.

Thank you.

Summary of the Commentary

Simon Hilpert

This book is based on presentations given at the joint conference on "The US Financial System—Five Years After the Crisis" of the Brookings Institution and the Hoover Institution on October 1, 2013. Questions and comments from members of the audience at both the Brookings Institution and the Hoover Institution followed the presentations. This chapter is a summary of the discussion, organized into sections that correspond to the four parts of this book.

Causes and Effects of the Financial Crisis

Commenting on Lawrence Summers's presentation (see chapter 2), **Peter Thiel** suggested that the decoupling of the real economy from the financial economy goes back further, starting with the recovery of the early nineties that was much slower than predicted by macroeconomic models. Even though the interest rate was very low for a long time back then, the transition mechanisms to the real economy were broken. In addition, Thiel pointed to the tech bubble in the late nineties as a predecessor to the bubble in the housing and financial markets in the 2000s.

Thiel further suggested heavy micro-regulation as an alternative to poor macroeconomic policies as a cause for the slow recovery. Even with low real interest rates, investors are not finding many good opportunities in the real economy, as evidenced by low capital expenditures. He noted that a lot of this micro-regulation comes under the header of environmental regulation, so that a debate on the cost of environmental regulation would be needed. As an example, he estimated that abandoning all zoning laws in the United States would lead to a rise in gross domestic product (GDP) growth in the following year by 6 percent.

Lawrence Summers pointed out that there were several years in the nineties with positive real interest rates, a robust economy, and no strong evidence of bubbles. Therefore, he doubted that the decoupling of the real and financial economies goes back twenty years. Summers agreed with the concerns about regulation. He pointed out that in 1903, before the bulldozer had been invented, the Harvard football stadium was conceived and built in just twenty-one months with a building time of just four and a half months. This would no longer be possible in today's regulatory environment, despite technological progress. However, he doubted that there was a discontinuity in regulatory policies between the years 1980 and 1989, given the political constellation in the United States. Hence, he did not fully agree with Thiel's theory that micro-regulations were causing slow recoveries but noted that regulatory issues can form a part of resolving slow growth. Summers also said that the burden of environmental regulation on investment is unlikely to be large enough to cause slow GDP growth. In addition, he noted that unprecedentedly punitive and burdensome regulation would be associated with low corporate profits as a share of corporate output, which is not supported by the data. However, Summers recognized the importance of the issue that Thiel was raising.

While **John Taylor** did not disagree with Thiel that increased micro-economic regulations were a factor in the slow recovery, he noted that Stanford had recently built its football stadium in only nine months, tearing down the old one after the end of the 2005 season and building a new one before fall 2006, notwithstanding modern environmental regulations. He further commented that the slow recovery from the deep downturn was very unusual in comparison with most of US history. In contrast, a mild recovery of the early 1990s was not unusual because it followed a mild recession. In his opinion, however, the causes for both the deep recession and the weak recovery were changes in policy that occurred more recently than the longer-term increases in environmental regulation.

Lee E. Ohanian brought up long-run supply-side policies. Indicators for many of the key drivers of economic growth—such as entrepreneurship, new business formation, job creation, and job reallocation (moving workers from less productive to more productive positions)—have deteriorated substantially since the 1990s. Traditional economics suggests a number of policies to address these issues. He said that there is broad consensus among economists about immigration reform to bring in high-skilled workers and entrepreneurs and a lot of discussion about corporate tax reform. Ohanian inquired whether these trends suggest significant, substantive problems with the underlying economy and what policies should be considered to alleviate them. He argued that these long-run problems were more important than the short-run demand issues highlighted by Summers.

Lawrence Summers agreed with economists' consensus on immigration reform, a general desire to have the economy function more efficiently, and a desire to remove tax barriers to investment. He noted that the economists at the Brookings Institution and the Hoover Institution might disagree on whether the economy is demand-constrained. If a market is constrained by a lack of demand and supply is increased, the level of output won't rise. He pointed to a recent study on training programs in different French localities.[1] The study found that in all localities, the people who got trained were more likely to get jobs than the people who did not receive training. In the localities that previously had full employment, more training led to more employment overall. However, in the localities with high unemployment previously, the training programs did not lead to an increase in the total level of employment, since those who received no training were less likely to find a job due to the stiff competition from people with training. This demonstrates that increasing supply does not matter when there is a constraint on demand. Summers argued that in the past several years and for several years in prospect, the US economy likely has been and will be substantially demand-constrained. Therefore, while he supports supply-side agendas, he did not think that they address the pressing near-term challenges. However, Summers also noted that focusing only on the near-term demand challenges would be a mistake, in particular since supply-side measures take years to implement. He also noted that the sense that successful long-run supply-side measures are being put in place contributes to confidence, which may lead to increased demand in the short run. Summers concluded that while supply-side policies are important, the current constraint on the economy stems from the side of demand.

Sheila Bair noted that one problematic aspect of loose monetary policy is that it papers over the underlying structural problems in the economy that can only be dealt with by elected officials. Therefore, it absolves political leaders of accountability to show leadership on these structural changes. Bair agreed that immigration reform is important. She also pointed to the importance of infrastructure improvements for the competitiveness of the US economy and emphasized that government

---

1. Bruno Crépon, Esther Duflo, Marc Gurgand, Roland Rathelot, and Philippe Zamora, "Do labor market policies have displacement effects? Evidence from a clustered randomized experiment," published as NBER Working Paper 18597, December 2012.

plays a necessary role in infrastructure repair. She added that the United States needs to become more competitive in the global economy so that there will be increased demand for its goods and services. However, competing on the basis of labor costs is difficult and undesirable. Bair instead pointed to a better-trained workforce, better infrastructure, and lower energy costs. She said these areas—in particular, infrastructure and job training—require the long-term commitment of elected officials, an effort that will pay off over time. In the shorter term, she noted that corporate tax reform is a low-hanging fruit, since there is a tremendous amount of inefficiency in the corporate code. By broadening the tax base, the top rate can be reduced. Bair pointed to very viable proposals for corporate tax reform put forward by very smart people and expressed her astonishment at the lack of progress in this area.

Bair said she wondered whether the political leadership can show the wherewithal to stand up to the special interests that benefit from various breaks in the corporate tax code. She argued in favor of closing loopholes and broadening the tax base, which would make the corporate tax rate more competitive. This would abolish a tremendous friction in the system and enable a substantial repatriation of foreign profits. There should be much more focus on corporate tax reform, she argued.

Paul Saltzman inquired whether more policymakers should have predicted the crisis and how the insights gained from the recent recession will affect our ability to predict future crises.

Kevin Warsh noted that the goal of the Dodd-Frank regulations and the burden assumed by the Federal Reserve is to make sure bad economic outcomes never happen again, using new power, authority, and macroprudential remit. He agreed that, coming out of the crisis, we have learned lessons about sources of instability in the economy. He expressed concern, however, that the Fed is over-promising and hence might under-deliver. Betting an institution's credibility on its ability to predict and prevent crises is risky, in particular for the Fed, whose institutional credibility is tested every day in financial markets.

Warsh also pointed to a second-order consequence of the current aggressive monetary policy: it removes a lot of volatility from financial markets. This might have benefits through wealth and confidence effects in the near term. However, he was concerned that markets are no longer able to point regulators and government officials to areas of the economy where problems are building up. Measures of volatility in equity markets, fixed income markets, and capital markets more broadly are low globally, but perceived risk from news reports is high. He concluded that risk is highest when measures of risk are lowest and that the aggressive central bank policy might therefore generate greater risks in the long run.

Finally, Warsh expressed great concern that the novelty and aggressiveness of the government's policy response in recent years may have fundamentally altered the behavior of businesses and households on the front lines of the economy. Hence, a reduction in our economy's dynamism would correspond to the weakness of the recovery to date.

John Taylor commented that financial crises are always very hard to predict. However, economic imbalances are what to look for, which was the case with Fed policy in the early 2000s. Taylor pointed to the yen/dollar exchange rate in 2012 as another example where economists were detecting imbalances. He cautioned that while it may be possible to detect imbalances, predicting the exact moment when markets will move to correct the imbalance is very hard.

Lawrence Summers argued that we can't expect to anticipate crises and forestall them with public policy. He gave two reasons. First, financial crises involve major movements in the price of some asset. Since vast fortunes can be made by reliably predicting major moves in asset prices, individuals who are smart enough to do that are likely to become investors and not regulatory officials. Thus, investors are likely to be better than regulators at predicting moves in asset prices. And if there were a consensus that a price was going to move in a major way, it would have already moved since the number of sellers exceeded the number of buyers. Summers concluded that the notion that public policy is able to predict crises is epistemologically problematic. Similarly, if there is an imbalance that predictably leads to a crisis, then noticing the imbalance is the basis for a sound trading strategy, which is more likely to be discovered by the private than by the public sector.

Second, Summers pointed out that the essence of a bubble is a widely shared and pervasive view that turns out to be wrong. In a democratic society, the government acts on prevailing and consensus beliefs. Asking the government to be a systematic opponent of prevailing consensus beliefs is not likely to be successful. Therefore, Summers argued that financial regulatory policy is unlikely to be able to anticipate and prevent crisis. Instead, we need to recognize that aspects of human nature such as greed, stupidity, herd behavior, fear, and revulsion will not change, and set up a regulatory system that is safe for a world with these features of human nature. This includes provisions for capital buffers and liquidity. Summers then drew an analogy to the late senator Daniel Patrick Moynihan's first major policy initiative, an essay on automobile safety. Before Moynihan's essay, the dominant paradigm for addressing automobile safety was drivers' education. Moynihan, however, realized that people have faults and they are going to drive too fast, get tired, or misuse the steering wheel. Even with excellent drivers' education, accidents are going to happen. Seatbelts, banked highway curves, guard rails, and crash-proof bumpers were a superior strategy. Since then, the fatality rate per vehicle mile has decreased by a factor of ten. Summers's vision of success for financial regulation was that a failsafe system is a system that's safe for failure, not one that can realistically aspire to avoid failure, accidents, and mistakes.

Sheila Bair commented that while it is not hard to see a crisis building, predicting the precise timing is hard. In the case of the recent crisis, it was not difficult to see a housing bubble and over-leveraged financial system. However, she argued that taking action before the crisis erupts is problematic since market participants are making a lot of money as long as the bubble is building, so regulators would have to fight popular sentiment.

Commenting on Summers's presentation, **Martin Baily** disagreed with the notion that the financial sector is fully restored, which would rule out problems in the financial sector as a cause for slow growth. Instead, he suggested that the financial sector is still focusing on fulfilling regulatory requirements, as opposed to evaluating the riskiness of loans and focusing on risk management. For that reason, the availability of funds from the financial sector has not yet been fully restored. In addition, Baily asked why the policies targeted at the lack of demand—both quantitative easing and fiscal stimulus—have not returned the economy to full employment. His reservation on this issue was that the United States has been running large trade deficits for a long time, and that people in the nineties and early 2000s have argued that there was too much consumption, suggesting excess demand, not excess supply. Even in the current environment, the US trade deficit is at 4 percent, which makes it hard for the US economy to get back to full employment. Baily suggested that this might be done by improving competitiveness, or by adjusting the dollar, or perhaps it would turn out not to be possible at all due to economic weakness in the rest of the world.

Lawrence Summers agreed with both points. He noted that there are regulatory headwinds that constrain lending by financial institutions. However, it can also be argued that these are necessary corrective regulations of pre-crisis excesses. He pointed out that if we returned to prudent behavior in the financial sector, similar issues on regulation would remain on the agenda. In commenting on the international aspect, Summers noted that he had urged the administration in early 2010 to set a goal of doubling exports over five years and to organize energy around that goal. He said that in comparison with the other countries in the industrialized world, the United States is a natural capital importer given its demographics and the capacity of the US economy to innovate. He also pointed out that there is a global aspect to the determination of the real interest rate. Summers said that the structure of the global economy and the US economy currently implies that full employment is only attained at real interest rates that are uncomfortably low from the point of view of financial stability. He suggested that the solution is to accept low interest rates, to promote various kinds of public investments, to reduce foreign surpluses, and to promote net exports. In addition, he suggested avoiding major fiscal contraction. However, he argued that the lesson from five years before and after the crisis is that business as usual does not necessarily produce a healthy, fully employed economy and that this lesson has not been drawn in the debate so far. He noted that policies involve trade-offs and expressed concern about a policy agenda solely pursuing financial stability, which seems to currently be congealing into conventional wisdom. The elements of this financial stability agenda are (1) that loose money needs to be avoided because it produces bubbles, (2) that more regulation is needed since insufficient regulation generates bubbles, and (3) that fiscal consolidation is required because long-term debts are a problem. Summers argued that this agenda does not add up to a growth strategy and that the economy has been demand-constrained for a long time. He stressed that the economy is not naturally fixing itself in the way one might have expected in an era of 4 percent inflation and 6 percent nominal rates that could freely be adjusted downward to accommodate demand constraints.

The Federal Reserve's Role

Following the presentations on the role of the Fed (chapters 5–8), **Donald Kohn** commented that although unconventional monetary policy might produce distortions in asset markets, it was also addressing a large distortion in the real economy—high unemployment and underutilized capital—and the costs of the asset distortions needed to be weighed against the problems in the real economy. From the presentations, he gathered that the prescription for monetary policy is to avoid using unconventional monetary policy. In the absence of unconventional monetary policy, interest rates would be higher. Kohn asked whether lowering the interest rate on excess reserves, as had been advocated in the presentations, and reducing uncertainty would be enough to offset the effects of the rise in the interest rate on economic activity that follows from withdrawing unconventional monetary policy in the face of current restrictive fiscal policy.

Peter Fisher pointed to the slope of the yield curve and expressed his objections to the Fed suppressing the term premium by buying long-term bonds and selling short-term bonds in Operation Twist. He noted that the Fed's model is that a reduction in interest rate will unequivocally lead to increased investment. However, this effect is lowered as the long end of the yield curve approaches zero because of portfolio investors' reasonable concerns about a future backup in rates. In addition, he expressed concern about the perverse effects of prolonged, low long-term rates on business investments.

Donald Kohn inquired whether Fisher wanted the yield curve to be more sloped and whether higher interest rates would be better for the economy. Fisher conceded that he thought somewhat higher and more predictable *long-term* interest rates would be better and argued that suppressing the term premium through extraordinary policies has discouraged business investment.

Alan Blinder disagreed and noted that, in his opinion, it was appropriate to decrease medium- and long-term interest rates, since these are the interest rates that matter for economic transactions—unlike the standard tool of monetary policy, the federal funds rate. He noted that the argument for reducing the interest on excess reserves (IOER) is that quantitative easing is a weak instrument. Since the Fed is rational, it picks the low-hanging fruit first and then moves to higher-hanging fruit. Now it is pretty high up in the tree, and the effects of additional quantitative easing are limited. So IOER is another potential tool for the Fed, though not a panacea. Blinder argued that the first-best solution would be to have additional room to decrease the federal funds rate but that this is not in the realm of choice, given the zero lower bound. So second- and third-best instruments need to be used, one of which is the IOER. He noted that using the IOER as a tool would also have the side benefit of calming critics who argue that the Fed's balance sheet is out of control, since the Fed could reduce its balance sheet as banks disgorge some of the reserves and still contribute positively to the economy. Blinder, however, cautioned that there is not much experience with these tools.

Allan Meltzer pointed out that he is not opposed to unconventional monetary policy and supports security purchases once the federal funds rate reaches the zero lower bound. He noted that buying longer-term securities has the same effects on the economy as conventional monetary policy via the federal funds rate, except in some long-run models. The Fed chooses not to do that, because it takes the first-round effects and then locks up the reserves as idle. Meltzer suggested the opposite: fewer increases in reserves and more increases in money growth. He referred to the case when Japan initiated quantitative easing: Japan's money supply growth increased and output rose more rapidly. In the United States, on the other hand, asset purchases only result in small output effects and large increases in stock prices and excess reserves; the monetary effects seen in Japan are absent. Meltzer agreed with Blinder on dropping the interest paid on excess reserves to zero. He argued that this had very good efficiency effects and pointed to the fact that half of the payments—$5 billion in interest and reserves—goes to foreign banks' branches in the United States. Blinder suggested that lowering the interest on excess reserves must be a non-controversial issue, given that both he and Meltzer agreed on it.

Michael Bordo agreed that keeping the interest rate on excess reserves high had been a mistake, citing the situation in the 1930s and the case of Japan as examples. With respect to interest rates, Bordo suggested that raising short-term rates to up to 2 percent could help normalize the situation in financial markets. The benefits of this normalization might outweigh the potential costs of a short-term slowing of the economy.

Paul Saltzman brought attention to the shadow banking system, pointing out that a significant portion of financial intermediation is provided by nonbanks. He inquired whether the notion that banks will continue to be the principal channel of monetary policy transmission is the working assumption of the presenters' opinions on monetary policy. He also asked how the growth of the shadow banking system might challenge this assumption.

Allan Meltzer said that the shadow banking system would not pose a problem if it were allowed to mark to market completely. The shadow banking system is a result of the Federal Reserve Board's regulation Q, which capped interest payments on checking and savings accounts. The government did not want to repeal or circumvent regulation Q, so it decided to allow mutual funds to create a separate banking system. Meltzer argued that this was a mistake that is still continuing today. Concerning the transmission of monetary policy, Meltzer argued that what mattered was the change in relative prices and the increase in money stock, not whether the transmission is done through commercial banks, savings and loan associations, or insurance companies.

Alan Blinder agreed that shadow banks are an important channel of monetary transmission. He deduced that the money supply, which is a product of banks, is less important than interest rates, since interest rates affect everybody. Therefore, moving interest rates affects the shadow banking system as well as the regular banking system, regardless of whether any particular definition of the money supply moves. Blinder added that since the shadow banking system is just as important, or more important, than the conventional banking system, a sensible regulatory regime for the shadow banking system is critical. Meltzer and Blinder both agreed that higher money growth would currently be preferable.

Kevin Harrington asked about ways to solve problems that would arise from ending quantitative easing. Blinder had asked why bond market participants believe that ending quantitative easing will steepen the yield curve. Harrington responded that one reason they expect this is that the Fed's quantitative easing policy is absorbing a lot of duration, thus performing a maturity transformation usually carried out by banks and bond investors in normal times. So ending the policy could be expected to steepen the yield curve, all other things equal, since other market agents need to be provided incentives to perform this maturity transformation function with the increased carry and roll-down that a steeper yield curve provides. Whether or not this proves to be the market-balancing mechanism, marginal buyers of some sort need to be found to absorb the bonds created by the large fiscal deficit. The banks probably won't be performing this function to the extent needed. Because banks are being regulated more aggressively and their capital requirements forced higher, their returns on equity will be much lower in the future, and so no new banks are being formed and existing banks cannot meaningfully expand their balance sheets. Thus the banking system's collective balance sheet is constrained.

So who will the marginal maturity transformers be when the Fed's balance sheet as well as the balance sheets of Fannie Mae and Freddie Mac are shrinking? Alternatively, sovereign reserve accumulators such as

China, Russia, the OPEC countries, and potentially Japan could absorb the excess supply of bonds. But taking this course will further increase the current account imbalance that had already been a major cause of the financial crisis in the first place. Harrington argued that if quantitative easing is ended, the problem of excessively easy monetary policy will just be transformed into the problem of substantial current account imbalances, setting up the United States for another big crisis in the future.

Alan Blinder noted that as the economy strengthens and people get richer, aggregate demand will increase and so will demand for bonds. This needs to be taken into account when determining the speed of the exit from quantitative easing. Blinder recommended not rushing into it as long as the economy stays weak.

Peter Fisher agreed with the concerns about current account imbalances. He argued that quantitative easing created both a stock and a flow effect and that the Fed had substantially underestimated the flow effect. Fisher said that he had no qualms about the expansion of the Fed balance sheet early on in the crisis in 2007–2008. However, the Fed's recent open-ended purchase program had an even larger flow effect, the unwinding of which risked washing out the effects that were previously obtained. He argued that the problem of having a significant flow effect is that the reversal of the flow effect cannot be avoided when it's time to exit.

Allan Meltzer argued that it will take years to unwind the balance sheet and that it has to be done slowly. The way to do it is to announce a path conditional on certain events and to subsequently stick to the path. Meltzer then challenged the current administration, inquiring why it does not seem to be aware of the fact that raising tax rates and regulating businesses, in the way that is currently done, burden the economy and slow the recovery. He noted that when Franklin Roosevelt was president, at the onset of World War II he swiftly abandoned populist policies, appointed two Republicans to his cabinet, and appointed the head of General Motors to be his production czar, even though he had previously called businessmen "economic royalists." Meltzer argued that this was a recognition that the president had abandoned populist policies, and concluded that we need a similar signal now.

Is "Too Big to Fail" Over? Are We Ready for the Next Crisis?

In the discussion following the presentations on "too big to fail" (chapters 9–12), a member of the audience inquired about demand deposits and time deposits, asking what kind of tool could be instituted to reduce the run for deposits.

John Cochrane answered that for demand deposits, a first-come, first-served system could be maintained. Money that is immediately available comes from a money market fund backed by short-term Treasuries. For a higher interest rate, one would have to opt for a different product, which would not allow the right to run. Cochrane noted that another standard tool for dealing with runs and crises, sometimes advocated for money market funds that hold illiquid assets, is to suspend convertibility. However, the problem with suspension of convertibility is that investors who anticipate an imminent suspension of convertibility withdraw their funds immediately. Cochrane pointed out that the suspension of convertibility, designed as the tool to stop the run, then creates the run in the first place.

Darrell Duffie added that the idea of having full reserve backing for deposits has been around for a long time, suggested by Milton Friedman (though he eventually recanted the idea). Duffie also noted that narrow banking is a closely related proposal.

Another member of the audience inquired about contingent convertible bonds (CoCos). **John Cochrane** questioned whether CoCos have any economic advantages. He noted that the reason to prefer CoCos over equity is that CoCos preserve the subsidy to debt implicit in their tax deductibility. Hence, CoCos would be a security that is really equity, but denominated as debt for reporting purposes at the IRS. Cochrane cautioned that similar window dressing was related to the financial crisis.

Sheila Bair noted that all four speakers were opposing the restrictions on the Fed's discretion under section 13(3) of the Federal Reserve Act. She explained that the Dodd-Frank Act was designed to allow the Fed to use 13(3) to generate lending programs that were generally available to a broad set of financial institutions in unusual circumstances. In the case of the idiosyncratic failure of a single institution, on the other hand, the institution would go into Title II or the bankruptcy process. She argued that this is the way in which Dodd-Frank bans bailouts and that many people believe that Title II is credible and provides a viable resolution strategy, with the potential of ending bailouts and the too-big-to-fail problem. Her concern was that reversing the ban on bailouts and giving the Fed wide discretion under 13(3) would lead to the market doubting that the government would use Title II, since a bailout by the Fed would be an easier approach. She asked the panelists how they would solve the too-big-to-fail problem if the ban on bailouts under 13(3) were abandoned and the Fed's unfettered discretion were restored. Bair also inquired about the panelists' comments regarding "flights to safety." Given the panelists' hypothesis that large banks now have huge capital cushions and are very safe, why would depositors run from a large bank to an institution that just entered a Title II resolution process?

Steve Strongin clarified that depositors would likely run to the systemically important financial institutions (SIFIs) in a period of stress, not to the specific SIFI in resolution but to other SIFIs because of their strong capital positions. However, the other SIFIs might well have to refuse those deposits so that they do not violate the new leverage restrictions—and this in turn could be systematically destabilizing in a new way.

Darrell Duffie asked Bair's opinion on whether providing liquidity to financial market infrastructure under emergency lending is a good or bad idea, and why. Bair responded that in her opinion, liquidity assistance to solvent institutions is a good idea. In a system-wide crisis, when healthy banks are under stress for reasons beyond their control, the Fed should be able to make assistance generally available. The restriction in the Dodd-Frank legislation bans one-off bailouts, such as the bailouts of mismanaged institutions like AIG, Bear Stearns, and Citigroup. The intention of the legislation was to keep the government, including the Fed, from doing these one-off bailouts. She argued that if this restriction is eliminated, the market is going to believe that the Fed is going to do bailouts. She asked how one would convince the market that "too big to fail" is over if the Fed has unfettered discretion to do bailouts.

Donald Kohn pointed out that the Fed was in favor of Title II and did not favor bailouts for individual institutions. **Martin Baily** added that the ability to provide liquidity to the system is desirable, but that this may mean providing liquidity to a particular institution. In this way, central banks provide liquidity to a bank that is suffering from a run but is not insolvent.

Steve Strongin pointed out that liquidity support in a single-point-of-entry (SPOE) resolution should be provided within the holding company at the point of recapitalization (for example to the new bridge holding company, see chapters 9–12) and not be limited to the bank's subsidiaries.

Sheila Bair pointed out that there is broad authority to provide liquidity assistance once an institution has entered a Title II resolution, with the shareholders and creditors responsible for any losses. She added that

13(3) restricts the Fed from providing one-off assistance to a troubled institution. She noted that according to her understanding, the panelists were all suggesting abandoning this restriction. She cautioned against that since it would hurt the progress made so far in limiting the problem of "too big to fail."

Donald Kohn added the following two points: first, the distinction between solvency and illiquidity is very difficult to make in the middle of a crisis. Making loans against good collateral is part of Bagehot's dictum, which prescribes that a central bank, in order to avert a panic, should act as the lender of last resort by lending freely at high rates to solvent firms with good collateral.[2] However, the collateral needs to be valued cautiously and at a haircut to normal market circumstances. Kohn noted that in a fire sale it is hard to know who is going to be solvent when the fire sale is over, exacerbating the distinction between solvency and illiquidity. Second, he expressed worry regarding the transparency of section 13(3). Every institution that borrows from the Federal Reserve will be identified to Congress and its name will be released to the public in no more than two years. From experience, it is known that there is a lot of stigma involved in borrowing from the Fed. He expressed concern that the ability of the Fed to play its Bagehot role of providing liquidity to prevent runs, or to intervene at the beginning of a run to prevent it from getting worse, will potentially be impaired by institutions' great reluctance to borrow from the Federal Reserve until they are in the process of failure. He added that, beyond the risk that the market finds out that the institution has borrowed from the Fed, thus reducing its liquidity, there is substantial political risk as well.

John Cochrane reminded the audience of the background of 13(3). In the crisis, the Fed took extraordinary measures by participating in the bailout of specific companies, which had political consequences. Therefore, Congress took away this power. Cochrane argued that with the Fed's macroprudential project, intense regulation of specific industries, allocation of credit flow, and popping bubbles, market participants will make and lose tens of billions of dollars. The ones who lose money will call their representatives in Congress. He noted that so far the Fed has had very limited power in return for great independence. He cautioned that as the Fed starts taking a lot of discretionary power that has strong effects

---

2. See *Lombard Street: A Description of the Money Market* (1873) by the English economist Walter Bagehot.

on people's bottom lines, it will lose this political independence. If the Fed is restricting credit to real estate in Palo Alto since it judges there to be a housing bubble, Congress is going to intervene as those who lose money from this policy will speak up. Cochrane said the loss of political independence as a response to the Fed taking discretionary power is a big danger in the pursuit of macroprudential policies.

Steve Strongin pointed toward the liquidity coverage ratio (LCR) as an implicit floor for the liquidity and the amount of stress that good collateral is under. If the regulator is only lending against collateral and against the LCR schedule, there are a lot of restrictions, so that government money is not at risk. The assets and haircuts are predetermined and sufficient for almost any circumstances. He noted that embedded in the LCR is hence the notion of what the liquidity floor could be without incurring significant government risk.

Sheila Bair agreed with these points, but stressed the question of why the Fed needs the ability to tailor an emergency measure to just one institution. She further asked why it would be insufficient in a severe liquidity situation to allow all solvent institutions that would otherwise be under stress to borrow against collateral under certain conditions.

J. W. Verret challenged the notion that the restrictions on 13(3) have actual restrictive content. He pointed out that Jeffrey M. Lacker, president of the Federal Reserve Bank of Richmond, had recently testified on this issue before a congressional committee. A simple rule from a legal standpoint, he said, is that a law that no one has the authority to sue under is not a law, but instead a mere aspiration, goal, or hope. The Fed still has a significant amount of discretion under the restrictions in section 13(3), given the gray area between insolvency and illiquidity. However, he pointed out that if the Fed chose to ignore the law and to lend to an individual institution, there would be political consequences but no legal consequences. He wondered whether the panel would consider the possibility of making restrictions self-executing, such as rights of action to seize the proceeds of support issued in violation of the restrictions or a mandatory minimum penalty for lending under 13(3). These would make the restrictions real from a legal standpoint.

Martin Baily said he considered it unlikely that the Fed would violate regulations which Congress has passed. He further expressed concern that the debate was focusing entirely on 13(3).

Russell Roberts challenged the panelists by noting that the debate so far had focused on financial regulation as an economics or engineering problem and had discussed progress achieved by tweaking a complex system. Roberts argued that instead of being an economics or engineering problem, the issue at hand is overwhelmingly a political problem. He pointed to the elephant in the room: the political power of the large banks in the United States. Due to this power, promises can't always be credible. Roberts noted that in the last twenty-five to thirty years of American discretionary policy, when push came to shove the large banks got their way. While this is not done in a transparent way, it seems that we make it easy for large financial institutions to use borrowed money rather than their own money. He argued that until this political problem disappears, we are living in a Kafkaesque world where the people who are not immersed in the debate on financial regulation see the charts and complexity that they don't understand, but know what is going to happen when the time comes. The people who have billions of dollars at stake are not going to stand for something else. He urged that this political problem be fixed before addressing the economic problems.

As a former banker, **Douglas Elliott** decided to comment on this point. He agreed with Roberts's concerns but argued that, notwithstanding the public focus on bailouts, the owners of the failed banks were wiped out. Those who had owned shares in Citigroup ended up with merely 5 percent of their initial value. Hence, Elliott pointed out that it is politically possible to do damage to the people who run the big banks. He did agree that in the United States, as in the rest of the world, rich people tend to have a lot of influence, so that it is reasonable to raise concerns about banks' political influence. He argued, however, that the fact that we have recently been through a financial crisis will lend political support to bankers' opponents. In addition, many restrictions will be embedded in the regulatory structures going forward. Elliott found it hard to envision that the equity holders of financial institutions would be rescued to any significant extent in some future financial crisis. He also pointed out that equity holders were not rescued in the recent financial crisis, but instead took very large hits.

Russell Roberts observed that equity holders are not the crucial decision-makers in the case of risk-taking. Instead, it is the creditors, since they have no upside and only the downside of bankruptcy. The equity holders have the upside. They also have downside risk but can diversify away. Hence, when taking away the downside risk to creditors, he argued that we are taking away the single most important watchdog in the financial system, because creditors overwhelmingly care about downside risk. Bailing out creditors without a haircut removes the crucial oversight creditors provide.

Martin Baily argued that one of the suggestions discussed in the presentations was to hit long-term debt with losses in the bankruptcy process, which is a change relative to the system prior to the crisis that would address Roberts's concern.

George Shultz agreed that big banks have a lot of power, but interpreted recent large fines to JPMorgan Chase and other financial institutions as a sign that this power is diminishing. JPMorgan now looks like a cash cow.

John Cochrane noted that, notwithstanding the large fines levied on large banks, in the end the government will not let them fail, which means really the government won't let them lose a lot of money. So it's a bit of a charade overall: levy big fines with one hand but subsidize and guarantee with the other.

Donald Kohn asked about Cochrane's proposal, under which there would be no deposits and debt would be taxed. He inquired whether this interpretation is correct and whether it would mean that there are indeed no deposits.

John Cochrane answered that there are demand deposits, but that these are guaranteed fully by short-term Treasuries. This allows for taxes on debt instead of capital requirements, since the latter leads to debates about how to risk-weight assets. As an economist, he preferred the use of a price rather than a quantity, so as to avoid the arguments about the exact quantity. An institution like Lehman Brothers with 30–1 leverage that is rolling over short-term funds every night will then pay a high tax for its capital structure and hence consider issuing more equity.

David Skeel noted that some of the speakers had criticized the leverage ratio as encouraging risk-taking. He therefore wondered whether the presenters would just get rid of it or whether the optimal solution would be to include both a risk-weighted measure of capital and a leverage ratio, as is done in Basel III, or to pair the leverage ratio with some other form of capital measurement.

Martin Baily argued that the leverage ratio is a useful backup measure but that it should be paired with other forms of capital. Purely using the leverage ratio leads to excessive risk-taking, so that employing risk weights adds an important dimension. However, he added that the leverage ratio should be a constraint that is not frequently binding.

Bankruptcy, Bailout, Resolution

Martin Baily took up the point mentioned by Michael Helfer on the advantage of cross-border agreements under Title II (chapter 16). He noted that Title II makes it easier to negotiate with foreign regulators. He then asked the members of the panel to comment on whether Title II needs to be available for global SIFIs, even if Chapter 14 is added to the bankruptcy code.

David Skeel answered by first noting that he agrees with Helfer in that he does not favor repealing Title II, but rather making it as unnecessary as possible by minimizing the likelihood that it needs to be used. He further noted that the notion that judges cannot coordinate as closely as regulators can is overstated. He mentioned projects on which judges in multiple countries work, including a project on cross-border principles in bankruptcy cases run by the American Law Institute. He cautioned, however, that mere handshake agreements like the one between the United States and the United Kingdom on whether single-point-of-entry measures will apply may not hold up in a financial crisis.

Ken Scott agreed with Skeel that substantial international cooperation in the court system does occur as well, pointing to a paper on dealing with cross-border issues by the American Law Institute.[3] He added that the situation in which a global SIFI fails and foreign governments engage in ring-fencing to protect subsidiaries and branches is only a subset of the issues that can arise with SIFIs that have global activities. Another example is a huge loss in a foreign subsidiary of a SIFI and the subsequent decisions that need to be made regarding whether the subsidiary should be kept in operation.

Randall Guynn added that Europeans are often confused about the meaning of the bankruptcy Chapter 14 alternative, which might pose a challenge in the case of a financial crisis. He argued that it is therefore easier for regulators to cooperate under Title II. Guynn agreed with Helfer in favoring an improved bankruptcy code. However, he argued that more work is needed to avoid confusion by foreign regulators about the two alternatives. One way to achieve this is by the process of drawing up living wills, in which regulators communicate with each other. In addition,

---

3. The American Law Institute and the International Insolvency Institute, "Transnational Insolvency: Global Principles for Cooperation in International Insolvency Cases," report to the American Law Institute, March 30, 2012.

under Chapter 14, regulators would have a role and the Chapter 14 proceedings could be used for cross-border cooperation.

Michael Helfer agreed with Guynn's assessment but argued in response to Scott that cross-border issues are not limited to situations in which a foreign subsidiary experiences a large loss. He said that many large institutions operate through branches outside the United States and argued that losses within the United States could lead to ring-fencing and similar actions by foreign regulators in the absence of clear understandings about how the branches would be kept open.

Kevin Harrington observed that significant mergers and acquisitions have the potential to move currencies substantially and that financial crises usually result in sizeable currency movements as well. He therefore inquired whether single-point-of-entry or Title II resolution mechanisms take account of the (possibly large) currency movements that would result from capital transfers between currency jurisdictions that are implicit in recapitalizing a foreign banking subsidiary. If such currency movements take place, then wouldn't such recapitalizations be a form of socializing banking losses in disguise, transferring them to trade-sensitive economic sectors via currency movements?

Randall Guynn answered that he could not immediately identify this problem, but cautioned that this may be due to its complexity. If a foreign subsidiary became undercapitalized, some debt or equity would need to be converted, or an asset from the holding company would need to be contributed to recapitalize the subsidiary. Even with the largest SIFIs, this transfer would amount to a couple of billion dollars or potentially a lot less. Therefore, it was not clear to him why a transfer of that size would move the currency. He was of the opinion that it would not pose an issue.

Finally, **David Skeel** noted a related concern pertaining to lengthy stays on derivatives: the continual currency movements and movements in the prices of other assets. This is an argument for keeping the stay short (one day in the Dodd-Frank Act and up to three days in the proposal for Chapter 14).

Discussion Commentators

Peter Thiel	Co-founder of PayPal, co-founder and chairman of Palantir Technologies, and managing partner of Founders Fund

Lee E. Ohanian	Professor of economics, University of California, Los Angeles, and senior fellow at the Hoover Institution
Donald Kohn	Senior fellow at the Brookings Institution and former vice chairman of the Board of Governors of the Federal Reserve
Kevin Harrington	Managing director, Thiel Macro LLC
J. W. Verrett	Assistant professor of law, George Mason University
Russell Roberts	John and Jean De Nault Research Fellow at the Hoover Institution

Glossary

Alt A mortgage   Alternative A-paper mortgage

AOCI   accumulated other comprehensive income

ARRA   American Recovery and Reinvestment Act

Basel III   international regulatory framework for banks

BHC   bank holding company

BP   basis point

CCAR   Comprehensive Capital Analysis and Review

CCP   central clearing party

CDO   collateralized debt obligations

CDS   credit default swap

CFMA   Commodity Futures Modernization Act

CoCo   contingent convertible bond

CP   commercial paper

CPSS-IOSCO   Committee on Payment and Settlement Systems (CPSS) and the Technical Committee of the International Organization of Securities Commissions (IOSCO)

DFA   Dodd-Frank Act, or Wall Street Reform and Consumer Protection Act of 2010

DFMU   designated financial market utility

DIP   debtor-in-possession

DSGE   dynamic stochastic general equilibrium

D-SIB   domestic systemically important bank

ECB   European Central Bank

FBO   foreign banking organization

FDIC   Federal Deposit Insurance Corporation

Fed   Federal Reserve System

FI   financial institution

FMI   financial market infrastructure

FOMC   Federal Open Market Committee

FSB   Financial Stability Board

FSOC   Financial Stability Oversight Council

GAAP   generally accepted accounting principles

GDP   gross domestic product

GSE   government-sponsored enterprise

G-SIB   global systemically important bank
G-SIFI   global systemically important financial institution
IAS   International Accounting Standards
IASB   International Accounting Standards Board
IIF   Institute of International Finance
IOER   interest on excess reserves
LCR   liquidity coverage ratio
LIBOR   London interbank offered rate
LSAP   large scale asset purchase
M2   measure of money supply
MBS   mortgage-backed securities
MEP   Maturity Extension Program
MMMF   money market mutual fund
MPOE   multiple point of entry
NAV   net asset value
NINJA loan   no income, no job, no assets
NO-DOC loan   no documentation
NSFR   net stable funding ratio
OCC   Office of the Comptroller of the Currency
OECD   Organisation for Economic Co-operation and Development
OFHEO   Office of Federal Housing Enterprise Oversight
OFR   Office of Financial Research
OIS   overnight indexed swap
OLA   Orderly Liquidation Authority
OLF   orderly liquidation fund
OTC   over-the-counter
OTS   Office of Thrift Supervision
QE   quantitative easing (QE1, QE2, and QE3)
QFC   qualified financial contract
Repos   repurchase agreements
ROE   return on equity
RWA   risk-weighted assets
SDR   special drawing right
SEC   Securities and Exchange Commission
SIFI   systemically important financial institution
SIFMA   Securities Industry and Financial Markets Association
SIFMU   systemically important financial market utility
SIV   special investment vehicle or structured investment vehicle
SPOE   single point of entry

SPV   special purpose vehicle

SVAR   stressed value at risk

TAF   Term Auction Facility

TARP   Troubled Asset Relief Program

TBTF   too big to fail

TCH   The Clearing House

TIPS   Treasury Inflation-Protected Securities

TNX   ten-year Treasury yields

TPR   tri-party repo

UMP   unconventional monetary policy

VAR   value at risk

VIX   Volatility Index

Contributors

Martin Neil Baily is a senior fellow in the Economic Studies Program at the Brookings Institution and the Bernard L. Schwartz Chair in Economic Policy Development. He is also the director of the Business and Public Policy Initiative. Baily rejoined Brookings in September 2007 to develop a program of research on business and the economy. He is studying growth, innovation, and how to speed the recovery. He is a senior adviser to the McKinsey Global Institute, a senior director of Albright Stonebridge Group, a member of the Squam Lake Group of financial economists, co-chair of the Bipartisan Policy Center's Financial Reform Initiative, and a director of the Phoenix Companies of Hartford, Connecticut. Baily earned his PhD in economics in 1972 at the Massachusetts Institute of Technology. After teaching at MIT and Yale, he became a senior fellow at the Brookings Institution in 1979 and a professor of economics at the University of Maryland in 1989. Baily was the Chairman of the Council of Economic Advisers under President Clinton from 1999 to 2001 and a member of the Cabinet. He is the author of many professional articles and books, testifies regularly to House and Senate committees, and is often quoted in the press.

Sheila C. Bair served as chairman of the Federal Deposit Insurance Corporation from June 2006 through July 2011. From 2002 to 2006, she was the Dean's Professor of Financial Regulatory Policy for the Isenberg School of Management at the University of Massachusetts-Amherst. She also served as assistant secretary for financial institutions at the US Department of the Treasury (2001 to 2002), senior vice president for government relations of the New York Stock Exchange (1995 to 2000), commissioner and acting chairman of the Commodity Futures Trading Commission (1991 to 1995), and research director, deputy counsel, and counsel to Senate Majority Leader Robert Dole (1981 to 1988). She received a bachelor's degree from the University of Kansas and a JD from the University of Kansas School of Law. She is a senior adviser to the Pew Charitable Trusts and heads the Systemic Risk Council, a group of former regulators and financial policy experts committed to addressing regulatory and structural issues relating to systemic risk in the United States. She serves on the boards of Host Hotels, Grupo Santander, the Rand Corporation, and the Volcker institute. She is also a member of the International Advisory Council to the China Bank Regulatory Commission.

Alan S. Blinder is the Gordon S. Rentschler Memorial Professor of Economics and Public Affairs at Princeton University. He also is vice chairman of the Promontory Interfinancial Network, a financial services company. He has been a member of the Princeton University faculty since 1971, taking time off from 1993 to 1996 for government service, where he served first as a member of President Bill Clinton's original Council of Economic Advisers and then as vice chairman of the Board of Governors of the Federal Reserve System. Blinder is the author or co-author of twenty books, including the textbook *Economics: Principles and Policy* with William Baumol, from which well over two and a half million college students have learned introductory economics. Blinder's latest book, *After the Music Stopped: The Financial Crisis, the Response, and the Work Ahead*, was published in January 2013. He also is a regular columnist for *The Wall Street Journal* and appears frequently on television and radio. He is a member of the board of directors of the Council on Foreign Relations and in 2011 he was elected a Distinguished Fellow of the American Economic Association. He earned his bachelor's degree from Princeton University, his master's degree from the London School of Economics, and his doctorate from the Massachusetts Institute of Technology, all in economics.

Michael D. Bordo is Board of Governors Professor of Economics and director of the Center for Monetary and Financial History at Rutgers University, New Brunswick, New Jersey, and a distinguished visiting fellow at the Hoover Institution. He has held previous academic positions at the University of South Carolina and at Carleton University in Ottawa, Canada. He has been a visiting professor at the University of California-Los Angeles; Carnegie Mellon University; Princeton University; Harvard University; Cambridge University, where he was the Pitt Professor of American History and Institutions; and the Hoover Institution, Stanford University. He has been a visiting scholar at the International Monetary Fund; Federal Reserve Banks of St. Louis, Cleveland, and Dallas; the Federal Reserve Board of Governors; the Bank of Canada; the Bank of England; the Reserve Bank of New Zealand; and the Bank for International Settlement. He also is a research associate of the National Bureau of Economic Research, Cambridge, Massachusetts. He has a BA from McGill University, an MSc (economics) from the London School of Economics, and a PhD from the University of Chicago (1972). He has published many articles in leading journals and twelve books on monetary economics and monetary history. He is editor of a series of books for Cambridge University Press: *Studies in Macroeconomic History*.

John H. Cochrane is the AQR Capital Management Distinguished Service Professor of Finance at the University of Chicago's Booth School of Business, a senior fellow at the Hoover Institution at Stanford University, a research associate of the National Bureau of Economic Research, and an adjunct scholar of the Cato Institute. He is a fellow and a past president of the American Finance Association. He earned a bachelor's degree in physics at MIT and a PhD in economics at the University of California, Berkeley. He is the author of academic articles on risk and liquidity premiums in stock and bond markets, the volatility of exchange rates, the term structure of interest rates, the returns to venture capital, the relation between stock prices and investment, option pricing, the fiscal theory of the price level, the effects of monetary policy, health insurance, time-series econometrics, and other topics. He is the author of the popular textbook *Asset Pricing* and a coauthor of *The Squam Lake Report*. He also writes occasional Op-Eds for the *Wall Street Journal* and other publications and blogs as "the Grumpy Economist."

Ricardo R. Delfin is the executive director of the Systemic Risk Council, a group of former regulators and financial policy experts committed to addressing regulatory and structural issues relating to systemic risk in the United States. Before joining the SRC, he was special counsel to the chair of the Securities and Exchange Commission (Mary Schapiro). In that role he advised the chair on a wide range of post-crisis financial reforms, including the implementation of the Dodd-Frank Act and the formation of the Financial Stability Oversight Council (FSOC). He was a member of several FSOC committees and was a point person on a variety of intergovernmental efforts, particularly those related to systemic risk. Delfin was also senior counsel to the House Committee on Financial Services (Barney Frank, chair). There he worked on emergency legislation to respond to the financial crisis as well as a wide variety of banking and other financial services legislation to reform mortgage finance, consumer credit, and corporate governance. Before going into public service, he was an associate with Wilmer, Cutler & Pickering LLP in Washington, D.C. He is a graduate of the Northwestern University School of Law and Cornell University College of Arts and Sciences.

Darrell Duffie is the Dean Witter Distinguished Professor of Finance at Stanford University's Graduate School of Business. He is a member of the Financial Advisory Roundtable of the Federal Reserve Bank of New York, a fellow and member of the Council of the Econometric Society, a research fellow of the National Bureau of Economic Research, a fellow of the American Academy of Arts and Sciences, a member of the Board of Directors of Moody's Corporation since 2008, and the 2009 president of the American Finance Association. Duffie's research and teaching focus on valuation and risk in financial markets. His recent books include *How Big Banks Fail and What to Do about It* (2010), *Measuring Corporate Default Risk* (2011), and *Dark Markets: Asset Pricing and Information Transmission in Over-the-Counter Markets* (2012). He is also a coauthor of *The Squam Lake Report: Fixing the Financial System* (2010) and a member of the Resolution Project at Stanford University's Hoover Institution. Duffie chairs the Market Participants' Group on Reference Rate Reform established by the Financial Stability Board.

Douglas Elliott is a fellow in economic studies at the Brookings Institution. A financial institutions investment banker for two decades, principally at J.P. Morgan, he was the founder and principal researcher for the Center On Federal Financial Institutions, a think tank devoted to the analysis of federal lending and insurance activities. At Brookings, he focuses primarily on financial institutions and markets and their regulation. He has written extensively on bank regulation and on international coordination of financial regulation. Elliott's work as a financial institutions investment banker over two decades has given him a wide-ranging and deep understanding of the industry. He has researched financial institutions or worked directly with them as clients in a range of capacities, including as: an equities analyst, a credit analyst, a mergers and acquisitions specialist, a relationship officer, and a specialist in securitizations. His work encompassed banks, insurers, funds management firms, and other financial institutions. In addition to fourteen years at J.P. Morgan, he worked as an investment banker with Sanford Bernstein, Sandler O'Neill, and ABN AMRO.

Peter R. Fisher is senior fellow at the Center for Global Business and Government at the Tuck School of Business at Dartmouth College, where he is also a senior lecturer. He is a member of the Board of Directors of AIG and also serves as a senior director of the BlackRock Investment Institute. Previously, he served as head of BlackRock's Fixed Income Portfolio Management Group and as chairman of BlackRock Asia. Before joining BlackRock in 2004, Fisher served from 2001 to 2003 as undersecretary of the US Treasury for domestic finance. He also worked at the Federal Reserve Bank of New York from 1985 to 2001, concluding his service as executive vice president and manager of the Federal Reserve System Open Market Account. Fisher earned a bachelor's degree in history from Harvard College in 1980 and a JD degree from Harvard Law School in 1985.

Randall D. Guynn is head of Davis Polk's Financial Institutions Group. He is widely recognized as one of the country's leading bank regulatory and bank merger and acquisition lawyers and a thought leader on financial regulatory reform. He has advised the Securities Industry and Financial Markets Association (SIFMA), the principal trade organization for US banks, securities firms, and asset managers, all the United States' six largest banks, and many non-US banks on the Dodd-Frank Act and its regulatory implementation. His practice focuses on providing strategic bank regulatory advice and advising on M&A and capital markets transactions when the target or issuer is a banking organization or other financial institution. He also advises on regulatory enforcement actions and white-collar criminal defense, bank failures and recapitalizations, corporate governance and internal controls, cross-border collateral transactions, credit risk management, securities settlement systems, and payment systems. He is co-chair of the Workstream on Failure Resolution within the Bipartisan Policy Center's Financial Regulatory Reform Initiative.

Michael S. Helfer was appointed vice chairman of Citigroup in June 2012, after being Citigroup's general counsel and corporate secretary for almost ten years. Before joining Citigroup in 2003, Helfer was president of Strategic Investments and chief strategic officer at Nationwide Insurance. He had previously been a partner and chairman of the Management Committee of Wilmer, Cutler & Pickering, clerked for Chief Judge David Bazelon (District of Columbia circuit), and served as counsel for the Subcommittee on Constitutional Amendments of the US Senate Judiciary Committee. Helfer is a member of the American Law Institute and the Council on Foreign Relations and served as chairman of the Clearing House Association. A founding member of the board of directors of Lawyers for Children America, he served as president of the Legal Aid Society in Washington, D.C., and is now a member of the advisory board of the

Legal Aid Society of New York. He received his JD from Harvard Law School and a BA in economics from Claremont Men's College.

Simon Hilpert is a PhD candidate in the Economics Department at Stanford University, where he is a Ric Weiland fellow. His research focuses on financial economics, using both theoretical and empirical tools. Currently he is researching the relevance of beliefs about future economic developments in the formation of bond prices, the impact of having children on households' financial choices, and new statistical methods to summarize household portfolio decisions. A national of Germany, he received an M.A. with distinction in economics from the University of Mannheim, Germany, and has worked in quantitative fixed-income research at BlackRock.

Allan H. Meltzer is the Allan H. Meltzer University Professor of Political Economy at the Tepper School of Business at Carnegie Mellon University and a distinguished visiting scholar at the Hoover Institution at Stanford University. His teaching and research interests include the history of US monetary policy, size of government, macroeconomics, and the relation of money to inflation and unemployment in open and closed economies. Meltzer has served as a consultant on economic policy for the US Congress, US Treasury, the Federal Reserve, the World Bank, and the US and foreign governments and was chair of the International Financial Institution Advisory Commission. He was founder and chairman of the Shadow Open Market Committee from 1973 to 2000 and honorary adviser to the Bank of Japan. He is the author of many books and papers in the field of economics.

Paul Saltzman is president of the Clearing House Association and executive vice president, general counsel, of the Clearing House Payments Company, the oldest and largest private- sector payments operator in the United States. Saltzman has twenty-five years of experience in financial services, industry association management, and emerging technology development. For nearly a decade Saltzman served as executive vice president and general counsel for the Bond Market Association (now SIFMA), where he developed and steered the regulatory and legal agenda for the fixed-income industry. Saltzman is a graduate of Clark University, received his Juris Doctor from Boston University School of Law, and was admitted to the bar in the state of New York.

Kenneth E. Scott is the Ralph M. Parsons Professor of Law and Business Emeritus and a senior research fellow at the Hoover Institution. His current research concentrates on legislative and policy developments related to the current financial crisis, comparative corporate governance, and financial regulation. He has extensive consulting experience, including work for the World Bank, Federal Deposit Insurance Corporation, Resolution Trust Corporation, and, most recently, the National Association of Securities Dealers (now the Financial Industry Regulatory Authority). He is also a member of the Shadow Financial Regulatory Committee, Financial Economists Roundtable, and the State Bar of California's Financial Institutions Committee. Before joining the Stanford Law School faculty in 1968, he served as general counsel to the Federal Home Loan Bank Board and chief deputy savings and loan commissioner of California and worked in private practice in New York with Sullivan & Cromwell.

George P. Shultz is the Thomas W. and Susan B. Ford Distinguished Fellow at the Hoover Institution. Among many other senior government and private-sector roles, he served as secretary of labor in 1969 and 1970, director of the Office of Management and Budget from 1970 to 1972, and secretary of the Treasury from 1972 to 1974. He was sworn in on July 16, 1982, as the sixtieth US secretary of state and served until January 20, 1989. In January 1989 he was awarded the Medal of Freedom, the nation's highest civilian honor. Shultz rejoined Stanford University in 1989 as the Jack Steele Parker Professor of International Economics at the Graduate School of Business and as a distinguished fellow at the Hoover Institution. Shultz is the advisory council chair of the Precourt Institute for Energy at Stanford, chair of the MIT Energy Initiative External Advisory Board, and chair of the Hoover Institution Task Force on Energy Policy. He is a distinguished fellow of the American Economic Association.

David A. Skeel Jr. is the S. Samuel Arsht Professor of Corporate Law at the University of Pennsylvania Law School. He is the author of *The New Financial Deal: Understanding the Dodd-Frank Act and Its (Unintended) Consequences* (Wiley, 2011); *Icarus in the Boardroom: The Fundamental Flaws in Corporate America and Where They Came From* (Oxford University Press, 2005); *Debt's Dominion: A History of Bankruptcy Law in America* (Princeton University Press, 2001); and numerous articles on bankruptcy, corporate law, financial regulation, Christianity and law, and other topics. Skeel has also written commentaries for the *New York Times, Wall Street Journal, Books & Culture,* the *Weekly Standard,* and other publications.

Steve Strongin is head of Global Investment Research at Goldman Sachs and a member of the firm's Management Committee. He has previously served as the global head of strategy research and co-chief operating officer of Global Investment Research, as well as the global head of commodities research. He joined Goldman Sachs in 1994 and became a partner in 2002. Strongin is on the Board of Directors of New York City's Fund for Public Schools, the Board of Directors of the Cahn Fellows Program, the Visiting Committee at the University of Chicago, and the advisory board to the RAND Center for Corporate Ethics and Governance. Strongin earned both undergraduate and graduate degrees in economics from the University of Chicago and earned a master's in management degree from the Kellogg School of Management at Northwestern University.

Lawrence H. Summers is the Charles W. Eliot University Professor and President Emeritus of Harvard University. During the past two decades, he has served in a series of senior policy positions in Washington, D.C., including as seventy-first Secretary of the Treasury for President Clinton, Director of the National Economic Council for President Obama, and Vice President of Development Economics and Chief Economist of the World Bank. He received a Bachelor of Science degree from the Massachusetts Institute of Technology in 1975 and was awarded a PhD from Harvard in 1982. In 1983, he became one of the youngest individuals in recent history to be named as a tenured member of the Harvard University faculty. In 1987, Summers became the first social scientist to receive the annual Alan T. Waterman Award of the National Science Foundation; and in 1993 he was awarded the John Bates Clark Medal, given every two years to the most outstanding American economist under the age of forty. He is also the Weil Director of the Mossavar-Rahmani Center for Business & Government at Harvard's Kennedy School.

John B. Taylor is the Mary and Robert Raymond Professor of Economics at Stanford University and the George P. Shultz Senior Fellow in Economics at Stanford's Hoover Institution. He is also the director of Stanford's Introductory Economics Center. He served as senior economist on the President's Council of Economic Advisers and as a member of the council.

From 2001 to 2005, he served as undersecretary of treasury for international affairs. Taylor was awarded the Hoagland Prize and the Rhodes Prizes for excellence in undergraduate teaching. He received the Bradley Prize for his economic research and policy achievements, the Adam Smith Award from the National Association for Business Economics, the Alexander Hamilton Award and the Treasury Distinguished Service Award for his policy contributions at the US Treasury, and the Medal of the Republic of Uruguay for his work in resolving the 2002 financial crisis. Taylor received a BA in economics summa cum laude from Princeton and a PhD in economics from Stanford.

Kevin M. Warsh serves as a distinguished visiting fellow at Stanford University's Hoover Institution and as a lecturer at its Graduate School of Business. In addition, he advises several companies, including serving on the board of directors of UPS. Warsh served as a member of the Board of Governors of the Federal Reserve System from 2006 until 2011, as the Federal Reserve's representative to the Group of Twenty (G-20), and as the board's emissary to the emerging and advanced economies in Asia. In addition, he was administrative governor, managing and overseeing the board's operations, personnel, and financial performance. Before his appointment to the board, from 2002 until 2006, Warsh served as special assistant to the president for economic policy and as executive secretary of the White House National Economic Council. Previously, Warsh was a member of the Mergers & Acquisitions Department at Morgan Stanley & Co. in New York, serving as vice president and executive director. Warsh was born in upstate New York. He received his bachelor's degree from Stanford University and his JD from Harvard Law School.

WORKING GROUP ON ECONOMIC POLICY
AT THE HOOVER INSTITUTION

The Working Group on Economic Policy brings together experts on economic and financial policy to study key developments in the U.S. and global economies, and develop policy proposals. John B. Taylor, the George P. Shultz Senior Fellow at the Hoover Institution and the Mary and Robert Raymond Professor of Economics at Stanford University, chairs the working group.

For twenty-five years starting in the early 1980s, the United States experienced an unprecedented economic boom. Expansions were stronger and longer than in the past. Recessions were shorter, shallower, and less frequent.

This quarter-century boom strengthened as its length increased. Productivity growth surged by one full percentage point per year. And the long boom went global with emerging market countries experiencing the enormous improvements in both economic growth and economic stability.

Economic policies that place greater reliance on the principles of free markets, price stability, and flexibility were the key to these successes. Recently, however, several powerful new economic forces have begun to change the economic landscape, and these principles are being challenged. A financial crisis flared up in 2007 and turned into a severe panic in 2008 leading to the Great Recession and a very slow recovery. How we interpret and react to these forces—and in particular whether proven policy principles prevail going forward—will determine whether strong economic growth and stability returns and again continues to spread and improve more people's lives or whether the economy stalls and stagnates.

Index